JESUS AMONG FRIENDS AND ENEMIES

JESUS AMONG FRIENDS AND ENEMIES

A Historical and Literary Introduction
to Jesus in the Gospels

Edited by Chris Keith and Larry W. Hurtado

B
Baker Academic
a division of Baker Publishing Group
Grand Rapids, Michigan

Published by Baker Academic
a division of Baker Publishing Group
P.O. Box 6287, Grand Rapids, MI 49516-6287
www.bakeracademic.com

Printed in the United States of America

Library of Congress Cataloging-in-Publication Data
    Jesus among friends and enemies : a historical and literary introduction to Jesus in the Gospels / edited by Chris Keith and Larry W. Hurtado.
        p.   cm.
    Includes bibliographical references and indexes.
    ISBN 978-0-8010-3895-2 (pbk.)
    1. Jesus Christ—Friends and associates—Biography. 2. Bible. N.T. Gospels—Biography. 3. Jesus Christ—Historicity. 4. Jesus Christ—Biography. I. Keith, Chris. II. Hurtado, Larry W., 1943–.
BT340.J47 2011
232.9′01—dc23   2011022323

In keeping with biblical principles of creation stewardship, Baker Publishing Group advocates the responsible use of our natural resources. As a member of the Green Press Initiative, our company uses recycled paper when possible. The text paper of this book is composed in part of post-consumer waste.

11   12   13   14   15   16   17   7   6   5   4   3   2   1

green press INITIATIVE

To our wives
Erin Keith
and
Shannon Hurtado

Contents

Part 2 The Enemies of Jesus

Illustrations

Preface

This book introduces students to the portrayals of Jesus in the Gospels of the New Testament by introducing them to the characters who surround Jesus in those narratives—his friends and enemies. Part 1 covers the friends of Jesus: God and the angels (chap. 1); John the Baptist (chap. 2); the disciples (chap. 3); the family of Jesus (chap. 4); other friends of Jesus—Mary Magdalene, the Bethany family, and the Beloved Disciple (chap. 5); and secret disciples—Nicodemus and Joseph of Arimathea (chap. 6). Part 2 covers the enemies of Jesus: Satan and demons (chap. 7); the Jewish leaders (chap. 8); the political authorities—the Herods, Caiaphas, and Pontius Pilate (chap. 9); and Judas Iscariot—the betrayer of Jesus (chap. 10). As is clear, not every character in the Gospels is covered. That would require a much larger book and likely would not contribute further to the most important point this book makes, which is (as the title "Jesus *among* Friends and Enemies" suggests) that if a reader truly wants to know what the Gospels say about Jesus, he or she should also pay attention to what the Gospels say about his friends and enemies. The friends and enemies chosen for discussion, then, are those whom we consider most important to the Gospels' portrayals of Jesus.

An introductory chapter will focus upon the main character of the Gospels, Jesus. This chapter will also introduce readers to the format of the book, first presenting the various images of Jesus that appear outside the canonical Gospels and then presenting the canonical portrayals of him. The concluding chapter returns to the topic of Jesus. Both the format of the book and the concluding chapter require a few more words.

The Format of the Book

The primary goal of this book is to bring readers as close as possible to understanding how the original audiences of the Gospels would have heard the stories of Jesus in Matthew, Mark, Luke, and John. This is a tall order, not least because knowing what an author intended or an audience would have understood with 100 percent certainty is ultimately impossible. Not being able to know the original meaning of a text with 100 percent certainty is not the same as not being able to know it at all, however, and it is our conviction that readers today can reconstruct and understand the messages of the Gospels competently, even if imperfectly.

In order to understand these texts, however, modern readers must understand (1) the historical contexts in which they were produced and circulated and (2) the intricate narratives of the Gospels. There are a number of manners in which scholars can introduce students to both of these important topics; we have chosen to split each chapter in half, dedicating the first half explicitly to historical context and the second half to the Gospel narratives. That is, the first half of each chapter presents what scholars can know about that character or group of characters from the broad historical record and the contexts of Jesus and the early church. The second half of each chapter then turns to consider the portrayals of that character or group of characters in the Gospels of Matthew, Mark, Luke, and John. (Obviously, multicharacter chapters will repeat this format for each character.) The payoff of this approach is that readers are able to compare what other people in the ancient world said about various characters before appreciating the claims of the canonical Gospels, which are unique in some cases. Each chapter then concludes with statements on what the character or characters under consideration contribute to the narratives' portrayals of Jesus.

In terms of method, then, each chapter includes both a sociohistorical section and a narrative-critical section. Importantly, this division does not reflect an assumed disjunction between history and story, implying either that histories cannot be narratives or that narratives cannot be historical. The division of each chapter as such indicates only a distinction between these characters' portrayals in the historical record generally and their portrayals within Matthew, Mark, Luke, and John specifically.

Additionally, readers unfamiliar with literary approaches to the Gospels such as narrative criticism (the formal literary-critical methodology of studying narratives) may initially misread the emphasis on the Gospels as "stories" and on figures in the Gospels as "characters" to mean that the texts are "tales" or "fables." Technically, however, narrative criticism is not in the business of making historical judgments. Rather, applied to the Gospels, its business is making explicit the complexity and sophistication with which the Gospel authors have crafted their images of Jesus, enriching readers' understandings of those portraits of him. Jesus's friends and enemies are major elements of the Gospels' portrayals of Jesus, and thus such a perspective is appropriate for this book.

Jesus among His Friends and Enemies and the Historical Jesus

It should be clear, then, that this is not a historical Jesus book. Its primary focus is on Jesus's friends and enemies and how the Gospel narratives portray them in order to make claims about Jesus's identity, rather than on whether the Gospel claims are correct. As editors of the volume, however, we are nevertheless convinced that its primary focus is relevant to certain discussions in historical Jesus research and that certain discussions in historical Jesus research are relevant to readers of this book. On a practical level, comparing the portrayals of Jesus, his friends, and his enemies in the canonical Gospels to portrayals of them outside those Gospels inevitably leads, for some students, to questions about which version is correct. In this sense, the approach of this book can be the first step on a path that leads to studying the historical Jesus and the nature of the Gospels as historical narratives.

Further, our emphases on Jesus's contemporaries and the narrative portrayals of their interactions in the canonical Gospels correspond with recent trends in historical Jesus scholarship. With regard to those surrounding Jesus, for example, the essays in Scot McKnight and Joseph Modica's *Who Do My Opponents Say That I Am?* study the reception of Jesus by his enemies.[1] With regard to the narrative portrayals of Jesus, one may note a recent upsurge in the importance of those narrative portrayals as sources for the life of Jesus in current critical Jesus scholarship. The reasons for this upsurge vary from scholar to scholar, as the conclusion will show. But the chapters of this book are relevant to current discussions of the historical Jesus in light of this trend, since they focus ultimately on how the narratives of the Gospels answer the question of Jesus's identity via their portrayals of those surrounding him.

For these reasons, instead of offering a typical concluding chapter at the close of the volume, we, the editors, offer a conclusion, "Seeking the Historical Jesus among Friends and Enemies," as a port of entry into the current state of critical Jesus studies. This "conclusion" differs from typical concluding chapters insofar as a typical concluding chapter to a book such as this might rehearse the previous chapters in a this-chapter-said-this and that-chapter-said-that fashion. In contrast to ending the book in this manner, as if coming to the end of a journey, our conclusion bridges this book and a student's future studies, inviting him or her into the next level of academic discussion about the identity of Jesus. We introduce the student to historical Jesus research, some of its central tenets, and recent developments that relate specifically to this book. As an epilogue, the final chapter is designed as a capstone reading for a class on Jesus and the Gospels, as an opportunity to see why the answers of Matthew, Mark, Luke, and John to the question "Who is Jesus?"—and

---

1. Scot McKnight and Joseph B. Modica, eds., *Who Do My Opponents Say That I Am? An Investigation of the Accusations against Jesus*, LHJS/LNTS 327 (London: T&T Clark, 2008).

their employment of Jesus's friends and enemies in their narratives in order to answer that question—are beginning to matter more to scholars' answers to the same question.

Along these lines, we should note that we cannot claim to speak for all the contributors to the volume, as they were not required to agree with our argument in that chapter. Indeed, far from inspiring or attaining consensus, a more modest goal for the conclusion may be explaining some reasons why scholars often disagree on the roles of the canonical Gospels in historical Jesus research.

This final chapter, however, arrives only after the bulk of the volume introduces readers to the canonical portraits of Jesus by introducing them to his friends and enemies, and purposefully so. Certainly, Jesus is the main star of the Gospels of Matthew, Mark, Luke, and John. His supporting cast of friends and enemies, however, play determinative roles for the images of him that appear in those texts. Their roles are so important that, for readers to know who Jesus is in the Gospels, they must know his friends and enemies. Thus, this book presents Jesus among his friends and enemies.

Acknowledgments

The present book began life as an idea floated from a doctoral student to his supervisors at New College, the School of Divinity at the University of Edinburgh. The original idea eventually matured into a particular shape—a textbook that combined the focus on the Gospel narratives in narrative criticism with the historical information in typical textbooks, using the characters of the Gospels as vehicles for introducing students to those narratives, the sociohistorical contexts in which they were crafted, and, in particular, Jesus himself. So far as we are aware, it is the only "introduction to Jesus and the Gospels" that combines these approaches in this particular manner. We leave it to readers and reviewers to decide whether such a combination of approaches is useful pedagogically.

Numerous individuals have had a hand in bringing that original idea to fruition, and it is our privilege to record a few of those names here. Jack Kragt expressed confidence in the project on a campus visit to Lincoln Christian University and communicated it to Baker Academic. Our editor at Baker Academic, James Ernest, showed enthusiasm for the project when it was no more formal than two sheets of paper, a handful of verbal commitments, and a conversation at the annual meeting of the Society of Biblical Literature. James's continued involvement has improved the quality and scope of the volume in numerous ways. A cadre of international scholars, representing a mix of senior, established figures and junior, younger figures carried out the authorship of the individual chapters in a timely and professional manner. We thank our colleagues for their involvement. Chris would also like to thank the administration of Lincoln Christian University for their vision, support, and leadership, in particular Karen J. Diefendorf, Dr. Clay Ham, and Dr. Keith Ray, as well as Dr. Neal Windham.

Finally, Chris dedicates this book to his wife, Erin, and Larry dedicates it to his wife, Shannon. We are grateful to have wives who put up with us.

Contributors

David M. Allen (PhD, University of Edinburgh) is tutor in New Testament studies at The Queen's Foundation for Ecumenical Theological Education and the author of *Deuteronomy and Exhortation in Hebrews* (Mohr Siebeck, 2008).

Richard J. Bauckham (PhD, University of Cambridge) is emeritus professor of New Testament studies at the University of St. Andrews and senior scholar, Ridley Hall, Cambridge University and the author of numerous books, including *Jude and the Relatives of Jesus in the Early Church* (T&T Clark, 1990), *Jesus and the Eyewitnesses: The Gospels as Eyewitness Testimony* (Eerdmans, 2006), and *The Testimony of the Beloved Disciple: Narrative, History, and Theology in the Gospel of John* (Baker Academic, 2007).

Michael F. Bird (PhD, University of Queensland) is lecturer in theology at Crossway College, honorary research consultant at the University of Queensland, and the author of multiple studies, including *Jesus and the Origins of the Gentile Mission* (T&T Clark, 2006) and *Are You the One Who Is to Come? The Historical Jesus and the Messianic Question* (Baker Academic, 2009).

Helen K. Bond (PhD, University of Durham) is senior lecturer in New Testament language, literature, and theology at the University of Edinburgh and the author of *Pontius Pilate in History and Interpretation* (Cambridge University Press, 1998), *Caiaphas: Friend of Rome and Judge of Jesus?* (Westminster John Knox, 2004), and *The Historical Jesus: A Guide for the Perplexed* (Continuum, forthcoming).

Holly J. Carey (PhD, University of Edinburgh) is associate professor of biblical studies at Point University and the author of *Jesus's Cry from the Cross: Towards a First-Century Understanding of the Intertextual Relationship between Psalm 22 and the Narrative of Mark's Gospel* (T&T Clark, 2009).

Warren Carter (PhD, Princeton Theological Seminary) is professor of New Testament at Brite Divinity School, Texas Christian University, and the author of numerous publications, including *John and Empire: Initial Explorations* (T&T Clark, 2008); *John: Storyteller, Interpreter, Evangelist* (Hendrickson, 2006), and *The Roman Empire and the New Testament: An Essential Guide* (Abingdon, 2006).

Edith M. Humphrey (PhD, McGill University) is William F. Orr Professor of New Testament Studies at Pittsburgh Theological Seminary and the author of several books, including *Ecstasy and Intimacy: When the Holy Spirit Meets the Human Spirit* (Eerdmans, 2006), *And I Turned to See the Voice: The Rhetoric of Vision in the New Testament* (Baker Academic, 2007), and *Grand Entrance: Worship on Earth as in Heaven* (Brazos, 2011).

Larry W. Hurtado (PhD, Case Western Reserve University) is professor of New Testament language, literature, and theology at the University of Edinburgh and the author of many studies, including *Lord Jesus Christ: Devotion to Jesus in Earliest Christianity* (Eerdmans, 2003) and *The Earliest Christian Artifacts: Manuscripts and Christian Origins* (Eerdmans, 2006).

Chris Keith (PhD, University of Edinburgh) is assistant professor of New Testament and Christian origins at Lincoln Christian University and the author of *The "Pericope Adulterae," the Gospel of John, and the Literacy of Jesus* (Brill, 2009), a winner of the 2010 John Templeton Award for Theological Promise, and *Jesus' Literacy: Scribal Culture and the Teacher from Galilee* (T&T Clark, forthcoming 2011).

Anthony Le Donne (PhD, University of Durham) is assistant professor of New Testament and Second Temple Judaism at Lincoln Christian University and the author of *The Historiographical Jesus: Memory, Typology, and the Son of David* (Baylor University Press, 2009) and *The Historical Jesus: What Can We Know and How Can We Know It?* (Eerdmans, 2011).

Dieter T. Roth (PhD, University of Edinburgh) is Wissenschaftlicher Mitarbeiter/Post-doctoral Fellow at Johannes Gutenberg Universität, Mainz, and the author of numerous articles in *Expository Times*, *Journal of Biblical Literature*, *Journal of Theological Studies*, and *Vigiliae Christianae*.

Loren T. Stuckenbruck (PhD, Princeton Theological Seminary) is Richard Dearborn Professor of New Testament at Princeton Theological Seminary and the author of numerous publications, including *1 Enoch 91–108* (De Gruyter, 2004) and *The Fall of the Angels*, edited with Christoph Auffarth (Brill, 2004).

Abbreviations

General

ca.	circa	i.e.	that is
cf.	*confer*, compare	ms(s).	manuscript(s)
chap(s).	chapter(s)	lit.	literally
cod.	codex	n.	note (i.e., footnote)
e.g.	for example	par(s).	parallel(s) (also //)
esp.	especially	p(p.)	page(s)
frg(s).	fragment(s)	repr.	reprint
Gk.	Greek	rev.	revised
Heb.	Hebrew	sg.	singular
ibid.	in the same source	v(v).	verse(s)
idem	by the same author	2X	twice

Ancient Texts, Text Types, and Versions

LXX	Septuagint
MT	Masoretic Text

Modern Versions

KJV	King James Version
NIV	New International Version
NRSV	New Revised Standard Version
RSV	Revised Standard Version

Papyri

P.Oxy.	Oxyrhynchus Papyri
P.Vindob.	Einige Wiener Papyri

Apocrypha and Septuagint

Add. Dan.	Additions to Daniel	Sir.	Sirach
Bar.	Baruch	Tob.	Tobit
Jdt.	Judith	Wis.	Wisdom of Solomon
1–4 Macc.	1–4 Maccabees		

Old Testament Pseudepigrapha

2 Bar.	2 Baruch (Syriac Apocalypse)
3 Bar.	3 Baruch (Greek Apocalypse)
4 Bar.	4 Baruch (Paraleipomena Jeremiou)
BW	Book of Watchers (in 1 Enoch)
1 En.	1 Enoch (Ethiopic Apocalypse)
2 En.	2 Enoch (Slavonic Apocalypse)
3 En.	3 Enoch (Hebrew Apocalypse)
4 Ezra	4 Ezra
Jub.	Jubilees
Mart. Ascen. Isa.	Martyrdom and Ascension of Isaiah
Pss. Sol.	Psalms of Solomon
T. 12 Patr.	Testaments of the Twelve Patriarchs

Dead Sea Scrolls and Related Texts

1Q19	Noah	4Q370	Exhortation Based on the Flood
1Q20	Genesis Apocryphon ar (unopened scroll)	4Q387	Apocryphon of Jeremiah
1Q24	Book of Giants	4Q390	Apocryphon of Jeremiah
1QH^a	Thanksgiving Hymns^a	4Q444	Incantation
1QS	Community Rule	4Q458	Narrative A
1QM	War Scroll	4Q480	Narrative F
4Q177	Catena^a	4Q491	War Scroll^a
4Q180	Ages of Creation	4Q521	Messianic Apocalypse
4Q201	Book of Giants	4Q510	Songs of the Maskil^a
4Q203	Book of Giants	4Q511	Songs of the Maskil^b
4Q213a	Aramaic Levi Document	4Q554	New Jerusalem^a ar
4Q225	Pseudo-Jubilees^a	4Q560	Exorcism (Aramaic)
4Q256	Community Rule^b	4QCatena^a	Catena^a
4Q266	Damascus Document^a	4QD^a	Damascus Document^a
4Q269	Damascus Document^d	4QD^d	Damascus Document^d
4Q270	Damascus Document^e	4QD^h	Damascus Document^h
4Q272	Damascus Document^g	4QD^g	Damascus Document^g
4Q280	Curses (olim Berakot^f)	11Q5	Psalms Scroll^a
4Q286	Blessings	11Q11	Apocryphal Psalms^a

Mishnah, Talmud, and Related Literature

b.	Babylonian Talmud	Sanh.	Sanhedrin
m.	Mishnah	Šeqal.	Šeqalim
t.	Tosefta	Soṭah	Soṭah
y.	Jerusalem Talmud	Sukkah	Sukkah
		Taʿan.	Taʿanit
Ber.	Berakot	Tamid	Tamid
Giṭ.	Giṭṭin	Tem.	Temurah
Ḥag.	Ḥagigah	Yebam.	Yebamot
Šabb.	Šabbat		

Other Rabbinic Works

Eccles. Rab.	*Ecclesiastes Rabbah*
Exod. Rab.	*Exodus Rabbah*
Lam. Rab.	*Lamentations Rabbah*

Apostolic Fathers

Herm. Sim.	*Shepherd of Hermas, Similitude*
Herm. Vis.	*Shepherd of Hermas, Vision*
Ign. *Eph.*	Ignatius, *To the Ephesians*
Ign. *Smyrn.*	Ignatius, *To the Smyrnaeans*
Ign. *Trall.*	Ignatius, *To the Trallians*
Mart. Pol.	*Martyrdom of Polycarp*

Nag Hammadi Codices

Gos. Phil.	II,3 *Gospel of Philip*
Gos. Thom.	II,2 *Gospel of Thomas*

New Testament Apocrypha and Pseudepigrapha

Acts Andr. Mth.	*Acts of Andrew and Matthias*	*Gos. Pet.*	*Gospel of Peter*
Acts Pet.	*Acts of Peter*	*Gos. Thom.*	*Gospel of Thomas*
Apoc. Pet.	*Apocalypse of Peter*	*Pist. Soph.*	*Pistis Sophia*
Ep. Apos.	*Epistula Apostolorum (Epistle of the Apostles)*	*Prot. Jas.*	*Protevangelium of James*
Gos. Mary	*Gospel of Mary*	*Ps.-Clem. Rec.*	*Pseudo-Clementine Recognitions*

Greek and Latin Authors

Ambrose
Exp. Luc.	*Expositio Evangelii secundum Lucam*

Augustine
Civ.	*De civitate Dei (The City of God)*

Cyril of Alexandria
Comm. Luke	*Commentary on Luke*

Epiphanius
Pan.	*Panarion (Refutation of All Heresies)*

Eusebius
Hist. eccl.	*Historia ecclesiastica (Ecclesiastical History)*

Hippolytus
In Cant.	*In Canticum canticorum*

Irenaeus
Haer.	*Adversus haereses (Against Heresies)*

Jerome
Epist.	*Epistolae*
Vir. ill.	*De viris illustribus*

Josephus
Ag. Ap.	*Against Apion*

Ant.	*Jewish Antiquities*
J.W.	*Jewish War*
Life	*The Life*

Justin
1 Apol.	*Apologia i (First Apology)*
Dial.	*Dialogus cum Tryphone (Dialogue with Trypho)*

Juvenal
Sat.	*Satirae*

Lactantius
Mort.	*De morte persecutorum*

Lucian
Peregr.	*De morte Peregrini (The Passing of Peregrinus)*

Origen
Cels.	*Contra Celsum (Against Celsus)*
Comm. Jo.	*Commentarii in evangelium Joannis*

Philo
Abraham	*On the Life of Abraham*
Dreams	*On Dreams*
Embassy	*On the Embassy to Gaius*
Flaccus	*Against Flaccus*

Philostratus
Vit. Apoll.	*Vita Apollonii*

Pliny the Younger
Ep.	*Epistulae*

Suetonius
Claud.	*Divus Claudius*

Tacitus
Ann.	*Annales*

Tertullian
Praescr.	*De praescriptione haereticorum (Prescription against Heretics)*

Secondary Sources

AB	Anchor Bible
ABRL	Anchor Bible Reference Library
AGJU	Arbeiten zur Geschichte des antiken Judentums und des Urchristentums
BBR	*Bulletin for Biblical Research*
Bib	*Biblica*
BibInt	*Biblical Interpretation*
BNTC	Black's New Testament Commentaries
BTB	*Biblical Theology Bulletin*
BZNW	Beihefte zur Zeitschrift für die neutestamentliche Wissenschaft
CBQ	*Catholic Biblical Quarterly*
CM	Christianity in the Making
COQG	Christian Origins and the Question of God
EKKNT	Evangelisch-katholischer Kommentar zum Neuen Testament
ESCJ	Études sur le christianisme et le judaïsme

ETL	*Ephemerides theologicae lovanienses*
FF	Foundations and Facets
HTKNT	Herders theologischer Kommentar zum Neuen Testament
ICC	International Critical Commentary
JBL	*Journal of Biblical Literature*
JR	*Journal of Religion*
JSHJ	*Journal for the Study of the Historical Jesus*
JSNT	*Journal for the Study of the New Testament*
JSNTSup	Journal for the Study of the New Testament: Supplement Series
LCL	Loeb Classical Library
LHJS	Library of Historical Jesus Studies
LNTS	Library of New Testament Studies
MNTS	McMaster New Testament Studies
NCB	New Century Bible
Neot	*Neotestamentica*
NHMS	Nag Hammadi and Manichaean Studies
NIGTC	New International Greek Testament Commentary
NovT	*Novum Testamentum*
NovTSup	Novum Testamentum Supplements
NTAbh	Neutestamentliche Abhandlungen
NTS	*New Testament Studies*
NTTSD	New Testament Tools, Studies, and Documents
RBS	Resources for Biblical Study
SBLEJL	Society of Biblical Literature Early Judaism and Its Literature
SBLMS	Society of Biblical Literature Monograph Series
SBT	Studies in Biblical Theology
SemEd	Seminar Editions
SemeiaSt	Semeia Studies
SHJ	Studying the Historical Jesus
SJT	*Scottish Journal of Theology*
SNTSMS	Society for New Testament Studies Monograph Series
StudMon	*Studia Monastica*
SUNT	Studien zur Umwelt des Neuen Testaments
TBei	*Theologische Beiträge*
TBN	Themes in Biblical Narrative
TS	*Theological Studies*
TSAJ	Texte und Studien zum antiken Judentum
VCSup	Vigiliae christianae Supplements
WBC	Word Biblical Commentary
WMANT	Wissenschaftliche Monographien zum Alten und Neuen Testament
WUNT	Wissenschaftliche Untersuchungen zum Neuen Testament
ZKG	*Zeitschrift für Kirchengeschichte*
ZNW	*Zeitschrift für die neutestamentliche Wissenschaft und die Kunde der älteren Kirche*

Introduction

Jesus outside and inside the New Testament

CHRIS KEITH

Any book on Jesus among his friends and enemies should start with Jesus himself. As a historical figure, Jesus of Nazareth casts a greater shadow over the history of Western culture than anyone who has ever lived. Although various aspects of his life and ministry remain hotly debated, all serious scholars, regardless of religious persuasion, acknowledge that Jesus lived and taught in Judea in the first century CE, and furthermore that he died on a Roman cross in Jerusalem at the order of the Roman prefect Pontius Pilate. In fact, as one scholar says, Jesus's crucifixion by Pilate "is one of the surest facts of Christian history."[1]

Important as they are, however, these barest of historical facts—his existence and crucifixion—provide mere starting points for answering the important question of Jesus's identity. Various groups and individuals, ancient and modern, have proceeded from these facts to offer substantially differing answers to the question "Who was (or is) Jesus?" This chapter will introduce many of the ancient answers to that question.

The first half of the chapter will present images of Jesus outside the four canonical Gospels from the first to the third centuries CE. Some of these sources say Jesus was killed because he was a wise man whom his own people rejected, as happened with other wise men. Others say Jesus was killed

---

1. Helen K. Bond, *Pontius Pilate in History and Interpretation*, SNTSMS 100 (Cambridge: Cambridge University Press, 1998), xi.

1

Canonical and Noncanonical Gospels

In reference to literature, a canon (from the Greek *kanōn*, "rule, standard") is an authoritative collection of texts. In Christian history it refers specifically to the texts in the Bible that make up the Old and New Testaments.[1] Although the earliest reference to the twenty-seven books that compose the New Testament as a canon was not until 367 CE (by Athanasius, bishop of Alexandria), some Christians were already recognizing Matthew, Mark, Luke, and John as an authoritative collection of their own by the time Irenaeus, bishop of Lyon, was writing almost two centuries earlier, about 180 CE.[2] By the mid-second century, then, it is historically appropriate to speak of these Gospels as the "canonical" Gospels, which represented some orthodox Christians, in contrast to other Gospels that were thus labeled "noncanonical" or "apocryphal."

1. See further Lee Martin McDonald, *The Biblical Canon: Its Origin, Transmission, and Authority*, 3rd ed. (Peabody, MA: Hendrickson, 2007).
2. Irenaeus of Lyon, *Haer.* 3.11.8–9.

because he was a mischievous charlatan, a deceiver of the people who led them away from worshiping the true God of Israel and got what he deserved for doing so. Still others were concerned more with Jesus's followers than Jesus himself, but count his crucifixion as an ignoble mark against those who later bore his name as "Christians." These images provide an important background for the general milieu in which Matthew, Mark, Luke, and John circulated.

The second half of the chapter will then focus on Jesus's identity inside the four canonical Gospels. This section will reflect the general theme of this book in approaching Jesus via the characters of the Gospels but will of course concentrate on Jesus himself. Since subsequent chapters focus on singular characters' contribution to Jesus's identity, therefore, I will here note how the narrators and various characters interact to answer the question of Jesus's identity, specifically in light of his death. These answers exhibit differences as well as similarities but stand together in stark contrast to the portrayals of Jesus and his death outside the Gospels. The characters play crucial roles in sharpening and clarifying these answers. They alternately understand and misunderstand who Jesus is, thereby enlarging readers' peripheral vision of Jesus's identity. In other words, the answer of the canonical Gospels to the question "Who was (or is) Jesus?" is not singular but multifaceted and comprises both correct and incorrect identifications by those around him, including both sympathetic and hostile characters.

The Historical Jesus

Scholars use the phrase "historical Jesus" either to refer to Jesus "as he really was" or, more precisely, to refer to scholarly reconstructions of Jesus "as he really was." To greater or lesser degrees, depending on the individual scholar, the "historical Jesus" stands in contrast to the portrayals of him by others, and especially the portrayals of the canonical Gospels. For more on the historical Jesus and an introduction to historical Jesus studies, see the epilogue of this book.

Historical Considerations: Jesus outside the Canonical Gospels

The four canonical Gospels are the earliest surviving sources for Jesus and offer the most robust statements on his identity They are not the only ancient sources for Jesus, however. Jesus appears outside the canonical Gospels in the writings of Jewish and Greco-Roman authors from the first to the third centuries CE, as well as noncanonical Christian writings from the same period.[2] Within the latter group of texts are noncanonical Gospels, which are largely late and creative rewritings or elaborations of the canonical Gospels and their stories. A few noncanonical Gospels are wildly fantastic, but most scholars agree that other noncanonical Gospels may contain genuine historical traces of Jesus. For this reason, they have become very popular in historical Jesus research. The matter of the historical Jesus is not unimportant, and the conclusion of this book will return to it. Since the main question at present is Jesus's identity in these sources, however, I will limit discussion of historical accuracy here. I begin with images of Jesus that look, in many ways, like the canonical Gospels' Jesus.

The Agrapha: Some of Jesus's "Many Other Things"

The Gospel of John closes by telling its readers: "But there are also many other things that Jesus did"[3] (John 21:25; see also John 20:30). Luckily, some of these "many other things" have been preserved, and scholars refer to them as *agrapha* (sg. *agraphon*), which literally means "unwritten things." This term is ironic since these Jesus traditions *were* written (and that is how we are aware of them), but it reflects the fact that they were "not written" in the

---

2. Clearly, sources for Jesus exist after 300 CE as well, but they are not the focus here. For further reading on noncanonical sources for Jesus, see the bibliography included at the end of this chapter, and particularly Robert E. Van Voorst, *Jesus outside the New Testament: An Introduction to the Ancient Evidence*, SHJ (Grand Rapids: Eerdmans, 2000).

3. Unless otherwise noted, all biblical citations in this book are from the New Revised Standard Version (NRSV).

canonical Gospels. At least one *agraphon* occurs outside the Gospels but still in the New Testament—Acts 20:35 preserves Jesus's saying "It is more blessed to give than to receive."

Other *agrapha* appear in manuscripts of the canonical Gospels as textual variants. A few of these *agrapha* occur in multiple New Testament manuscripts and have become so popular that most English Bibles still print them, although often with notes explaining their secondary nature. Examples of such variants are the stories of the angel and the agony (Luke 22:43–44), the angel troubling the water (John 5:3b–4), and the adulterous woman (John 7:53–8:11).[4]

Codex Bezae (D), a bilingual Greek and Latin manuscript dated to 400 CE, preserves two *agrapha* that apparently did not enjoy as widespread an acceptance as the previous examples.[5] Bezae is the sole witness for an *agraphon* about a man working on the Sabbath between Luke 6:4 and 6:6[6]: "On the same day, seeing one working on the Sabbath day, Jesus said to him, 'Man, if you know what you are doing, you are blessed; but if you do not know, you are accursed and a transgressor of the law.'" Bezae is also one of only two Greek manuscripts (the other being sixth-century Codex Beratinus [Φ]) that preserve a statement of Jesus placed after Matthew 20:28: "But seek to increase from that which is small, and to become less from that which is greater."

Codex Bezae's *agrapha* may seem odd to readers familiar primarily with stories of Jesus from the canonical Gospels, but one cannot consider them uncommon. Hundreds of *agrapha* occur in the writings of early Christian fathers or manuscripts.[7] Perhaps the most widely circulated *agraphon* in the early church, cited by multiple early church fathers, is Jesus's teaching "Be competent money changers." Another interesting *agraphon* appears in a fragmentary manuscript dated to 200 CE known as Papyrus Egerton 2, or the "Egerton Gospel."[8] This text is dependent upon the canonical Gospels but also includes an otherwise unattested miracle of Jesus at the Jordan River.[9]

---

4. Another possible example is the longer ending of Mark (Mark 16:9–20), although this passage is a compilation of other Jesus traditions rather than a true *agraphon*.

5. For brief discussion of both *agrapha* and Codex Bezae, including a picture of the page including the Luke 6 *agraphon*, see Bruce M. Metzger and Bart D. Ehrman, *The Text of the New Testament: Its Transmission, Corruption, and Restoration*, 4th ed. (New York: Oxford University Press, 2005), 70–72, from which the English translations in the main text are taken.

6. Luke 6:5 occurs after 6:10 in this codex.

7. See the extensive collection in William D. Stroker, *Extracanonical Sayings of Jesus*, RBS 18 (Atlanta: Scholars Press, 1989).

8. Convenient English translations are in Ron Cameron, ed., *The Other Gospels: Non-Canonical Gospel Texts* (Philadelphia: Westminster, 1982), 74–75; Robert J. Miller, ed., *The Complete Gospels: Annotated Scholars Version*, rev. and exp. ed. (Santa Rosa, CA: Polebridge, 1994), 416.

9. P.Egerton 2, fragment 2, verso, lines 65–70 (following the versification of Cameron, *Other Gospels*, 75).

Some *agrapha* are undoubtedly more likely than others to have originated with Jesus, but in general the *agrapha* demonstrate the truth of John 21:25—Jesus did indeed do and say more than the canonical Gospels record.

Jesus the Executed Wise Man

Several ancient authors describe Jesus as a Jewish "wise man." Such an identification of Jesus, while positive and reflecting his renown, is certainly not an inherently Christian one. Augustine (early fifth century) reports that even staunch pagan critics of Christianity were willing to recognize Jesus as a wise man,[10] including the third-century pagan critic Porphyry, who affirmed that "the gods have declared that Christ was very pious" and that Jesus was one of "the wise men of the Hebrews."[11]

At least two other ancient authors describe Jesus as "wise," but do so in the context of describing his execution. The first is Josephus, a first-century Jewish historian and contemporary of the apostle Paul. Josephus had lived in Galilee during his early life as a military officer and thus was familiar with the social and historical context in which Jesus and his disciples operated. He mentions Jesus twice in his *Jewish Antiquities*. In one reference, he identifies James as "the brother of Jesus who was called the Christ."[12] A few scholars have thought the Christian scribes who preserved Josephus's writings may have inserted this reference. The majority, however, affirm that this phrase was in Josephus's original text, primarily because Josephus does not identify Jesus directly as *the* Christ but as someone *called* the Christ. If later Christians had modified the text, they likely would have identified Jesus as Christ rather than as a messianic claimant.

More open to the charge of later Christian modification is Josephus's fuller reference to Jesus, which is where he refers to Jesus as a wise man. This text is known as the *Testimonium Flavianum* ("testimony of Flavius") and reads as follows in the Greek text as we have it.

> About this time there lived Jesus, a wise man, if indeed one ought to call him a man. For he was one who wrought surprising feats and was a teacher of such people as accept the truth gladly. He won over many Jews and many of the Greeks. He was the Messiah [*christos*]. When Pilate, upon hearing him accused by men of the highest standing amongst us, had condemned him to be crucified, those who had in the first place come to love him did not give up their affection for him. On the third day he appeared to them restored to life, for the prophets of God had prophesied these and countless other marvelous things about him. And the tribe of Christians, so called after him, has still to this day not disappeared.[13]

10. Augustine, *Harmony of the Gospels* 1.7.11.
11. Augustine, *Civ.* 19.22–23 (Dods, NPNF[1]).
12. Josephus, *Ant.* 20.200 (Feldman, LCL).
13. Josephus, *Ant.* 18.63–64 (Feldman, LCL).

Flavius Josephus

According to his own writings, Josephus was a Jewish commander in Galilee during the great revolt against Rome that began in 66 CE. As a priest, he became involved in the conflict as a result of his service (*Life* 7) and, despite working to calm Jewish resistance, eventually led troops. Upon capture, Josephus appealed to his captor Vespasian and prophesied that he would become emperor (*J.W.* 3.8.9). Once Vespasian became emperor, Josephus returned to Jerusalem with Titus, Vespasian's son, and worked further to calm the Jewish resistance to Rome. Once again unsuccessful, Josephus returned to Rome after the destruction of the temple in 70 CE and lived the rest of his days there, being supported by the emperor and taking the name "Flavius." While in Rome, he wrote an account of the Jewish revolt (*Jewish War*), a history of the Jewish people (*Jewish Antiquities*), an autobiography (*The Life of Flavius Josephus*), and an apologetic work (*Against Apion*), explaining Jews and Jewish customs for the Roman aristocracy. His writings are one of the most important sources for understanding the Judaism of Jesus and early Christianity.

Although scarcely anyone doubts that Josephus wrote something about Jesus and his followers here, scholars are rightly skeptical that he wrote these exact words. Among other elements of the *Testimonium*, Josephus's reference to Jesus as a wise man and miracle worker and his reference to Christians as a "tribe" have a greater claim to originating with Josephus.[14] These references to Jesus fall far short of being full faith statements, and the description of Christians as a "tribe" is not a typical Christian way of referring to Jesus followers.

Other more explicitly Christian elements, however, and especially his identification of Jesus *as* Christ and a fulfillment of prophecy, are likely Christian interpolations for the following reasons. First, if Josephus did in fact believe Jesus was Israel's messiah, it is difficult to explain why he does not say more about him in his writings and why elsewhere he identifies Jesus as one *called* Christ (*Ant.* 20.200). Second, it is also difficult to explain why he elsewhere views the Roman emperor Vespasian as the divinely appointed deliverer of the Jews, even confessing him as "master not of me only, but of land and sea and the whole human race."[15] Third, the *Testimonium*'s context in the *Antiquities* makes it unlikely that Josephus said anything exceedingly positive about Jesus. He mentions Jesus as part of a larger discussion of failed Jewish rebellions

14. Cf., however, Ken Olson, who argues that the *Testimonium* as we have it reflects so much Eusebian influence that Josephus's original is unrecoverable ("A Eusebian Reading of the *Testimonium Flavianum*" [paper presented at the annual meeting of the Society of Biblical Literature, New Orleans, LA, November 23, 2009]).

15. Josephus, *J.W.* 3.402 (Thackeray, LCL).

and disturbances during Pilate's term as prefect. He has little positive to say about Pilate, but he also does not see his seditious countrymen as worthy of emulation. In fact, Josephus introduces the next event after his reference to Jesus as "another outrage [that] threw the Jews into an uproar," suggesting that he understood the events of Jesus's life in a similar light as an unhelpful disturbance.[16] Finally, translations of Josephus's work into Arabic and Slavonic demonstrate conclusively that scribes have indeed modified the textual tradition at different stages, making the possibility that scribes altered the Greek text all the more likely.[17]

For these reasons, one can affirm that Josephus did write about Jesus and his followers and likely considered Jesus a wise man and worker of miracles. It is highly unlikely, however, that he affirmed that Jesus *was* the Christ, although he likely knew that others thought he was.

The British Museum in London contains a letter written sometime after the Jewish revolt ended in 74 CE that likewise refers to Jesus as wise, specifically as a "wise king."[18] The author, Mara bar Serapion, waxes eloquent to his son on the unfortunate fate of famous wise men, as well as the inevitable divine retribution persecutors of the wise receive.

> For what advantage did the Athenians gain by the murder of Socrates, the recompense of which they received in famine and pestilence? Or the people of Samos by the burning of Pythagoras, because in one hour their country was entirely covered with sand? Or the Jews *by the death* of their wise king, because from that same time their kingdom was taken away? For with justice did God make recompense to the wisdom of these three: for the Athenians died of famine; and the Samians were overwhelmed by the sea without remedy; and the Jews, desolate and driven from their own kingdom, are scattered through every country. Socrates is not dead, because of Plato; neither Pythagoras, because of the statue of Juno; nor the Wise King, because of the laws which he promulgated.[19]

In Mara's letter, Jesus joins the ranks of Socrates and Pythagoras as a wise man whose own people rejected and murdered him. Admittedly, Mara does not refer to Jesus by name. Nevertheless, Jesus is certainly the person to whom

16. Josephus, *Ant.* 18.65 (Feldman, LCL).

17. For succinct discussion of the Arabic and Slavonic versions of the *Testimonium Flavianum*, including English texts, see Craig A. Evans, "Jesus in Non-Christian Sources," in *The Dictionary of Jesus and the Gospels*, ed. Joel B. Green, Scot McKnight, and I. Howard Marshall (Downers Grove, IL: InterVarsity, 1992), 364–65; Van Voorst, *Jesus*, 81–104.

18. The original editor and translator, William Cureton, posits dates for the letter from the end of the first century CE to the latter half of the second century CE (*Spicilegium Syriacum: Containing Remains of Bardesan, Meliton, Ambrose and Mara Bar Serapion* [London: Rivingtons, 1855; repr., Lexington: American Theological Library Association, 1965], xiv–xv). F. F. Bruce dates the letter to the "second or third century" (*Jesus and Christian Origins outside the New Testament* [Grand Rapids: Eerdmans, 1974], 31n31).

19. Cureton, *Spicilegium*, 73–74 (translator's italics).

he is referring. There is widespread tradition that Jesus was crucified as "King of the Jews" or "King of Israel."[20] And even Josephus knew that some people identified Jesus as "Christ," which means "anointed one" in Greek (*christos*) and in the Hebrew Scriptures refers to Israel's kings.[21] Mara also likely reflects a distinctively Christian interpretation of the results of the Jewish war as retribution for rejection of Jesus.[22]

Mara makes no mention of Pilate's role in Jesus's crucifixion, blaming it instead solely on Jesus's fellow Jews. Like Josephus and Porphyry, however, Mara views Jesus as a wise man.

Jesus the (Foolish) Founder of (Foolish) Christians

Several Greco-Roman writers refer to Jesus as the founder of Christianity, using "Christ" as a proper name for him. Since they are responding to the religion and its adherents, they reveal essentially no new information about Jesus's life. These writers do, however, reveal what later members of Greco-Roman elite society thought about the idea of a crucified messiah, which is important for understanding the background against which the canonical Gospels were read and understood by the imperial audience at large.

Some authors' comments about Jesus are only mildly derogatory. For example, Pliny the Younger, in a letter to the emperor Trajan written around 112 CE, describes Jesus as the focus of Christian worship services and as someone whom Christians deify. He claims that, when interrogated, Christians "also declared that the sum total of their guilt or error amounted to no more than this: they had met regularly before dawn on a fixed day to chant verses alternately among themselves in honour of Christ as if to a god."[23]

Suetonius, a contemporary of Pliny who was also writing in the early second century, refers to Jesus as the cause of disruption in the Jewish community in the city of Rome. He says of the emperor Claudius, "Since the Jews constantly made disturbances at the instigation of Chrestus, he expelled them from Rome."[24] Suetonius's Latin text refers to *Chrestus* rather than *Christus*, which one would expect for a Latinizing of the Greek *Christos*. The two spellings would have been pronounced almost identically, however, and scholars generally

20. "King of the Jews": Matt. 27:11, 29, 37; Mark 15:2, 9, 12, 18, 26; Luke 23:3, 37–38; John 18:33, 39; 19:3, 14–15, 19, 21. "King of Israel": Matt. 27:42; Mark 15:32; *Gos. Pet.* 3:2; 4:2.
21. See the anointing of Saul, David, and Solomon in 1 Sam. 10:1; 16:13; 1 Kings 1:39, respectively. Note also that "Christ" and "King of Israel" are synonymous in Mark 15:32 (cf. Luke 23:2).
22. Among others, Matt. 23:37–38; 27:25; Luke 19:41–44; John 11:47–50; 1 Thess. 2:14–16; Justin Martyr, *1 Apol.* 32, 47–49, 53; *Dial.* 25, 108.
23. Pliny the Younger, *Ep.* 96 (Radice, LCL). This is the earliest pagan reference to a Christian worship service.
24. Suetonius, *Claud.* 25.4 (Rolfe, LCL). Van Voorst translates *impulsore Chresto* as "because of the instigator Chrestus" rather than "at the instigation of Chrestus" (*Jesus*, 31).

agree that Suetonius is referring to "Christ" being a source of disturbance in Jewish synagogues that were just beginning to distinguish between Christian Jews and non-Christian Jews. Indeed, this is likely the same edict of Claudius that caused Aquila and Priscilla to move to Corinth (Acts 18:2).

Jewish Christians presumably would have been able to return to Rome when Claudius died in 54 CE. According to another contemporary of Pliny, the historian Tacitus (writing ca. 116 CE), however, ill fortune awaited them only ten years later. Describing the aftermath of the great fire of 64 CE, Tacitus claims that the emperor Nero, unable to stop the rumor that he had set the fire himself, made Christians the scapegoats:

> Therefore, to scotch the rumour, Nero substituted as culprits, and punished with the utmost refinements of cruelty, a class of men, loathed for their vices, whom the crowd styled Christians. Christus, the founder of the name, had undergone the death penalty in the reign of Tiberius, by sentence of the procurator Pontius Pilate.[25]

Thus, Tacitus's account of Jesus and Christians contrasts with those of Pliny and Suetonius in two ways. On the one hand, Tacitus reveals that members of Greco-Roman society actively disdained Christians. Granted, neither Pliny nor Suetonius is quick to cast Christians in a positive light; but Tacitus claims that Christians are "loathed" for adhering to a "pernicious superstition."[26] He also mentions an event from Jesus's life (his death at the hands of Pilate). In the next two sources, the disdain for Christianity and Jesus is even more explicit.

In the late second century, Lucian of Samosata satirized Jesus and Christians in his *Passing of Peregrinus*. He portrays Peregrinus as capable of duping a group of Christians based upon their gullibility.[27]

> In a trice he made them all look like children; for he was prophet, cult-leader, head of the synagogue, and everything, all by himself. He interpreted and explained some of their books and even composed many, and they revered him as a god, made use of him as a lawgiver, and set him down as a protector, next after that other, to be sure, whom they still worship, the man who was crucified in Palestine because he introduced this new cult into the world.[28]

Lucian considers Christians detestable for being conned by Peregrinus, so much so that he attributes Jesus's death to nothing other than his having

25. Tacitus, *Ann.* 15.44 (Jackson, LCL). The earliest manuscript of Tacitus's *Annals*, dated to the eleventh century, makes a spelling error similar to that made by Suetonius when claiming that the crowd identified Christ followers as "Chrestians." Van Voorst believes "Christians" is original (*Jesus*, 43–44). Regardless, it is clear that Tacitus is referring to Jesus and Christians.
26. Tactitus, *Ann.* 15.44 (Jackson, LCL).
27. Similarly, Celsus (discussed below) claimed Christianity was "successful only among the uneducated because of its vulgarity and utter illiteracy" (Origen, *Cels.* 1.27 [Chadwick]).
28. Lucian, *Peregr.* 11 (Harmon, LCL).

founded Christianity. Elsewhere, Lucian has equally
derogatory language for Jesus
and his followers when he
refers to Jesus as Christians'
"first lawgiver . . . [who] persuaded them that they are all
brothers of one another after
they have transgressed once for
all by denying the Greek gods
and by worshipping that crucified sophist himself and living
under his laws."[29]

Figure I.1. "Alexamenos worships (his) god."

The Alexamenos graffito
provides another Roman witness to the sentiment Lucian
expresses (fig. I.1). This carving was found on a stone in a
guardroom on Palatine Hill
and is difficult to date but falls
generally into the time period
under consideration (first to
third centuries CE).[30] It shows
an opinion of Jesus and his later worshipers in Rome that, again, was not
very positive.

In the graffito, Jesus hangs on a cross, having an ass's head where his human
head should be. Just below him, another man, presumably Alexamenos, looks
up at the crucifixion victim and raises a hand in worship. The Greek inscription mockingly reads, "Alexamenos worships (his) god."

Taken together, these Greco-Roman authors demonstrate the truth of Paul's
claim that the idea of a crucified messiah was "foolishness to Gentiles" (1 Cor.
1:23). To accept the testimony of the canonical Gospels in the pre-Constan-
tinian Roman Empire was also to be an object of scorn.

Jesus the Son of Pantera

While the Greco-Roman authors discussed above concentrate their in-
flammatory comments on Christians and mention Jesus in passing, other
ancient critics of Christianity focus on Jesus himself. One of the more stinging

---

29. Lucian, *Peregr.* 13 (Harmon, LCL).
30. Graydon F. Snyder: "No fixed date can be given for this drawing" (*Ante Pacem: Archaeological Evidence of Church Life before Constantine* [Macon: Mercer University Press, 1985]), 28.

criticisms is that, far from being born of a virgin, Jesus was the product of an act of adultery by his mother, Mary. This accusation appears in the work of Celsus and in later rabbinic tradition.

Celsus was a prominent second-century pagan critic of Christianity. His writings survive only in excerpts from Origen, a church father who, around a century after Celsus, still found it necessary to respond to his attack. In Origen's *Against Celsus*, he addresses Celsus's acceptance of a Jewish accusation that Jesus "fabricated the story of his birth from a virgin" and actually "came from a Jewish village and from a poor country woman who earned her living by spinning . . . who was driven out by her husband, who was a carpenter by trade, as she was convicted of adultery."[31] The accusation goes on to claim that while Mary "was wandering about in a disgraceful way she secretly gave birth to Jesus" and that Jesus then went to Egypt and acquired magical powers.[32] A little later in his response to Celsus, Origen reveals more of the accusations against Mary: "The mother of Jesus . . . had been convicted of adultery and had a child by a certain soldier named Panthera."[33] Origen's defense of the Gospel accounts of Jesus's miraculous birth occupies the next couple chapters of his work. He even responds to Celsus's scoffing at the idea of divine conception because God could not have possibly been attracted to Mary since she was not wealthy or royalty![34]

Celsus's claim that some Jews believed that Jesus was the son of Mary and a Roman soldier named Pantera is likely accurate, for the response of the Jews in John 8:41—"*We* are not illegitimate children"—may hint that Jesus was being called a bastard child already in the first century. Later Jewish tradition contains the same charges as Celsus, referring to Jesus as Jesus ben Pantera ("Jesus son of Pantera"; e.g., *b. Šabb.* 104b and the medieval *Toledot Yeshu*).[35] One prominent explanation for this Jewish code name for Jesus is that it arose as a wordplay on the Greek word for virgin used in Matthew 1:23, *parthenos*.[36] Under this view, the Jewish charge intentionally contradicts the early Christian belief that Jesus was born of a virgin and accuses Christians of simplemindedness, having confused Jesus son of *parthenos* with Jesus son of Pantera.

31. Origen, *Cels.* 1.28.
32. Ibid.
33. Ibid., 1.32.
34. Ibid., 1.39.
35. For full discussion of Jesus in rabbinic tradition and the *Toledot Yeshu*, see Peter Schäfer, *Jesus in the Talmud* (Princeton: Princeton University Press, 2007); Van Voorst, *Jesus*, 104–34.
36. See Schäfer, who observes, "This story of the adulterous mother and her bastard son is the perfect counternarrative to the New Testament's claim that Jesus was born of a virgin betrothed to a descendent of the house of David" (*Jesus*, 97–99, at 97–98). Schäfer argues more broadly that the talmudic stories of Jesus "presuppose a detailed knowledge of the New Testament, in particular the Gospel of John, presumably through the Diatessaron and/or the Peshitta, the New Testament of the Syrian Church" (8–9).

The Babylonian Talmud, a body of Jewish teachings that reached its written form around 500 CE, provides a statement on Jesus with which Celsus would have agreed and sums up the later rabbis' opinion of Jesus: "Yeshu . . . has practiced sorcery and enticed Israel to apostasy" (*b. Sanh.* 43a).[37] Celsus and these Jewish writers thus join the previous Greco-Roman authors in portraying Jesus and his followers negatively.

Jesus the Mischievous Little Boy

If Jewish portrayals of Jesus at the time of Celsus downplayed the miraculous elements of Jesus's young life, a couple of early Christian texts from around the same time period, the *Infancy Gospel of Thomas* and *Infancy Gospel of James*, go to the other extreme.

The *Infancy Gospel of Thomas*, so named because the text identifies its author as "Thomas the Israelite" (1:1), is one of the most interesting early Christian texts we possess.[38] It portrays a young and temperamental Jesus who alternately uses his divine powers for good or mischief, moving over the course of the narrative from receiving harsh criticism to receiving worship. The story opens with a five-year-old Jesus causing trouble when he breaks the Sabbath by turning clay sparrows into live ones (2:1–7) and closes with an account of the twelve-year-old Jesus in the Jerusalem temple that mirrors the same story in Luke 2:41–51 (19:1–13). In between are many extraordinary tales, including one in which Jesus strikes dead one of his playmates for annoying him (3:1–3), Joseph pulling Jesus by the ear when he gets into trouble (5:4), Jesus knocking out and reviving his teacher (14:4; 15:7), and Jesus healing his brother James from a viper bite (16:1–2).

The *Infancy Gospel of Thomas* is not alone in the infancy gospel genre, as the *Infancy Gospel of James* (or *Protevangelium of James*) has also survived. The *Infancy Gospel of James* focuses, however, more upon the miraculous circumstances of Jesus's conception and birth and also the virginal conception of his mother Mary.[39] I will thus not dwell upon it here. Both these infancy gospels are dependent upon the infancy narratives of Matthew and Luke and are best viewed as creative enhancements of those narratives. They attempt to pacify early Christian curiosity by filling in some gaps in the Matthean and Lukan infancy narratives with dramatic details.

37. Translation is that of Schachter, reproduced in Jacob Neusner, trans., *The Babylonian Talmud: A Translation and Commentary*, vol. 16, *Tractate Sanhedrin* (Peabody, MA: Hendrickson, 2005), 220. Schäfer provides in his front matter an interesting image of a manuscript of the Babylonian Talmud where censors have erased this reference to Jesus.

38. Here and below I follow the versification of Ronald F. Hock, trans., "The Infancy Gospel of Thomas," in Miller, *Complete Gospels*, 371–79.

39. *Prot. Jas.* is the earliest text to reflect the doctrine of the perpetual virginity of Mary and claims that Jesus's brothers and sisters are from Joseph's previous marriage (9:2).

The Passion Narrative

A "passion narrative" is a Gospel account of Jesus from the Garden of Gethsemane until his death on the cross. The word "passion" here does not, as in everyday language, refer to what Jesus was passionate about. (No one was passionate about being crucified!) Rather, "passion" derives from the Latin *passio*, "suffering," and designates the sections of the Gospels that narrate Jesus's final acts of suffering. Many scholars believe the passion narratives were the earliest pieces of Jesus tradition to circulate in the young church.

There are dozens of other noncanonical Gospels. One scholar estimates that there are at least forty (a number with obvious and purposeful biblical overtones) other "gospels."[40] Two of those are important for present purposes because of their dates, the image of Jesus they offer, and the scholarly discussion surrounding them: *Gospel of Peter* and *Gospel of Thomas*.

Jesus in the Gospel of Peter

The *Gospel of Peter*, so named because it identifies its author as "Simon Peter" (14:3), survives only in fragments. What remains of the primary manuscript witness to the *Gospel of Peter* is a version of the passion and resurrection narratives that clearly is literarily related to the canonical versions but contains interesting differences from them. For example, Jesus, instead of shouting from the cross, "My God, my God, why have you forsaken me?" (Mark 15:34; Matt. 27:46), shouts, "My power, my power, you have forsaken me!" (5:5).[41] Also, the *Gospel of Peter* claims Pilate gave the Jewish leadership a Roman centurion named Petronius to guard Jesus's tomb (8:4; cf. Matt. 27:65). One of the most spectacular sections of the *Gospel of Peter* is when Jesus emerges from his tomb, his head reaching higher than the skies and alongside two gigantic angels only slightly shorter, followed by a cross that speaks (*Gos. Pet.* 10:2–5).

The *Gospel of Peter* emphasizes Jewish responsibility for Jesus's death more than the canonical Gospels. The first line of the surviving fragment notes, "of the Jews no one washed his hands" (1:1), in contrast with Pilate's handwashing in Matthew 27:24 (cf. *Gos. Pet.* 11:4). Immediately after this verse, the text says Herod—not Pilate, as in all four canonical Gospels—ordered Jesus's crucifixion (1:2). At several places the Jewish leadership confesses its collective guilt and Jesus's innocence (7:1; 8:1). The Jesus of the *Gospel of*

---

40. Christopher Tuckett, "Forty Other Gospels," in *The Written Gospel*, ed. Donald A. Hagner and Markus Bockmuehl (Cambridge: Cambridge University Press, 2005), 238–53.

41. Modified from Arthur J. Dewey, trans., "The Gospel of Peter," in Miller, *Complete Gospels*, 403.

Peter is therefore characteristically a Jesus killed by his own countrymen, who state as much themselves. Rome's guilt is absolved, as Pilate does not give the execution order and in fact acknowledges Jesus as "son of God" (11:4).

The *Gospel of Peter* has garnered significant scholarly attention because of Jesus scholar John Dominic Crossan's theory that the *Gospel of Peter* contains within it an earlier text (Crossan calls it the *Cross Gospel*) that is the original source for all four canonical Gospels and the *Gospel of Peter*.[42] Further research has discredited this theory and identified the *Gospel of Peter* as a second-century Gospel that is creatively rewriting (and thus dependent upon) the canonical Gospels.[43] (Alternatively, one scholar has questioned cogently whether most of the fragmentary manuscripts scholars typically identify as the *Gospel of Peter* are witnesses to the same text that early church fathers called the *Gospel of Peter*.[44])

Jesus in the Gospel of Thomas

The *Gospel of Thomas*, which identifies its author as "Didymos Judas Thomas" and should not be confused with the infancy gospel by that name, has produced a tsunami of scholarly discussion. The text survives in three early third-century Greek fragments from Oxyrhynchus and a fourth-century Coptic manuscript from Nag Hammadi.[45] Proposed dates for the composition of the *Gospel of Thomas* differ, but it can generally be dated to the late first century or second century CE.[46] The complete Coptic manuscript contains 114 freestanding sayings of Jesus that occur with no surrounding narrative, revealing a Gospel that is related to the canonical Gospels but ultimately unique.[47]

---

42. John Dominic Crossan, *The Cross That Spoke: The Origins of the Passion Narrative* (San Francisco: Harper & Row, 1988), esp. 17–18.

43. Alan Kirk, "The Johannine Jesus in the Gospel of Peter: A Social Memory Approach," in *Jesus in Johannine Tradition*, ed. Robert T. Fortna and Tom Thatcher (Louisville: Westminster John Knox, 2001), 313–21; Charles L. Quarles, "The Gospel of Peter: Does It Contain a Precanonical Resurrection Narrative?" in *The Resurrection of Jesus: John Dominic Crossan and N. T. Wright in Dialogue*, ed. Robert B. Stewart (Minneapolis: Fortress, 2006), 106–20.

44. Paul Foster, "Are There Any Early Fragments of the So-Called *Gospel of Peter*?" *NTS* 52 (2006): 1–28.

45. Oxyrhynchus and Nag Hammadi are archaeological sites in Egypt where scholars discovered many ancient manuscripts, both Christian and non-Christian.

46. Uwe-Karsten Plisch, *The Gospel of Thomas: Original Text with Commentary*, trans. Gesine Schenke Robinson (Stuttgart: Deutsche Bibelgesellschaft, 2008), 15–16.

47. The majority of scholars would cite the Q source as a "sayings" Gospel like *Gospel of Thomas*. "Q" (from the German *Quelle*, "source") is an appellation given to an otherwise unknown source that, according to certain solutions for the Synoptic Problem (which deals with the similarities and differences between the Gospels of Matthew, Mark, and Luke), is the source of the material Matthew and Luke share that is absent in Mark. Since, however, no manuscript evidence for Q exists and it is thus a hypothetical document, the *Gospel of Thomas* remains unique as a Gospel that presents Jesus exclusively through his sayings.

The *Gospel of Thomas*'s Jesus often utters sayings that also appear on the lips of Jesus in Matthew, Mark, Luke, and John. For example, the *Gospel of Thomas* includes the parable of the sower (*Gos. Thom.* 9; Matt. 13:3–9) and Jesus's common rejoinder from the Synoptics, "Let anyone with ears listen" (*Gos. Thom.* 21; Matt. 11:15; 13:9; Mark 4:9, 23; Luke 8:8; 14:35).[48] The *Gospel of Thomas* preserves Jesus's comparison of the kingdom of God to a mustard seed (*Gos. Thom.* 20; Matt. 13:31–32) and his statement that "the Son of Man has no place to lay his head and rest" (*Gos. Thom.* 86; Matt. 8:20). Also like the canonical Jesus, Jesus in the *Gospel of Thomas* teaches on the kingdom of heaven (e.g., 20, 22) and the Sabbath (27), says the famous "Blessed are the poor, for yours is the Kingdom of Heaven" (*Gos. Thom.* 54; Matt. 5:3//Luke 6:20), and claims, "Give Caesar what belongs to Caesar, give God what belongs to God." (*Gos. Thom.* 100; cf. Mark 12:17).[49] Additionally, some of Jesus's companions from the canonical Gospels also appear in the *Gospel of Thomas*, including James (12), the disciples (13), the Pharisees and the scribes (39), John the Baptist (46), Salome (61; cf. Mark 16:1), Jesus's brothers and mother (99), and Mary Magdalene (114).

Despite these similarities, however, the *Gospel of Thomas* is "a very different, indeed a dissonant, portrait of Jesus."[50] First, it contains several teachings of Jesus that appear nowhere else, some of which are very strange. For example, according to *Gospel of Thomas* 28, Jesus taught, "I took my place in the midst of the world, and I appeared to them in flesh. I found them all intoxicated; I found none of them thirsty." *Gospel of Thomas* 108 claims Jesus said, "He who will drink from my mouth will become like me. I myself shall become he, and the things that are hidden will be revealed to him." Finally, in one of the strangest sections in the text, Peter says, "Let Mary leave us, for women are not worthy of Life," to which Jesus responds, "I myself shall lead her in order to make her male. . . . For every woman who will make herself male will enter the Kingdom of Heaven" (*Gos. Thom.* 114). Needless to say, Jesus turning women into men is a miracle unattested in any other Jesus tradition, canonical or noncanonical!

Second, the *Gospel of Thomas* is devoid of an interconnecting story and consists of repeated aphorisms with the stock formulaic introduction "Jesus said . . ." Jesus's sole function in the *Gospel of Thomas* is thus to offer aphoristic teaching. The other characters in the document appear in a similar light, simply as prompts who ask questions that lead to one of Jesus's sayings. This is one stark difference between the *Gospel of Thomas* and the canonical

48. Here and below, with slight modifications, I follow the English translation of Thomas O. Lambdin, trans., "The Gospel of Thomas," in *The Nag Hammadi Library in English*, ed. Marvin W. Meyer (Leiden: Brill, 1977), 118–30.

49. *Gos. Thom.* 100 continues, "and give me what is mine."

50. Larry W. Hurtado, *Lord Jesus Christ: Devotion to Jesus in Earliest Christianity* (Grand Rapids: Eerdmans, 2003), 453.

Gospels; in the latter, characters are used to make important statements on Jesus's identity.

Third, the *Gospel of Thomas* has *gnostic* tendencies, or at least a gnostic veneer to its theological outlook in the form in which we have it.[51] The Coptic manuscript of the *Gospel of Thomas* was in fact discovered alongside numerous other gnostic works. Gnosticism, from the Greek word *gnōsis* ("knowledge"), viewed attainment of secret knowledge as the key to salvation. The Jesus of many of the sayings in the *Gospel of Thomas* is therefore a revealer of such salvific knowledge, providing salvation through his teachings rather than through his sacrificial death, as in other versions of the Jesus story. This alternative inter-pretation of Jesus as Savior is evident from his first saying, "Whoever finds the interpretation of these sayings will not experience death" (*Gos. Thom.* 1). The *Gospel of Thomas*'s theological outlook also explains its genre as a collection of sayings—for this Jesus need do nothing else in order to offer his followers salvation—and thus its omission of Jesus's death and/or resurrection.

There is little about the *Gospel of Thomas* that scholars do not debate, including its date, whether it represents an incipient or fully developed Chris-tian gnosticism (or none at all), and whether it is dependent upon the canoni-cal Gospels or vice versa.[52] Although some sayings in the *Gospel of Thomas* may represent a stage of Jesus tradition that is independent of the canonical Gospels, the weight of scholarly opinion is that other sayings in the *Gospel of Thomas* are revisionist history of Jesus that is dependent upon the canonical Gospels. Thus, these sections purposefully rewrite, or co-opt, the canonical image of Jesus into an alternative theological framework.

The *Gospel of Thomas* is an appropriate place to end the sampling of noncanonical images of Jesus in the first to third centuries CE because the rest of this chapter and book will focus specifically upon what the *Gospel of Thomas* either removes or omits from the canonical portrait in order to offer its alternative sayings-salvation Jesus—the narrative and full cast of charac-ters surrounding Jesus. It is important to bear in mind, however, that early Christians first encountered the canonical stories of Jesus in a larger cultural context that viewed (or would come to view) Jesus as a wise man who was executed; as the founder of an ill-educated, silly superstition; as the product of an illicit affair between his mother and a Roman centurion; as a supernatural god-man who could do miracles as a youth or whose height reached into the heavens after his resurrection; and as a speaker of wisdom who bestowed secret salvific knowledge.

---

51. Plisch, recognizing the complicated tradition history of the disparate sayings in the *Gospel of Thomas*, observes, "The *Gospel of Thomas* in its entirety can hardly be defined as Gnostic" (*Gospel of Thomas*, 33). That is, although some elements of the *Gospel of Thomas* comport with gnosticism, some do not, and thus one must be cautious in viewing it against a gnostic background.

52. See ibid., 9–36.

Narrative Considerations: Jesus inside the Canonical Gospels

The Gospels of Matthew, Mark, Luke, and John all were likely written before 100 CE. Scholars' proposed specific dates for the writing of each Gospel differ one from another, sometimes by a few decades. Mark, however, is generally considered to be the first written Gospel and dated around 65–75 CE. Matthew and Luke, whom most scholars agree used Mark in writing their Gospels, are dated after him, around 70–85 CE. John is generally considered to be the last of the canonical Gospels to have been written and dated around 80–100 CE. The canonical Gospels are therefore the earliest extant accounts of Jesus's life.

The Earliest Gospel Narratives

Perhaps more important, the canonical Gospels are the earliest *narrative* accounts of Jesus's life, since each offers its image of Jesus in the form of a story. As we have seen, this was not a universal practice for early Christians, since the Christians responsible for the *Gospel of Thomas* present their image of Jesus in the form of a catalogue of his sayings. In contrast to the *Gospel of Thomas*, the canonical Gospels have *narrators* who tell the story of Jesus, *characters* who enliven the story of Jesus, *settings* that situate the story of Jesus, *plots* that direct the story of Jesus, and *conflict* that drives the story of Jesus to its resolution.[53] To ask about the identity of the canonical Jesus, then, is to ask how the Gospel *narratives* generate their respective images of Jesus. And, as discussed at the beginning of this chapter, to ask how the narratives generate their portraits of Jesus is to ask how the narrators and characters within the narrative provide ways of grasping that identity.

Before we proceed, however, the phrase "canonical Jesus" needs to be clarified. On the one hand, since Matthew, Mark, Luke, and John attained a collective identity as the canonical Gospels (at least by shortly before 180 CE), one can rightly refer to their joint presentation of Jesus as "the canonical Jesus." On the other hand, this can be a misleading description, since the canonical Gospels do not jointly present *an* image of Jesus but rather *four* images. The canonical presentations of Jesus have tremendous similarities, of course. Each begins with Jesus in Galilee, mentions John the Baptist's early role in his life, and describes Jesus's subsequent ministry of teaching and healing, including his conflict with the Jewish political and religious authorities. Each also ends with Jesus's death in Jerusalem at the hands of Pontius Pilate, which the Jewish authorities instigate and Judas enables through his betrayal. That all four tell the same broad story is therefore obvious.

---

53. To an extent, the *Gospel of Thomas* does have a narrator and characters. They are not situated in a connected narrative, however, and so the *Gospel of Thomas* does not have other narrative dynamics such as plot, setting, conflict, etc.

Nevertheless, one should not overlook or diminish the fact that each canonical Gospel tells Jesus's story in its own distinct way that does not always
line up with the other accounts. Some contain events that the others do not.
For example, Matthew and Luke contain Jesus's genealogy and stories of
his birth (Matt. 1:1–2:23; Luke 2:1–38; 3:23–38), while Mark and John begin
with Jesus as a grown man; Luke alone records the story of Jesus's postres-
urrection appearance to disciples on the road to Emmaus (Luke 24:13–35);
and John alone records Jesus's conversation with the Samaritan woman at
the well (John 4:7–26). At other times, two or more Gospels may contain the
same story, but disagree on details. For example, the Synoptic Gospels place
Jesus's disruption of the temple at the end of his ministry (Matt. 21:12–13;
Mark 11:15–19; Luke 19:45–46), whereas John places it at the beginning
(John 2:13–22);[54] Mark claims Jesus healed blind Bartimaeus on the way
out of Jericho (Mark 10:46), whereas Luke claims he healed an anonymous
blind man on the way into Jericho (Luke 18:35), and Matthew claims Jesus
healed two anonymous blind men on his way out of Jericho (Matt. 20:30);
and all four Gospels narrate Jesus's Jewish trial and Roman trial, but only
Luke relays that Pilate sent Jesus to Herod before pronouncing judgment
himself (Luke 23:6–12).

That each Gospel has its own unique way of telling Jesus's story should
therefore caution readers against conflating the four versions into a single
"canonical Jesus" in an uncritical manner. To do so would be not only to
ignore the richness and integrity of each Gospel but also to ignore the historical and theological statement of the early church in its acceptance of all
four Gospels—similarities and differences in tow—as the official image(s) of
Jesus. Thus, as we consider the Gospels in the rough chronological order of
Mark, Matthew, Luke, and John, I will note especially how each Gospel's
narrator, characters, and readers converge in the narrative in order to answer
the question "Who was (or is) Jesus?" in a way that is both distinctive from
and similar to other canonical Gospels.

Jesus in the Gospel according to Mark

In his capacity as authoritative and trustworthy narrator, Mark opens his
Gospel by speaking directly to readers a resounding proclamation of Jesus's
identity: "The beginning of the good news of Jesus Christ, the Son of God"
(Mark 1:1).[55] Seemingly insignificant, this short sentence is packed with im-

54. Some scholars argue that the Synoptic Gospels refer to a different disruption of the temple
than John does, but I remain convinced that the texts refer to the same event.

55. Since some important ancient manuscripts omit "Son of God" in Mark 1:1 and other
important manuscripts include it, whether it is part of the original text is unclear. See R. T.
France, *The Gospel of Mark: A Commentary on the Greek Text*, NIGTC (Grand Rapids:
Eerdmans, 2002), 49.

portant information concerning Jesus. It identifies Jesus as the long-awaited Christ (*christos*, "Messiah") and Son of God. With both these titles, Mark taps into Jewish expectations of a kingly deliverer who would rid Jews of foreign domination and reestablish Israel by reestablishing God's reign in Jerusalem. As already discussed,[56] the Greek word for Christ, *christos*, which translates the Hebrew word for "Messiah," literally means "anointed one" and referred primarily to Israel's kings. "Son of God" also could refer to Israel's king, as indicated by one of the most prominent Old Testament texts that created messianic expectations for the Christ and/or Son of God—2 Samuel 7.

In 2 Samuel 7, God promises David that one of David's descendants will build the temple in Jerusalem and that he will establish this king's—this anointed one's—throne as eternal: "Your house and your kingdom shall be made sure forever before me; your throne shall be established forever" (2 Sam. 7:16). In addition, God identifies this son of David as his own son, that is, "Son of God": "I will be a father to him, and he shall be a son to me" (2 Sam. 7:14).

As the story continues, Solomon builds God's temple. Solomon does not, however, establish an eternal Davidic kingdom. Far from it, David's kingdom subsequently falls into disarray and splits into the northern kingdom of Israel and the southern kingdom of Judah. Eventually, both kingdoms are carried into exile away from Jerusalem and the promised land—Israel by the Assyrians in 722 BCE; Judah by the Babylonians in 586 BCE. Even worse, the Babylonians raze to the ground Solomon's temple (2 Chron. 36:18–19), the physical locus of God's promises in 2 Samuel 7. Since Solomon was therefore not the promised Christ, Son of God, or Son of David from 2 Samuel 7, later Jews experiencing foreign oppression looked for such an individual as a deliverer from their current circumstances and as the one who would establish David's eternal throne.

A Jewish text dated to the first century BCE, *Psalms of Solomon*, testifies to the expected fulfillment of God's promises in 2 Samuel 7. Its author eagerly anticipates the Messiah/King who will "destroy unrighteous rulers" and "purge Jerusalem from gentiles" (*Pss. Sol.* 17:22). That is, *Psalms of Solomon* expects the coming Messiah to establish his kingdom by banishing non-Jews from Jerusalem. These messianic expectations were still alive and well in Jesus's time, as the promised land was part of the Roman Empire and thus under the thumb of gentiles. By telling his reader in the first sentence of the narrative that Jesus is the Christ/Messiah and Son of God, then, Mark is claiming that a lengthy history of Jewish messianic expectations has come to fulfillment in the figure of Jesus of Nazareth—Jesus is the promised Son of David who will sit on David's eternal throne, ruling over an eternal kingdom.

Mark's presentation of Jesus's identity as the Christ/Messiah and Son of God, however, is more complex than Mark 1:1 initially indicates. For Mark,

---

56. See under "Jesus the Executed Wise Man" above.

Psalms of Solomon and
First-Century Jewish Messianic Expectations

Psalms of Solomon reveals what some Jews near the time of Jesus expected of the Messiah, and thus its text provides helpful background in understanding why the canonical Gospels are careful in their claims that Jesus was in fact the promised Messiah. Note how the author's expectations derive directly from 2 Samuel 7 but have evolved to take the shape of removal of gentile presence from the land.

> Lord, you chose David to be king over Israel,
> and swore to him about his descendents forever,
> that his kingdom should not fail before you. . . .
>
> See, Lord, and raise up for them their king,
> the Son of David, to rule over your servant Israel
> in the time known to you, O God.
> Undergird him with the strength to destroy the unrighteous rulers,
> to purge Jerusalem from gentiles
>   who trample her to destruction;
>   in wisdom and in righteousness to drive out
>   the sinners from the inheritance;
> to smash the arrogance of sinners
>   like a potter's jar;
> To shatter all their substance with an iron rod;
> to destroy the unlawful nations with the word of his mouth;
> At his warning the nations will flee from his presence;
>   and he will condemn sinners by the thoughts of their hearts.[1]

Pss. Sol. 17:4, 21–25

1. R. B. Wright, trans., "Psalms of Solomon: A New Translation and Introduction," in James H. Charlesworth, ed., *The Old Testament Pseudepigrapha* (Garden City, NY: Doubleday, 1985), 2:639–70.

readers must understand exactly what type of Christ and Son of God Jesus is, because he was not the type that Jews like the author(s) of *Psalms of Solomon* expected. One way in which Mark offers precision to Jesus's identity is through the appearance of "Christ" and "Son of God" on the lips of the characters in the course of the story. Peter, for example, identifies Jesus as Christ/Messiah in his famous confession of Jesus in Mark 8:29: "You are the Messiah."[57] Mark informs readers that Jesus then ordered the disciples not to reveal his identity to anyone (Mark 8:30), implying that Jesus accepted the identification. Immediately after accepting Peter's designation of him as Christ,

57. In Matthew's version of Peter's confession, he confesses Jesus as Christ and Son of God (Matt. 16:16).

however, Jesus clarifies that his messianic mission is very different from that of the Christ in *Psalms of Solomon* 17. For, he says, he must suffer and die (at the hands of fellow Jews!) and be raised (8:31). Peter cannot accept suffering and death—and the defeat they imply—as tasks for the anticipated king and Messiah. Peter rebukes Jesus for his words and, in turn, receives a rebuke from Jesus (8:32–33). As readers watch this unfold, they realize that Peter's confession of Jesus as Christ is correct in one sense, for Mark has already said as much in 1:1. But—and critically—it is incorrect in another sense because Peter misunderstands what type of Christ Jesus is.

Mark narrates Peter's misunderstanding in order to lead readers into a correct interpretation of Jesus as the Christ; for readers see Jesus accept this title only when he can define it in light of his messianic mission of death and resurrection. As we have already seen, the idea of a crucified messiah was ludicrous to Greco-Roman culture. The narrative of Mark, however, asserts that, far from disqualifying Jesus as a legitimate Christ/Messiah, his death and resurrection are where his identity as Christ is displayed most clearly. Through the character Peter, however, Mark shows that this identity of Jesus was next to impossible to accept.

Mark's narration of Jesus as "Son of God" also claims that Jesus's exalted identity is best understood in light of his crucifixion. After Mark identifies Jesus as Son of God in 1:1,[58] the title is restricted to usage by supernatural characters, God (1:11; 9:7) and demons (3:11; 5:7). The first and only occurrence of a human character calling Jesus Son of God comes from the centurion who watches Jesus breathe his last from the cross and responds, "Truly this was a/the Son of God" (15:39).[59] Mark's portrayal of a character's recognition of Jesus as Son of God provides a powerful statement on Jesus's identity to readers. Human characters' knowledge of Jesus *as* Son of God can come only by viewing him as a crucifixion victim. Therefore, and again, far from disqualifying Jesus from being the expected Son of God, Mark portrays his crucifixion as the place where Jesus most reveals that he is.

Despite common Christian convictions, Mark's identification of Jesus as Christ/Messiah and Son of God does not directly attribute to him a divine identity, since Scripture also refers to Israel's human king (anointed one) as God's son (e.g., Ps. 2:7). Mark does, however, raise the question of Jesus's relationship with God in other ways. Mark 2:6, 8 portrays Jesus as having Godlike omniscience in the story of the healing of the paralytic. In the same story, Jesus forgives the man's sins (2:5, 10), which readers overhear other

58. On the text-critical issue, see n. 55 above.

59. In Greek, the centurion's statement could be "a son of God" or "the Son of God." Mark may be exploiting the ambiguity in the Greek phrase to claim that the centurion confesses more than he knows; that is, by recognizing Jesus as a son of God, the centurion also unwittingly acknowledges his true identity as the Son of God.

characters claim is something that God alone does (2:7).[60] Mark also tells readers that Jesus controls the weather and sea (4:39), to the extent that he can walk on water (6:48–49). The Old Testament reserves these abilities for God alone (Job 9:8; 38:8–11, 16, 34; Pss. 65:7; 77:19; 89:9). In several places, then, Mark describes Jesus with categories that the Old Testament applies only to God. That is, he applies God's qualities to Jesus and asks his readers to connect the dots. Mark is also, however, at pains to portray Jesus with human qualities. Mark's Jesus gets angry and sad (3:5), falls asleep (4:38), and despite seeming omniscience, also confesses a lack of knowledge (13:32).

According to the Gospel of Mark, therefore, Jesus is the Christ and Son of God, titles that must reflect his messianic mission of crucifixion and resurrection in order to be understood properly. In addition, Mark narrates his story in such a way as to suggest that, though Jesus was recognizably a human, his identity was, in some ways, comparable with God's identity. Significantly, Mark never attempts to explain this theological conundrum.

Jesus in the Gospel according to Matthew

Although Matthew, like Mark, begins by identifying Jesus as Christ/Messiah (Matt. 1:1), he is also an excellent example of how a narrator can offer a statement on Jesus by telling his story in a particular way. Matthew works hard to paint a picture of Jesus as the fulfillment of Old Testament Scripture, and specifically the fulfillment of Moses's promise in Deuteronomy 18:15 that God would send another prophet like Moses (still unfulfilled in Deut. 34:10). Two places where Matthew portrays Jesus along these lines are his account of Jesus's birth and infancy and his narration of Jesus's Sermon on the Mount.

Matthew strategically narrates Jesus's young life in such a manner as to mimic Moses. Jesus's birth is surrounded by a tyrant's slaughter of infants (2:16) as was Moses's (Exod. 1:15–22). Jesus narrowly escapes the slaughter (2:13–14a), as did Moses (Exod. 2:1–10). So, Jesus spends his youth in Egypt (2:14b–15, 19), as did Moses (Exod. 2:11). Matthew even applies Hosea 11:1 ("out of Egypt I called my son"), originally a reference to the Hebrews leaving Egypt under Moses's leadership, to Jesus (2:15).

In a similar manner, Matthew narrates Jesus's famous Sermon on the Mount (5:1–7:29) in such a way as to show that Jesus as the new lawgiver replaces Moses, who originally brought the covenant law to Israel. Just as Moses went up the mountain (Exod. 19:20) and came down (Exod. 19:25) with the Ten Commandments, Matthew tells his reader that Jesus "went up the mountain" (5:1) and, by the time he "had come down the mountain"

---

60. Similarly, see Jesus's forgiving of the sinful woman in Luke 7:47–50.

The Beatitudes

Jesus's Sermon on the Mount (Matt. 5:1–7:29) opens with a section called "the Beatitudes." There are nine beatitudes, which include statements like "Blessed are the poor in spirit, for theirs is the kingdom of heaven" (Matt. 5:3) or "Blessed are the pure in heart, for they will see God" (Matt. 5:8). Church teachers everywhere often explain their name by claiming this is how one's "attitude" should "be." Although this is creative and perhaps true, the name "beatitude" actually derives from the first word in each Beatitude in the Latin Bible, *beati*, "blessed."

(8:1) at the end of his sermon, Israel had a new set of instructions. This new set of laws for the kingdom of God that Jesus preaches begins with the Beatitudes (5:3–12). By placing Jesus on a mountain in the giving of his law, then, Matthew deliberately describes Jesus with language reminiscent of the giving of the Mosaic law.

In this light, although Matthew never allows his opinion to rise to the surface of the text with a statement like "Jesus was the promised prophet like Moses," it is clear from his narration of Jesus's story—what he relays and how he relays it—that he wants his readers to reach that conclusion. If his readers stopped there, however, they would miss an important nuance in the Matthean portrayal of Jesus. For, while Matthew portrays Jesus as the prophet *like* Moses, he also portrays him as someone who far exceeds Moses. Matthew does not want his readers to miss the importance of the name "Emmanuel" in a prophecy he claims Jesus fulfills (1:22–23). Thus, he translates the Hebrew name for his Greek-speaking audience—"God with us" (1:23). Readers are thus alert to the fact that Jesus's arrival in the world is somehow to be understood also as God's arrival. Additionally, although Jesus goes up the mountain and comes down, like Moses did, his law supersedes the Mosaic law (5:21–44). Further, Matthew indicates Jesus's superior status to Moses and shared identity with God (and thus authority to override Mosaic law) by portraying Jesus as giving the Sermon on the Mount while still on a mountain (5:1; 8:1). The only one who gave the Mosaic law *while on a mountain* was God himself (Exod. 31:18; 34:27); Moses gave it to the Israelites only once he had come down from Mount Sinai (Exod. 32:15; 34:29; 35:1).[61] Like Mark, Matthew also portrays Jesus as someone who has the divine abilities to walk on water and control the weather (14:25, 32).

Therefore, for Matthew, Jesus is the promised prophet like Moses, as long as readers simultaneously recognize that Jesus is in a category Moses never was. This in itself is a startling statement, since there was never a prophet

61. Luke has Jesus come down from a mountain (Luke 6:12, 17) and reside on a "level place" (Luke 6:17) before he gives the Beatitudes.

like Moses (Deut. 34:10–12). Jesus, however, is more than a prophet—he is "God with us."

Jesus in the Gospel according to Luke

Luke's opinion of Jesus is also visible in the manner in which he narrates Jesus's story. Among other agreements,[62] Luke agrees with Mark that Jesus is the Christ. Instead of announcing that at the beginning in a direct statement to readers, however, he allows characters to identify Jesus as such. An angel claims Jesus is the Christ (2:11), as does the elderly Simeon upon seeing Jesus (2:29–32). In a similar example that is also unique to Luke's Gospel, the two thieves crucified on either side of Jesus disagree as to Jesus's identity as Christ.[63] The first chastises Jesus for claiming to be the Christ (23:39), while the second rebukes the first thief and pronounces Jesus's innocence, asking Jesus to remember him when he comes into the kingdom (23:40–42). The second thief functions similarly to the Markan centurion, who correctly identifies Jesus while Jesus is hanging on the cross. Luke thus presents two interpretive options for his readers as they view a crucified Jesus: his crucifixion is the ultimate means by which Jesus's messianic mission failed (the first thief); or his crucifixion is the ultimate means by which Jesus's messianic mission succeeded (the second thief).

A distinctive of Luke's image of Jesus is his emphasis on him as a Christ who attracts outcasts. Luke explains the reasons why large numbers of socially insignificant individuals came to Jesus: "And all in the crowd were trying to touch him, for power came out from him and healed all of them" (6:19). Other narrators describe Jesus as a healer as well, but Luke shows an affinity for portraying Jesus as such and populates his narrative with less-than-desirable characters. He describes Jesus healing unclean individuals, such as the hemorrhaging woman (8:43), the ten lepers (17:12–19), or a demon-possessed mute (11:14), or associating with tax collectors and sinners (5:30; 7:34; 15:1), such as the woman who washes his feet (7:36–50) or Zacchaeus the tax collector (19:2–10).

Luke's narration of Jesus's ministry thus leads readers to the conclusion that the kingdom of God that Jesus proclaims is open to exactly those marginalized Israelites whom the reigning authorities consider inadequate for God's kingdom. It was precisely the sinners and unrighteous gentiles (who employed the likes of Zacchaeus) whom, according to *Psalms of Solomon*,[64] some Jews expected the Messiah to remove from the land (*Pss. Sol.* 17:20, 23, 25). Luke's Jesus, however, says he came "to call not the righteous but sinners

---

62. For example, Luke 1:31–35 identifies Jesus as the Davidic heir and Son of God.
63. In Matt. 27:44 and Mark 15:32, the two thieves both chastise Jesus. They are silent in John (19:18, 32).
64. See "*Psalms of Solomon* and First-Century Jewish Messianic Expectations" earlier in this chapter.

Purity, Jesus, and the Kingdom of God

Some Jews at Jesus's time believed that Jewish society had become too impure for a pure God to live among, and that once that purity was restored, God would again reside with them.[1] The ostracizing of many of the individuals whom Jesus attracts was therefore not a personality defect on the part of Pharisees and other Jewish groups, but a matter of purity and religious convictions. The hemorrhaging woman was impure according to Leviticus 15:25; the ten lepers were impure according to Leviticus 13–14; the woman who washes Jesus's feet, if a prostitute, was impure according to Leviticus 15:17–18; and Zacchaeus was likely considered impure because he consistently came in contact with impure gentiles and handled their money. Jesus's healing of the bleeding woman, lepers, and sinful woman thus restores their purity, just as dining with Zacchaeus as a legitimate "son of Abraham" symbolically restores Zacchaeus to Israel.

Jesus's healing and teaching caused turmoil for Jewish leaders because it created a point of access—Jesus himself—to forgiveness and purity outside the sacrificial system and the temple. It also therefore created alternative definitions for who is in God's community, who is out, and who decides. Jesus placed himself at the center of God's restoration of Israel, a place that Jewish tradition reserved for God. These symbolic claims from Jesus, among other aspects of his ministry, are what infuriated the Jewish leadership in the Gospels.

1. One group in this category is the one responsible for the *Community Rule* discovered at Qumran. They set forth thorough purity regulations and believed that their pure society would constitute a temple and holy of holies (1QS VIII, 5–6), and applied Isaiah 40:3 ("prepare the way of the Lord") to themselves and their activity (1QS VIII, 14). Such statements are, of course, implicit criticisms of the temple and holy of holies in Jerusalem, where God was supposed to reside.

to repentance" (5:32) and "to seek out and to save the lost" (19:10). Jesus's interaction with these characters inevitably raises a question for readers: "Who is Jesus, that he can determine who is in and out of God's kingdom?" Luke's answer to this question, in the form of the story of Jesus he narrates, reveals one of his most sophisticated methods of presenting Jesus's identity.

Like the other canonical narrators, Luke tells his story in such a way as to suggest that, in some way, Jesus's identity is intertwined with God's identity. Luke does this, as recent research has demonstrated, by consistently referring to Jesus as *kyrios* ("Lord") in a deliberately ambiguous manner.[65] *Kyrios* in common parlance meant nothing more than "sir" or "master,"[66] but it

65. C. Kavin Rowe, *Early Narrative Christology: The Lord in the Gospel of Luke* (Grand Rapids: Baker Academic, 2006), 10.

66. Luke reflects the more common meaning of *kyrios* in Luke 19:33, but does so as a wordplay with v. 34, contrasting the colt's "masters/lords" with Jesus, "the Lord." See Rowe, *Early Narrative Christology*, 159–63.

also had a more exalted meaning in the Septuagint, the Greek translation of the Old Testament used by early Christians. The Septuagint uses *kyrios* to translate the Hebrew word for "God" and even uses it to translate the divine name of God.[67]

Luke uses *kyrios* in this latter, more exalted sense in order to refer to both God *and* Jesus. The opening chapters of the narrative demonstrate this usage of *kyrios*. Luke uses the word to refer unambiguously to God, unambiguously to Jesus, and ambiguously to either/both. At the beginning of his story, Luke refers to the "commandments of the Lord [*kyrios*]" (1:6), the "sanctuary of the Lord [*kyrios*]" (1:9), and an "angel of the Lord [*kyrios*]" (1:11). Readers know that these references are to Yahweh, the God of Israel, for that is the only entity to whom they could refer. Before readers emerge from the first chapter, however, Luke creates confusion by using *kyrios* to refer to Jesus. Elizabeth refers to Mary as "the mother of my Lord [*kyrios*]" (1:43). And, at Luke 2:11, Luke relays an angel's proclamation that the unborn Jesus will be "the Messiah, the Lord [*kyrios*]." He therefore refers to the God of Israel *and* the human Jesus, Joseph and Mary's son, as *kyrios*, rendering the question "Is *kyrios* God, as in the Old Testament, or Jesus?" seemingly unanswerable.

Luke exploits the confusion he has created by preserving the deliberate ambiguity in the term. For example, he reports that Zechariah prophesied about his son John the Baptist with these words: "And you, child, will be called the prophet of the Most High; for you will go before the Lord [*kyrios*] to prepare his ways" (1:76). Isaiah 40:3, the verse to which Zechariah alludes and which Luke applies directly to John the Baptist in 3:4–6, claims that the voice in the wilderness "prepare[s] the way" for God himself upon his return to Jerusalem. In Luke's narrative, however, John the Baptist does not precede God, but rather quite specifically Jesus. According to Luke, then, Jesus fills the role that Isaiah 40:3 attributes to God, so that, when the passage appears in Luke's narrative, *kyrios* possibly refers to either or both.

By employing *kyrios* in this manner, Luke strategically overlaps the characters to whom it refers: sometimes it refers clearly to God; sometimes it refers clearly to Jesus; other times it could (or must) refer to both. By so constructing his story, Luke forces his readers to think of Jesus in terms of God and pronounces that any answer to the question "Is *kyrios* God or Jesus?" that excludes either is inadequate. Luke's answer is "both," even though he consistently portrays Jesus and God as separate characters in the story. In the words of C. Kavin Rowe, "Luke uses *kyrios* to make an essential claim about the relation of Jesus and the God of Israel: Jesus of Nazareth is the movement of God in one human life so much so that it is possible to speak

---

67. Some manuscripts of the Greek Old Testament retain the Hebrew יהוה for the divine name in the Greek text. Scholars normally assume these are Jewish copies of the Greek Old Testament rather than Christian, although it is not always clear. See Larry W. Hurtado, *The Earliest Christian Artifacts: Manuscripts and Christian Origins* (Grand Rapids: Eerdmans, 2006), 18.

of God and Jesus together as *kyrios*."[68] Therefore, to return to the question that Luke's portrait of Jesus's association with sinners and other undesirables raises—who is Jesus that he can establish the boundaries of God's kingdom? He is *kyrios*, the Lord.

Jesus in the Gospel according to John

John's first fourteen verses are a direct address from the narrator to readers *à la* Mark and boldly declare, "In the beginning was the Word [*logos*], and the Word was with God, and the Word was God" (1:1). These words are bold statements from John because they deliberately mimic the opening line of Genesis 1:1, which similarly starts, "In the beginning . . . ," and is one of the primary texts that reflect Judaism's monotheism (belief in one god). John's further statement that "all things came into being through him, and without him not one thing came into being" (1:3) describes Jesus as the agent of creation, an action that Genesis attributes to God alone. Thus, the Johannine narrator starts his story by claiming that Jesus does what the one God does, is eternal as the one God is eternal, and, as the Word, "was God."

Nevertheless, John does not conflate the identities of Jesus and God completely, despite their overlap. Jesus as Son is the true revelation of the Father (1:18) but is nevertheless distinct from the Father. They function as separate characters, with Jesus appearing as a human being (1:14), who even weeps (11:35). Indeed, Jesus the Son prays to the Father (17:1–26), and the Son and Father speak to one another (12:27–28). The relationship between Jesus as Son and God as Father is one of the central themes in the narrative. Several passages demonstrate further how John leads his readers to identify Jesus as separate from God, but nonetheless as sharing in God's unique identity.

Similar to Matthew, John portrays Jesus as the prophet like Moses who is superior to Moses. Already in the first chapter, John tells his readers, "The law indeed was given through Moses; grace and truth came through Jesus Christ" (1:17). John's direct statement of Jesus's superiority to Moses takes narrative form in John 6. In the preceding context, Jesus argues with the Jews over his relationship to Moses, claiming, "If you believed Moses, you would believe me, for he wrote about me" (5:46). This argument sets the immediate narrative background for Jesus's miraculous feeding of a large group of people (6:1–13). His miracle mirrors the supernatural provision of manna when Moses led the Israelites in the wilderness (Exod. 16). The similarity in the miracle is not lost on Jesus's audience, who then proclaim, "This is indeed the prophet who is to come into the world" (6:14), a reference to the promised prophet like Moses from Deuteronomy 18:15. John would agree with the identification of Jesus as the prophet like Moses, but only with a

---

68. Rowe, *Early Narrative Christology*, 217–18; see also 27.

qualification. For, as narrator, he is clear that Jesus himself provided the food (6:11), whereas Moses was not the provider of food in the wilderness; God was. Later, John makes his point clear through the words of Jesus: "It was not Moses who gave you the bread from heaven, but it is my Father who gives you the true bread from heaven" (6:32). Like other canonical narrators, John uses the crowd's insufficient identification of Jesus to provide for his readers an example of how *not* to identify Jesus. John thus leads readers to think of Jesus in terms of God the provider, not Moses the agent, and thereby parallels Jesus's identity with God's identity.

As other examples of John's sophisticated presentation of Jesus's identity, several verses overlap Jesus's identity as Son with God's identity as Father. When asked why he is healing a man on the Sabbath, and thus working, Jesus responds by claiming he is doing nothing less than what the Father is doing: "My Father is still working, and I also am working" (5:17). As narrator, John then informs his readers that Jesus's alignment of himself with God, and especially his reference to God as *his* Father (instead of "our Father") had deadly consequences: "For this reason the Jews were seeking all the more to kill him, because he was not only breaking the sabbath, but was also calling God his own Father, thereby making himself equal to God" (5:18). John, of course, has already affirmed Jesus's status as parallel to God in the opening of the narrative, but readers see now that some characters' inability to grasp Jesus's identity will inevitably lead to his death. For John too Jesus's true identity is inextricably connected to his death.

An even more explicit example of the deliberate overlapping of the Son's and Father's identities is John 10:30. Similar to John's usage of the Genesis creation account in John 1, Jesus's response to the Jews request for him to identify himself (10:24) employs a traditional Jewish statement of monotheistic belief in order to include Jesus in the identity of the one true God. Jesus closes his response by climactically asserting, "The Father and I are one" (10:30). The Jews' response—an attempted stoning—demonstrates that Jesus crossed a sacrosanct line. The line he crossed was Deuteronomy 6:4.[69] Known as the "Shema," after the first word in the verse in the Hebrew text (*šĕma'*), Deuteronomy 6:4 states: "Hear, O Israel: The LORD our God, the LORD is one" (NIV). Jesus thus recites the last clause of this affirmation of the one true God's unique identity, as observant Jews were supposed to do daily (Deut. 6:7; see also *y. Ber.* 1.5, *b. Ber.* 9a–b), but does so by including himself in that identity. The Jews in the story do not miss the significance of what Jesus does: "It is not for a good work that we are going to stone you, but for blasphemy, because you, though only a human being, are making yourself God" (10:33).

_____

69. Similarly, Richard Bauckham sees the Shema behind John 10:30 ("Monotheism and Christology in the Gospel of John," in *The Testimony of the Beloved Disciple: Narrative, History, and Theology in the Gospel of John* [Grand Rapids: Baker Academic, 2007], 250–51).

John thus narrates his story of Jesus in such a way that the Father and Son have separate identities but nonetheless a shared identity. He uses his narrator's voice, and characters within the story, to present Jesus as the prophet like Moses, but greater than Moses, and as someone to whom the Shema—the quintessential Jewish monotheistic confession—refers. Significantly, John's presentation of Jesus's modification of the Shema in John 10:30 suggests that Jesus's divine identity does not compromise the monotheism that passage asserts; nor does Jesus's presence at creation as the Word compromise the role that passage asserts for God. Indeed, John's rhetoric demands the full force of those passages in order to make its point about Jesus, which is that, in some way, Jesus's identity parallels the identity of the one true God who created the universe and whom Jews confess as the only God. As with the other canonical narrators, John makes no attempt to unravel this theological riddle.

Therefore, the answer to the question "Who was (or is) the canonical Jesus?" is complex and multifaceted. Among many other things, he is the Christ and Son of God, God with us, the prophet like Moses who is greater than Moses, the *kyrios*, the preexistent Word, and the Son who uniquely reveals the Father. Furthermore, the canonical Jesus is a human who eats, sleeps, gets angry, and cries but also someone whose identity parallels the identity of God himself. Jesus does things only God does, such as forgive sins, restore purity, and walk on water, and occupies positions that only God occupies, like Creator of the universe and referent of the Shema. The Gospel narrators thus strategically encourage readers to identify Jesus with, or even as, God but never collapse the identities of the two into one in such a way as to obliterate either's distinct identity. Thus, and although the narrators do not attempt to explain how it could be that a person could exhibit a divine identity, it is clear they believed Jesus did.

In this light, the canonical gospels make a startling claim about Jesus's identity implicitly that John 1:18 makes explicit—God's identity is revealed through Jesus's identity. Combined with each Gospel's emphasis that Jesus's identity is most accurately apprehended via his crucifixion and resurrection, then, the Gospels make an even more startling claim—God's identity is revealed through the actions of someone who has power over the grave but nonetheless submits to a torturous death on behalf of God's people.

Conclusion

Christians and pagans alike struggled with the idea of a messiah and/or god who reveals himself in the weakness of a shameful death. Indeed, as we have seen, many, from the apostle Peter to the inscriber(s) of the Alexamenos graffito, scoffed emphatically at the idea of a crucified man being worthy of adulation.

This reaction should not surprise modern readers; it certainly would not have surprised the Christians responsible for the canonical Gospels. Although the canonical narratives are unapologetic in offering the startling answers to the question of Jesus's identity that they do, they also forthrightly claim that Jesus's presence evoked multiple responses from his contemporaries, a fact the broader historical record confirms.

Further, in their own stories, the canonical narrators' portrayals of the multiple responses to Jesus reveal their strategic usage of characters in offering their image of Jesus. Those characters with a divine or supernatural perspective—God, angels, and demons—identify Jesus accurately and provide readers with an authoritative affirmation of the narrators' own statements. The human characters, however, struggle with Jesus's identity. True enough, some, like Simeon in Luke, recognize Jesus immediately. But others, like most of the Jewish leadership, consistently fail to grasp Jesus's identity. Peter's confession of Jesus as Christ shows that a character can even simultaneously correctly and incorrectly identify Jesus. By employing such a wide cast of characters, and thus showcasing a wide range of responses to Jesus, the narrators provide their readers with interpretive options. In some cases, the narrators lead readers to a particular identification of Jesus via characters. This is particularly clear, for example, in the Lukan story of the two thieves crucified next to Jesus, or Peter's misguided confession of Jesus, without which readers would not know what type of Christ Jesus is, what Mark means by identifying him as such in Mark 1:1, and why Jesus's death is part of the messianic mission rather than evidence that it has failed.

Therefore, the characters of the canonical narratives are invaluable to the narrators' overall portrayals of Jesus. Their misunderstandings and affirmations of Jesus are central dynamics of each narrative that enable readers to decipher his identity as the story progresses. In other words, without the characters, the Gospel narratives cannot offer the robust answers to the question "Who was (or is) Jesus?" that they do. And, needless to say, this chapter has featured only a selection of the characters in the Gospels. Still awaiting discussion are enigmatic characters like John the Baptist, Judas, Nicodemus, and many others. With that in mind, the rest of this book will further introduce readers to Jesus by introducing them to the friends and enemies who surround him in the canonical narratives.

Suggestions for Further Reading

Jesus outside the Gospels

Bruce, F. F. *Jesus and Christian Origins outside the New Testament*. Grand Rapids: Eerdmans, 1974.

Cameron, Ron, ed. *The Other Gospels: Non-Canonical Gospel Texts*. Philadelphia: Westminster, 1982.

Evans, Craig A. "Jesus in Non-Christian Sources." In *The Dictionary of Jesus and the Gospels*, edited by Joel B. Green, Scot McKnight, and I. Howard Marshall, 364–68. Downers Grove, IL: InterVarsity, 1992.

France, R. T. *The Evidence for Jesus*. The Jesus Library. Downers Grove, IL: InterVarsity, 1986.

Van Voorst, Robert E. *Jesus outside the New Testament: An Introduction to the Ancient Evidence*. SHJ. Grand Rapids: Eerdmans, 2000.

Jesus inside the Gospels

Bock, Darrell L. *Jesus according to Scripture: Restoring the Portrait from the Gospels*. Grand Rapids: Baker Academic, 2002.

Burridge, Richard A. *Four Gospels, One Jesus? A Symbolic Reading*. 2nd ed. Grand Rapids: Eerdmans, 2005.

Culpepper, R. Alan. *Anatomy of the Fourth Gospel: A Study in Literary Design*. FF. Philadelphia: Fortress, 1983.

Rhoads, David, Joanna Dewey, and Donald Michie. *Mark as Story: An Introduction to the Narrative of a Gospel*. 2nd ed. Minneapolis: Fortress, 1999.

PART 1

The Friends of Jesus

1

God and Angels

EDITH M. HUMPHREY

Anyone who has taught Sunday school knows about the little girl who has a stock one-word answer for every question: "God!" With this response, seven-year-old Emily figures that she has a good chance of answering correctly—though not with any depth.

This chapter faces the same dilemma. How can we talk with any substance about God in the Gospels, since God is the main actor and the initiator of every action, not only in the Gospels but also in the entire scriptural library? The other heavenly characters, the angels, are not so prominent, but they appear at key points in the biblical narrative; moreover, the corpus of literature that provides the background for their appearances in the Gospels is varied and vast. To class the almighty God alongside other characters in stories about Jesus may appear impudent; to trace the mysterious force of the angels risks speculation. Yet we will see that the connection of God and the angels with Jesus coheres well with the main theme of this volume—surely Jesus is in the company of his *friends*.

We begin by looking at key concepts of God and of the angels that informed the Evangelists and that occasionally provide a foil against which they react. In writings that circulated prior to the Gospels, we find customary titles, various descriptions of God and the angels, and stories in which they precipitate or perform characteristic action. (At times we also will consider writings concurrent with or postdating the New Testament, because these may preserve for us ways of speaking about God and the angels that come from an earlier time but that are available to us only through such later documents.) With this

Protology and Eschatology

Eschatology is a word heard frequently today, due to end-of-the-world theories taught in several American denominations and sensationalized in novels and film. The word *eschaton* refers to the end; so *eschatology* (sometimes confused with *apocalyptic*) is the study of those things connected with "the end." However, *eschatology* is a slippery term in the hands of theologians, as G. B. Caird demonstrates in his cogent book *The Language and Imagery of the Bible*,[1] where he adduces at least seven different meanings of the term. After all, to which "end" are we referring—the end of an era or the absolute end of the space-time universe? The term *protology* is the mirror opposite of *eschatology*, referring to the dawn of creation, even to the "time" before that. In this category belongs the fall of rebel angels (cf. *1 Enoch* 6–9; *2 Apoc. Bar.* 56:12–14; 2 Pet. 2:4; Jude 6), who make their influence felt in the human realm (e.g., Dan. 10:13, 20; Wis. 2:24; Tob. 3:8; Eph. 6:12, Gal. 4:3–9). Alternately, there are clues concerning "good angels," as in Job 38:7, where they are called the "morning stars." (Astral imagery is often used for minor deities and angels.) These sang for joy at the creation, but Job knows nothing of this mystery, since protology is beyond the ken of humanity. Secrets about time, protological and eschatological, as well as mysteries about unseen worlds are seldom disclosed in the Bible, but are partially unveiled in those strange books called "apocalypses" (e.g., Daniel, Revelation, *1 Enoch*, *4 Ezra*, *Apocalypse of Abraham*), whose generic title means "an unveiling" or "revelation."

1. G. B. Caird, *The Language and Imagery of the Bible* (London: Duckworth, 1980), 243–71.

context in place, we will read Mark, Matthew, Luke, and John with an eye to where God and the angels make their impact, both separately and together, but always in connection with Jesus himself.

It is clear from the outset of each Gospel that the main denotation given to God is that of the supreme Deity associated with the drama of humankind and especially of Israel, beginning with the creation stories in Genesis. References to God's *angels* push further back to what we may call "protological time," adding a mysterious "apocalyptic" dimension to this story. That is, the narrative of God's dealings with humankind and with Israel sometimes is prefaced and bordered by an earlier and parallel narrative involving angels. This dimension is memorialized in Western culture by the epic poem of John Milton, whose *Paradise Lost* commences not with the human plight but with the rebellion of Satan.

Historical Considerations: God and the Angels in the Biblical and Later Traditions

First we will consider the portrayal of God and angels in the biblical and later traditions that informed the authors of the canonical Gospels.

Ēl and *ʾĔlōhîm*

The simplest Hebrew form of the word for God is *ēl*, incorporated in the names "Isra*el*," "Micha*el*," "Rapha*el*." *ʾĔlōhîm* is the plural and can accurately be translated "gods" (Ps. 82:1b). Commonly, it is used in the Bible to refer to the singular God of the Hebrew people, with the plural ending perhaps suggesting God's majesty (thus sometimes called the "majestic plural"), similar to the English royal use of "we."

God in the Biblical and Later Traditions

Let us follow the contours of the Bible, starting with God's active engagement with the seen world: "In the beginning God created" (Gen. 1:1 RSV). We may trace this drama, along with N. T. Wright[1] and others, as an open-ended five-act play: creation, the fall, the call and history of Israel, the climax of the story in Jesus, and the continuing drama of God's people in a world that God promises to judge and renew. The first three acts of this story were not clearly discerned as such by the Hebrew, Israelite, or Jewish people who related and transmitted these narratives. This is the shape, however, implied by the Evangelists, who craft their narratives with the previous "acts" in view, and with a defined hope for the future. They consider themselves inheritors of a tradition in which God's character has been revealed: God is Creator of the world and Sovereign over history; God is also the "LORD of hosts" (1 Sam. 1:3; 2 Kings 19:31; Ps. 24:10; cf. 2 Kings 6:17), commanding unseen forces whose actions have a bearing on the space-time world. He is Lord of all.

So impressive is this God that, in the Hebrew Bible, his generic title, *ʾĕlōhîm*, takes a plural form. *ʾĔlōhîm* is a classifying noun ("God") rather than a name: so beyond human understanding is God that his full nature cannot be named by human beings (not even by his specially chosen people), nor fully conceived. Moses does not name God, for to name is to dominate. Rather, God reveals his mysterious "name" as *YHWH* (Exod. 3:14).

In the Hebrew/Israelite/Jewish tradition, *YHWH* is held in such great respect that the name is not uttered. When reciting Scripture in Hebrew, the reader encounters *YHWH* adorned with the vowel-pointings for the word *ʾădōnāy* ("Lord"), and by this convention is cued to substitute *ʾădōnāy* orally in its place. In the mature Jewish tradition (from the first century CE and afterward), the sense of holiness is amplified: not only *YHWH*, but even *ʾădōnāy* is avoided (except for prayer), and terms such as *haššēm* ("the Name"), "Heaven," "Glory," "Power," and "Abode" come into currency. (See Matt. 5:34, which already may reflect this practice in the phrase swearing "by Heaven.") Other

---

1. See the structural narrative that informs N. T. Wright, *The New Testament and the People of God*, COQG 1 (Minneapolis: Fortress, 1992).

YHWH

The four Hebrew consonants transliterated *YHWH* form what is known as the "tetragrammaton" ("four-lettered word"). This holy "name" (commonly pronounced "Yahweh" in academic circles) may be discerned in English translations of the Old Testament when the word "Lᴏʀᴅ" is printed in small capitals, and the name is associated with the verb "to be" (Exod. 3:14). Its precise sense remains unknown: "I am," "I will be," or even perhaps "I cause to be." In the Hebrew Bible, *YHWH* is found often in combination with *'ĕlōhîm* ("the Lᴏʀᴅ God"). The varied combinations of *'ĕlōhîm* and *YHWH* form a key plank in some scholarly theories concerning the compilation of the *Torah* (the Pentateuch, the first five Old Testament writings). The short form for *YHWH* is *yāh*, which appears in a number of biblical names (e.g., "Eli*jah*") and in the cry "Hallelu-jah!" (= "Praise Y/Jah!").

alternative titles for God use periphrasis: "Father of the sons of truth" (the Qumran community), "Prince of gods," "King of majesties," "Ruler of all creatures," "God of gods," "King of kings," "Ruler over all earthly kings," and "God of knowledge." These substitutes for *YHWH* (and *'ădōnāy*) and descriptive expansions of the generic *'ĕlōhîm* are not all found in the Gospels but are consonant with the character of God expressed there.

Besides the trio of *YHWH*, *'ĕlōhîm*, and *'ădōnāy*, there are common biblical titles that evoke images or contexts: "God Most High" (*'ēl 'elyôn*) places God over other super-human beings, probably over rival tribal deities; "Lord of hosts" (*YHWH ṣĕbā'ôt*) pictures a warrior leading the heavenly armies; "Holy One of Israel" associates him with Israel; "God of the fathers/patriarchs" or "the God of Abraham, Isaac and Jacob" recalls Hebrew history. The Lᴏʀᴅ God, though exalted, reaches into human affairs—breathing life into Adam, calling Israel into being, writing the Ten Commandments on stone tablets by means of "his finger" (Exod. 31:18), and inspiring Israel's leaders by his presence, or "Spirit" (e.g., Num. 11:25; 2 Sam. 23:10).

For hundreds of years, it seems, the Hebrews (and then Israelites) as a group did not deny outright the existence of other deities. Rather, they positioned their Lᴏʀᴅ above all others, practicing an exalted "henotheism" (the *choice* of one supreme God among others, e.g., Ps. 82:1) instead of the absolute monotheism now expressed in Judaism and Christianity. Even while the Shema (Deut. 6:4) and other passages imply a *practical* monotheism, we see a continuing Israelite admission that other deities exist in the proscriptions of biblical prophets against the worship of Baal and Molech. However, the association of the term *YHWH* with the verb "to be" came to involve an implicit denial of the "being" of other deities. The trajectory moves toward an acknowledgment of YHWH alone, emerging full-blown in the pointed sarcasm of (deutero-) Isaiah: "Who would fashion a god or cast an image that can do no good? . . .

He plants a cedar. . . . Part of it he takes and warms himself. . . . The rest of it
he makes into a god, his idol, bows down to it and worships it. . . . [A] deluded
mind has led him astray, and he cannot save himself or say, 'Is not this thing
in my right hand a fraud?'" (Isa. 44:10–20).

Probably by the Persian period (fifth century BCE), and certainly by the
Common Era, Jews and then Christians were known for what others regarded
as their eccentric notion that there is only one God worthy of worship—indeed,
Christians came to be charged as "atheists," as we see in the second-century
Martyrdom of Polycarp.[2] At that time, Christian apologists also faced off
with the gnostic movement, some of whose writers radically reinterpreted the
Hebrew Scriptures, as we can verify from the cache of texts found in 1945 at
Nag Hammadi. Gnostics reanimated the biblical stories with various deities,
including a creator (the "Demiurge") who is not the supreme God. When the
biblical deity's words "I alone am God" are placed in the mouth of the Demiurge, they are heard by readers no longer as a call to monotheistic faithfulness,
but "as the height of . . . hubris and stupidity."[3] Even in the wider religious
setting of the second century, Jewish and Christian monotheism continued
to be a curiosity.

We must also consider the Greek expression of biblical names for God.
Both Hellenistic Jews and Christians throughout the empire mainly read their
Scriptures in Greek translation called the Septuagint (abbreviated LXX), and so
the Greek titles and phrases used for God were appropriated in the New Testament and Christian tradition. *'Ĕlōhîm* becomes *theos*, YHWH (with *'ădōnāy*)
is generally rendered *kyrios* ("Lord"), "the Most High" is rendered *hypsistos*,
and "Lord of Hosts" is rendered *kyrios pantokratōr* (literally, "Lord–Ruler
over all"). Interestingly, the "to be" connotation of YHWH comes to the fore
in the participial Greek title *ho ōn* ("the One who is," "the Existing One"),
used in Christian worship and on icons of Jesus.

Especially notable is the tradition whereby two of God's primary attributes
came to be pictured as agents of God, beginning with Proverbs and Psalms and
then developed in the rabbinic tradition, as well as in the Deuterocanonical
writings. God's "Word" (Hebrew, *dābār*; Greek, *logos*; and the associated Aramaic *memra* in the targumim) and God's "Wisdom" (Hebrew, *ḥokmâ*; Greek,
sophia) began as poetic personifications (e.g., Word in Ps. 33:6; Wisdom in
Proverbs 8), which were then vividly amplified so that in the texts they seem
to assume will and personality as quasi-independent beings alongside God.

In Wisdom of Solomon, we read: "For while gentle silence enveloped all
things . . . your all-powerful Word leaped from heaven, from the royal throne,
into the midst of the land that was doomed, a stern warrior carrying the sharp

2. *Mart. Pol.* 9.2
3. Larry W. Hurtado, *Lord Jesus Christ: Devotion to Jesus in Earliest Christianity* (Grand
Rapids: Eerdmans, 2003), 526.

Deuterocanonical/*Anagignoskomena*/Apocryphal, Pseudepigraphal Writings and Parabiblical Writings

The term *parabiblical* refers to a myriad of writings that are connected by theme or narrative with the books that were eventually recognized as sacred by the Jewish rabbis, or as canonical by Christians. (The term *canonical*, or "according to the 'rule' of faith," is a specifically Christian term, whereas rabbis, when they debated the limits of the Hebrew Bible, spoke of those books that required a ceremonial washing of hands.) Parabiblical books were written at various times and in various genres: some pieces were more popular (e.g., *Joseph and Aseneth*), while others offered serious reflections upon theology and sacred history. Some of these books (e.g., Wisdom of Solomon, Susanna, Judith, Tobit, Bel and the Dragon, the books of the Maccabees, *4 Ezra*) were honored by inclusion in the Septuagint, the Greek translation of the Hebrew Bible, before rabbis of the late first century CE delimited those sacred "books that rendered the hands unclean." Because the earliest Christian communities were separating from Jewish circles during the time that the rabbis were making these decisions, they were not subject to the rabbinic decision. In many Christian circles, "extra" books of the Old Testament were retained until the time of the Reformation, when Protestants rejected them. These books (the list varies between Roman Catholic and Orthodox traditions) are known as the "Deuterocanonical" writings ("Second-Canon," Roman Catholic term), *Anagignoskomena* ("Knowable" or "Readable" Books, Eastern Orthodox term) or "Apocrypha" ("hidden away," the pejorative Protestant term). Other parabiblical books, called *Pseudepigrapha*, not included in any "canon," continued to be read (and written) as pious, imaginative minds filled in "gaps" in the biblical stories or meditated upon biblical themes. Some of these may be found in the two-volume work *The Old Testament Pseudepigrapha*, by James Charlesworth. (Christian Pseudepigrapha are called *New Testament Apocrypha* and have been edited by Wilhelm Schneemelcher.)[1]

1. Wilhelm Schneemelcher, ed., and R. McL. Wilson, trans., *New Testament Apocrypha*, rev. ed., 2 vols. (Louisville: Westminster John Knox, 1991).

sword of your authentic command, and stood and filled all things with death, and touched heaven while standing on earth" (Wis. 18:14–16). Here the "Word" depicts both the Exodus "angel of death" and the LORD, who is sovereign over world history. Like the angel in Exodus, the Word enacts God's commands; like the Lord, the Word is both transcendent and immanent. A similar phenomenon occurs in the figure of Wisdom (Wis. 7:22–8:8), who "is a breath of the power of God, and a pure emanation of the glory of the Almighty" (7:25), but who (like the LORD) is "one" (7:27). Thus, Wisdom demonstrates some of the characteristics of God but also provides a link between God and humanity, making them "friends of God." Again, in Sirach 24, Wisdom dwells with Israel, especially in Jerusalem, while in Baruch 4:1, Wisdom is equated with the Torah, given to Israel from God by the hand of the angels. Wisdom and Word are strongly linked together, a bond implied in the poetic doublet of Wisdom of Solomon 9:1–2: "O God . . . who have made all things by your Word, and by your wisdom have formed humankind." *First Enoch*, however, relates a more pessimistic story in which Wisdom cannot find a dwelling place on earth (not even in Israel) and so returns to heaven, allowing "Folly" full reign on the earth (*1 En.* 42).

We have lingered over these figures of Wisdom and Word because they provided material for Christian expressions of the Son's deity (beginning in the New Testament with John 1:11–18; Col. 1:15–20); in later Christian tradition, the Wisdom motifs are connected with the Holy Spirit. Christians were not alone in exploiting these images. Contemporaneous with earliest Christianity, the Jewish philosopher Philo engages in dialogue with Greek philosophers, tracing the activity of a divine "Word" (*logos*) alongside God, as well as God's "words" (*logoi*), which he says are known among the common people as angels.[4] These *logoi*, explained Philo, are sent by God as helpers of the righteous, physicians for the soul and guides to morality.[5] With Word and Wisdom, then, we encounter two striking figures that bring together divine, angelic, and human categories and that are explained variously by Jewish and Christian writers.

The traditions to which the Gospel writers laid claim thus included a variety of titles for God and descriptions of God's activity, all of which underscored God's ineffability alongside his intimate relationship with Israel. While the Lord is described throughout the Hebrew Bible in anthropomorphic ("human-shaped") terms (he can be angry, can change his mind, uses his "right arm," and so on), he remains "holy" and separate. So the prophet declares: "For my thoughts are not your thoughts, nor are your ways my ways, says the Lord. For as the heavens are higher than the earth, so are my ways higher than your ways and my thoughts than your thoughts" (Isa. 55:8–9). Various metaphors become favorites in describing this dynamic God, who is holy, righteous, and in covenant relationship with Israel: "Fortress," "Rock," "God of my Right," "the Judge of [all] the earth" (Gen. 18:25; Ps. 94:2), "Help," "Refuge," "Shield," and "Deliverer." During the time when the New Testament books were being written, Philo reconstrued such ideas, referring to God as "Architect" (*On the Creation* 15–25) and "the Unoriginate" (*Migration* 89–93), and recasting the name YHWH in philosophical terms as "the Existing One" (*That the Worse Attacks the Better* 160).

The Deuterocanonical and Pseudepigraphal writings refer to God in various ways—"God of the Universe," "the Holy Great One," "Most High," "Lord of the Spirits," "the Great King" (*1 Enoch* 1:3; 10:1; 47:1; 92:14); "Antecedent of

4. Philo, *Dreams* 1.19.
5. Philo, *Dreams* 1.12.

Time" (*1 Enoch* 46:1, cf. Dan. 7:9); "Imperishable God" or "Immortal God" (*Sibylline Oracles* 1:55; 1:155 and throughout); "Mighty One," "Inscrutable One," "Living One," "Immortal One" (throughout *2 Bar.*); "God of Heaven," "the Great One in Israel," "God of peace" (*T. 12 Patr.*); "God, who oversees all things, . . . holy among the holy ones" (3 Macc. 2:21); "the only living God" (4 Macc. 5:24). Some of these titles are polemical, reacting to the polytheism of the Roman and Hellenistic context round about. Though not all these come into the New Testament, they inform the character of the God who is depicted there.

Perhaps the most poignant metaphor used for this God is the "Father" of Israel, found in the Hebrew Bible in Exodus 4:22, Deuteronomy 32:6, Isaiah 63:16, Jeremiah 31:9, and Hosea 11:1. Though the later Jewish books usually speak more reverentially of God as "the Most High," this tradition of God's fatherly intimacy with Israel continues. In 3 Maccabees 7:6 (from perhaps ca. first century BCE), a pagan king concedes that the "God of heaven surely defends the Jews, always taking their part as a father does for his children." Again, God is wholly involved in the affairs of humanity and especially with Israel, yet is beyond human knowledge. This mysterious tension between transcendence and immanence is central to the highly influential vision of Isaiah 6 (cf. Mark 4:12; Matt. 13:15; John 12:40; Acts 28:27; Rom. 11:8): there God is depicted as "high and lofty," even while "the hem of his robe filled the temple," and he gave directions concerning "blind" Israel to his prophet, through his angels.

Angels in the Biblical and Later Traditions

Angels illustrate both the holiness and the engaged character of the LORD. Some scholars have seen angels (and demons) as a convenient category into which the Jewish people placed demoted "deities" once the monotheism of Judaism was established. While there may be truth to this, the logic of angels coheres well with the dual nature of God, who is separate but deeply concerned for his people. This transcendent God who remains intimately involved in human affairs is well served by agents who are neither human nor divine. As the first-century writer to the Hebrews would later interpret the ancient stories, angels are "spirits in the divine service, sent to serve for the sake of those who are to inherit salvation" (Heb. 1:14). However, because of the proximity of these beings to divinity on the one hand and to humanity on the other, there are places in the biblical writings where the delineation between God, the angels, and humanity is not crystal clear. Some Old Testament texts blur the line between God and his angel, whereas in the New Testament angels are not always clearly distinguished from humans. Such lack of precision gives rise to various readerly responses: an angel may appear as an extension of God's own being, character, and power; angels may remain anonymous, thus adding to their mystique; or we may not be certain whether we have encountered an angel in the text, and so redirect our attention to the less ambiguous elements of the story.

Especially known for mystery is "the Angel of YHWH." In the story of the three who visit Abraham (Gen. 18), there is a fluidity between "the LORD" who appears to Abraham, the "three men" whom he entertains, the "two angels" of this trio who speak to Lot, and the singular "Lord" who remains to consult with Abraham. When Hagar is sustained in the wilderness, there is a similar movement back and forth between "God" and "the angel of God" (Gen. 21:15–19). Again, in Genesis 32, Jacob (Israel) wrestles with a "man" whom he has no power to name, receives a blessing, and calls the place "Peniel" since he has "seen God face to face" (32:30). In Exodus 23:20–22, the LORD himself speaks about the angel who will go before Israel, whom they must obey, and who bears "in him" God's name. Centuries later, apocalyptic and rabbinic writers speculated about this "Name-bearing angel" in proximity with God's mysterious *merkabâ*, or chariot-throne, calling him "The Prince of the Presence," "Metatron," or even "the lesser YHWH" (cf. *3 Enoch*).

Besides the angel of the Lord, there are also groupings of angels and named angels in the pre-Christian traditions. Only Gabriel and Michael are specified

Merkabah Mysticism

Visionary rabbis engaged in Merkabah mysticism, a speculative tradition beginning at least by the Common Era. (Paul seems to intimate such practices in Rom. 10:6 and 2 Cor. 12:1–9.) *Merkabâ* was the name given to the chariot-throne of God, understood to be composed of orders of angels ("wheels" and "eyes") and portable—it visited Ezekiel on the Chebar River (Ezek. 1:1). A practice of meditation, fasting, and bodily positions was developed whereby the mature rabbi (at least of the age of thirty), in the company of visionary adept, "descended to the chariot" (paradoxically, a spiritual ascent!), glimpsed the heavenly world, and so understood the deeper meaning of Torah. Another type of mystical meditation, called *Bereshit* (literally "in the beginning"), focused on *protology* (see sidebar "Protology and Eschatology"). Evidence of these esoteric traditions is seen in apocalypses not included in the Hebrew Bible (e.g., the many extracanonical writings mentioned in *4 Ezra* 14:46), in the Enochic literature that details ascents through the heavens (e.g., *1 En.* 14:9–25), and in later references to first-century mystical rabbis (e.g., *Hekhalot Rabbati* 5 [107]). But Mishnah Ḥagigah 2.1 issues a warning: "Whosoever gives his mind to four things it were better for him if he had not come into the world—what is above? what is beneath? what was beforetime? and what will be hereafter? And whosoever takes no thought for the honor of his Maker, it were better for him if he had not come into the world." For more on Enoch in the apocalypses, Metatron, and rabbinic mysticism, see Gershom Scholem, *Major Trends in Jewish Mysticism* (New York: Schocken, 1995).

in the Hebrew Bible, bearing names that call attention to the Almighty, rather than to the figures themselves, Gabriel meaning "Strong Man / Hero of God" and Michael meaning "Who is like God?" The word "angel" is not actually applied to them when they appear in Daniel. Rather, the reader must infer their identity: Gabriel interprets visions at the command of God, appears in a vision that levels Daniel to the ground, and flies swiftly (Dan. 8:16–17; 9:21); Michael stupefies Daniel with his appearance and is the "chief" or "prince" who protects and "stands for" Israel (Dan. 10:13; 10:21; 12:1). These references are notable for their reserve. Little description is given, and the angels' functions are subordinate to the LORD, for the sake of God's people.

We must also note the strange attendants at God's throne, labeled as "seraphim" in Isaiah 6:2–7 and described along the lines of ancient "cherubim" (Mesopotamian winged animals) in Ezekiel 1:5–12. Both groups are associated with fire and adorned with wings. These figures are described more extensively than either Gabriel or Daniel, but since they are not named personally, there is still no explicit encouragement given to the reader who would collect "angel lore." Rather, the purpose of seraph and cherub is to mark the holy presence of God. In Isaiah, the seraphim actively defer by covering themselves and by their song of praise. In Ezekiel, the "living creatures" glorify the Lord over creation, attending YHWH as he visits the prophet for the sake of exiled Israel.

Certainly not all who read these visions heeded the biblical reserve, for a speculative tradition grew concerning the seraphim, the cherubim, the seven archangels, and so on. In Deuterocanonical and Pseudepigraphal books, we meet others. In the domestic story of Tobit, the incognito angel Raphael plays a key role as healer and protector. In *4 Ezra* (ca. 100 CE), Uriel is "Ezra's" philosophical sparring partner and interprets visions. *First Enoch* 20:1–8 lists seven archangels with various spheres of influence: Uriel, Raphael, Raguel, Michael, Saraqael, Gabriel, and Remiel. In popular books such as the Hellenistic Jewish novel *Joseph and Aseneth* (date uncertain, but by many assigned from 150 BCE to early second century CE), angels are paired with human beings: Joseph's heavenly counterpart is the unnamed "Anthropos" (human-shaped angel) who visits Aseneth (chaps. 14–17); the gentile princess Aseneth has a double in heaven called "Metanoia" (Repentance or Penitence); and other figures (Metanoia's companions) are also intimated (chap. 15).[6] Similarly, in

---

6. Various versions of *Joseph and Aseneth* illustrate different ways that ambiguous angels may be understood. Comparing the two strongest manuscript traditions, we see in chaps. 14–17 two different tendencies. In the short version, there is a brief glossing over of the angel's importance, where he briefly identifies himself as an army captain, and the focus turns back to Aseneth herself. In the long version, Aseneth makes much of asking the angel's identity, which she never learns, but she herself is given a new name. The first version pictures the angel as a bit player to rescue Aseneth from idolatry. The second version leaves open the question as to whether this is an angel, and surrounds this "Man" with an aura of divine mystery. His action of feeding Aseneth, renaming, and reclothing her proved irresistible for Christian communities, who discerned in the figure a type of Christ. An English translation of the short text taken from David Cook, "Joseph

apocalyptic and later mystical traditions (e.g., in 2 and 3 Enoch), angels assume great importance, set as guardians over the spheres of the heavens. In such books we find details about the fall of angelic orders (1 Enoch 6; Jub. 5:1; Pirqe Rabbi Eliezer 22) or the angelic role in giving the Torah to Israel (Jub. 1:29), and other historical or cosmic functions.

The Qumran community, too, understood life as intertwined with angelic activity. It is difficult to know what kind of influence such groups as the Essenes might have had on any of the New Testament writers, or how much of their perspective was paralleled by earliest Christian communities. At the very least, we see by means of the Qumran scrolls a community roughly contemporaneous with the New Testament that paid a good deal of attention to the unseen world. This is clear both in the books preserved at Qumran (e.g., 1 Enoch and the thirteen Songs of the Sabbath Sacrifice / Angelic Liturgy) and in the works that were more likely written by the sectarian community that lived there—the Thanksgiving Psalms, the War Scroll, and others.[7]

So then, both in esoteric and popular circles, angels were well known by the time the Gospels were written. Presumably only Gabriel and Michael are detailed in the canonical books because they rule over human affairs, whereas other archangels have more esoteric functions, and domestic angels (those assigned to individuals) did not merit recognition. But some of the traditions permeating the nonbiblical books were known to the New Testament and early Christian writers. Jude 9 refers to an apocryphal story about the angel Michael in The Assumption of Moses, while both Luke and Paul describe the Torah as given by angels (Acts 7:53; Gal. 3:19). Paul also refers to the presence of angels in the worship gathering (1 Cor. 11:10) and explains that Christians will, in the eschaton, "judge angels" (1 Cor. 6:3; cf. the "Watchers" story of 1 Enoch 1–36). Indeed, the interchange between the human and angelic world is mentioned in Ephesians 3:10, where the church is described as showing to the heavenly "powers" the mysteries of God, and in Revelation 12:7–12, where a heavenly battle between angels is paralleled by the human struggle to remain

---

and Aseneth," in H. F. D. Sparks, ed., The Apocryphal Old Testament (Oxford: Oxford University Press, 1984), 473–503, is available online at http://www.markgoodacre.org/aseneth/translat.htm, while the longer (and in my view, more authentic) text is Christoph Burchard, trans., "Joseph and Aseneth: A New Translation and Introduction," in James H. Charlesworth, ed., The Old Testament Pseudepigrapha (Garden City, NY: Doubleday, 1985), 2:177–247.

7. On the understanding of angels at Qumran, and a careful distinction between what seems to have been the angelology of the Dead Sea community, on the one hand, and perspectives found in 1 Enoch, on the other, see Maxwell G. Davidson, Angels at Qumran: A Comparative Study of 1 Enoch 1–36, 72–108 and the Sectarian Writings from Qumran, Journal for the Study of the Pseudepigrapha: Supplement Series 11 (Sheffield: JSOT Press, 1992). Scholars continue to debate concerning the community or communities that lived at Qumran, and also concerning which of the works found were penned by the Qumran community and which they inherited. I am assuming, with Davidson and others, that the Qumran community was a group of Essenes who preserved documents congenial to their teaching and worldview, while producing others.

faithful. Slightly later, in the second-century Christian apocalyptic work the *Shepherd of Hermas*, the Son of God is ranged alongside six "first-created" beings in a tableau that recalls the seven archangels (*Vis.* 3.4.1; *Sim.* 5.5.3). So then, earliest Christian writers were informed by this lore of angels and expected their readers to understand such tantalizing details. Let us turn now to the Gospels themselves to see the Holy One and these holy angelic ones acting "in character" as powerful friends of Jesus.

Narrative Considerations: God and the Angels in the Gospels

All four Gospels present God, or the Lord, as the initiator of their action. There is a complication, however, with the title "Lord" (Greek *kyrios*). It is used in the Gospels both for God and for the main human actor, Jesus. "Lord" served as an honorific tag for a human being in the Greek cultural context. However, since *kyrios* was pronounced aloud whenever the tetragrammaton was encountered in early Greek Old Testament texts, and since *kyrios* was actually written in the later Christian Septuagint as a translation for *YHWH*, we cannot be wholly certain as to what "the Lord" connoted for a first-century Christian readership. In the Gospels, "the Lord" acts—sometimes that Lord refers to the unseen God and sometimes to Jesus in particular. The ambiguity proves pregnant in suggesting a concerted action (or even a stronger identity) between Jesus and God. Let us look at beginnings and endings of the four Gospels to disclose how God and the angels act.

Beginnings and Endings

We begin with Matthew. After a genealogical preface, recalling the Lord's action through the stars (and otherwise!) of Israelite history, Matthew establishes the initiative of the Holy Spirit of God before any human response. Mary is "found" already expectant by the Spirit, as we are told both by the omniscient narrator (Matt. 1:18) and by an "angel of the Lord" (1:20). Immediately after this, we are reminded about what has been spoken "by the Lord" in the prophets concerning the name of the Messiah, "God-with-us." Within Matthew's first chapter, "the Lord," the Holy Spirit, and "Emmanuel" are brought together, a dynamic that matches the Gospel's concluding instructions that the apostles "baptize in the name of the Father and of the Son and of the Holy Spirit" (28:19). An ancient reader with background in biblical or parabiblical writings would not be surprised to hear about the initial action by God's Spirit; by the end of the Gospel, however, something new has happened. This Spirit is more clearly identified in terms of the baptismal "Name" and thus can no longer easily be interpreted as merely the strength or force of God.

As for angelic action, Matthew introduces this in terms reminiscent of Genesis, as the "angel of the Lord" appears to Joseph in dreams, catalyzing the action. By the angel's instruction, the Lord guides the plot, so that the infant Jesus retraces the steps of the people of Israel—fleeing to Egypt and recalled to the holy land. An angel of the Lord (the same one?) also appears to the two Marys at the tomb on Easter morning (28:2–5), announcing that they, like Joseph at the beginning, need not fear, for God has acted. However, at the resurrection the angel quickly cedes to Jesus, who greets his disciples with words about his own authority and the ongoing task that he has for them. It is not an angel but Jesus who has all authority, whose name joins that of the Father, and who is with them until the end of the age. Hence, a subtle shift in the meaning of "God" has taken place, beginning with the expected (the ministration of a go-between angel) and culminating in the figure of Jesus, who is "worshiped" (28:17).[8]

Luke's style is more reminiscent of stories in biblical and Jewish tradition. We begin with the domestic troubles of a barren woman, whose priestly husband meets an angel of the Lord, subsequently self-identified as Gabriel (1:19). The angelic action is sustained as Gabriel appears to the young woman Mary, engaging in extensive conversation with her. This scene recalls some of the most central episodes of the Scriptures—for example, the story of Hannah and Samuel. However, its homey touches (questions and answers, the internal doubts and questions of main actors and crowds, verbal reflections by characters on what has happened) echo scenes in the books of Tobit, Judith, and Susanna. Intertwining the human and divine realm, beginning with those who are "righteous before God" (1:6), Luke *shows* as well as *tells* how the God who performs "strength with his arm" (1:51) is working intricately, bringing the fortunes of righteous Israelites together.

Luke employs many of the common names of God—God, Lord, Lord God, Most High, Mighty One, Lord God of Israel—thus linking his Gospel with the extended history of Israel. Angels are furiously busy, visiting Zechariah and Mary and startling shepherds. The Holy Spirit, too, is ubiquitous—preparing the way for John's birth, overshadowing Mary, filling Elizabeth, putting words in Zechariah's mouth, informing Simeon, and inspiring Anna. By way of conclusion, Luke's Gospel is equally dramatic—the women are terrified by two dazzling "men" (24:4, later interpreted as "angels" at 24:23) who mark Jesus's resurrection. Yet the angels merit all of two verses. Instead, it is the revelatory activity of Jesus that dominates: the walk to Emmaus with the meal (24:13–32), the appearance to Simon and the Twelve (24:33–42), the closing interpretation of these God-directed events (24:45–47), the commission coupled with a promise of "power" to come (24:48–49), and the final

---

8. Though the word used here for worship (*proskyneō*) is not reserved for God, in the context of Jesus's declaration of authority, and adjacent to the command to baptize in the name of Father, Son, and Holy Spirit, we may discern that the author of the Gospel has in mind more than deference to a human being. English translations such as the NRSV rightly translate "worship" and not simply "did reverence to" in describing the actions of those gathered around the Lord.

ascension and blessing (24:50–53). The attribution of this action to the God of Israel, of David, and of the prophets is confirmed in the closing sentence, where Jesus's followers occupy the same initial position as Zechariah, Gabriel, Simeon, and Anna: they tarry within the temple of God and bless the Holy One. They wait, knowing that God is active.

Mark's version is more circumspect, matching its deceptive simplicity—no prenatal stories, no visions of angels. Instead, God sends a human *angelos* ("messenger," 1:2), John the Baptist, who prepares the way for the main actor, the Lord (1:3), who "will baptize . . . with the Holy Spirit" (1:8).[9] God speaks for himself in this initial scene, rending open the heavens, descending by means of the Spirit, and proclaiming this one "my Son" (1:11). It is the Holy Spirit who sustains the action, driving Jesus out to the wilderness, alone with Satan—but not alone, for the angels serve him (1:13). The ending of Mark is difficult to delineate, given the alternate endings that come to us through various manuscripts. However, even the shortest ending emphasizes the action of God—the women are worrying about who will roll the stone away, but discover that the task has already been accomplished, and are delivered a message from Jesus via a terrifying "young man" who "alarm[s]" the women (16:5).[10] The women, seized with terror because of this announcement that Jesus is raised, are seemingly paralyzed;[11] yet even their paralysis highlights God's sovereign action. In the longer endings, their inactivity is followed by appearances of Jesus, who again takes central stage.

The Fourth Gospel is even more extreme in its portrayal of the One who initiates and fulfills. We begin in protological time, with the actions of the Word and God, the coming of light into darkness, and the archetypical witness of John the Baptist, who claims only "I am not" (1:21) in contrast

9. Christine E. Joynes mounts the unlikely hypothesis that Mark's Gospel identifies John the Baptist as an angel ("The Returned Elijah? John the Baptist's Angelic Identity in the Gospel of Mark," *SJT* 58, no. 4 [2005]: 455–67). Instead, Mark's John is earthy in his context of water, honey, and camel's hair and calls attention not to any supposed angelic status of his own, but to the Coming One.

10. Philip Oakeshott argues unconvincingly that the young man has "not even one" of the attributes associated with an angel, that the "women's flight is irreconcilable with angelic invitation," and that Mark cannot have intended the young man to be an angel, despite the clear interpretation of Matthew and Luke in this regard ("How unlike an Angel: The Youth in Mark 16," *Theology* 111, no. 863 [September/October 2008], 321, 367). Unfortunately, he offers no other Markan intent. And we have noted already that angels are not always clearly distinguished from either God or humanity as they are depicted in the Bible: Jacob did not recognize his divine wrestling partner until dawn broke; there is a whole tradition of "entertaining angels unawares" (cf. Heb. 13:2). Surely the lack of attention to the young man's angelic appearance coheres with Mark's overall reserved tendency in describing mystery, which serves to highlight Jesus himself and the actions associated with him rather than other potentially impressive figures or experiences.

11. For an alternative reading of this passage, see Larry W. Hurtado, "The Women, the Tomb, and the Climax of Mark," in *A Wandering Galilean: Essays in Honour of Seán Freyne*, ed. Zuleika Rodgers, Margaret Daly-Denton, and Anne Fitzpatrick McKinley (Leiden: Brill, 2009), 427–51.

to Jesus's "I am" (4:26; 6:35; 8:12, 18, 24, 28, 58; etc.). The unique Son (1:18), the Spirit, who "remained on him" (1:32), and the "Father" have a common work before them—they will show "glory" and work signs so that the hidden Father can be "made . . . known" (1:18) and so that worshipers can be gathered "in spirit and truth" (4:23). Angels have a negligible, minor role in John's Gospel, for it is the Son and the Father who love each other as friends and are always "working" together (5:17–20), the Greek verb *phileō* ("to love as a friend") expressing this partnership. Except for the resurrection, the only uncontested references to angels in John's Gospel are Jesus's enigmatic reference to Jacob's ladder (which we will consider later) and the uninformed comment from some in the crowd who say, when God acknowledges the Son, that "an angel has spoken" (John 12:29). The angels' words are hardly required, for the Son is present to reveal all. Some might cite also John 5:4, regarding the angel who "stirred up the water" at the pool of Bethesda/Bethsaida/Bethzatha, but this detail is not found in the best manuscripts. Even accepting this reading, the episode mutes such impressive traditions concerning angelic healing, for one who works by the Spirit and not simply by water is here to heal, and does so.

The climax of the Fourth Gospel also spurs the reader to see God-in-Jesus as the divine actor. Two angels appear in the tomb, but their question "Why are you crying?" is eclipsed by the personal appearance of Jesus to Mary, who tells her about "my Father and your Father, my God and your God." Immediately afterward, when Jesus greets Thomas, offering his hands and side, Thomas exclaims, "My Lord and my God!" And then, the risen Jesus looks forward to others who will believe and be blessed. The emphasis on divine initiative is maintained until the final verse: "There are also many other things that Jesus did; if every one of them were written down, I suppose that the world itself could not contain the books that would be written" (John 21:25). Herein is the paradox of the Fourth Gospel: the world itself is too small to contain God; yet God has come to inhabit it.

All the Gospels, then, feature God as the primary actor and make Jesus complicit with that divine action, while also appealing to the Holy Spirit. Indeed, where angels appear at the beginning and end of these narratives, they mark a special intersection of boundaries between the human and divine realm and underscore the solemn significance of God's very own actions. In John's Gospel, their ministrations are barely engaged. More often, John encourages the reader to deal with the Light (John 8:12) without, so to speak, any recourse to sunglasses.

Angels in Their Places and "the Many-Splendoured Thing"

Let us probe a little more deeply into the Gospels, noting those places where angels indicate God's concern for humanity and signify his connection with the human realm. One Jewish scholar describes the way that he understands this in Hebrew and (especially later) Jewish texts:

> The truth is that God was in many senses brought very near, and the angel was but an aspect of this "nearness." God was immanent as well as transcendent, and the angel was a sort of emanation of the Divine, an off-shoot of Deity, holding intimate converse with the affairs of the world. . . . God did not really come into contact with the world, but His angels did—and His angels are really part and parcel of His own being, emanations of His own substance.[12]

This description may very well be an accurate portrayal of some Jewish approaches to angelology. It is consonant with the connection of angelic names to the divine (Micha-el, Gabri-el, Rapha-el, Uri-el) and follows the same pattern as the increasingly vivid personification of God's Wisdom and Word. As we have seen, Philo, who spoke of the mysterious "Logos" as a second power besides the Most High, also spoke of the angels as God's "logoi." However, the Hebrew tradition was able to speak about God's immanence alongside of God's transcendence without recourse to angelic agency: God's glory fills the temple, Moses speaks with YHWH, "mouth to mouth" (Deut. 34:10), and God himself addresses the prophets.

The Gospels sustain this mystery of the transcendent and immanent God and deepen this by means of their narratives concerning Jesus. That is, the Gospels either intimate or, in some cases, directly state that God is among the people, or near, in the person of Jesus:

> "The time is fulfilled, and the kingdom of God has come near." (Mark 1:15)
>
> "The kingdom of God is not coming with things that can be observed. . . . For, in fact, the kingdom of God is among you." (Luke 17:20)
>
> "If it is by the finger of God that I cast out the demons, then the kingdom of God has come to [or come upon] you." (Luke 11:20)
>
> "If it is by the Spirit of God that I cast out demons, then the kingdom of God has come to you." (Matt. 12:28)
>
> "Whoever has seen me has seen the Father." (John 14:9b)

Given the new episode of "Emmanuel" (God-with-us), which the Gospels narrate as a climax to the biblical story, we cannot say that angels continue to be involved in human affairs because their mediation is *required* by the supposed problem of a distanced God. These Gospels show the heavens torn open, the plunging of God's Son into human elements, and the human longing for God's presence (and vice versa) requited. Why, then, angels? Are these

---

12. J. Abelson, *Jewish Mysticism: An Introduction to Kabbalah* (London: Bell and Sons, 1913), 54.

simply a "reversion" to folk explanations as to how the holy God can bear human creaturely and sinful presence? That is hardly plausible, nor was that explanation really adequate to the passionate God of the Hebrew people, who in former times walked with Adam and sought Israel as a jilted lover or tender father (Hos. 2:14; 11:1). In prophetic identification with YHWH, Jesus cries out, "How often have I desired to gather your children together as a hen gathers her brood under her wings, and you were not willing!" (Luke 13:34// Matt. 23:37). (John's Gospel, identifying "his own" with all of humanity—John 1:10–11—neutralizes any anti-Judaic interpretation: what we see in Israel's sin is the *human* tendency to reject God, up close and personal.)

What, then, of the angels in the Gospels? It is perhaps helpful to approach this in terms of that enigmatic statement of Jesus near the beginning of John's Gospel. In John 1:47, Jesus encounters the skeptical Nathanael, after "seeing" him under the fig tree. Nathanael is amazed by Jesus's discernment and acclaims him Messiah, to which Jesus responds (in so many words), "You think that is amazing! Just wait!" What Jesus actually says is, "You [singular] will see greater things than these." Then, embracing his disciples, and perhaps the reader too, he solemnly declares, "You [plural] will see heaven opened and the angels of God ascending and descending upon [or "to"] the Son of Man" (John 1:50–51). This promise is never kept, at least literally, in the Gospel. Angels of God are not seen ascending and descending, unless somehow the appearance of the two angels where the body of Jesus was (20:12) is intended as a fulfillment. One scholar sensibly suggests that since "the apparent promise of future angelophanies [manifestations of angels] remains unfulfilled from the perspective of the reader of John . . . the focus of the vision must be the Son of Man and not the angels."[13]

This is indeed true. What, then, is the point of bringing together the image of Jacob's ladder at Bethel ("the house of God" [Gen. 28:17, 19]) with that strange Son of Man from Daniel 7:13, who comes with the clouds before the Ancient of Days (God) and is honored? In the Synoptic Gospels, Isaiah's Suffering Servant (Isa. 42; 44; 49; 52–53) is merged with this "Son of Man" in Jesus's astounding statements that the Son of Man must suffer (cf. Mark 8:31; 9:12; Matt. 17:12; Luke 9:22); nowhere in Daniel is it said that the Son of Man suffers. The fusion inextricably links suffering with glory—a double theme essential for the narrative of the cross and resurrection, but also of significance for those surrounding Jesus, who are called to take up their cross. After all, Daniel's Son of Man is a corporate figure, standing for the people of God (cf.

13. Jennifer K. Berenson MacLean, "The Divine Trickster," in *Feminist Companion to John*, ed. Amy-Jill Levine and Marianne Blickenstaff (London: Sheffield Academic Press, 2003), 1:57. For this scholar, one possible reading of the text is "descending to" where the Son of Man is, and she believes that Jesus's statement recalls a rabbinic tradition in which Jacob's sight of the heavenly ladder was honored even by the angels, who made pilgrimage to see this blessed patriarch. Thus, in John's Gospel, Jesus as Son of Man replaces the honorable Jacob.

Dan. 7:27), just as the Suffering Servant is corporate, standing for the righteous in Israel (Isa. 44:1). Appropriately, the knitting together of these figures says something first about Jesus but also something about Jesus's followers.

A similar strategy seems to be at play in this provocative link of the Son of Man with Jacob's vision (Gen. 28:11–22). Jesus's statement suggests that the "ladder of angels" was of benefit for Israel (Jacob) but that something far more weighty is here. There is now a deeper point of contact between the heavens and God's people—that is, "the Son of Man." Those gathered around Jesus (the "you" plural) will see far more than "father Jacob," as Jesus also points out two chapters later to the bemused Samaritan woman. He it is "who will proclaim all things" (John 4:25–26) and who is the perfect nexus between heaven and earth. It is by means of the embodied, dying, rising, and glorified Son that they will not simply "see" a mystical descent and ascent but be brought into communion with the Father of the Son, as their own "Father" (1:12; 20:17b). Jacob recognized, "Surely the LORD is in this place—and I did not know it!" (Gen. 28:16). Nathanael, too, has had a shock—but for the reader of the Gospel, there is even more to contend with than a "portal" to the heavens, the gate of angels. In distinction to a singular place of access that can be memorialized with a pillar, in distinction to Wisdom, who fled the realm of humanity in despair of finding a home (1 En. 42), God the Word has come to "dwell" (John 1:14), and Wisdom's glory can be seen. Where the Sun shines, the stars fade out—so then, the angels play a minor role to the Son of glory.

Yet the angels keep their ancient places. They linger at their post where Jesus's body was, redirecting weeping eyes. In the Synoptic Gospels, their appearance is a little more frequent. Especially they are said to have a special ministry to Jesus himself, who has no need of them as go-betweens with "Abba," his Father, but who nonetheless receives their service and their homage too—with reserve. A delicate balance is preserved in the Synoptic Gospels, keeping the spotlight squarely upon Jesus himself. In Jesus's initial skirmish with Satan in the wilderness, the ministration of angels is both eschewed (Matt. 4:6–7// Luke 4:9–12) and welcomed (Mark 1:13; Matt. 4:11). This tension is especially evident in Matthew 4:6–11, which retains both Jesus's demurral to call upon the angels for protection and the service of the angels at the conclusion of his trial. And there lurks another subtlety: Jesus's words "Do not put the Lord your God to the test" (Matt. 4:7) may be read both in terms of his own refusal to force God's hand and as an ironic judgment upon Satan, who is testing Jesus! The ambiguity of "Lord" thickens the interpretive possibilities. The angels serve this one, as they serve YHWH and as they served Elijah in the wilderness, yet Jesus's humble service forbids that he should force their aid in the wrong manner. Indeed, by means of the temptation episodes the reader is afforded both a positive and a negative angelology. Jesus is typed as undergoing temptation for the sake of Israel and humanity, as the centerpiece

The Angels Keep Their Ancient Places

The Victorian poet Francis Thompson, better known for his semiautobiographical "Hound of Heaven," expresses the immanence of God in his poem "The Kingdom of God." The last three stanzas call attention to "the many-splendoured" wisdom of God (cf. Eph. 3:10), seen not in the angels (though they are present) but in Jesus, whose coming has hallowed the entire world as a ladder of access, and whose healing is available to any who would "cry" out and cling to the hem of his garment (Matt. 9:20; 14:36):

> The angels keep their ancient places;—
> Turn but a stone and start a wing!
> 'Tis ye, 'tis your estrangèd faces,
> That miss the many-splendoured thing.
>
> But (when so sad thou canst not sadder)
> Cry,—and upon thy so sore loss
> Shall shine the traffic of Jacob's ladder
> Pitched betwixt Heaven and Charing Cross.
>
> Yea, in the night, my Soul, my daughter,
> Cry,—clinging Heaven by the hems;
> And lo, Christ walking on the water,
> Not of Genesareth, but Thames!

of the great cosmic battle between heaven and earth.[14] Part of his righteousness is not to presume upon angelic help; yet God has his means of ministering to the faithful.

Jesus's temptation, then, translates into cosmological terms the dual principle of community found in the Pauline letters: "bear one another's burdens. . . . All must carry their own loads" (Gal. 6:2, 5). The *koinōnia* ("communion") of personal role and solidarity is extended into the fellowship between heaven and earth. (In terms of this dynamic, the absence of ministering angels in John's Gospel appears to be consonant with the absence of Simon of Cyrene in this Gospel: Jesus is the sole actor, bearing his suffering and cross alone.) In this vein, we can appreciate the instinct of those who were responsible for adding the details of Jesus's agony (Luke 22:43–44) found in some ancient manuscripts (and in Bibles such as the KJV, which are based on older editions of the Greek New Testament). Sweating drops of blood,

14. For an intriguing discussion of the temptation in connection with the cosmic battle, the arriving kingdom of God, and the title "Lord of Hosts," see Craig A. Evans, "Inaugurating the Kingdom of God and Defeating the Kingdom of Heaven," *BBR* 15, no. 1 (2005): 49–75.

Jesus is strengthened in Gethsemane by an angel of the Lord. Surely this is the least that can be done for the One who alone remains vigilant, while all others are sleeping, and whose ordeal is merely beginning. Jesus *could*, in communion with his Father, summon twelve legions of angels to come to his aid (Matt. 26:53); but he will not. This is the beginning of a work that is to be done by himself, helped by "the finger of God" (Luke 11:20), but not in conjunction with the lesser angels.

So, then, when we see angels appearing or not appearing in the Gospels, we encounter an ancient Christian "discussion" concerning the role of Jesus, his "friendship" with heaven, his solidarity with earth, and his unique identity both in heaven and on earth. References to the angels mark the boundaries and the astonishing points of crossover, as the heavenly (and satanic) realms weigh down upon human affairs. But the different stance of the Evangelists toward the angels, on the one hand, and toward God-in-concert-with-his-Son, on the other, illustrates the difference between mere go-betweens and the deep solidarity of Jesus with both heaven and earth. The angels are helpful; God (with Jesus) initiates and effects all the action, and thus elicits human praise.

We are left with several typical positions that the angels occupy in the Synoptic Gospels: they are associated with future matters, and they are associated with life in the presence of God. Frequently Jesus speaks in the Synoptics of the coming of the Son of Man "with the holy angels" for the purpose of judgment: Matthew 13:39, 41, 49 (the parable of the weeds); Mark 8:38//Matthew 16:27//Luke 9:26, Mark 13:27//Matthew 24:31 (reaping angels); Matthew 25:31, 41 (the parable of the sheep and goats). Associated with these verses is also that scene where the Son of Man will "acknowledge before the angels" those who have previously acknowledged Jesus and deny those who have denied him (Luke 12:8–9).

Judgment, the Angels, and Apocalyptic Reality

Let us leave aside entirely the question of the "historical Jesus questers" as to whether Jesus identified himself with the Son of Man or whether this was a later move in the church. From the perspective of the Evangelists, the Son of Man is none other than Jesus himself; as Son of Man, his future role is to judge (Matt. 16:27–28; 25:31; Mark 8:38; Luke 9:26). References to the "holy ones" and to the "court sitting in judgment" in Daniel 7:26–27 may well have given rise to the belief that angels also participate in or at least will attend this final accounting. After all, the kingly judge must have his retinue. Moreover, there are stories where angels appeared wielding the sword to act on behalf of (i.e., to judge *for*) God's people in past battles (Josh. 5:13–15; Dan. 12:1), and there is the rabbinic tradition concerning Sennacherib's destruction (*Exod. Rab.* 18.5), which may have ancient roots. The connection in folk wisdom of angels with individual judgment may also be glimpsed in Jesus's parable about Lazarus (Luke 16:22), where the angels escort the dead to his place of rest.

In the Gospels, however, neither personal nor corporate judgment has simply a future aspect, since God has acted decisively in Jesus: the Son of Man will therefore speak up for those who *in this life* acknowledged or helped him and his followers (Luke 12:8–9; Matt. 25:40). As John's Gospel puts it, the time "is coming *and is now here*, when the dead will hear the voice of the Son of God, and those who hear will live" (John 5:25). In Matthew's Gospel, Jesus's resurrection is accompanied by the opening of the tombs and the rising of those "holy ones"—a curious apocalyptic scene indicating the present effect of Jesus's victory (Matt. 27:52–53). This present aspect appears also in the unique saying of the Gospel of Luke that the angels *now* rejoice over the repentance of even one who turns (Luke 15:10). Friends of Jesus, these strange beings share his joy and the joy of those who are "in the presence of God." Yet the accent falls not upon the holy ones, but upon the Most High, and how he has brought life through the anointed One.

The association of the angels with the future is also seen in the saying of Jesus concerning "giving and taking in marriage" found in all three Synoptic Gospels. In controversy with the Sadducees, whose constructed "hard case" of the multiply married woman aims to ridicule the doctrine of the final resurrection, Jesus directs attention away from this most intimate form of human communion to deep communion with God. The angels are known for ministering in the presence of the Lord, and so may be appealed to as those who already, in some measure, know this form of fellowship. In the resurrection, says Jesus, the issue will not be "Whose wife is she?"; for glorified human beings will stand before God himself, the source of all communion and love. They will be "like" the angels (Mark 12:25; Matt. 22:30), or, in Luke's terminology, "equal-to-angels" (*isangeloi*, 20:36)—even the women, who are merely given and taken in first-century Palestinian society! This adaptation of Daniel's promise that the wise will "shine . . . like the stars" (Dan. 12:3) demonstrates an exalted status in the resurrection, but not a transformation into angels. (This kind of transformation is, however, envisioned in such Pseudepigraphal books as *1 Enoch*.)

Finally, there is Matthew 18:10, a passage that is alternately ignored or the cause of much speculation:

> He called a child, whom he put among them, and said, "Truly I tell you, unless you change and become like children, you will never enter the kingdom of heaven. . . . Whoever welcomes one such child in my name welcomes me. If any of you put a stumbling block before one of these little ones who believe in me, it would be better for you if a great millstone were fastened around your neck and you were drowned in the depth of the sea. Woe to the world because of stumbling blocks! Occasions for stumbling are bound to come, but woe to the one by whom the stumbling block comes! . . . Take care that you do not despise

one of these little ones; for, I tell you, in heaven their angels continually see the face of my Father in heaven. . . . So it is not the will of your Father in heaven that one of these little ones should be lost."

Matt. 18:2–3, 5–7, 10, 14

It is from this passage that Christians through the ages taught the protective presence of "guardian angels," particularly those assigned to children. Jesus's saying about "their angels" finds its context in a lengthy composite passage about greatness and humility, stumbling blocks and welcoming, the danger of judgment because of the human condition, God's concern for even one out of the hundred, and the will of God for "little ones"—whether these are understood as young in age or in spiritual condition. The discourse does not read smoothly as a unit, but such coherence as it has is established by the repeated theme of "little ones" and God's care for them. Interestingly, the disciples' concern for human hierarchy ("Who is the greatest?" [18:1]) is both overturned by Jesus's *leveling* action (he "put [a child] among them" [18:2]) and challenged by an appeal *to* a mysterious unseen hierarchy ("their angels continually see the face of my Father"). Those who follow Jesus must not despise those who seem insignificant because, according to the apocalyptic logic, which connects this world to the unseen realms, more is going on than seems to be going on.

Whatever *else* "their angels" are doing in heaven—pleading for their human charges, representing their cause before the LORD, accusing those who would harm the little ones?—they are engaged in an activity not vouchsafed to many. For they "continually behold" God's face. Not even the seraphim do that: "With two [wings] they covered their faces" (Isa. 6:2b). The exalted position and privilege of these angels, it would seem, is directly proportionate to the humility of those with whom they are paired. "Whoever becomes humble . . . is the greatest in the kingdom of heaven" (18:4) and so, it seems, will "see God" (cf. Matt. 5:3, 8). Is what their angels do a picture of what these "little ones" will do, once they enter into life?[15] For, says Jesus, it is the will of the Father to "find them," that they might "enter life" intact with feet, with hands to lift to God, and with both eyes to see the great glory (Matt. 18:8–14).

So it is that we come full circle. The station of the angels marks those places where heaven and earth come together. In the Hebrew Bible, these places were varied, but focused especially on the mountain where the Torah was given and in the temple where God's great glory touched into the life of Israel. In continuity, the Gospel of Luke begins as an angel again appears in the temple to forewarn Zechariah. Yet angels also appear in the dreams of Joseph, on

---

15. Indeed, could it be that the term "their angels" evokes the same idea as is seen in such popular understanding as Acts 12:15 and *Joseph and Aseneth*, where each person is believed to have a doppelgänger—a heavenly twin or double—who is both their representative and their alter ego?

the plains before the poor who are guarding sheep, and in a small northern town where a young woman dwells. The overshadowing of the Holy Spirit is proclaimed by Gabriel, who "stand[s] in the presence of God" (Luke 1:19) in the heavenly temple. Yet this very announcement means that any angel's name and station will fade in importance. Like the Baptist (John 3:30), the angels will decrease, as the One named Jesus will increase. Even the characteristics associated with the angels will be bent to the purpose of proclaiming this One, who is, according to the Gospels, both old and new.[16]

Conclusion

In the final analysis, it is not angels who display God in the Gospels, but this other "sent" One. Perhaps the angels of the Gospels do not suffer as radical an eclipse as they do with St. Paul, for whom, as two scholars cogently argue, the centrality of the Christ was such that "the angels lost their ultimate significance."[17] However, as Susan Garrett aptly puts it, in the Gospels the angels assume the role of "supporting players and bit characters who seldom steal the limelight."[18] Of course, in each of the Gospels, the angels are used differently, according to the flavor of each work. Yet nowhere do we see an angel engage in healing, teaching, or even leading the way. Rather, they take on the same modest role that Paul assigns to Torah in 2 Corinthians 3: they are pointers to that One who himself "exegetes" the Father, so that believers may become God's own children, as John 1:12–13 claims.

Nor is the centrality of the Son a Johannine eccentricity. To be sure, it is John's Jesus who breathes the Holy Spirit upon the disciples as that life-giving Breather of the new creation (Gen. 2:7; John 20:22, cf. 1 Cor. 15:45–49). It is John's Jesus who implies that he is now the ladder, the wellspring, and the house

16. We have seen already that God's mysterious agents of Word and Wisdom come to have a life of their own in the Jewish tradition. Both agents are, of course, proclaimed by the early Christians to find their true identity in Jesus, the Word of the Fourth Gospel, and the Wisdom of, for example, Matthew 11:29–30. Good arguments have been made by several scholars that the characteristics and roles attributed to the angels are also used to fill in the understanding of Jesus, God's true Agent, or "Sent One," who announces the rule of God, heals, confronts, and wins battles over the rebel hosts. See Bogdan G. Bucur, "Matthew 18:10 in Early Christology and Pneumatology: A Contribution to the Study of Matthean *Wirkungsgeschichte*," *NovT* 49 (2007): 209–31.

17. Dominika Kurek-Chomycz and Reimund Bieringer, "Guardians of the Old at the Dawn of the New: The Role of Angels according to the Pauline Letters," in *Angels: The Concept of Celestial Beings—Origins, Development and Reception*, ed. Friedrich V. Reiterer, Tobias Nicklas, and Karin Schopflin, Deuterocanonical and Cognate Literature Yearbook 2007 (Berlin: De Gruyter, 2007), 350.

18. Susan R. Garrett, "Jesus and the Angels," *Word and World* 29, no. 2 (Spring 2009): 162. See also her very helpful *No Ordinary Angel: Celestial Spirits and Christian Claims about Christ* (New Haven: Yale University Press, 2008).

of God. And it is John's Jesus who declares unequivocally the Divine Name as his own, relishing the "I Am" so reverently avoided by the rabbinic readers. But it is Mark's Jesus who declares "I Am" before the high priest himself (Mark 14:62). And, despite Matthew's preserved circumlocution "kingdom of heaven" (over against "kingdom of God"), the Jesus of both Matthew and Luke utters that shocking word: "All things have been handed over to me by my Father; and no one knows the Son [who the Son is] except the Father, and no one knows the Father [, or who the Father is] except the Son and anyone to whom the Son chooses to reveal him" (Matt. 11:27//Luke 10:22, the latter version in square brackets).

Jesus, then, makes concrete the character of the unseen God, who everywhere initiates action, superintends the story, and verifies the significance of what is going on. We can see this in two complementary actions, witnessed to by all four Evangelists—God's own action of bearing solemn witness, and the human response of worship. It is no ministering angel, but God himself who ratifies Jesus's authority by his own voice at the baptism (Matt. 3:17//Mark 1:11//Luke 3:22) and at the Transfiguration (Matt. 17:5//Mark 9:7//Luke 9:35); this same "ultimate reliable voice"[19] of the Father makes a pronouncement in John's Gospel (John 12:28) as Jesus prepares for his crucifixion and prays that God will glorify him. Ironically, some of the crowd, not understanding the uncontested significance of this voice from heaven, interpret it as the word of an "angel" only (John 12:29). They do not understand that only the Father's testimony is a match for the Son (8:18). From the human side, all four Gospels also show that worship is due to God alone—yet this worship includes giving glory to Jesus (Matt. 28:17; Mark 14:62; Luke 24:52; John 20:28). Both by divine fiat and by human response, Jesus is ranged not with the angels but alongside the Most High—and yet he is in the midst of God's people, content to do the will of the Father, who alone knows the detailed outcome of the drama (Mark 13:32).

Angels, then, may serve as bookends to the Gospels, beginning and ending their solemn pages. However, the content of the good news is that Jesus is the Son, come in the crucial act of God's great cosmic drama to make children and informed en-Spirited worshipers for the Father. That announcement is made by means of the words and actions of Jesus himself. It is this One, and not the angels, who, in the words of John's Gospel, "made [God's] name known" to those who belong to the Father.[20] That name, once the inscrutable I Am,

19. Larry Hurtado notes this dynamic especially in the Synoptic Gospels in his article "God," in *Dictionary of Jesus and the Gospels*, ed. Joel B. Green, Scot McKnight, and I. Howard Marshall (Downers Grove, IL: InterVarsity, 1992), 273.

20. We have seen already that the metaphor of "father" was a favorite among others in the Jewish tradition for God's relationship to Israel. In Acts 17:22–31 Paul, quoting Epimenides's *Cretica* 4 ("In him we live and move") and Aratus's *Phaenomena* 5 ("We are his offspring"), indicates how this metaphor would have been appealed to in a gentile context. However, for the

is now filled out with vital metaphors—life, truth, way, door, Shepherd, and Vine—and with signs that speak of Wisdom, the Law, and the Prophets. The divine Name has now been given content by the life of the Son, to the glory of the Father, and vivified by the Holy Spirit, who is given to "those who ask" (Luke 11:13) and who leads into all truth (John 16:13).

Though angels may tarry in the sequel offered by the Evangelist Luke, offering a word of explanation at the ascension (Acts 1:11) or loosening prison bolts for an apostle (Acts 12:7), it is Jesus himself who remains the great exegete (Luke 24:27), and it is Jesus who has undergone the new exodus (Luke 9:31, where NRSV's "departure" translates the Greek *exodos*) to deliver God's people. By means of him, even the children of humanity may assume the "face of an angel" (Acts 6:15). This is what happens to the first martyr, Stephen, that "little one" who sees the Son of Man standing to welcome him, shining-faced and filled with the Holy Spirit, into the very presence of the God (Acts 7:55). Angels may be the sign of momentous events, but it is not the angels who are "man's best friend."[21] Rather, it is Jesus who as the true Wisdom "makes them friends of God, and prophets" (Wis. 7:27), in partnership with himself and the Father: "I do not call you servants any longer . . . but . . . friends" (John 15:15). Or perhaps it is better to adopt the Gospels' more poignant language (e.g., Matt. 6:9; Mark 11:25–26; Luke 6:36; John 20:17), which insists that the transformation is not merely from servants into friends or prophets (nor even into the form of angels!), but into God's own children. "Abba," on the lips of Jesus and his followers, ceases to be a metaphor among others, and becomes their family name for God.

Suggestions for Further Reading

Bucur, Bogdan G. "Matthew 18:10 in Early Christology and Pneumatology: A Contribution to the Study of Matthean *Wirkungsgeschichte.*" *NovT* 49 (2007): 209–31.

Caird, G. B. *The Language and Imagery of the Bible.* London: Duckworth, 1980.

Charlesworth, James H, ed. *The Old Testament Pseudepigrapha.* 2 vols. Garden City, NY: Doubleday, 1985.

Davidson, Maxwell G. *Angels at Qumran: A Comparative Study of 1 Enoch 1–36, 72–108 and the Sectarian Writings from Qumran.* Journal for the Study of the Pseudepigrapha: Supplement Series 11. Sheffield: JSOT Press, 1992.

Gospel writers, "father" has ceased to be a metaphor but has become the proper name for God because of the unique link of Jesus to God and belief that those who follow Jesus participate in this relationship.

21. One very curious element of the book of Tobit, in which the angel Raphael is clearly the best friend and guardian of the hero and heroine, is that a dog also accompanies the actors, appearing at random points without any discernible purpose (Tob. 6:2; 11:4). Here biblical lore and folklore come together—celestial and creaturely "best friends" together with God's people!

Evans, Craig A. "Inaugurating the Kingdom of God and Defeating the Kingdom of Heaven." *BBR* 15, no. 1 (2005): 49–75.

Garrett, Susan R. "Jesus and the Angels." *Word and World* 29, no. 2 (Spring 2009): 162–69.

———. *No Ordinary Angel: Celestial Spirits and Christian Claims about Christ.* New Haven and London: Yale University Press, 2008.

Humphrey, Edith M. *And I Turned to See the Voice: The Rhetoric of Vision in the New Testament.* Grand Rapids: Baker Academic, 2007.

Hurtado, Larry. "God." In *Dictionary of Jesus and the Gospels*, edited by Joel B. Green, Scot McKnight, and I. Howard Marshall, 270–76. Downers Grove, IL: InterVarsity, 1992.

———. *Lord Jesus Christ: Devotion to Jesus in Earliest Christianity.* Grand Rapids: Eerdmans, 2003.

Reiterer, Friedrich V., Tobias Nicklas, and Karin Schopflin. *Angels: The Concept of Celestial Beings—Origins, Development and Reception.* Deuterocanonical and Cognate Literature Yearbook 2007. Berlin and New York: De Gruyter, 2007.

Scholem, Gershom. *Major Trends in Jewish Mysticism* (New York: Schocken, 1995).

Wright, N. T. *The New Testament and the People of God.* Minneapolis: Fortress, 1992.

2

John the Baptist

Michael F. Bird

John the Baptist, or the Baptizer as he was sometimes called (Mark 1:4; 6:14, 24),[1] stands as a unique figure in both Jewish history and Christian tradition. He is historically significant as a forerunner to Jesus of Nazareth, who led a call for covenantal renewal in Judea and proclaimed an apocalyptic message. He is also an important figure for understanding Judean social prophets in the

---

1. Notable studies on John the Baptist include C. H. Kraeling, *John the Baptist* (New York: Scribner's, 1951); C. H. H. Scobie, *John the Baptist* (Philadelphia: Fortress, 1964); Walter Wink, *John the Baptist in the Gospel Tradition*, SNTSMS 7 (Cambridge: Cambridge University Press, 1968); Johannes Ernst, *Johannes der Täufer: Interpretation—Geschichte—Wirkungsgeschichte*, BZNW 53 (Berlin: De Gruyter, 1989); idem, *Johannes der Täufer: Der Lehrer Jesu?* (Freiburg, Germany: Herder, 1994); Jerome Murphy-O'Connor, "John the Baptist and Jesus: History and Hypothesis," *NTS* 36 (1990): 359–74; Robert L. Webb, *John the Baptizer and Prophet: A Socio-Historical Study*, JSNTSup 62 (Sheffield: Sheffield Academic Press, 1991); idem, "John the Baptist and His Relationship to Jesus," in *Studying the Historical Jesus: Evaluations of the State of Current Research*, ed. Bruce Chilton and Craig A. Evans, NTTSD 19 (Leiden: Brill, 1994), 179–230; Bruce Chilton, "John the Purifier," in *Judaic Approaches to the Gospels* (Atlanta: Scholars Press, 1994), 1–37; Colin Brown, "What Was John the Baptist Doing?" *BBR* 7 (1997): 37–50; Joan E. Taylor, *The Immerser: John the Baptist within Second Temple Judaism* (Grand Rapids: Eerdmans, 1997); Dale C. Allison, "The Continuity between John and Jesus," *JSHJ* 1 (2003): 6–27; Catherine M. Murphy, *John the Baptist: Prophet of Purity for a New Age* (Collegeville, MN: Liturgical Press, 2003); Daniel S. Dapaah, *The Relationship between John the Baptist and Jesus of Nazareth: A Critical Study* (Lanham, MD: University of America Press, 2005); G. H. Twelftree, "Jesus the Baptist," *JSHJ* 7 (2009): 103–25

first century. John the Baptist plays a significant role in Christian tradition as well, as all four Gospels associate John with the "beginning of the gospel" and regard him as a central witness to Jesus's identity as the "One to Come" and the "Lamb of God." He remains theologically significant for Christian doctrines of baptism and culturally significant for groups such as the Mandaeans of Iraq and Landmark Baptists of the southern United States, who both trace their religious ancestry all the way back to John the Baptist. The Baptizer is also regarded as a prophet by Christian, Muslim, and Baha'i religious traditions. However, a number of complex issues beset study of John the Baptist. There are differences between the accounts in Josephus, the Synoptic Gospels, and the Fourth Gospel about John. Then there are questions about whether John the Baptist was ever part of the Qumran sect, which also engaged in baptismal practices. Finally, there is the matter of the relationship of Jesus to John: Were they relatives; was John the mentor of Jesus; did Jesus start a rival breakaway baptismal ministry from John's group; did Jesus abandon John's message of apocalyptic judgment; and are there traces of rivalry between Jesus-believing groups and followers of John the Baptist behind the Fourth Gospel? The aim of this chapter is to examine such questions so as to identify the place of John the Baptist in Judean history and in Christian testimony, and to indicate how this figure contributes to our understanding of Jesus in the Gospels. It will be seen that John the Baptist was a significant religious figure in his own right and that he plays a crucial role in the Gospels as the eschatological forerunner of Jesus.

Historical Considerations: John the Baptist according to the Earliest Sources

Our primary sources for excavating information about John the Baptist are limited to a single entry in Josephus's *Jewish Antiquities* and the several accounts in the four canonical Gospels. Yet in all cases these sources have inherent biases, seen not least in Josephus's attempt to translate John's message into philosophical categories and in the Evangelists' christianizing of John. In addition, Josephus and the Gospels offer different reasons for why Herod Antipas had the Baptizer executed. Additional background information for understanding John's ministry can be found in a study of prophetic movements in first-century Judea, archaeological evidence on baptismal pools in Galilee and Judea, and a comparison of the Baptizer with other Judean figures such as Bannus the Ascetic and the Qumranites. Equally noteworthy is the presence of disciples of John the Baptist in Ephesus as narrated in the Acts of the Apostles (Acts 18:24–25; 19:1–5).

Josephus

Josephus is among our most important witnesses to Judaism and Judean history in the pre–70 CE period. In book 18 of the *Antiquities of the Jews*,

Josephus mentions John the Baptist in a parenthetical remark about the defeat of Herod Antipas's army by the Nabataean king Aretas IV. There Josephus says of the Baptizer:

> But to some of the Jews the destruction of Herod's army seemed to be divine vengeance, and certainly a just vengeance, for his treatment of John, surnamed the Baptist. For Herod had put him to death, though he was a good man and had exhorted the Jews to lead righteous lives, to practice justice towards their fellows and piety towards God, and so doing to join in baptism. In his view this was a necessary preliminary if baptism was to be acceptable to God. They must not employ it to gain pardon for whatever sins they had committed, but as a consecration of the body implying that the soul was already cleansed by right behavior. When others too joined the crowds about him, because they were aroused to the highest degree by his sermons, Herod became alarmed. Eloquence that had so great an effect on mankind might lead to some form of sedition, for it looked as if they would be guided by John in everything that they did. Herod decided therefore that it would be much better to strike first and be rid of him before his work led to an uprising, than to wait for an upheaval, get involved in a difficult situation and see his mistake. Though John, because of Herod's suspicions, was brought in chains to Machaerus, the stronghold that we have previously mentioned, and there put to death, yet the verdict of the Jews was that the destruction visited upon Herod's army was a vindication of John, since God saw fit to inflict such a blow on Herod.[2]

From Josephus we can deduce the following:

1. John was regarded as a Judean holy man, popular with the masses, and he attracted large crowds;
2. He was known for and named after his activity as a "baptizer" (*bapistēs*);
3. John exhorted the Jews to return to appropriate covenantal behavior marked by righteous conduct, justice, and reverence for God;
4. A commitment to righteous living was a prerequisite for baptism and not a license for lawlessness, implying that baptism was for the remission of sins;
5. Josephus links baptism to purification, though he adds a gloss in couching this activity in Hellenistic philosophical terms by regarding it as a symbol of the soul that has been cleansed by right conduct;
6. Herod Antipas imprisoned John because he feared the influence of John over the masses, who might be led into rebellion; and
7. It was a commonly held view that the defeat of Antipas's army by King Aretas of Arabia was a sign of God's disfavor with Antipas for executing the Baptizer.

2. Josephus, *Ant.* 18.116–19 (LCL).

The Canonical Gospels

The presentation of John the Baptist in the canonical Gospels is to some degree manufactured, insofar as the Baptist is placed in the service of their narratival and christological interests. Yet even given their theological character, and despite the differences between them on John's message and relationship to Jesus, there remains an authentic historical component to their overall presentation.

The Synoptic Gospels all provide a condensed narration of John's activity, apparel, message, and baptism of Jesus (cf. Mark 1:1–11; Matt. 3:1–6; Luke 3:1–6). John is unanimously located in the Judean "wilderness" proclaiming a "baptism of repentance for the forgiveness of sins" and attracting people from all over Judea and Jerusalem who were coming to the Jordan River to be baptized by him (Mark 1:4–5). This is followed with a brief description of the Baptizer's attire and diet, which consists of wearing "camel's hair, with a leather belt around his waist," and eating "locusts and wild honey" (Mark 1:6). The reference to "camel's hair" and a "leather belt" is reminiscent of 2 Kings 1:8, where Elijah was a "hairy man" or perhaps known for wearing hairy garments and having a "leather belt around his waist" (Mark follows the Septuagint—the Greek translation of the Hebrew Bible—of 2 Kings 1:8 very closely in the wording about the belt). In other words, John the Baptist is dressed like Elijah the Tishbite. The significance of John's diet is difficult to determine,[3] though it may indicate no more than his ascetic lifestyle.

The Gospels agree that John forecast the coming of a "more powerful" figure who would dispense the Holy Spirit (Mark 1:7–8; Matt 3:11; Luke 3:16; cf. John 1:32–33). There is no indication that "more powerful" (*ischyroteros*; lit., "stronger one") is a messianic title, as it might simply denote charismatic power and divine authority. The Baptizer appears to be deliberately ambiguous about the identity of the stronger one, but the epithet most likely refers to some divine agent of a prophetic, messianic, or transcendent quality who executes the eschatological separation of the righteous from the wicked. The contrast of baptism with "water" and baptism with "Spirit" is based on a juxtaposition of the Baptizer's ministry as one of preparation with that of the "stronger one" who implements the eschatological judgment. Unlike Mark 1:8, in the double tradition (that is, material common to both Luke and Matthew often regarded as belonging to a literary source or cluster of sources called "Q")[4] the "stronger one" is said to baptize with the Holy Spirit *and with fire*.[5] The image of fire could imply either judgment (e.g., Isa. 10:17; 29:6; 66:15–16; Jer.

---

3. Cf. James A. Kelhoffer, *The Diet of John the Baptist: "Locusts and Wild Honey" in the Synoptic and Patristic Interpretation*, WUNT 176 (Tübingen: Mohr Siebeck, 2005).

4. Cf. Clare K. Rothschild, *Baptist Traditions and Q*, WUNT 190 (Tübingen: Mohr Siebeck, 2005).

5. There is considerable debate among scholars as to whether or not the Baptizer spoke originally of a baptism of "Spirit *and fire*" (Q) or only of a baptism of "Spirit" (Mark).

21:12; Ezek. 22:31) or purification (e.g., Isa. 4:4) in Israel's sacred literature. If, however, we link "baptism" to the idea of a flood, associate "Spirit" with God's own breath, and link "fire" to the eschatological judgment, then perhaps the Baptizer refers to one who will effectively plunge the people into the fiery breath of God, bringing about either purification or destruction.[6] In the same unit of Q material, John also states that this coming figure has as his vocation the task of harvesting God's people like wheat and burning the residue like chaff.[7]

Figure 2.1. Picture of the Jordan River and the type of place where John may have been baptizing. (Photo by David Bjorgen, Wikimedia Commons.)

Jesus's baptism by John (Mark 1:9–12) is almost universally recognized as a historically reliable event since it is attested in Mark and Q and is simply assumed in early Christianity (see *Gospel of the Ebionites* 4–5; *Gospel according to the Hebrews* 6). What is more, given that the baptism could imply the subordination of Jesus to John, the event was *potentially* embarrassing to the Evangelists, which is why the tradition tended to emphasize the Baptizer's unworthiness to baptize Jesus (Matt. 3:14–15) or, in the case of the Gospel of John, omitted the baptismal episode altogether.[8]

At one point, it is reported that the Baptizer accuses his audience of being a "brood of vipers" who come to him only because they wish to flee from God's wrath, much like a few snakes recoiling from danger; they act only out of a desperate urge for self-preservation (Luke 3:7–9, 15–18//Matt. 3:7–12). In Israel's sacred traditions God's wrath was thought of as the response of his holiness to moral evil, and it could be likened to the destructive and consuming forces of a raging fire, scorching heat, and blasting wind (e.g., Isa. 13:9; Ezek. 7:19; Zeph. 1:14–16; 2:2). John also demanded that his audience produce "fruits worthy of repentance" (Luke 3:8), signifying that the exterior rite of baptism is effective only if accompanied by a resolute interior transformation. That means visible evidence of a return to God is necessary as per the calls for "repentance" in the prophetic writings. The Baptizer accentuates the

6. Cf. James D. G. Dunn, *Jesus Remembered*, CM 1 (Grand Rapids: Eerdmans, 2003), 366–69.

7. One can cross-reference Luke 3:16–17//Matthew 3:11–12 with Mark 1:7–8; Acts 13:25; and John 1:26–27, 33. These are therefore among our most secure remarks about the Baptizer's teaching.

8. Cf. Webb, "John the Baptist," 215–17.

warning by referring to the imminence of divine judgment ("even now the ax is lying at the foot of the trees"), highlighting the shortness of time to react.

There is an account of John, while in prison, sending a delegation to Jesus inquiring whether Jesus really is "the one to come" (Luke 7:18–28, 31–35// Matt. 11:2–19). The outline of the pericope is very likely to be authentic, since it implies that the Baptizer had doubts about the identity of Jesus, whereas, in the tendency of the tradition, John is presented as a key witness to Jesus's messianic identity and heavenly origins. What is more, Jesus's response to the Baptizer echoes a number of texts drawn from Isaiah, which coheres with the strong Isaianic themes in Jesus's teachings and activities. In the first part of the unit (Luke 7:18–23//Matt. 11:2–6), John's disciples relay a question to Jesus, "Are you the one who is to come, or are we to look for another?" Although "the one to come" (*ho erchomenos*) was not a technical title for a messianic deliverer, it was readily applicable to a messianic figure who "comes" to rescue the Jewish nation. Here "the one to come" is arguably parallel to "the stronger one" about whom the Baptizer prophesied. Jesus responds to the question by quoting a series of texts taken from Isaiah 29, 35, and 61 about the signs that accompany the dawn of restoration, such as healing of the lame and preaching good news to the poor. Significantly, a similar list of "deeds" is also attributed to the Messiah in the *Messianic Apocalypse* from Qumran (4Q521 II, 1–14). Jesus's reply is obliquely affirmative, but he also urges John not to be impatient or discouraged, since the signs of restoration are clearly present in his deeds and preaching.[9] Jesus's response closes with a beatitude addressed specifically to John in the hope that his onetime teacher will not be scandalized by his claim.

This exchange provides occasion for Jesus to speak about the significance of the Baptizer in Israel's religious history in Luke 7:24–28//Matthew 11:7–11. Jesus thus asks the crowd why they went into the wilderness to see John and what they thought they were seeing. The Baptizer was evidently not "a reed shaken by the wind" (Luke 7:24). Herod Antipas minted coins with reeds on them, and Luke's version accentuates the contrast of Herod and John further with the reference to fine clothes and palaces. As a political commentary, the statement seems to mean that John did not bend to Herod. Instead, John is a prophet, but no ordinary prophet, as his prophetic work is qualitatively above and beyond that of the prophets who went before him. The Baptizer's prophetic work is associated with a text ("See, I am sending my messenger ahead of you, who will prepare your way before you") that appears to be a conflation of Exodus 23:20 (LXX) and Malachi 3:1 (MT). It underscores John's preparatory role for the eschatological events about to unfold. John is thus greater than all those born of women, and yet the least in the kingdom of God is greater than

---

9. Cf. Michael F. Bird, *Are You the One Who Is to Come? The Historical Jesus and the Messianic Question* (Grand Rapids: Baker Academic, 2009), 98–104.

he: "Even the most insignificant Israelite who has entered into the eschatological kingdom of God that Jesus announces enjoys a privilege and a standing greater than John's."[10]

The Synoptic Gospels (Mark 6:17–28; Matt. 14:3–11; Luke 3:19–20) recount that the Baptizer had criticized Antipas for marrying his brother Philip's wife Herodias, contrary to Levitical law (Lev. 18:16; 20:21), and historically this need not be doubted. The occasion for John's death seems somewhat contrived by the macabre and malicious de-

Figure 2.2. Bronze Galilean coin minted at Tiberias in 30 CE with Greek inscription reading *Hērōdou Tetrarchou* (Herod the Tetrarch) with a palm branch symbolizing Herod's reign. (Photo by Zev Radovan, www.BibleLandPictures.com.)

signs of women at Herod's court (see Esth. 5:1–8). When Herodias's daughter Salome dances for Herod at his birthday party and Herod promises the young girl whatever she asks, she, having consulted with her mother, asks for the head of John the Baptist. This leaves Herod notably grieved, but he agrees to it nonetheless in order to preserve his honor before his guests.

It is quite plausible, as Mark and Matthew narrate, that at some point Jesus was asked by his disciples, "Why do the scribes say that Elijah must come first?" (Mark 9:11//Matt. 17:10). That question relates to Malachi 4:5, which concerns the return of Elijah before the "day of the Lord." Jesus in turn affirms that Elijah does indeed come first, but he vaults over the standard scribal reference to Malachi 4:5 and enlarges Elijah's role to include making preparations for the future age. Jesus also retorts with his own question: "How then is it written about the Son of Man, that he is to go through many sufferings and be treated with contempt?" (Mark 9:12). Jesus locates his own messianic travails as the penultimate stage before the kingdom's arrival. Questions over the role of John (Elijah) and Jesus (Son of Man) in the consummation of Israel's history are entirely plausible topics in the course of Jesus's teaching to his disciples, and they correspond to other questions from the disciples about when and how the new age will begin (e.g., Mark 13:4; Acts 1:6).

In the parable about the marketplace, Jesus likens his critics' objections to him to a children's game where a cohort of children sing and dance a wedding dance and perform a funeral dirge, and other children refuse to play along (Luke 7:31–35//Matt. 11:16–19). Then he states that John "came neither eating nor drinking" and yet is accused of being demon possessed. In contrast, the Son of Man came "eating and drinking" and is accused of being a "glutton and a drunkard." The contrast of John and Jesus here shows a slight discontinuity in their method and message. John is ascetic, whereas Jesus engages in open table-fellowship as a living parable of the openness of the kingdom. John's

10. John P. Meier, *A Marginal Jew: Rethinking the Historical Jesus*, ABRL (New York: Doubleday, 1994), 2:144.

message is one of judgment and warning, while Jesus declares a message of jubilant restoration and eschatological joy.

The final reference to the Baptizer appears in a story of conflict between Jesus on the one hand and the chief priests, scribes, and elders on the other over the source of Jesus's authority (Mark 11:27–33//Matt. 21:23–27//Luke 20:1–8). When asked about the source of his authority, Jesus responds by asking whether John's baptism was of human or heavenly origins. His interlocutors are caught in a trap, as they can neither affirm nor deny the heavenly origins of John's baptism without losing their own credibility in front of the crowds. They therefore answer, "We don't know." The story, inherently plausible again, assumes the widespread popularity of John's baptism, Jesus's affirmation of John's ministry, and the Judean religious hierarchy's ambivalence toward John.

Early Church

The influence and memory of John did not die out quickly. John evidently had disciples (Luke 7:18–19//Matt. 11:2; Luke 11:1; John 1:35; 3:25–26), and, according to Acts, in the 50s CE followers of John were to be found as far as Ephesus, where persons still esteemed John's preaching and practice of baptism (Acts 18:25; 19:1–7). A further and much later reference to his disciples is found in the *Pseudo-Clementine Recognitions*, which note that John's disciples claim that the Baptizer was the Messiah (*Ps.-Clem. Rec.* 1.60). Luke's description of early Christian preaching highlights the role of the Baptizer as a forerunner of Jesus and thereby ensures Christian appropriation of John's memory (Acts 1:5, 21–22; 10:37–38; 11:16; 13:24–25; 19:4–5; cf. Justin Martyr, *Dial.* 50.1). Scholars often posit, on the basis of a reconstructed situation behind the Fourth Gospel, a supposed internecine conflict between followers of the Baptizer and members of the Johannine community. However, this view stems from an illegitimate attempt at mining the Gospel of John for intracommunal debates between entities that we cannot prove even existed, namely, a Johannine community in a fractious relationship with a Baptist community. What is more, the tradition tended to claim the Baptizer for the Christian cause rather than polemicize against the Baptizer. Although the Evangelists endeavor to show the superiority of Jesus over John, they still retain Jesus's own positive evaluation of the Baptizer's work. It is also noteworthy that the Baptizer was prominent in works by later Christian writers such as Justin Martyr, Tertullian, Hippolytus, and Origen. John is referred to in several noncanonical works such the *Gospel of Thomas*, the *Protevangelium of James*, and the *Gospel of the Ebionites*, who revered the memory of John the Baptist.

Relationship of John to Jesus

The question of the historical relationship of John to Jesus arises naturally. In the Lukan tradition they are relatives (Luke 1:36). Scholars, however, either

The Baptism of Jesus in the *Gospel of the Ebionites*?

The *Gospel of the Ebionites*, known exclusively through citations by the church father Epiphanius, has this narration of Jesus's baptism from that text:

> After the people had been baptized, Jesus came also, and was baptized by John. And as he came out of the water, the heavens opened, and he saw the Holy Spirit descending in the form of a dove and entering into him. And a voice was heard from heaven, "You are my beloved Son, and in you am I well pleased." And again, "This day have I begotten you." And suddenly a great light shone in that place. And John, seeing him said, "I pray you, Lord, baptize me." But he would not, saying, "Suffer it, for thus it is fitting that all should be accomplished."[1]

Note three things here:

- This account is probably not an independent version of the same event recorded in the Gospels, but reflects an embellishment of Matthew 3:14–15.
- The addition of "This day have I begotten you" is a quotation from Psalm 2:7, and the same addition is found in some ancient manuscripts of Luke 3:22.
- The reference to a "great light [that] shone in that place" is also found in two Latin manuscripts and Tatian's *Diatessaron*, and was known to Justin Martyr as well. It likely reflects a tradition that developed in the second century that tried to enhance the miraculous events surrounding Jesus's baptism.

1. J. K. Elliott, ed., *The Apocryphal New Testament: A Collection of Apocryphal Christian Literature in an English Translation Based on M. R. James* (Oxford: Clarendon, 1993), 15.

postulate Jesus as a maverick offshoot from John's baptismal movement or else think of John as the mentor of Jesus. It is clear that there are elements of continuity and discontinuity between the two figures. Though Jesus may have spent some time baptizing (John 3:22), this was apparently not a major part of his work. Whereas John preached a message of judgment and repentance, Jesus preached judgment, social justice, and vindication for the faithful. John was location-bound to places near water, whereas Jesus was an itinerant preacher. John stood in the prophetic tradition, while Jesus was much like a rabbi in his teaching to his disciples; he resembled a healer/exorcist in his works, a prophet in his preaching to the crowds, and a messianic claimant in his view of his own role in ushering in the kingdom. Jesus can also contrast John's ascetic lifestyle with his own more euphoric table fellowship with sinners (Luke 7:33–34// Matt. 11:18–19). Deeply engrained in the Jesus tradition is John's witness to Jesus as a significant eschatological figure, Jesus's affirmation of the validity of John's baptism, and Jesus's identification of John as Elijah. It is rather difficult, then, to assert that Jesus's ministry represented a radical departure from the Baptizer's teachings and practice, especially over the apocalyptic message that both prophets proclaimed. In the words of John Meier:

If Jesus accepted John's message and baptism, presumably he affirmed John's basic eschatological outlook. To be sure, Jesus may have developed or even moved away from John's eschatology later on. But a totally un-eschatological Jesus trips over the very stumbling-stone early Christianity found so difficult: John the Baptist, the independent Jewish prophet of fiery imminent eschatology, to whom Jesus himself adhered.[11]

We can summarize the testimony from our sources about Jesus's relationship to the Baptizer in the following way:[12]

- Jesus submitted to John's baptism, and John marked Jesus out as an anointed figure (Mark 1:9–11).
- Jesus commenced a ministry similar to that of John about repentance and God's kingdom (Mark 1:14–15), and he may have had his own initial baptismal ministry that overlapped with John's for a time (John 3:22–26).
- John's imprisonment was a decisive turning point in the beginning of Jesus's ministry (Mark 1:14–15).
- John expressed doubts about Jesus's identity as the "coming one" (Matt. 11:2–3).
- Jesus claimed that John was more than a prophet (Luke 7:26, 28//Matt. 11:9, 11).
- Jesus claimed that John was the eschatological prophet Elijah *redivivus* (Mark 9:12–13; Matt. 11:14).
- Some thought Jesus was John the Baptist come back from the dead (Mark 6:14).
- At the end of his ministry Jesus expressed his own purpose and authority by comparing and contrasting himself with John and suggested that they were part of the single effort of God (Luke 7:31–35//Matt. 11:16–19 and Mark 11:27–33).

John the Baptist: A Sketch

If our sources are taken together, we can offer an overview of John the Baptist in this way. John was possibly born from a priestly family settled in Galilee. Some time around 28 CE he appeared on the outskirts of the Judean wilderness near the Jordan River as an ascetic holy man dressed like Elijah and preaching an Isaianic message of God's judgment. The location

11. Meier, *Marginal Jew*, 2:31–32.
12. See similarly Ben Witherington, "John the Baptist," in *Dictionary of Jesus and the Gospels*, ed. Joel B. Green, Scot McKnight, and I. Howard Marshall (Downers Grove, IL: InterVarsity, 1992), 383–84.

by the Jordan was deliberate too, as the Baptizer was inviting a purified and prepared Israel to reenter the land along the lines of a new exodus (Exod. 7–19) or perhaps a new conquest (see Josh. 3–4). To onlookers he acted, looked, and spoke like a prophet. The description of him as the "Baptist" or "Baptizer" was appended to his name because of his distinctive practice of water baptism for devotees to his message. This baptism functioned as a sign of turning away from past sins and as a symbol of cleansing and release from moral impurity, and conveyed a determination to live in an upright manner thereafter. This baptism was related to John's message of repentance and judgment, as it was a necessary rite of preparation to face the day of the Lord. For the Baptizer, ethnicity and election were not a shield against divine judgment—only an inward, heartfelt transformation would suffice. In his proclamation, then, John was a preacher of righteousness and repentance, announcing these in light of the imminent coming of Yahweh's eschatological wrath upon the wicked.

John can be placed in relation to other figures from Israel's sacred history and other contemporary Judean groups of the first century. The Baptizer stood in the prophetic tradition with a message apparently indebted to the eschatological perspective of Isaiah, but with additional apocalyptic motifs about judgment. Although there were various prophetic movements in the first century,[13] John was among what Robert Webb calls the "popular leadership prophets," who modeled themselves on patterns from the classical prophets with an announcement directed to Israel.[14] John is partially reminiscent of Bannus the Ascetic, who, according to Josephus, "lived in the desert, and used no other clothing than that which grew upon trees, and he had no other food other than that which grew of its own design, and he often bathed himself in cool water, both by night and by day, in order to preserve his purity," and drew to himself disciples some time in the 40s CE (Josephus, *Life* 11). Analogous to the ministry of John the Baptist and Jesus of Nazareth was Jesus ben Ananias, who prophesied against the temple and was killed by a Roman catapult (Josephus, *J.W.* 6.300–310). Very interesting points of contact also exist between John and the Qumran community, not least concerning their physical location near the Jordan, use of Isaiah 40:3, baptismal practices, and apocalyptic outlook, though it remains unlikely that John was ever a member of the Qumranite sect.[15]

The Baptizer also appears to have deliberately excited apocalyptic and messianic hopes about a coming deliverer who would follow after him. Among those whom he baptized was Jesus from Nazareth, a Galilean craftsman who

---

13. Cf. W. J. Heard and Craig A. Evans, "Revolutionary Movements, Jewish," in *Dictionary of New Testament Background*, ed. Craig A. Evans and Stanley E. Porter (Downers Grove, IL: InterVarsity, 2000), 939–41.

14. Webb, *John the Baptizer and Prophet*, 333–46.

15. Ibid., 351n4.

John the Baptist and Qumran?

A number of scholars have proposed that John the Baptist was a onetime member of the sect of Judeans who lived on the shores of the Dead Sea at Qumran. Such a relationship is certainly possible, for a number of reasons. First, John's ministry on the Jordan took place in an area that was at best a day or two's walk from the Qumran settlement. Luke reports that as a child John grew up in spiritual strength and "was in the wilderness until the day he appeared publicly to Israel" (Luke 1:80), and we know from Josephus that the Essenes[1] often adopted children and trained them in their customs (Josephus, *J.W.* 2.12). Second, if we compare John as he is portrayed in the Gospels with themes and motifs drawn from the Dead Sea Scrolls, then a number of striking similarities emerge. Both John and the Qumranites practiced a form of ritual baptism, both separated themselves from ordinary Palestinian life, both practiced a form of religious devotion independent of the institutions of Judaism, such as the temple and its cultus, both pronounced woes of judgment upon their contemporaries for moral laxity, both looked ahead to God's imminent and dramatic intervention in Israelite history to effect deliverance, both possessed an apocalyptic worldview with messianic themes about coming deliverers, and—most importantly of all—both saw in Isaiah 40:3 the task of their calling as preparing the way for the Lord out in the wilderness. However, a number of key differences are apparent as well. John's ministry was public, whereas the Qumranites were largely secluded. The character of John's ministry was prophetic, while the Qumranites were largely priestly. John interacted with persons who would have been regarded as morally and ceremonially impure by the Qumranites (e.g., ritually unclean Jews, non-Jews, prostitutes, tax collectors). The baptism of John was for eschatological preparation, while baptism at Qumran was part of initiation into the community and part of a daily regime of purity and ritual. The "stronger one" spoken by John was a dispenser of the Spirit, whereas the messianic figures attested in the Qumran writings are Davidic and priestly. John looks to the deliverance of all of Israel, while the Qumranites anticipate only a remnant of themselves being saved.

Isaiah 40:1–3	Mark 1:2–4	1QS VII, 14–16
Comfort, O comfort my people, says your God.　Speak tenderly to Jerusalem, and cry to her that she has served her term, that her penalty is paid, that she has received from the Lord's hand double for all her sins.　A voice cries out: "In the wilderness prepare the way of the Lord, make straight in the desert a highway for our God."	As it is written in the prophet Isaiah, "See, I am sending my messenger ahead of you, who will prepare your way; the voice of one crying out in the wilderness: 'Prepare the way of the Lord, make his paths straight,'"　John the baptizer appeared in the wilderness, proclaiming a baptism of repentance for the forgiveness of sins.	When such men as these come to be in Israel, conforming to these doctrines, they shall separate from the session of perverse men to go to the wilderness, there to prepare the way of truth, as it is written, "In the wilderness prepare the way of the Lord, make straight in the desert a highway for our God." This means the expounding of the Law, decreed by God through Moses for obedience, that being defined by what has been revealed for each age, and by what the prophets have revealed by His holy spirit."[2]

1. I am assuming that the Qumranites were at least "Essenic" (i.e., exhibited views and practices analogous to the Essenes) in some respects, although they might have included Pharisaic and Sadducean elements as well.
2. M. Wise, M. Abegg, and E. Cook, trans., *The Dead Sea Scrolls: A New Translation* (San Francisco: HarperSanFrancisco, 1996), 138.

later led a prophetic/messianic renewal movement and was eventually handed over by the Judean leadership to the Romans and crucified as a messianic pretender. It may be the case that Jesus, Jesus's followers, and even John himself thought of Jesus as the "one" who would inaugurate the eschatological time of Israel's deliverance.

The apocalyptic message of John, along with the gathering of very large crowds, disturbed the authorities, who saw this as a potential cause of social unrest and political upheaval. In particular, Herod Antipas, tetrarch of Galilee and Perea, undertook preventive measures and had John arrested and then executed some time around 30 CE. According to Christian authors, the Baptizer had criticized Herod for marrying his brother Philip's wife, Herodias.

Yet, even after his death, followers of John did not completely die out, as some continued to venerate the Baptizer and to keep his message alive in Palestine and even in Asia Minor. Some Judeans also thought that Antipas's defeat by King Aretas IV of the Nabataeans was a sign of divine judgment upon Antipas for his execution of John. After Jesus's death, a group of Jesus's followers reconstituted themselves in Jerusalem as a messianic movement, and key figures in this group saw the Baptizer as an important precursor to the ministry of Jesus. It also possible (though far from certain) that followers of John and Jesus came into some kind of critical interaction in the mid- to late first century that shaped oral and written traditions about the relationship between the two as they appear in the canonical Gospels.

Narrative Considerations: John the Baptist according to the Canonical Gospels

The Evangelists do not simply report John's activities as a matter of antiquarian interest. They also interweave traditions about the Baptizer into their own narratives in order to present him as a crucial figure in God's revelation of his Son to Israel. Their theological configuration of John the Baptist is interesting in its own right, as John's ministry and testimony is freighted with christological significance in their account of him. Moreover, John also provides a link between Jesus and Israel's sacred literature through John's role as a prophetic forerunner of the Messiah.

Mark

In the Gospel of Mark, the Evangelist utilizes the Baptizer's testimony to serve his own interest in the messianism of Jesus, and he situates the Baptizer in relation to his "new exodus" motif drawn from Isaiah.[16] The "beginning

16. Cf. Rikki E. Watts, *Isaiah's New Exodus in Mark* (Grand Rapids: Baker Academic, 2000).

of the gospel" opens with Old Testament quotes that portray the Baptizer as the prophetic forerunner of Jesus (Mark 1:2–3). In the Markan account the Baptizer is somewhere between a proto-Jesus and Elijah incognito, and the joint efforts of John and Jesus contribute to the inauguration of the age of deliverance.

Mark summarizes the Baptizer's message as follows: "The one who is more powerful than I is coming after me; I am not worthy to stoop down and untie the thong of his sandals. I have baptized you with water; but he will baptize you with the Holy Spirit (Mark 1:7–8).[17] The baptism in/with/by the Holy Spirit probably suggests some sort of purifying and cleansing power. Ironically, though, John himself never really penetrates into the mystery surrounding Jesus's identity, even though he baptized him. Thus: "The messianic secret is kept even from the Messiah's forerunners" (Mark 1:4–11).[18]

According to Mark, the story of the Baptizer's martyrdom is a crucial indicator of the nature of kingdom mission and kingdom discipleship. Herod's execution of John (Mark 6:14–29) is sandwiched between the sending out of the twelve disciples to preach and exorcise unclean spirits (Mark 6:7–13) and the return of the apostles to report to Jesus all that they had done (Mark 6:30–31). In the middle we find Herod's statement: "John, whom I beheaded, has been raised" (Mark 6:16). It is unclear whether this refers to belief in an actual resurrection of John the Baptist who appears *redivivus* in Jesus of Nazareth or whether it refers to the same power of God, like the "spirit of Elijah" (cf. 2 Kings 2:15), that has been transferred from John to Jesus. The observation assumes continuity between John and Jesus and a supernatural element that brings John to new life through Jesus.[19] Clearly, however, the arrangement of material is far from accidental. Mark has deliberately organized this unit in such a way so as to show what commitment to the kingdom means. John's death foreshadows the passion of Jesus and underscores the cost of discipleship. Those who follow Jesus, announce the kingdom, and adhere to Jesus's teachings will find themselves at odds with local and provincial rulers, perhaps even to the point of death (see Mark 8:34–38; 13:9–13).

In addition, the secret of Jesus's messianic identity is paralleled by John's secret Elijanic identity and his role to "restore all things" (Mark 9:12). Jesus's own time line for the eschatological denouement is that it will not transpire until after Elijah comes and suffers and not until the Son of Man has also been rejected and entered his travails as written about in Scripture. Jesus contends

---

17. This coming figure cannot be God because it makes no sense of John's comparison ("greater than I") and John's unworthiness to attire his footwear ("sandals I am not fit to untie"). John has in mind a person, not a theophany. See further Webb, "John the Baptist," 200–201.

18. Meier, *Marginal Jew*, 2:21.

19. Cf. Klaus Berger, *Die Auferstehung des Propheten und die Erhöhung des Menschensohnes: Traditionsgeschichtliche Untersuchungen zur Deutung des Geschickes Jesu in frühchristlichen Texten*, SUNT 13 (Göttingen: Vandenhoeck and Ruprecht, 1976).

that Elijah has already come—an implicit allusion to the Baptizer—and that he suffered as it was written about him in Scripture (Mark 9:13). In other words, Jesus affirms the story of Scripture as teaching that Elijah effects a prior restoration, but before the end the Son of Man must also enter his sufferings, and only then will the end finally come. That is part and parcel of Mark's apocalyptic framework, in which Jesus comes to a world permeated with evil in order to activate the divine plan for salvation. Thus, for Mark, the Baptizer is not accidentally prior to Jesus but necessarily precedes Jesus, as the work of the Son of Man cannot begin until Elijah has performed his antecedent tasks. In the confrontation with the chief priests, scribes, and elders, Jesus takes the Baptizer's side by affirming the heavenly origins of his baptism, while his interlocutors must retreat to an uncommitted answer (Mark 11:27–33). In hindsight, then, Jesus received a heavenly baptism and a heavenly voice at his baptism, and this interweaves his messianic ministry and the preparatory ministry of the Baptizer together.

Matthew and Luke

The portrait of John the Baptist in the Gospels of Matthew and Luke is hardly uniform, but they both incorporate material from Mark and adapt material from a shared Q tradition.

The portrait of the Baptizer in the Gospel of Matthew includes John's awareness of Jesus's inherent dignity, and John accordingly confesses his own inferiority to Jesus at Jesus's baptism: "I need to be baptized by you, and do you come to me?" (Matt. 3:14). Yet Jesus exhorts him to do it anyway, "for it is proper for us in this way to fulfill all righteousness," which John reluctantly consents to do (Matt. 3:15). In Matthew's Gospel the Baptizer is twice associated with "righteousness." In context, "righteousness" implies the fulfillment of God's plan of salvation (Matt. 3:15) and the upright conduct of the Baptizer (Matt. 21:32). John and Jesus stand together against the official establishment of Judaism at the popular (Pharisees) and aristocratic (Sadducees, Herodians) levels, as is seen in the abrasive nature of the preaching of both figures. While Mark veils the reference to John as Elijah, Matthew makes the connection explicit, and in his Gospel the disciples comprehend that "he was speaking to them about John the Baptist" (Matt. 17:13), which emphasizes the John-Elijah connection all the more. John in many ways can be contrasted with Jesus by Matthew (e.g., Jesus's frivolous engagement with sinners and John's ascetic lifestyle), yet both pave the way of righteousness and represent not the antithesis of the Law and Prophets but the ushering in of their climactic fulfillment (Matt. 21:32).

In the Lukan account the Baptizer first appears as a relative of Jesus (Luke 1:36). In the birth narrative, John, even while in utero, leaps for joy in Elizabeth's womb at the presence of Jesus, who is also in utero in Mary (Luke 1:41–44).

Why Was Jesus Baptized?

If John's baptism was a "baptism of repentance for the forgiveness of sins" (Mark 1:4), then why did Jesus need to be baptized? In Christian thought Jesus is the sinless savior, the unblemished Lamb of God, so why would he need to be baptized? Was Jesus a "sinner"? Did he need to repent? The problem is reflected in the Gospels themselves. Matthew notes John's reluctance to baptize Jesus: "I need to be baptized by you, and do you come to me?" (Matt. 3:14). Mark and Luke balance the subordination in baptism with the descent of the Spirit upon Jesus and the words of the divine voice to Jesus when he comes up out of the water. And the Gospel of John omits the baptism story altogether. The answer to our question is perhaps threefold: (1) Jesus's baptism was an act of solidarity with exiled Israel and fallen humanity. In entering into the waters of baptism Jesus was identifying himself with Israel, who needed to repent of her sins and to experience a new exodus. Baptism also shows Jesus identifying with corporate humanity, which is alienated from God. Baptism marks out his willingness to be the true Israel and the second Adam, which is why after his baptism a voice from heaven declares, "This is my Son, the Beloved, with whom I am well pleased" (Matt. 3:17; both Israel and Adam were a "son" of God [Gen. 5:1–3; Exod. 4:22; Luke 3:37]). (2) Matthew adds his own reason, that Jesus's baptism was to "fulfill all righteousness" (Matt. 3:15). The meaning of "righteousness" (*dikaiosynē*) here is terribly vague, and we should resist reading a Pauline meaning into it. I propose that it stems from a Hebraic tendency to view "righteousness" as equivalent to "salvation" (e.g., Pss. 40:10; 51:14; 71:2; 143:11; Isa. 51:5–8; 61:10; Jer. 23:5). Thus, "righteousness" here has a salvation-historical meaning, as Jesus's baptism fulfills God's plan of salvation. (3) There is potentially a priestly Christology lurking in the background of the baptism story as well. For instance, priests had to be ceremonially washed with water (Exod. 29:4; Lev. 8:6) and ceremonially anointed for their work (Exod. 29:7; Lev. 8:12), according to the Torah. Both elements, washing and anointing, are apparent in Jesus's baptism, and they show him suitably qualified for his role as intercessor and priest (note the priestly themes in Mark 1:40–44; 2:26–27; 12:35–37).

This is the only time that John and Jesus come into direct contact in the Gospel of Luke. Somewhat strangely, Luke describes John's imprisonment before the baptism of Jesus, and in his account of Jesus's baptism does not refer to John as the one who baptized him in the Jordan (Luke 3:19–21). Luke says that the "word of God came to John," meaning that he received his prophetic call at this time to go into the wilderness to proclaim his message (Luke 3:2). John appears in a vital chain of events leading to the revelation of the Son of God to Israel and a revelation for the gentiles. Luke also has carefully noted the broader context of John's calling in the theater of the wider Roman Empire (Luke 3:1). John's ministry is eschatological, full of moral exhortation, and yet in Luke's summary, "So, with many other exhortations, he proclaimed the good news to the people" (Luke 3:18). Jesus and the apostles also proclaim "good news," which demonstrates a unified theme in Luke-Acts, where the announcement of God's kingdom is made by the Baptizer, Jesus, and the Apostles. This shows that their preaching, however diverse in content, is part of the one act of God to bring salvation to the ends of the earth. Luke's salvation-historical perspective shines through in Luke 16:16, where John is the *last* of the Old Testament prophets, but simultaneously the *first* preacher of the kingdom of God and a cotestifier with Jesus to the saving action of God that is now manifested.

Matthew and Luke revise the Q tradition in different ways. For case in point, noticeable differences appear in the speech about John the Baptist in Luke 7:24–30//Matt. 11:7–10. Luke adds a parenthetical remark about the Baptizer's reception among the tax collectors, who received John's baptism, and the Pharisees and scribes, who rejected it (Luke 7:29–30). In contrast, Matthew proceeds to add further remarks about the Baptizer's place in Israel's sacred history (Matt. 11:12–15), while Luke places some similar material much later on (Luke 16:16). In the Matthean sequence,[20] Jesus states that from the period of John to the present time the "kingdom of heaven has suffered violence, and the violent take it by force." The meaning of the Greek about the "violence and the violent" (*biazetai kai biastai*) is uncertain, but it may indict those who wanted to usher the kingdom in through revolution.[21] After this statement, Matthew's Jesus says that the "prophets and the law prophesied until John came," indicating the penultimate role of the Baptizer in Israel's sacred history (though the authenticity of this statement is questioned by many as too "Christian").[22] Finally, the Matthean Jesus declares that John is "Elijah who is to come." Whereas this last statement is more explicit about the Baptizer-Elijah connection than the private and veiled reference in Mark 9:11–13, it is no less authentic, since it evidently coheres with the overall pattern in the Jesus tradition that paints John as the eschatological forerunner to the advent of the kingdom (e.g., Mark 1:1–8; 11:32; Luke 3:15; 7:29–30; John 1:6–7, 15, 23–40; 5:35; Acts 1:5).

In material unique to Matthew and Luke (derived from their own respective sources or else stemming from their own creation), we find several units dealing with the Baptizer. Matthew, in the parable of the two sons (Matt. 21:28–32), reports that Jesus referred to the unfavorable reception of the Baptizer by the temple authorities: "John came to you in the way of righteousness and you did

---

20. Luke inverts the order of the saying about Law/Prophets/John and the kingdom suffering violence, and he adds the gloss "good news." Therefore, Luke's version is probably secondary to Matthew.

21. Cf. Michael F. Bird, "Jesus and the Revolutionaries: Did Jesus Call Israel to Repent of Nationalistic Ambitions?" *Colloquium* 38 (2006): 129–30.

22. Cf. Rudolf Bultmann, *The History of the Synoptic Tradition*, trans. John Marsh (New York: Harper & Row, 1963), 164–65; but see in contrast Meier, *Marginal Jew*, 2:157–64, and Dunn, *Jesus Remembered*, 452–53.

not believe him, but the tax collectors and the prostitutes believed him; and even after you saw it, you did not change your minds and believe him" (Matt. 21:32). The unit is probably authentic because it corresponds to other material about the error of disbelieving John (e.g., Mark 11:31) and lacks any signs of christianization. In context, the "way of righteousness" is John's message and conduct; that is, he practiced what he preached.[23] Distinctive Lukan material about appropriate responses to John's message (Luke 3:10–15) appears sandwiched between two Q units (Luke 3:7–9, 16–18). In response to the question "What should we do?" the Baptizer accordingly advises the crowds, tax collectors, and soldiers to undertake actions that promote compassion and justice. On the one hand, this account sounds very much like Luke's own manifesto for communities of mutual care and God-driven compassion. Still, Jewish teachers generally provided guidance for how life should be lived before God, and there is no sufficient reason to think that the picture of John as a teacher of morality is purely a "product of that notorious bourgeois Christian and peddler of early Catholicism, Luke."[24]

What Matthew and Luke share (mainly via the Q tradition) is that John was an apocalyptic preacher of repentance and judgment. He testified to a stronger one/coming one, who would unleash the Holy Spirit as a purifying and purging power. He appears to have identified this figure with Jesus and then had second thoughts about it. The Baptizer was also remembered for his ascetic lifestyle, in contrast to Jesus's open commensality with sinners.

John

The peculiar fact of the Fourth Gospel is that John is never called the "Baptist," but is known simply as "John." In the prologue, John is said to be "sent from God" and to have come "as a witness to testify to the light" even though "he himself was not the light" (John 1:6–8). John also attests the preexistent being of the Word, who comes and dwells among Israel (1:14–15). This captures the main function of John in the Fourth Gospel: he is principally a witness to the messianic identity and soteric task of Jesus rather than a prophetic contemporary of Jesus.

Beyond the mention of John in the prologue, the Fourth Gospel contains a section on the "testimony" of John (John 1:19–39). In this unit, which is a mix of historical tradition and theological confession, the Baptizer testifies to Jesus as the Lord (1:23), the Lamb of God who takes away the sin of the world (1:29), the anointed Spirit-dispenser who is sent to Israel (1:33), and the Son of God (1:34). Although the Synoptic Gospels call John "Elijah" (e.g., Mark

23. Benno Przybylski, *Righteousness in Matthew and His World of Thought*, SNTSMS 41 (Cambridge: Cambridge University Press, 1980), 94–96.
24. Meier, *Marginal Jew*, 2:41 (Meier is being sarcastic against those who contest Luke's historical utility).

9:13 and Matt. 11:14; 17:12–13), in the Gospel of John, the Baptizer is quite explicit in his denial that he is Elijah, the Messiah, or the Prophet. He then defines his role along the lines of Isaiah 40:3 (as per Mark 1:2–3, 8–9), as that of preparing the way for the Lord (1:19–23).

The same witness motif occurs elsewhere in the Gospel of John. The Baptizer states that Jesus is the bridegroom, who increases, while the Baptizer himself decreases (3:29–30). In the discourse of John 5:33–47, John the Baptist, the Father, and the Scriptures all testify to Jesus's identity and authority, yet all three are ignored by "the Jews," who reject the claims of the Johannine Jesus. Finally, though the Baptizer's work is not attested by signs, his testimony to Jesus is said to be entirely authentic (10:41).

In sum, in the Fourth Gospel, John the Baptist is principally a witness to the christocentric revelation of the Word, rather than a baptizing prophet. However, rather than polemicizing against John, the Gospel of John holds up John as the quintessential testimony (*martyria*) that Jesus is the Messiah sent by God (see esp. John 5:33–37).

Conclusion

John the Baptist has an eminent place in Palestinian history and early Christian literature. What, then, does John the Baptist contribute to the identity of Jesus in the theater of Christian discourse? First, John is part of the "beginning of the gospel," as he is the prophetic predecessor who paves the way for Jesus. He is the "Elijah to come" who announces the "way of the Lord" and identifies Jesus as the "stronger one" and "coming one." He is the last of the Old Testament prophets and the first proclaimer of the kingdom of God. Second, John is the witness par excellence to Jesus's messianic mission and heavenly origins. Though expressing doubts himself about this identification just before his death, John is principally remembered for confirming God's appointment of Jesus for his redemptive task, a point clearly accentuated in Johannine tradition. Third, John's martyrdom highlights the link between God's kingdom and suffering, since those who announce God's saving reign, as John and Jesus did, can expect hostility in this life. Fourth, Jesus's ministry and message in many ways form a continuation of John's. Though Jesus seemed to have accentuated eschatological joy rather than eschatological judgment in his teaching, both Jesus and John set before Israel a dire warning that the hour of decision had come. Accordingly, the nation had to choose how it would respond to the dawning hour of judgment, and whether they would enter the reign of God or not. Finally, John's significance is perhaps best summarized with a paraphrase from the Fourth Gospel: "John performed no sign, but everything that John said about this man was true" (John 10:41).

Suggestions for Further Reading

Murphy, Catherine M. *John the Baptist: Prophet of Purity for a New Age*. Collegeville, MN: Liturgical Press, 2003.

Taylor, Joan E. *The Immerser: John the Baptist within Second Temple Judaism*. Grand Rapids: Eerdmans, 1997.

Webb, Robert A. *John the Baptizer and Prophet: A Socio-Historical Study*. JSNTSup 62. Sheffield: Sheffield Academic Press, 1991.

Witherington, Ben, III. "John the Baptist." In *Dictionary of Jesus and the Gospels*, edited by Joel B. Green, Scot McKnight, and I. Howard Marshall, 383–91. Downers Grove, IL: InterVarsity, 1992.

3

The Disciples

WARREN CARTER

The focus in this chapter concerns Jesus's disciples. In part 1, we will explore some historical questions: Did Jesus have disciples; if so, who were they, and what do we know about them? In part 2, we will examine the presentation of the disciples in each of the canonical Gospels.

Historical Considerations: The Twelve (or Fifteen)

This section concerns the historical Jesus and his disciples. How do we know that Jesus had disciples? If so, did he have a fixed and clearly defined number? If he did, what happened to this group after Jesus's crucifixion? What reliable historical information do we have?

Jesus's Disciples

The criterion of multiple attestation (see the sidebar on criteria) indicates that Jesus had disciples.[1] Accordingly, we find references to Jesus's disciples in

---

1. For discussion, see E. P. Sanders, *Jesus and Judaism* (Philadelphia: Fortress, 1985), 98–106; Bart Ehrman, *Jesus: Apocalyptic Prophet of the New Millennium* (New York: Oxford University Press, 1999), 185–87.

Criteria Used in the Quest for the Historical Jesus

The main sources for information about Jesus are the canonical Gospels. The Gospels, however, are not primarily historical writings, though they contain historical material. They were written some fifty to seventy years after Jesus's crucifixion, and they each employ a distinct perspective. They do not pretend to be "neutral" about Jesus. They are pastoral-theological stories written from the perspective of commitment to Jesus. They express insights into Jesus to shape faithful discipleship. The Gospel writers edit (or redact) their accounts, including historical material, to carry out this goal. This pastoral-theological-historical mix and fifty- to seventy-year gap between the time of Jesus and the Gospels make the task of identifying historical information about the historical Jesus difficult.

Historians have developed various criteria or "rules of evidence" to guide this inquiry. One of those criteria is called "multiple attestation." If a saying or action appears in different traditions—two or more of Paul, Q (material common to Matthew and Luke but not in Mark), Mark, L (special only to Luke), M (special only to Matthew), and John—it is judged to be probably authentic to the historical Jesus. Likewise, if material appears in multiple forms or types of writing, it probably comes from Jesus. As noted already, the application of this criterion of multiple attestation indicates that Jesus had disciples.

Below we will employ another criterion, that of dissimilarity, to establish a special group comprising "the Twelve." The criterion of dissimilarity says that if material is not influenced by either Jesus's cultural context or the post-Jesus situations of the early church, it probably comes from Jesus. Another criterion is that of embarrassment. Some material would likely have been somewhat embarrassing for key figures in the early Jesus-believing communities, such as Peter's denial of Jesus, Judas's betrayal of Jesus, and Jesus's declaration that the Twelve, including Judas, would rule Israel. It is most unlikely that the church would invent such material after Jesus's death. It is, therefore, probably authentic to the historical Jesus.

several writings of early Jesus followers. The earliest reference comes in Paul. Writing in the early 50s CE about Jesus's resurrection appearances, Paul says, "and . . . he appeared to Cephas, then to the twelve" (1 Cor. 15:5). In addition, the Gospels, written in the late first century CE, provide independent accounts concerning the call of disciples:

- Mark 1:16–20 (Simon, Andrew, James, John; which Matt. 4:18–22 follows),
- Luke 5:1–11 (Simon Peter, James, John; the source L comprising material exclusive to Luke's Gospel),
- John 1:35–51 (Andrew, Simon Peter, Philip, Nathanael).

In these accounts, several disciples are fishermen, people of low status whose occupation embeds them in the Roman Empire's economy (likewise Matthew the tax collector).[2]

These accounts not only come from varying traditions but are also themselves of different kinds. Paul includes "the twelve" in a list of recipients of resurrection appearances. Mark and Matthew employ the form of a call narrative. The L account in Luke uses a miracle story, and John employs a quest story in which intermediaries bring people to Jesus. These independent accounts and these different forms or types of writing provide multiple attestation for Jesus's practice of calling disciples.

A second factor indicates that Jesus had "disciples." In the Greek and Roman worlds, philosophers and religious teachers had committed followers or adherents.[3] These followers were frequently identified as *mathētai*, the word the Gospels use for "disciples." Moreover, in Jewish traditions, prophets (1 Sam. 10:5–8; 19:20–21; Isa. 8:16) and wise men and scribes (Sir. 51:23) assembled adherents, or followers and learners, to pass on their craft. The account of the prophet Elijah summoning Elisha from his work and parents to follow Elijah as a prophet appears somewhat analogous to Jesus's call of disciples (1 Kings 19:19–21). The Gospels themselves attest the practice of key figures other than Jesus gathering disciples: John the Baptist (John 1:35; Matt. 11:2; Acts 19:3—multiple attestation), Pharisees (Matt. 22:15–16; Luke 5:33; Josephus, *Ant.* 13.289; 15.3), and Moses (John 9:28). It was thus common practice for a teacher to gather adherents and disciples, making Jesus's adoption of the practice fully plausible and thoroughly compatible with his setting.

How Many Disciples?

So how many disciples did Jesus have? Influenced by the Gospels' presentation, many speak of a fixed group of "the disciples" or "the twelve disciples." While the Gospels use the term "disciples" often to refer to this group, they also indicate that the term had significant flexibility.

The first indication of this flexibility emerges in the lists of "the disciples" found in the Synoptic Gospels and Acts.

	Mark 3:16–19	Matt. 10:2–4	Luke 6:14–16	Acts 1:13, 26
Simon named Peter	1	1	1	1
James son of Zebedee	2	3	3	3

2. For discussion, see K. C. Hanson and Douglas E. Oakman, *Palestine in the Time of Jesus* (Minneapolis: Fortress, 1998), 106–10.

3. Michael J. Wilkins, *Discipleship in the Ancient World and Matthew's Gospel* (Grand Rapids: Baker, 1995), 11–125.

	Mark 3:16–19	Matt. 10:2–4	Luke 6:14–16	Acts 1:13, 26
John his brother	3	4	4	2
Andrew	4	2	2	4
Philip	5	5	5	5
Bartholomew	6	6	6	7
Matthew	7	8	7	8
Thomas	8	7	8	6
James son of Alphaeus	9	9	9	9
Thaddaeus	10	10		
Simon the Zealot			10	10
Simon the Cananaean	11	11		
Judas son of James			11	11
Judas Iscariot who betrayed him	12	12	12	
Matthias				12

Although the Gospels commonly refer to "twelve disciples," there are actually fifteen names here. Mark and Matthew have the same twelve names. Luke does not include Thaddaeus and Simon the Cananaean but does include Simon the Zealot and Matthias. This variety suggests that, although the number "twelve" was fixed, there was less agreement on who composed the Twelve. The different orders for the names support this observation. Peter always appears first. Within the first nine, Andrew's place varies, and Matthew and Thomas switch places. Numbers 10 and 11 are unsettled, with four contenders for these two places. Judas Iscariot is consistently last, and does not appear on the list in Acts. John's Gospel complicates the picture. It does not list "twelve disciples" and refers to "the twelve" only four times (6:67–71; 20:24). In various passages, John's Gospel identifies nine male disciples (Andrew, Philip, Peter, the Beloved Disciple, Nathanael, Thomas, Judas, and the sons of Zebedee, presumably James and John). Nathanael appears only in John.

Further, though the term "disciple" often refers to this group of twelve followers, it is not restricted to them.

- Matthew 5:1 says Jesus went up a mountain and "his disciples came to him." Jesus then preached the Sermon on the Mount. This is the first time the term "disciples" appears in the Gospel. Seven verses previously, Jesus has called Peter, Andrew, James, and John, but clearly the sermon presupposes a larger audience than merely these four disciples.
- In Mark 2:13–14, Jesus calls Levi the tax collector. The scene resembles the call of the first four disciples (Mark 1:16–20), and we would expect

Levi to be one of the twelve listed in 3:16–19. But he is not there (likewise Luke 5:27–29)!

- Mark 4:10 links "those who were around him" with "the twelve," while at the same time distinguishing the two groups. "Those who were around him" are not simply the twelve and are not identified as disciples, and yet they act like disciples in seeking explanation of Jesus's parables. Subsequently, after identifying and naming the twelve (3:13–19), Mark's Jesus goes on calling other followers (8:34; 10:21).
- Luke identifies "a great crowd" of disciples (6:17; 19:37), "seventy others" (10:1), as well as the Twelve (Luke 9:1).

Beyond this use and nonuse of the word "disciple," other characters exhibit features of discipleship even though they are not called "disciples." For example, Jesus commends the faith of the centurion who seeks Jesus's healing for his sick slave (Q—Matt. 8:5–13; Luke 7:1–10), of the woman whom he heals (Mark 5:21–43 par.), and of blind Bartimaeus (Mark 10:46–52 par.). None is identified as a "disciple," though they all exhibit qualities of disciples and receive Jesus's healing and commendation.

Women are also among Jesus's followers, although the Gospels do not use the term "disciple" for them. No women are included in the lists of "the Twelve." A focus on male followers is not surprising given that the world in which the Gospels were written was an androcentric world. This means that male concerns were central, that public space and leadership were often, though not exclusively, the realm of males, while domestic space was often, though not exclusively, the realm of females. Yet despite this pervasive social structuring, several traditions (multiple attestation) indicate the significant role that women disciples played in Jesus's activity. Luke 8:1–3 declares that "the twelve were with him, as well as some women who had been cured of evil spirits and infirmities: Mary, called Magdalene . . . and Joanna, the wife of Herod's steward Chuza, and Susanna, and many others." Here, these women use their resources to support Jesus's ministry, obedient to his teaching about using resources for the good of others (Luke 6:30–36). Mark 15:40–41 (with parallels in Matt. 27:56) identifies women present at Jesus's crucifixion: "Among them were Mary Magdalene, and Mary the mother of James the younger and of Joses, and Salome. These used to follow him and provided for him when he was in Galilee; and there were many other women who had come up with him to Jerusalem." John's Gospel provides further evidence: "Standing near the cross of Jesus were his mother, and his mother's sister, Mary the wife of Clopas, and Mary Magdalene" (John 19:25). Also, the resurrection narratives include a prominent role for women disciples (Mark 16:1–8; Matt. 28:1–10; Luke 24:1–10).

Further, Jesus defines a new household or family that is not constituted by birth. When Jesus's mother, brothers, and sisters come to get him because some are saying he is mad, Jesus resists their attention and responds by re-defining his family: "Whoever does the will of God is my brother and sister and mother" (Mark 3:35 par.). In Luke's version, the new family comprises "those who hear the word of God and do it" (Luke 8:21). The terms of redefinition are inclusive—"whoever"—and the criteria of "hearing and doing God's will" are broad. These qualities are central features of being a disciple, though that term is not used. A similar familial redefinition is evident when, in response to Peter's declaration that he and others have "left everything" to follow Jesus, Jesus promises, "There is no one who has left house or brothers or sisters or mother or father or children or fields, for my sake and for the sake of the good news, who will not receive a hundred-fold now in this age—houses, brothers and sisters, mothers and children, and fields, with persecutions—and in the age to come eternal life" (Mark 10:28–30). He promises that disciples join a new family now and that they will be part of the "age to come." He uses the language of household rela-tions, not that of discipleship, though clearly, following Jesus and learning from him are in view.

The upshot of these observations is that although the Gospels present a group of characters called "the (twelve) disciples," these same texts also indicate that the historical Jesus had more than twelve disciples. The notion of "disciples" seems to have been much more porous. Numerous people—women and men—followed him. Such a conclusion raises an interesting question: among these followers, did Jesus have a special group of twelve disciples?

A Special Group of Twelve?

Several criteria indicate that Jesus probably did have an inner group of twelve disciples, even if we cannot be exactly sure of their names. The criterion of multiple attestation points to references to the twelve disciples in multiple traditions: Paul (1 Cor. 15:5), the common synoptic tradition (Mark 3:14; Matt. 10:1–2; Luke 6:13), John (6:67–71; 20:24), and Acts (6:2). Further, the criterion of dissimilarity alerts us to an interesting Q saying from Jesus: "When the Son of Man is seated on the throne of his glory, you who have followed me will also sit on twelve thrones, judging the twelve tribes of Israel" (Matt. 19:28; Luke 22:30). Jesus's addressees are the twelve, including Judas Iscariot. A saying appointing the betrayer Judas as part of a reconstituted Israel and to rule over Israel in God's reign would not be created later in the tradition! It is too embarrassing. Rather, the saying most likely comes from Jesus and attests an inner group of twelve disciples.

Jesus, then, chose twelve disciples as an inner group among a wider circle of disciples. But why did he want a group of twelve rather than eleven or thirteen? This Q saying clarifies his choice. Israel comprised twelve tribes, and in the new age dawning in Jesus's ministry and when God's reign will be established in its fullness, the twelve represent Israel and will exercise God's reign. Jesus calls the twelve to participate in the final and full establishment of God's reign. Anticipating this powerful and privileged role, however, seems to have provoked inappropriate ambition and rivalry among some of them (Mark 10:35–45 par.).

What Happened to These Twelve/Fifteen Disciples?

In the resurrection narratives, Jesus rehabilitates the disciples, commissioning them to mission (Matt. 28:19–20; Luke 24:48–49; John 20:21). But what happens to them subsequently is not clear. The Acts of the Apostles purports to narrate their activities, but Acts has eyes for only a few of them. John figures a bit (Acts 3–4), Peter much more so, at least through chapter 15, after which Paul (not one of the twelve) takes center stage. Subsequently, numerous legends emerge about these figures. Developing traditions, for example, claimed that Peter was martyred in Rome, crucified upside down.[4] He was also supposed to be the leading source for Mark's Gospel. Matthew and John are identified as Gospel writers late in the second century, though neither probably wrote the Gospel with which his name is linked. The same is true for other Gospels that subsequently emerged claiming the authority of Thomas, Peter, Philip, Andrew, Bartholomew, and Judas. Numerous traditions attribute extensive missionary preaching to several disciples: John in Ephesus, Philip in Hierapolis (Asia Minor) and France, Thaddaeus in Edessa, Bartholomew in Armenia and India, Thomas in Babylon (Iraq) and India, Peter in Britain and France, Andrew in southern Russia (where he was stoned and crucified), Greece (according to the *Acts of Andrew and Matthias*), and Asia (especially Ephesus).[5] Traditions also commonly claim that many of them were martyred. These traditions are of limited historical value, but they illustrate how a tradition can give a significant afterlife to important historical figures.

To summarize, there is good historical reason to conclude that Jesus gathered disciples. Likewise, among his followers was a special group of twelve, even though the traditions are not entirely agreed on those who constituted this group. Jesus chose twelve to represent the restoration of the twelve tribes of Israel and, at the final establishment of God's reign, to rule Israel. Numerous later traditions attest extensive literary, missionary, and martyr activity for the members of this group, though the historical value of these traditions is generally dubious.

4. See, for example, *Mart. Ascen. Isa.* 4:2–3; *Apoc. Pet.* 14:4; *Acts Pet.* 35–40; Lactantius, *Mort.* 2:5–8; Jerome, *Vir. ill.* 1.
5. For some discussion, see Edgar J. Goodspeed, *The Twelve: The Story of Christ's Apostles* (New York: Collier, 1962), 77–104.

Narrative Considerations: The Disciples in the Canonical Gospels

We look now at ways in which each canonical Gospel presents "the disciples" as a character group. We will focus on the term "disciple/s," recognizing that this focus does not include every "disciplelike" character in the Gospels, nor does it include all of Jesus's instruction about discipleship. We will begin with the earliest Gospel, Mark (ca. 70 CE), and then turn to Matthew, Luke, and John (ca. 80s–100 CE).

Mark: Sustained Failure

Mark's presentation of the disciples is very distinct. After an initially positive characterization, their performance deteriorates significantly and their characterization becomes quite negative as they fail to be faithful to Jesus. What would have been the rhetorical effect of this presentation on the Gospel's audience, most of whom would also consider themselves to be disciples of Jesus?

Disciples are introduced in two short scenes in Mark. At the outset of his public activity, Jesus calls two sets of brothers, Simon and Andrew (1:16–18) and James and John (1:19–20). The scenes have identical structures.

Jesus in motion: "passed along"; "he went"	1:16a	1:19a
"he saw"	1:16b	1:19b
Identification of brothers	1:16c	1:19c
Description of fishing activity	1:16d	1:19d
Jesus's initiative: speaking, calling	1:17	1:20a
Immediate response: leave work; "they . . . followed him"	1:18	1:20

Jesus's summons disrupts the fishing activity of their daily lives and the familial (1:20: "Zebedee their father") and imperial economic structures of contracts and taxes in which such activity was embedded. His call to "follow me" disorients and reorients, summoning them to a new loyalty. There is no indication that they have met or heard of Jesus previously. Their response is instant and radical. Jesus has just finished speaking about God's reign, saying, "The kingdom of God has come near" (1:15), urging people to repent and believe. In Jesus's call, the men encounter and embrace God's reign with its different priorities and focus. They abandon their possessions ("nets"), family (father), workforce ("hired hands"), and occupation (fishing; cf. 10:28). They receive a new family comprising one another and centered on Jesus, as well as a new task, to "fish for people" (1:17). The metaphor indicates mission/recruitment work, so that people are to encounter God's rule, either for salvation or condemnation, through these disciples.

Readers who also follow Jesus admire this immediate and faithful response, and understand its significance. The Gospel's opening fifteen verses identify significant affirmations about Jesus. He is God's agent (1:1, 7–8), sanctioned by God and empowered by God's spirit (1:10–11), sustained by God against the devil (1:13), a messenger of God's good news that God's rule is at hand (1:14–15). On this basis, readers can assess that the four have made a good decision to commit themselves to Jesus.

These four disciples, along with others, now accompany Jesus until near the end of the Gospel (14:50). They witness him perform impressive, powerful acts involving preaching, teaching, exorcisms, and healings (1:21–3:35). These powerful acts include healing Simon's mother-in-law (1:29–31) and, in terms reminiscent of the call of the first four disciples, calling Levi the tax collector to "follow me" (2:13–14). Levi is presumably one of the "sinners" whom Jesus calls (2:17). In 3:13–19, Mark names the twelve disciples and presents their threefold mission: "to be with him, and to be sent out to proclaim the message, and to have authority to cast out demons" (3:14–15).

But all is not well. In 4:3–9 Jesus tells his first parable about the sower who sows seeds in different types of ground with very different survival and production results. The twelve and others request an explanation (4:10). Jesus's response is surprising.

First, Jesus indicates that disciples have a privileged place in understanding God's purposes: "To you has been given the secret of the kingdom of God" (4:11). The passive construction "has been given" refers to God's activity of revealing to disciples a "secret" concerning God's reign or empire. The secret is that God's reign has broken into human lives in the ministry of Jesus in anticipation of its future completion in full (1:14–15). Jesus has enacted this reign in his actions and teaching in chapters 1–3. The disciples have encountered it in their lives and in the mission Jesus has entrusted to them (3:13–15).

Second, Jesus draws a line between the disciples as recipients and "those outside," for whom "everything comes in parables; in order that 'they may indeed look, but not perceive, and may indeed listen, but not understand; so that they may not turn again and be forgiven'" (4:11b–12). The characteristic distinguishing disciples from "those outside" is understanding. Disciples understand Jesus as the revealer of God's reign ("the secret"); outsiders do not.

This division is evident in chapters 1–3. Whereas demons understand Jesus's identity, those in the Capernaum synagogue do not (1:21–28). The scribes judge Jesus's declaration of forgiveness to be blasphemy (2:5–12) and do not understand his eating with "tax collectors and sinners" (2:15–17). The Pharisees dispute his disciples' action of plucking grain on the Sabbath (2:23–28). They so resent his restoring the withered hand on the Sabbath that with "hardness of heart" they, along with the Herodians, plot to kill him (3:1–6). The scribes from Jerusalem declare him to be demon possessed (3:20–27).

Third, having established this line between understanding and nonunderstanding, Jesus immediately blurs it. Addressing the disciples to whom God has given understanding, he says to them, "Do you not understand this parable?

Then how will you understand all the parables?" (4:13). Jesus expects them to understand, but they do not.

The subsequent scenes show that even though Jesus continues to instruct them (4:33–34), the disciples do not understand who Jesus really is and what he is about. So in 4:35, in the first of three boat scenes, the disciples, beset by storms and threatened with sinking, fail to understand that Jesus's manifestation of God's power over the sea reflects God's control of all creation. This assertion of sovereignty over creation including the sea is consistent with God's work of creation (Gen. 1) and implicitly contests Roman claims to be masters of earth and sea (Philostratus, *Vit. Apoll.* 7.3, where the emperor Domitian is "master of sea and land"; Juvenal, *Sat.* 4.83–84; Josephus *J.W.* 3.402, Vespasian rules land, sea, and people). Once Jesus has calmed the sea, he poses a stark alternative to his disciples: "Why are you afraid? Have you still no faith?" (Mark 4:40). The disciples have chosen fear, not faith. In verse 41 their lack of understanding is manifest as they ask one another—not Jesus—about Jesus's identity: "Who then is this?" They do not seem to have discerned any revelation of Jesus as agent of God's reign in this scene.

In chapter 5 they witness Jesus manifest God's powerful rule over demons and Roman rule (5:1–20) and over disease and death (5:21–43). Jesus commends both Jairus, the ruler of the synagogue, and the woman who has been sick for twelve years for showing faith (5:34, 36). These supposed outsiders have faith, while the insider-disciples, who are supposed to have it, do not. In 6:7–13, however, Jesus shows faith in them, sending them on a mission journey, preaching, exorcising, and healing. These are the same tasks that Jesus performs in revealing God's reign and which he appointed the Twelve to perform (3:14–15). In 6:30–44, a scene that echoes the feeding of the people in the wilderness after the exodus from Egypt, they witness the miracle of Jesus multiplying five loaves and two fish to feed "five thousand men."

A second boat scene (6:45–52) indicates that, despite these new revelations and displays of power, the disciples have gained no understanding. Again in a storm, Jesus approaches them, walking on the water. After the first boat scene (4:35–41), we might expect the disciples to cry out, "Praise God. We knew that Jesus would manifest God's reign over the water and rescue us." Instead, "they thought it was a ghost and cried out . . . and were terrified." Again they fail to perceive accurately who Jesus is. Again they choose fear. Again they lack faith. Jesus reveals himself to them and urges them to reject fear ("Take heart, it is I; do not be afraid" [6:50]). They show only astonishment, not understanding (6:51).

The next verse, however, explains their astonishment: "for they did not understand about the loaves, but their hearts were hardened" (6:52). Readers might have expected a flashback to the previous boat scene (4:35–41), but instead the narrator evokes the feeding of the five thousand. The disciples are a scene behind! They did not understand in that scene the revelation of

God's life-giving power and reign in supplying people with food to eat. They cannot understand here God's reign over creation and the sea. But worse, Mark's narrative had used the term "hardness of heart" in 3:5–6 to describe the Pharisees and Herodians who were plotting to destroy Jesus! Disciples who are insiders and supposed to understand and have faith behave as outsiders marked by fear, nonunderstanding, and hardened hearts.

The same themes of their lack of understanding (7:18) and the appearance of faith in unlikely people (7:24–37) continue. In 8:1–10 the disciples participate in a second feeding scene. When Jesus points out to them the need for food (8:1–3), we might expect them to recall the feeding of the five thousand from 6:30–44 and to respond, "You can feed them, Jesus; the crowd is a bit smaller this time, only four thousand, not five thousand, and there's more bread, seven loaves, not five. You can work another catering miracle." But instead, without a clue, "his disciples replied, 'How can one feed these people with bread here in the desert?'" (8:4). The subsequent miracle again brings no comprehension that Jesus is the agent and revealer of God's reign.

The scene, however, ends ominously: "And immediately he got into the boat with his disciples" (8:10). We know from the two previous boat scenes (4:35–41; 6:45–52) that things do not go well for disciples in a boat. This third boat scene (8:14–21) starts badly with their having "forgotten to bring any bread." They then misunderstand his warning about "the yeast [or harmful influence] of the Pharisees and the yeast of Herod" (cf. 3:5–6). Jesus rebukes them: "Why are you talking about having no bread? Do you still not perceive or understand? Are your hearts hardened? Do you have eyes, and fail to see? Do you have ears, and fail to hear?" (8:17–18). Again he identifies their lack of understanding, rendering them outsiders, and observes their hard hearts, a characteristic of his enemies and killers (cf. 3:5–6). Jesus's language recalls 4:11–12 and his description of nonunderstanding outsiders, from whom disciples are supposed to be different. After reminding them of God's powerful rule demonstrated in the two feedings, Jesus again observes their lack of understanding (8:21).

Thereafter he asks the disciples whether people discern his identity (8:27–28). After several responses, he presses them for their opinion (8:29). Have they understood anything of his identity and mission? Peter, as representative disciple, declares, "You are the Messiah." Jesus's response is underwhelming at best. Instead of saying, "Thank God you've gotten a little insight," he "sternly ordered them not to tell anyone about him" (8:30). Why the command to not tell? Because although the term *christ* (the Greek form of the Hebrew *messiah*) means "anointed one," it did not have one fixed meaning indicating what this person was anointed to do.[6] Peter has gotten the right category—God has anointed or commissioned Jesus—but he and the disciples do not understand

6. Marinus de Jonge, "Messiah," in *Anchor Bible Dictionary*, ed. David Noel Freedman (New York: Doubleday, 1992), 4:777–78.

what Jesus is commissioned to do. Mark's Jesus reveals that he must now go to Jerusalem to die and be raised (8:31–32a). But Peter resists it. "And Peter took him aside and began to rebuke him" (8:32). Jesus's rebuke of Peter is again strong. "Get behind me, Satan! For you are setting your mind not on divine things but on human things" (8:33).

Jesus sets up two contrasting dualisms, God and Satan, and "divine things" and "human things." Peter is on the wrong side of the contrasts, unable to understand what God is doing. His link with Satan, enemy of God and God's purposes (3:20–27), might reflect another reality. Previously, several demons have declared Jesus's identity: "the Holy One of God" (1:24), "the Son of God" (3:11), "Son of the Most High God" (5:7). These confessions have come in the context of power, but now Jesus identifies weakness and crucifixion as a further context in which God's reign will be manifested. Peter resists the notion that God's reign embraces power *and* suffering.

Further misunderstandings follow even though the disciples go with Jesus to Jerusalem. In the transfiguration, they fail to perceive Jesus's identity as God's agent chosen to reveal divine presence and purposes (9:2–8). They again fail to understand his teaching about having to die (9:32). They dispute about who is the greatest (9:33–37). They attempt to keep children from being blessed by Jesus (10:13–16). James and John want places of honor when God's reign is established, whereas Jesus indicates that his disciples are to be slaves to one another, each seeking the other's good (10:35–45). Judas offers to assist the Jerusalem chief priests in putting Jesus to death by betraying him for a price (14:10–11). He betrays Jesus (14:43–46), as Jesus predicted (14:18–21); the disciples abandon him (14:50), as Jesus predicted (14:27); and Peter denies him three times (14:66–72), as Jesus predicted (14:30). At the cross, a centurion, not one of the Twelve, becomes the first human being (rather than a demon) to declare Jesus's identity as "God's son" (15:39). Whether this declaration is to be taken as a genuine confession or an ironic statement is debated. Either way, knowingly or not, his words agree with God's verdict that Jesus is God's son or agent (1:11; 9:7).

The final reference to the disciples comes in the resurrection chapter. At Jesus's empty tomb, the angel tells the women, "Go, tell his disciples and Peter that he is going ahead of you to Galilee; there you will see him, just as he told you" (16:7). The "as he told you" line refers to Jesus's words in 14:27–28 (citing Zech. 13:7), where he said that he as the shepherd would be "struck," the sheep/disciples would be scattered, but he would go before them to Galilee. But it is not clear that all will work out well. Jesus had previously warned the disciples that persecution lay ahead (13:9–13); will they respond with fear or faith, with misunderstanding or understanding? And what about the women? The women who have been faithful in following Jesus up to this point succumb to fear: "and they said nothing to anyone, for they were afraid" (16:8). Mark ends with this note of uncertainty, though the fact that readers get to read the Gospel suggests that someone said something to someone, that faith overcame fear, and that understanding got the better of misunderstanding.[7]

What is the effect of Mark's frequently negative presentation of the disciples? One way to think about it is that Mark employs this negative depiction to instruct readers about discipleship. How does he do it? Readers begin by identifying with disciples. Readers, too, have heard the call to follow Jesus and have committed themselves to him. But then the narrative, having divided insiders and outsiders, those who understand and those who do not (4:11–12), unsettles that identification and raises questions. "Do you not understand?" (4:13). The disciples' downhill spiral requires readers to examine their own discipleship. Having identified with them, readers do not want to be like them! Just what do readers understand about Jesus, about the ways in which God's reign is at work in the world through power and suffering, about the way of life that God's reign is creating? Do readers understand the difference between power that is destructive (as exercised among the gentiles by "their great ones" [10:42]) and life-giving power that overcomes suffering and death and is at work in the world for the good of others (10:43–45)? Are readers' lives marked by fear or by faith? That is, Mark's rhetorical strategy is to have readers initially identify with the disciples and then, by presenting the disciples' failures, to cause readers to examine their own discipleship.[8]

Matthew and Luke Redacting Mark's Presentation

Most scholars agree that both Matthew and Luke use Mark's Gospel as a source. What do they do with Mark's presentation of the disciples? Do they

7. For a more positive evaluation of the role of the women, see Larry W. Hurtado, "The Women, the Tomb, and the Climax of Mark," in *A Wandering Galilean: Essays in Honour of Seán Freyne*, ed. Zuleika Rodgers, Margaret Daly-Denton, and Anne Fitzpatrick McKinley (Leiden: Brill, 2009), 427–50.

8. Scholars have generally understood Mark's presentation of the disciples in one of two ways. One approach, a "historical-transparency" approach, sees the disciples representing conflict among early believers in which the Gospel writer takes sides, using the disciples to reject a particular understanding and to advocate for another view. Often the conflict is understood as involving the church in Jerusalem and Mark's community, with the disciples representing inadequate theology or Christology, which Mark attacks. A second approach, a "pastoral" approach, sees the disciples as characters in the story, in which Mark is instructing readers on living as faithful disciples. Instead of offering the disciples as a positive example, he presents them essentially as *failures* so that readers will learn from them and be more faithful. The approach here belongs with the second category. For discussion of the two options, see Frank Matera, *What Are They Saying about Mark?* (New York: Paulist Press, 1987), 38–55. For the second approach, Robert Tannehill, "The Disciples in Mark: The Function of a Narrative Role," *JR* 57 (1977): 386–405; Ernest Best, *Following Jesus: Discipleship in the Gospel of Mark*, JSNTSup 4 (Sheffield: Sheffield Academic Press, 1981); Jack Dean Kingsbury, *Conflict in Mark: Jesus, Authorities, Disciples* (Minneapolis: Fortress, 1989), 89–117; Larry W. Hurtado, "Following Jesus in the Gospel of Mark—and Beyond," in *Patterns of Discipleship in the New Testament*, ed. Richard N. Longenecker (Grand Rapids: Eerdmans, 1996), 9–29.

Reading Strategies

In our discussion of Mark and now Matthew's Gospel, we are using two quite different reading strategies or methods. The discussion of Mark uses "narrative criticism." The word "criticism" here means an approach or strategy. Narrative criticism focuses on the finished and final form of the text. This approach, for example, attends to the Gospel's plot, notably the sequencing and prioritizing of events. It also focuses on characters. In the preceding analysis of Mark, we concentrated on the features or characteristics of the disciples as they emerged through the Gospel narrative.

In discussing Matthew's Gospel, we will use a different reading strategy or method called "redaction criticism." This approach focuses on the way that Matthew edits or "redacts" Mark's Gospel. Matthew uses Mark's Gospel as a source but reworks or redacts it. Redaction criticism particularly pays attention to these changes and interprets their significance for Matthew's different presentation of the disciples.

also present disciples as constant failures, or do they change or redact the characterization? We will look briefly at Matthew first, and then Luke.

Matthew: Learning from Jesus

Matthew generally presents the disciples more positively than Mark, though without eliminating all the negative features.[9] Rather, inconsistency and fickleness emerge as key characteristics. Matthew's redaction of Mark's presentation of disciples is linked with other changes Matthew makes in presenting his story of Jesus.[10]

Immediately evident is Matthew's emphasis on the disciples as those whom Jesus instructs about God's rule or empire. As in Mark, their first appearance comes at the commencement of Jesus's public activity. Matthew provides a much longer lead-in to Jesus's ministry than does Mark. Matthew expands Mark's thirteen verses of establishing Jesus's identity and mission into a three-and-a-half-chapter statement (Matt. 1:1–4:16). As in Mark, Matthew shows

9. For discussion, see Warren Carter, *Matthew and the Margins: A Sociopolitical and Religious Reading* (Maryknoll, NY: Orbis, 2000); also idem, "Power and Identities: The Contexts of Matthew's Sermon on the Mount," and "Embodying God's Empire in Communal Practices: Matthew 6:1–18," in *Preaching the Sermon on the Mount: The World It Imagines*, ed. David Fleer and David Bland (St. Louis: Chalice, 2007), 8–21, 22–35.

10. For Matthew, see Richard Edwards, "Uncertain Faith: Matthew's Portrait of the Disciples," in *Discipleship in the New Testament*, ed. Fernando F. Segovia (Philadelphia: Fortress, 1985), 47–61; Jack Dean Kingsbury, *Matthew as Story* (Philadelphia: Fortress, 1986), 103–19; Terence L. Donaldson, "Guiding Readers–Making Disciples: Discipleship in Matthew's Narrative Strategy," in Longenecker, *Patterns of Discipleship*, 30–49; Warren Carter, *Matthew: Storyteller, Interpreter, Evangelist*, rev. ed. (Peabody, MA: Hendrickson, 2004), 215–27.

Jesus beginning his ministry with a one-verse announcement that God's reign is at hand (4:17; Mark 1:14–15), and then, as does Mark, follows it with a scene that demonstrates God's reign claiming human lives in the double call story of the first disciples (Mark 1:16–20; Matt. 4:18–22). But whereas Mark proceeds with his account of Jesus's ministry at 1:21, Matthew follows the call story with a three-chapter block of teaching material on discipleship, the Sermon on the Mount (chaps. 5–7). These chapters, comprising Q and M material,[11] and with no parallel in Mark, present a radical vision of what life for the community of disciples shaped by God's empire looks like. The chapters offer a vision significantly at odds with established values, practices, and structures of the Roman Empire. This teaching material presents disciples as not only committed to Jesus but also learning about living in God's empire.

Subsequently, Matthew includes four more major blocks of teaching material addressed to disciples. Two expand Mark's material, and two have no Markan parallel. In chapter 10, Jesus instructs disciples about continuing his mission (10:7–8). In chapter 13 (expanding Mark 4), the sequence of his parables concerning God's reign or empire shows disciples how God is at work in the world now and in the future. They explain why people welcome and reject Jesus's manifestation of God's empire. Chapter 18 instructs disciples about their life together in an under-pressure community. Care for one another, accountability, and forgiveness are key practices for sustaining discipleship. Chapters 24–25 provide instruction on eschatological matters, the completion of God's purposes, including the final judgment.

The addition of so much teaching material indicates, perhaps, Matthew's sense that Mark does not provide enough teaching content to shape discipleship. Although Mark mentions Jesus teaching some fifteen or so times, frequently he provides no content of what Jesus taught.[12] Matthew compensates for this lack with additional teaching material and heightened emphasis on Jesus as a revealer of God's will and saving presence (1:21–23).

Along with this emphasis on Jesus's role as revealer, Matthew presents disciples as evidencing some understanding, and he removes some aspects of Mark's presentation of disciples as not understanding Jesus. In Mark 4:13, having drawn the line between the understanding disciples and nonunderstanding outsiders, Mark's Jesus blurs the division, asking the disciples, "Do you not understand this parable? Then how will you understand all the parables?" Matthew makes three changes to this section. First, he replaces Mark's allusion

---

11. Scholars use the symbol Q (from the German word *Quelle*, meaning "source") to refer to material that is common to Matthew and Luke but is not in Mark. Scholars speculate that this material was a written or oral source of Jesus's teachings used by Matthew and Luke to expand Mark's account. The symbol M refers to material exclusive to Matthew's Gospel, perhaps deriving, at least in part, from another collection of material known only to the author of Matthew's Gospel.

12. See Mark 1:21–22; 2:13; 6:2, 6, 34; for exceptions, 4:1–32; 8:31.

to Isaiah 6:9 with an extended quotation of Isaiah 6:9–10 to emphasize the nonunderstanding of the crowds (13:14–15). Second, he omits the question about the disciples not understanding the parable, thereby not blurring the line between them and the crowds. And third, Matthew's Jesus emphasizes the disciples' understanding and reception of his revelation of God's purposes by adding a blessing: "But blessed are your eyes, for they see, and your ears, for they hear" (13:16).

Matthew's disciples also do better in the boat scenes. In the first boat scene, Mark's disciples awaken Jesus with the disrespectful and accusatory question, "Teacher, do you not care that we are perishing?" (Mark 4:38). Matthew's disciples are more respectful and devout, liturgically praying (see Ps. 69:1), "Lord, save us! We are perishing!" (Matt. 8:25). Mark's Jesus responds to the frightened disciples, "Why are you afraid? Have you still no faith?" (Mark 4:40), whereas Matthew's Jesus recognizes that disciples have at least some faith, modifying the address, "Why are you afraid, *you of little faith*?" (Matt. 8:26; emphasis added). Matthew uses this designation "little faith" rather than "no faith" in three other instances (6:30; 14:31; 16:8). Matthew's disciples, however, are not entirely exonerated. Their final question indicates that their faith and understanding are not complete. They ask not, "Who . . . is this?" (Mark 4:41), but, "What sort of man is this?" (Matt. 8:27).

Matthew leaves much of the second boat scene relatively untouched, with the disciples failing, as in Mark, to recognize Jesus and fearfully wondering if he is a ghost (Matt. 14:22–27; Mark 6:45–52). But Matthew makes four significant changes. First, Matthew adds a scene: Peter tries to walk on the water, but his faith fails him, and Peter the rock sinks like a stone (Matt. 14:28–31). Second, when Matthew's Jesus calms the storm, his disciples are not "utterly astounded" as in Mark 6:51. Instead, "those in the boat worshiped him" (Matt. 14:33). Third, Matthew adds to Mark's account a confession whereby the disciples acknowledge Jesus: "Truly you are the Son of God" (Matt. 14:33). With this confession, Matthew's disciples discern Jesus's identity accurately, since this is how God views Jesus (3:17; 17:5). Nor is this confession a fluke, since Peter will make it again in 16:16, where Jesus confirms that it is known only through God's revelation (16:17). The disciples are, in terms of an earlier passage that has no parallel in Mark, "infants" to whom God has revealed these things while hiding them "from the wise and the intelligent" (Matt. 11:25). And fourth, Matthew deletes Mark's concluding comment about the disciples not understanding "about the loaves" and being hard-hearted. Matthew also deletes Mark's two other references to hardness of heart (Mark 3:5; 8:17; compare Matt. 12:9–14; 16:8).

The third boat scene is also a mixture of affirmative and critical references to the disciples (Matt. 16:5–12; cf. Mark 8:14–21). Matthew's Jesus again rebukes the disciples for being "of little faith" in not perceiving, but the rebuke is softened by Matthew's elimination of Mark's three harsh clauses asserting nonunderstanding and being hard-hearted (Matt. 16:9; cf. Mark 8:17b–18a). The scene ends with Matthew adding a verse which declares that they do understand: "Then they understood that he had not told them to beware of the yeast of bread, but of the teaching of the Pharisees and Sadducees" (Matt. 16:12).

This mix of affirmative and critical references continues throughout the Gospel. As with Mark, Matthew's disciples do not do well in the feedings of the five thousand and four thousand (Matt. 14:13–21; 15:32–39). Yet Matthew deletes the disciples' question from the end of the transfiguration scene regarding "what this rising from the dead could mean" (Mark 9:10; Matt. 17:9). But just a couple of verses later, the disciples' "little faith" means that they cannot cast out a demon (17:20), something Jesus has commissioned them to do (10:7–8). Matthew softens the ambition of James and John to have the prime seats of power in God's empire by having their mother ask Jesus to give her sons this honor rather than having James and John ask it for themselves (Matt. 20:20; Mark 10:35). But in the Passion Narrative, Matthew's disciples fail to be loyal to Jesus in the same way as in Mark. Having shown these failures, however, Matthew ends with a much less ambiguous restoration scene than Mark. Matthew's Jesus, risen from the dead, meets the "eleven disciples" in Galilee and commissions them to worldwide mission, promising, "I am with you always" (28:16–20).

We should note briefly three further features of the presentation of the disciples in Matthew. Matthew's Jesus defines disciples as those who hear and obey his teaching (7:24–27; 12:46–50). By contrast, "hypocrites" (a word used only once in Mark, for an actor playing a part) are more concerned with their own interests and public recognition (6:2, 5, 16; 7:5). Matthew uses the term to denote groups that are not disciples, those who "teach human precepts as doctrines" (15:9) in opposition to God's will revealed by Jesus (15:7; 22:18; 23:13, 15, 23, 25, 27, 29).

Second, Matthew's Jesus constantly warns disciples that they will be held accountable for their discipleship in the final judgment. Each of the five major blocks of Jesus's teaching ends with an "eschatological" warning that disciples who do not live according to God's will will face condemnation in the judgment (7:24–27; 10:40–42; 13:47–50; 18:21–35; 25:31–46). These scenes dramatically underscore for the disciples the importance of obedience to Jesus's teaching.

Third, Matthew's Gospel continues to present Peter as the leading or representative disciple. For both Matthew and Mark, he is the first disciple called to follow Jesus (Matt. 4:18–19; 10:2). Matthew adds the story of Peter's failure to walk on water (Matt. 14:28–31) and expands Peter's role as the spokesperson for the disciples (Matt. 15:15; 17:24; 18:21, not in Mark). One important expansion concerns the confession of Jesus's identity (Matt. 16:16; Mark 8:29). Matthew adds a blessing for Peter as the recipient of divine revelation, declares his confession to be the rock on which Jesus will build his church, and gives him (along with all the disciples in 18:18) the task of interpreting

Jesus's teaching for the community of disciples (Matt. 16:17–19). Both Matthew and Mark narrate his rejection of Jesus's teaching about suffering in Jerusalem and being rebuked by Jesus (Matt. 16:22–23) and his central role in the transfiguration (Matt. 17:1–9) and in the passion (Matt. 26).[13]

Luke: On the Journey

Luke's presentation of the disciples resembles that of Matthew in that it is more positive than Mark's, although Luke's disciples are far from perfect. Luke's disciples, though clearly committed to Jesus, are quite inconsistent in their discipleship, at times clearly understanding Jesus's identity and mission, and at other times failing miserably. As in Matthew, their depiction ends on a strong note.[14]

As in Matthew and Mark, the disciples first appear in a call story (Luke 5:1–11, 27–28; 6:12–16). In both Matthew and Luke, their call is followed by an extended body of teaching material. In Matthew it is "the Sermon on the Mount" (Matt. 5–7); in Luke it is "the Sermon on the Plain" (6:20–49). Initially the disciples are simply "with" Jesus as he carries out his mission (8:1). Jesus subsequently declares them recipients of divine revelation (8:10) and scolds them for their lack of faith while in the storm-tossed boat (8:22–25). In chapter 9, after having them "with him" throughout chapters 6–8, Jesus sends them in mission (9:1–6), giving them "power and authority over all demons and to cure diseases," and sends them out "to proclaim the kingdom of God and to heal" (9:1–2). Significantly, this commission resembles closely the work that Jesus does in preaching, exorcising, and healing (cf. 4:38–44). That is, the disciples participate in and extend Jesus's mission. In chapter 10, a group of seventy is similarly commissioned to share in Jesus's mission (10:9). Response to their mission is the same as response to Jesus's mission. People encounter God's presence and power in both, according to Jesus's instruction, "whoever listens to you listens to me, and whoever rejects you rejects me, and whoever rejects me rejects the one who sent me" (Luke 10:16).

The disciples have mixed success in being faithful to these tasks. Although they fail to look to Jesus to feed the crowd (9:12–17), Peter confesses Jesus's identity correctly (9:18–20). Yet Peter, John, and James are sleepy during the transfiguration (9:28–36); all the disciples fail to understand Jesus's teaching about suffering in Jerusalem (9:44–45; 18:31–34); they cannot cast out a demon (9:37–43); they squabble about who is the greatest (9:46–48; 22:24–27).

13. Matthew writes Peter out of several passages: see Mark 5:37//Matt. 9:22–23; Mark 11:21// Matt. 21:20; Mark 13:3//Matt. 24:3; Mark 16:7//Matt. 28:7.
14. Charles Talbert, "Discipleship in Luke-Acts," in Segovia, *Discipleship*, 62–75; Jack Dean Kingsbury, *Conflict in Luke: Jesus, Authorities, Disciples* (Minneapolis: Fortress, 1991), 109–39; Joel B. Green, *The Theology of the Gospel of Luke* (Cambridge: Cambridge University Press, 1995), 102–21; Richard N. Longenecker, "Taking Up the Cross Daily: Discipleship in Luke-Acts," in idem, *Patterns of Discipleship*, 50–76.

Once Jesus sets out on his journey to Jerusalem to die (9:51), they want to call down fire from heaven to consume an unbelieving Samaritan village (9:51–56), and they attempt to turn children away from Jesus (18:15–17). Nevertheless, they go with Jesus to Jerusalem (9:52–54; 19:28–40), having left all behind and taken up their crosses (14:25–33). Traveling to Jerusalem, they receive his teaching concerning prayer (11:1–4), hypocrisy (12:1–4), anxiety (12:22–34), and readiness for his eventual, not immediate, return to establish God's empire (12:35–48; 17:20–37; 19:11–27). They overhear his denunciation of the scribes and Pharisees for their unjust societal vision and practices (11:37–54). They witness his condemnation of meal practices that uphold a hierarchical and exclusionary social structure and his advocacy of inclusive and compassionate practices (14:1–24). They hear his teaching on the use of possessions and wealth to welcome the marginal, especially the poor, who cannot reciprocate invitations or gifts (chap. 16).

This exacting challenge to learn to live in ways appropriate to "the good news of the kingdom [i.e., empire/reign] of God" (4:43) continues in Jesus's last days in Jerusalem. They obey Jesus's commands to secure a donkey for his entry to Jerusalem (19:29–40) and to prepare a place to eat Passover (22:7–13). They receive Jesus's commendation for being with him "in my trials" (22:28) and his affirmation of their future vindication in God's empire (22:29–30). They also hear his denunciation of the scribes, part of the Jerusalem power group (20:45–47). Yet "Satan entered into Judas called Iscariot, . . . one of the twelve," to betray Jesus (22:3–6). They argue about who is the greatest (22:24–27) and sleep while Jesus prays (22:39–46). Judas betrays Jesus (22:47–53), and Peter denies Jesus, as Jesus predicted (22:31–34, 54–62). Yet though they betray Jesus, they do not abandon him as in Mark (14:50) and Matthew (26:56; cf. Luke 22:53). While Jesus was crucified, writes Luke, "all his acquaintances, including the women who had followed him from Galilee, stood at a distance, watching these things" (Luke 23:49), and the women gathered at Jesus's tomb (23:55).

As with Matthew, Luke's final resurrection chapter places great confidence in the disciples. The chapter opens by depicting the disciples unfavorably, as not believing the women's report of the angel's announcement that Jesus was risen (Luke 24:5–11). Shortly after, "the eleven and their companions" (24:33) hear the testimony of two other disciples, one of whom is called Cleopas, that "the Lord has risen indeed" (24:34–35). Jesus "stood among them" (24:36) and "opened their minds to understand the scriptures" (24:45). He declares that "repentance and forgiveness of sins is to be proclaimed in [the Messiah's] name to all nations, beginning from Jerusalem. You are witnesses of these things" (24:47–48). They are to wait for the Holy Spirit, and the risen Jesus commissions them to worldwide mission: "And you will be my witnesses in Jerusalem, in all Judea and Samaria, and to the ends of the earth" (Acts 1:8).

John's Gospel: Bearing Witness

John's Gospel refers to "the twelve disciples" only four times. Yet it uses the term "disciples" more than seventy times for a group extending beyond the Twelve and including both men and women. The Johannine disciples do better than Mark's but, as in Matthew and Luke, struggle to understand Jesus's identity and mission.[15]

Disciples first appear in 1:35–51, but unlike the disciples in the Synoptics, they follow Jesus not because of his call but because others bear witness about him. This role of bearing witness to Jesus is central to John's Gospel. Disciples discern Jesus's identity as God's agent and as revealer of God's life-giving purposes in his sign or work of power in turning water into wine at Cana (2:11). By contrast, in 2:23–25, some commit themselves to Jesus on the basis of his "signs" or works of power without discerning his identity, but John's Jesus remains suspicious of them. Disciples accompany Jesus in chapters 3–6 and witness the extensive teaching of chapters 5–6. Yet despite the affirmation of 2:11, disciples often lack understanding, as for example in scenes concerning Jesus's action in the temple (2:20–22), Jesus's mission (4:31–34), Jesus's power to feed the crowd (6:5–10), Jesus's walking on water (6:16–21), and Jesus's detection of a plan to make him king (6:15). Having heard Jesus reveal his identity as the one sent from God to reveal life that lasts forever (6:25–59), some take offense and abandon him (6:60–66). The twelve who remain confess his identity (6:68–69), but Jesus warns that one of them, a devil, will betray him (6:70–71). In chapters 11–12, they fail to understand Jesus's speech (11:11–13), Thomas lacks faith (11:15–16), Judas is a betrayer (12:4) and thief (12:6), and they fail to understand Jesus's entry into Jerusalem (12:16).

Chapters 13–17 have no parallel in the other Gospels. These chapters, sometimes called the farewell discourse or Jesus's last testament, appear just before Jesus's arrest and crucifixion. Jesus instructs the disciples on how to live in his absence. He assumes the role of a slave and washes their feet, exemplifying his service of giving his life and the service they ought to render one another out of love (13:4–20, 34–35; 15:12–17). He assures them that he prepares a place for them, will return to take them to the Father, and in the meantime sends them the *paraklētos* (= "Counselor," the Holy Spirit) to be with them and teach them (14:16–17, 26; 15:26; 16:7, 12–13). He instructs them to abide or remain in him and the Father, obeying Jesus's commands, especially the command to love one another (15:1–17), continuing his mission, doing "greater works" (14:12), and bearing fruit (15:8).

15. Fernando F. Segovia, "'Peace I Leave with You; My Peace I Give to You': Discipleship in the Fourth Gospel," in idem, *Discipleship*, 76–102; Melvyn R. Hillmer, "They Believed in Him: Discipleship in the Johannine Tradition," in Longenecker, *Patterns of Discipleship*, 77–97; Warren Carter, *John: Storyteller, Interpreter, Evangelist* (Peabody, MA: Hendrickson, 2006), 73–85.

Yet again, however, they do not do entirely well. Satan enters Judas to betray Jesus (13:2), something Jesus knows (13:27–30). Peter cannot receive Jesus's self-giving action in washing his feet (13:6–8) but then, lacking insight, overcompensates by demanding that Jesus wash all of him (13:9–11). Jesus predicts Peter's denial (13:36–38). Thomas does not know where Jesus is going or that he reveals how to encounter God (14:5). Philip does not know that Jesus has revealed God to him (14:8–13). Others do not understand Jesus's teaching about his destiny and his return to them (16:17–18).

The downhill journey continues in the Passion Narrative in chapters 18–19. Judas betrays Jesus (18:1–5). Peter continues to resist Jesus's destiny by drawing his sword to attack those who arrest Jesus (18:10–11). Peter denies Jesus three times as predicted (18:15–27). The disciples go into hiding (20:19), except for "the disciple whom Jesus loved," Jesus's mother, his sister, and Mary Magdalene (19:25). A secret disciple, Joseph of Arimathea, buries Jesus (19:38).

The resurrection narrative presents Jesus's restoration of disciples and their future roles. Jesus appears to Mary Magdalene, who, as a model disciple, bears witness and testifies to other disciples, "I have seen the Lord" (John 20:18). The risen Jesus appears to the disciples (20:19–23), including Thomas (20:24–29), and commissions them to continue his mission to reveal or bear witness to God's presence and life-giving purposes. "As the Father has sent me, so I send you" (20:21). In chapter 21, Jesus challenges Peter three times to express his love (after three denials earlier in John 18) and commissions him to a future role as a leader and a martyr (21:15–19).

Also prominent in these last two chapters is the mysterious "disciple whom Jesus loved." This disciple is never named in John's Gospel and does not appear in the other Gospels. He is always identified as the object of Jesus's love, thus emphasizing his relationship with Jesus more than his identity. He first appears in 13:21–30 as Jesus instructs the disciples. As in other scenes, he is linked with Peter. Because he is reclining closer to Jesus than Peter is, Peter wants him to find out from Jesus the identity of the betrayer. In 19:26–27, he is with Jesus's mother, his mother's sister, and Mary Magdalene at the cross. In 20:2–10, he outruns Peter to reach the empty tomb; "he saw and believed" (20:8), something not said of Peter. In 21:7, while fishing, this disciple recognizes the risen Jesus on the shore and bears witness to Peter. In 21:20–23, Jesus does not predict the destiny of this disciple, though a rumor develops that he will not die before Jesus returns. But as a prototypical disciple, he continues to bear witness, enabling the writing of the Gospel (21:24–25).

Conclusion

In this chapter we have focused on Jesus's disciples. Under "Historical Considerations," we concluded that Jesus did gather disciples, particularly a group of twelve. The Gospel traditions, though, have not remembered their names in a consistent way. Under "Narrative Considerations," we looked at the presentation of the disciples in each of the canonical Gospels. Mark's Gospel uses the rhetorical strategy of presenting noncomprehending and fearful disciples to challenge the Gospel's original audience to examine its own discipleship. Matthew and Luke give the disciples a makeover, improving their image without idealizing them. In Matthew they are especially presented as learners and doers of Jesus's teaching. In Luke they walk the way of the cross, understanding and misunderstanding Jesus until after his resurrection, when they are commissioned to worldwide mission. In John, they are witnesses (albeit imperfectly) to and participants in Jesus's mission to reveal God's life-giving purposes.

In each Gospel the presentation of disciples contributes to the presentation of Jesus. In Mark the portrayal of noncomprehending disciples emphasizes understanding and following Jesus as the powerful and authoritative one, yet also as the crucified one. Matthew's makeover of the disciples, whereby they exhibit both understanding and failure, heightens Jesus's role as a teacher who in five big blocks of teaching material (Matt. 5–7; 10; 13; 18; 24–25) reveals God's will and purposes. Luke also extends Jesus's teaching role, as the disciples accompany Jesus on his lengthy journey to Jerusalem to die. John's Gospel presents them as witnesses to Jesus's life-giving ministry who, as witnesses, are charged by Jesus in a lengthy "farewell discourse" to bear that witness by continuing Jesus's works and teaching. In all of these presentations, Jesus appears as a compelling figure who calls disciples to participate in God's life-giving purposes for the world.

Suggestions for Further Reading

Carter, Warren. *John: Storyteller, Interpreter, Evangelist.* Peabody, MA: Hendrickson, 2006.

———. *Matthew: Storyteller, Interpreter, Evangelist.* Rev. ed. Peabody, MA: Hendrickson, 2004.

Kingsbury, Jack Dean. *Conflict in Luke: Jesus, Authorities, Disciples.* Minneapolis: Fortress, 1991.

———. *Conflict in Mark: Jesus, Authorities, Disciples.* Minneapolis: Fortress, 1989.

———. *Matthew as Story.* Philadelphia: Fortress, 1986.

Longenecker, Richard N., ed. *Patterns of Discipleship in the New Testament.* Grand Rapids: Eerdmans, 1996.

Segovia, Fernando F., ed. *Discipleship in the New Testament.* Philadelphia: Fortress, 1985.

4

The Family of Jesus

RICHARD J. BAUCKHAM

In the first part of this chapter, we shall draw on the evidence both of the New Testament and of sources outside the New Testament to reconstruct what we can know about members of Jesus's family: his family background, his parents, his brothers and sisters, and other relatives. We shall be concerned with the parts Jesus's relatives played in the early church, up to the end of the first century, as well as their relationship to Jesus during his ministry. In the second part of the chapter we shall examine the parts that relatives of Jesus play in the narratives of each of the four Gospels.

Historical Considerations of Jesus's Family

Jesus was born into a family that traced their descent from King David, though the line to which they belonged was a very minor one. Certainly this illustrious ancestry made no difference to their social status as a very ordinary family in the small village of Nazareth in Galilee, far from the ancestral homeland of the Davidic clan. Many scholars have thought that Davidic descent was attributed to Jesus only retrospectively, when the early Christians identified him as the royal Messiah predicted by the prophets and therefore necessarily a descendant of David. The Gospel passage in which Jesus appears to disagree with the scribes who say that the Messiah is the son of David (Mark 12:35–37) may seem to support this view, but it is likely that Jesus meant to suggest, not that the Messiah is not descended from David, but that the Messiah is a greater figure than mere descent from David could make him. All our relevant evidence is unanimous in affirming Jesus's Davidic descent, and the genealogy that Luke provides (Luke 3:23–38) has the marks of an authentic traditional genealogy that was probably preserved by Jesus's family.[1] Matthew supplies a different genealogy (Matt. 1:1–16), which may represent something more like an official list of the heads of the clan of David, the heirs apparent to David's throne.

Both genealogies are said to belong to Jesus's father Joseph, even though both Luke and Matthew claim that Jesus was conceived by Mary miraculously, so that Joseph was not his biological father. But both of these Gospel writers clearly indicate that Jesus was known as the son of Joseph and Mary (Matt. 13:55; Luke 2:41–50), implying that the miraculous conception was a family secret. So it is not likely, as some have argued,[2] that Jesus was regarded as illegitimate, with the social and legal disadvantage such a status would have given him. Joseph was for all ordinary purposes his father. It would not have made sense for Matthew or Luke to provide Mary's genealogy, even if she were descended from David (as later Christian writers certainly thought),[3] because in Jewish society legal inheritance, along with family and tribal membership, had to be traced through the male line.

Joseph was a "carpenter" (Matt. 13:55: the word *tektōn* is a rather general one that could refer to someone who works in metal and/or stone as well as wood), and Jesus learned his father's trade (Mark 6:3). (Matthew may have modified Mark's text, preferring to attach the designation to Joseph rather than Jesus, but it would in any case be very probable that, if Jesus practiced as a carpenter, he would have learned to do so from his father.) It may be that this trade was not the family's sole source of income but merely a way of supplementing the produce of the family's small holding. In Nazareth almost everyone would have been a farmer, whereas only Joseph was also a carpenter, and so he would naturally be known there as "the carpenter."

If this was the case, we do not have to imagine Joseph as an itinerant journeyman, finding work around a wide circle of Galilean villages or even in the nearby city of Sepphoris (as many have speculated). The demand for his services in Nazareth would not have been great, but it could have been sufficient to provide a useful supplement to his income from the farm.

Evidence that there was a family farm is found in Hegesippus, a second-century Christian writer who preserves for us some stories from Palestinian Jewish Christian tradition (extracts from his writings are preserved by the later

1. See Richard Bauckham, *Jude and the Relatives of Jesus in the Early Church* (Edinburgh: T&T Clark, 1990), chap. 7.
2. See Scot McKnight, "Calling Jesus Mamzer," *JSHJ* 1 (2003): 73–103.
3. The earliest is Ignatius, *Eph.* 18.2; *Trall.* 9.1; *Smyrn.* 1.1.

Figure 4.1. A house of the first century CE recently excavated in Nazareth. (Photo by Assaf Peretz, courtesy of the Israeli Antiquities Authority.)

church historian Eusebius). Hegesippus relates a story about two grandsons of Jesus's brother Judas (Jude), said to have been leaders in the Christian movement in Jewish Palestine at the end of the first century (quoted in Eusebius, *Hist. eccl.* 3.19.1–3.20.7; 3.32.5–6). According to the story, they were brought before Emperor Domitian, suspected of political subversion, because they were known to be descendants of David. Asked about their possessions, they claimed to own in common a farm worth 9000 *denarii*, thirty-nine *plethra* in size, and to prove that they were hardworking peasant farmers (not political revolutionaries), they showed their tough bodies and the hardened skin of their hands. Although the story may be legendary, the details about the farm are so specific and precise that it is likely that they rest on accurate tradition. The size of the farm must have been still well known in Palestinian Jewish Christian circles whose tradition Hegesippus drew upon a century after Jesus's time. It was not divided between the brothers, but owned jointly, no doubt because this family continued the old Jewish tradition of keeping a small-holding undivided as the joint property of the extended family rather than dividing it between heirs. So, three generations back, this same farm would have belonged to Joseph and his brother Clopas (about whom, see below). Unfortunately, because there are two possible sizes of the *plethron*, it seems impossible to be sure of the size of the farm: it may have been either about twenty-four acres or about twelve acres. But in either case this is not much land to support two families, and Joseph, as we shall see, had at least seven children to feed. Supplementing the family income by working as a carpenter would have made much sense.

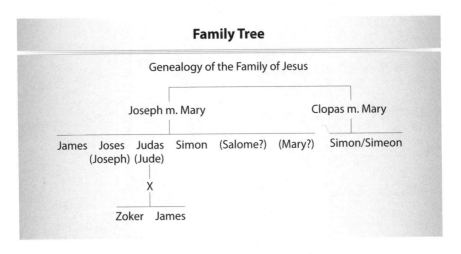

Family Tree

Genealogy of the Family of Jesus

Joseph m. Mary   Clopas m. Mary

James   Joses   Judas   Simon   (Salome?)   (Mary?)   Simon/Simeon
(Joseph) (Jude)

X

Zoker   James

The family tree shows those members of the family whose names and relationship to Jesus are definitely known. Joseph makes no appearance in the Gospels' narratives after the events Luke narrates when Jesus was twelve (Luke 2:41–51), and the conclusion most scholars have drawn, that Joseph had died before the beginning of Jesus's public career, is probably correct. (His absence from the list of Jesus's relatives in Mark 6:3 is especially significant.) The four brothers of Jesus are named in the Gospels of Matthew (13:55) and Mark (6:3). The order of the names in these lists makes it likely that James was the eldest. The second name is given as Joseph by Matthew, Joses by Mark. Joses was a common abbreviated form of Joseph and was presumably used to distinguish this man from his father Joseph. From the same Gospel passages we learn that Jesus had at least two sisters. Later Christian traditions name them as Mary and Salome (*Prot. Jas.* 19:3–20:4; *Gos. Phil.* 59:6–11; Epiphanius, *Pan.* 78.8.1; 78.9.6).

The four brothers of Jesus were known as "the brothers of the Lord" in early Christian circles (Gal. 1:19; 1 Cor. 9:5), but since the term "brother" by no means necessarily refers to a full blood brother, the question of their precise relationship to Jesus, along with that of Jesus's sisters, arises. Since at least the fourth century CE this issue has been much debated, mainly because of its implications for the traditional doctrine of the perpetual virginity of Mary. The three major views have come to be known by the names of their fourth-century proponents: Helvidius, Epiphanius, and Jerome. The Helvidian view, which probably most modern exegetes, even including some Roman Catholic scholars, hold, is that the brothers were sons of Joseph and Mary, born after Jesus. The Epiphanian view, which is the traditional view in the Eastern Orthodox churches, is that they were sons of Joseph by a marriage prior to his marriage to Mary, and so were older than Jesus. The Hieronymian view, which through Jerome's influence became the traditional Western Catholic view, is that they were first cousins of Jesus.

We cannot here enter this debate in any detail. Although the Hieronymian view still has its advocates, it must be said to be the least probable. The Greek word for "brother" can be used for relationships more distant than the modern English "brother," but the brothers of Jesus are invariably called his brothers in early Christian literature (both within and outside the New Testament), and the second-century writer Hegesippus, who calls James and Jude "brothers of the Lord," calls Simeon the son of Clopas the "cousin of the Lord," evidently distinguishing the two relationships. It is less easy to decide between the Helvidian and Epiphanian views, since the New Testament evidence is consistent with either, while the Epiphanian view is found in Christian literature as early as the middle of the second century (for example, the *Protevangelium of James*).

One of the women disciples of Jesus in the Gospels has sometimes been claimed to be a relative of Jesus. She is called, most fully, "Mary the mother of James the little[4] and of Joses" (Mark 15:40; so also Matt. 27:56, but with "Joseph" for "Joses"), more briefly "Mary [the mother] of Joses" (Mark 15:47; the words "the mother" are not in the Greek), "Mary [the mother] of James" (Mark 16:1; Luke 24:10; the words "the mother: are not in the Greek), or simply "the other Mary" (Matt. 27:61; 28:1; "other" because she accompanies Mary Magdalene). This Mary has sometimes been thought to be the mother of Jesus, because the eldest two of Jesus's brothers were also called James and Joses/Joseph. But these were extremely common names. There is no other evidence that James the brother of Jesus (to whom there are many references in Christian literature) was ever called "the little." The point of referring to these two sons, or to one of them, is to distinguish this Mary from other Marys, and it must have been the standard way in which this Mary was known within the early Christian movement. But Jesus's mother is elsewhere always identified as Mary the mother of Jesus. And it seems inconceivable that Matthew could have called the mother of Jesus "the other Mary."

Another way of including this "other Mary" in the family of Jesus has been taken by advocates of the Hieronymian view of Jesus's brothers, who have supposed this Mary's two sons (James the little and Joses/Joseph) to be the same men as their namesakes among Jesus's list of brothers, but have distinguished their mother from Jesus's mother. By means of yet another identification, between this Mary and Mary the wife of Clopas, the sister of Jesus's mother (John 19:25),[5] they have concluded that Jesus's "brothers" were actually his

4. NRSV has "James the younger," following many earlier translations, some of which call him "James the lesser." But the Greek word is not a comparative. It does not compare him with some other James. It is a nickname given presumably because of his height.

5. Probably "his mother's sister" and "Mary the wife of Clopas" are the same person, though grammatically they could be distinct. This Mary was the wife of Jesus's mother's husband's brother, and so could easily be described vaguely as her sister.

cousins. While this view avoids the improbability that Jesus's mother would be described as Mary the mother of James and Joses, it misses the fact that Mary, James, and Joseph were all extremely common Jewish names (Mary by far the most common feminine name, Joseph the second most common masculine name, and James the eleventh most common masculine name).[6] "Mary the wife of Clopas" will have been so called within the Christian movement precisely to distinguish her from other Marys, such as the woman commonly known as "Mary the mother of James and Joses."

For help with identifying other relatives, we must turn again to Hegesippus, who conveys Jewish Christian traditions about relatives of Jesus. These traditions tend to be legendary, but the legends are attached to historical figures who were revered as Christian leaders and martyrs in the memory of the Jewish Christian communities of Palestine. That these persons existed and were related to Jesus in the way Hegesippus claims we can be sure.

According to Hegesippus, Jesus's putative father Joseph had a brother named Clopas. Since this is a rare name, it is very likely that he is the same person as the Clopas mentioned in John 19:25, as well as the Cleopas (the Greek equivalent of the Semitic form *Clopas*) whom Luke names as one of the two disciples who met the risen Christ on the way to Emmaus (Luke 24:18). In John 19:25 it is probably his wife who is called "Mary of Clopas" in a list of three or four women who were present at the death of Jesus and who included also Jesus's mother. Thus it seems that at least three of Jesus's relatives—his mother and his uncle and aunt—were in Jerusalem with him on his last visit to the city. Probably his brothers were there too (cf. Acts 1:15).

Of the relationship between Jesus and his relatives—his mother and brothers in particular—during the period of his ministry, the Gospels offer a quite variegated picture, as we shall see in more detail in the second part of this chapter. Mark's Gospel gives the impression of a complete rift between Jesus and his immediate family (see Mark 3:20–21, 31–35; 6:1–4), and the same picture appears in Matthew, though with less emphasis (Matt. 12:46–50; 13:54–57). In Luke's Gospel, on the other hand, no hint of such tensions appears (see Luke 8:19–21; 11:27–28). Only in John's Gospel do we find Jesus's mother and brothers actually accompanying him along with his disciples at the beginning of his itinerant ministry in Galilee (2:12). Only rather late in his ministry does John indicate that Jesus's brothers were not entirely happy with the path he was taking (7:1–10), but this does not necessarily imply that they no longer counted themselves among his disciples.

What we should probably conclude is that there were serious tensions between Jesus and his relatives at some point or points during the period of his ministry, to which Jesus himself may have contributed by his insistence that

6. See Richard Bauckham, *Jesus and the Eyewitnesses: The Gospels as Eyewitness Testimony* (Grand Rapids: Eerdmans, 2006), 85–89.

service of the kingdom of God and relationships within the new community of his followers took precedence over natural family ties. It has usually been supposed that at the end of Jesus's earthly life his brothers were alienated from him and that they became his followers only after the resurrection, when, as we know, not from the Gospels but from Paul (1 Cor. 15:7), James was one of those to whom the risen Jesus appeared. However, as we have noticed, by the time of Jesus's death his uncle Cleopas/Clopas counted himself among Jesus's faithful disciples (Luke 24:18–24), and his mother and his aunt (Clopas's wife Mary) were present at the cross (John 19:25). Jesus's brothers were probably also in Jerusalem at the time (Acts 1:15), and it seems likely that, however problematic their relationship to Jesus might have been at some times previously, by this time they were once again among his disciples. The resurrection appearance to James also favors this view, since all other recipients of such appearances were already followers of Jesus, with the exception of Paul, who himself admits the exceptional nature of his case (1 Cor. 15:8).

That the Gospels give no account of the resurrection appearance to James is no more surprising than that they do not narrate the appearance to Peter. There is an account of the appearance to James in a fragment of an apocryphal Gospel that Jerome, who quotes it (*Vir. ill.* 2), calls "the Gospel according to the Hebrews." It describes Jesus breaking bread with his brother, who had sworn, at the Last Supper, not to eat bread until he saw Jesus risen from the dead. This looks like an equivalent to Jesus's vow at the Last Supper (Mark 14:25). The account reflects the unique esteem in which James was held within Palestinian Jewish Christian circles, but is unlikely to preserve historically authentic material other than the tradition of the appearance to James itself.

Jesus's brothers all became prominent leaders in the early Christian movement. From the New Testament and from later sources, we know most about James, whom some of the later sources call the first bishop of Jerusalem. The actual term "bishop" may not go back to his lifetime, but there is no doubt that it is appropriate in the sense that for a considerable period up to his death in 62 CE, James had a singular and unrivaled position as head of the Jerusalem church, with the status in the wider Christian movement that was also implied by his position as head of the mother church of the whole movement. Some traditions suggest that he occupied this position of eminence from the beginning. Clement of Alexandria, for example, wrote that, after the ascension of Jesus, the apostles Peter, James (the son of Zebedee), and John appointed James the Lord's brother bishop of Jerusalem (quoted in Eusebius, *Hist. eccl.* 2.1.3). In Acts, however, apart from the reference to the brothers of Jesus in 1:14, James goes unmentioned until 12:17, at the point in Luke's narrative where Peter leaves Jerusalem. Probably we should think of James only gradually reaching the position of preeminence in the church that he appears to have in Acts 15 and certainly has in Acts 21. He was already a significant figure when Paul paid his first visit to Jerusalem after his conversion (Gal. 1:19). Paul's reference to the three "pillars" with whom he consulted in Jerusalem—James, Cephas (Peter), and John (Gal. 2:9)—seems, with its striking positioning of James first, to document a stage in this rise of James to preeminence in Jerusalem. It seems likely that, when many members of the Twelve were no longer permanently resident in Jerusalem and at least one had died (Acts 12:2), James stepped into the leadership gap.

A minor indication of James's uniquely authoritative position is the fact that, although the name *James* was common, this James could be identified simply as "James," with no need for further explanation (Acts 12:17; 15:13; 21:18; 1 Cor. 15:7; Gal. 2:12; James 1:1; Jude 1). He also has the distinction of being the only Christian mentioned by name in a first-century source not written by a Christian. The Jewish historian Josephus records his martyrdom, in 62 CE (*Ant.* 20.200). The high priest Ananus II (son of Annas and brother-in-law to Caiaphas) had him executed by stoning, probably under the law that prescribed this penalty for someone who entices the people to apostasy (Deut. 13:6–11). The more legendary account in Hegesippus (quoted in Eusebius, *Hist. eccl.* 2.23.4–18) agrees that he suffered death by stoning.

James's eminent place in the early Christian movement is also reflected in an apocryphal saying of Jesus in the *Gospel of Thomas* (12):

> The disciples said to Jesus: We know that you will depart from us. Who is to be great over us?
> Jesus said to them: Wherever you shall have come, you are to go to James the Righteous, for whose sake heaven and earth came into being.

The saying most likely derives from the early Christian mission to the area of east Syria (hence its presence in traditions associated with Thomas), and it may well go back to James's own lifetime. The quasi-surname "the Righteous," which is widely attested for James in early Christian literature (though not in the New Testament), is no mere tribute to his personal piety. Only a few great biblical figures (Enoch, Noah, and especially Abraham) were commonly accorded this epithet, which must therefore ascribe to James a central role in salvation history, as the man who oversaw the establishment of the messianic people of God and whose exemplary righteousness modeled its life. It follows that it could be said of him, as Jewish theology said of Abraham, the representative righteous person: "James the Righteous, for whose sake heaven and earth came into being."

Still other traditions about James, preserved by Hegesippus and others, probably tell us little more about the historical James, but they amply testify to the reverence with which he was regarded by later Christians, especially the Jewish Christians of Palestine. His reputation also made him a figure to whom gnostic writers felt it appropriate to ascribe literature (the *First* and *Second Apocalypse of James*).

At this point, mention should be made of the ossuary (bone box) that has been alleged to be that of James. It bears the inscription "James, son of Joseph, brother of Jesus." If this inscription is authentic, it very likely refers to the James we have been discussing, since, although all three names were very common, it is very unusual for an ossuary inscription to mention the brother of the deceased (there is only one other example). There would need to be a particular reason for mentioning the brother, and the relationship of the famous James to the famous Jesus provides such an obvious reason. Unfortunately, however, the authenticity of the inscription is still debated. There is no doubt that the ossuary itself is a genuinely ancient one, from the vicinity of Jerusalem in the first century CE, but its exact provenance is unknown. As to whether the inscription or part of it ("brother of Jesus") is a modern addition, the evidence appears to be conflicting, and a court case in which the ossuary's owner (a private collector) is on trial for forging antiquities began in 2004 and is still ongoing. The legal proceedings have interrupted and frustrated appropriate debate among scholars, and for the time being it is wise to leave open the question of the authenticity of this intriguing inscription.

While James presided at the center of the Christian movement, the other brothers of Jesus worked as traveling missionaries. We know this from an incidental, but revealing, reference to them by Paul. Arguing that, like other apostles, he has the right to material support from his churches and to be accompanied by a wife, Paul cites, as examples of other apostles who were accorded such a right, Peter and the brothers of Jesus (1 Cor. 9:5). The latter must have been so well known as traveling missionaries that they were obvious examples for Paul to choose, even when speaking to the Christians in Corinth.

To fill out just a little more this tantalizing reference to the brothers of Jesus as traveling missionaries, we have just one other piece of credible information. It comes from Julius Africanus, who lived at Emmaus in the early third century CE and reports, as coming from the relatives of Jesus, information that he probably took from a written source of Palestinian Jewish Christian origin. He says that the relatives of Jesus were known as the *desposynoi*, a term that means "those who belong to the Master," and reports of them, "From the Jewish villages of Nazareth and Kokhaba they travelled around the rest of the land and interpreted the genealogy they had [from the family traditions] and from the Book of Days [i.e., the Old Testament books 1–2 Chronicles] as far as they could trace it" (quoted in Eusebius, *Hist. eccl.* 1.7.14). The meaning is probably that members of the family of Jesus, traveling around the land of Israel and preaching the gospel to their fellow Jews, used a family genealogy, like that in Luke 3:23–38, as a way of explaining the Christian claim that Jesus was the messianic Son of David. Kokhaba is most likely the Galilean village of that name (modern Kaukab), about ten miles north of Nazareth. We are given here a rare glimpse of Christianity in Galilee, showing us that not only Jerusalem, where James was leader, but also Nazareth and Kokhaba, where other members of the family were based, were significant centers of early Christianity in Jewish Palestine. Moreover, this report preserves the term *desposynoi*, which is not found in any other source and demonstrates that not only Jesus's brothers but also a wider circle of relatives—"the Master's people"—played a leadership role in the movement.

We know a little about some of these other relatives. According to Eusebius, the second "bishop" of Jerusalem, after James, was Simeon or Simon, the son of Joseph's brother Clopas (Eusebius, *Hist. eccl.* 3.11; 4.22.4). The model that perhaps best explains the role of Jesus's relatives in the leadership of the Palestinian church is not that of dynastic succession but that of the association of a ruler's family with him in government. Just as it was normal practice in the ancient Near East for members of the royal family to hold high offices in government, so Palestinian Jewish Christians felt it appropriate that Jesus's brothers, cousins, and other relatives should hold positions of authority in his church. If so, it is interesting that James himself, if the letter attributed to him in the New Testament is authentic, claimed authority not as brother but as servant of the Messiah (James 1:1), mindful perhaps of Jesus's own depreciation of family relatedness to him (Mark 3:32–35; Luke 11:27–28).

Simeon the son of Clopas was leader of the Jerusalem church—and doubtless the most important figure in Jewish Christianity—for at least forty years, until his martyrdom in the reign of Trajan (either between 99 and 103 CE or between 108 and 117 CE). Hegesippus's account of Simeon's death (quoted in Eusebius, *Hist. eccl.* 3.32.3, 6)—at the age of 120!—has legendary elements, but it is most likely true that he was arrested by the Roman authorities on a charge of political subversion, since he was of a Davidic family and supported the alleged Davidic king Jesus, and was put to death by crucifixion. Also from Hegesippus we learn of Zoker and James, grandsons of Jesus's brother Judas, who have been mentioned earlier in this chapter.

Narrative Considerations of Jesus's Family

In this section we shall consider how the relatives of Jesus and Jesus's relationship to them are portrayed in each of the four Gospels.

The Gospel of Mark

It is not surprising that in this shortest of the Gospels the family of Jesus is less prominent than in any of the others. His putative father Joseph (named in all of the other three Gospels) is never once mentioned, but his mother, his brothers, and his sisters appear in two of the Gospel's stories (3:19b–35; 6:1–6). More remarkable is the fact that Mark gives the impression of a complete rift between Jesus and his family, which is not healed within the narrative of the Gospel, though Mark's hearers and readers would certainly have known that Jesus's brothers had become prominent leaders in the early Christian movement within Jewish Palestine. James in particular had been one of the best-known and most influential leaders in the early Christian movement and had only quite recently been executed in Jerusalem (62 CE), as every Christian community in Mark's time would certainly have known.

Jesus first appears in Mark's narrative in the statement that he "came from Nazareth of Galilee" to be baptized in the Jordan by John (1:9). It is assumed that Nazareth is his hometown, and accordingly he is called "Jesus the Nazarene" by characters in the Gospel who need to identify him (1:24; 10:47; 14:67; 16:6). But once he has left it, he does not return until the visit Mark recounts in 6:1–6. Rather, he makes his home in Capernaum (1:21; 2:1; 3:20; 7:17; 9:33).

Mark 3:20–35 is probably an instance of Mark's so-called sandwich (or intercalation) technique of narration, which inserts one narrative between the two halves of another (cf. 5:21–43; 6:7–30; 11:12–25; 14:1–11). In this case, the story of the scribes' accusation against Jesus (3:22–30) is inserted within the story of his relatives' misunderstanding of him (3:20–21, 31–35). The phrase *hoi par' autou* in verse 21, which the NRSV translates "his family," could mean "his adherents" or "his followers," but they seem to be distinguished from the disciples in 3:13–19, and the "sandwich" structure helps to confirm that they are the same people as "his mother and his brothers" in verse 31 (probably the best textual reading in verse 32 adds "and his sisters"). Admittedly, a first-time hearer or reader of Mark might not too easily be able to identify them as such (since the phrase *hoi par' autou* is so vague), but no other reading seems to account for what Mark says in this brief statement.

Evidently Jesus's relatives have heard that he is devoting himself so single-mindedly to ministering to the crowds that throng him wherever he goes (cf. 3:7–9) that he and his disciples have no time to eat. The relatives take this to indicate that Jesus "has gone out of his mind" (more literally, "he is beside himself"), and they have come over from Nazareth to take him back home. Their conclusion that Jesus has gone mad seems an extreme one, but it may be intentionally hyperbolic (as we might say, "he must be mad to . . ."). They probably think that Jesus is being swept along by a situation that is getting out of control. They want to protect him from himself.

The effect of the sandwich construction is to put in parallel the view of Jesus's relatives ("he has gone out of his mind") and the accusation by the scribes (that "he has Beelzebul" [v. 22] or "he has an unclean spirit" [v. 30]). Both are in effect denying the divine authority that impels Jesus's activity, but this does not imply that the family is as culpable as the scribes. Unlike the scribes, they are acting out of concern for Jesus's welfare, and they do not go so far as to suggest that Jesus is in league with the devil. So they are not condemned by Jesus in the way that the scribes are. But the parallel highlights the two forms of opposition that Jesus has to contend with at this stage of his mission: misunderstanding from his closest relatives and the worst sort of slander from his religious opponents.

This little story about Jesus's relatives turns out, in verses 31–35, to be a pronouncement story that leads up to Jesus's statement about his true family in verses 34–35. To the news that Jesus's mother and siblings are asking for him, Jesus's response is virtually to disown them. At least, their familial relationship with Jesus gives them no right to remove him from those who constitute his real family—those who do the will of God. Given a choice between relatives who fail to recognize his mission and those who crowd around him in their eagerness to hear his teaching and thereby to do God's will, the latter are Jesus's true family. The natural family is replaced by the new family, the people of God that Jesus's preaching and activity are calling into being.

The impression of a complete rift between Jesus and his family is confirmed by Mark's account of Jesus's visit to Nazareth, when he preaches in the synagogue. The Nazarenes find it difficult to accept Jesus as a prophet because they know his origins as a member like themselves of their small community: "Is not this the carpenter, the son of Mary and brother of James and Joses and Judas and Simon, and are not his sisters here with us?" (6:3). Jesus's mother and siblings are present in this congregation, but we might not suppose that they share the general attitude of disbelief toward Jesus, were it not that Jesus quotes the proverb "A prophet is not without honor, except in his own country, and among his own kin, and in his own house" (6:4 RSV). When this proverb appears on Jesus's lips in the Gospels of Luke, John, and *Thomas*, it refers only to the prophet's country, not to his family or house (Luke 4:24; John 4:44; *Gos. Thom.* 31; *P.Oxy.* 1.32–33). Mark's longer version makes it clear—and could even be said to stress the fact—that Jesus's own family refuses to recognize him as an inspired prophet.

Of all the Gospels, Mark's has the most negative characterization of Jesus's family. Some scholars have supposed that this characterization is polemical. Mark intends the family of Jesus to represent the Jerusalem church, whose jurisdictional role in the early Christian movement Mark rejects. (By such scholars Mark's negative portrayal of the Twelve is similarly explained. Note that such a view requires a date for the Gospel before 66 CE.) But that kind of ecclesiastical polemic is alien to the character of Mark's Gospel. Much more likely, Mark wishes to portray Jesus as setting the example for his followers, who also have to face misunderstanding and opposition from their families and to renounce natural family ties that would hinder their discipleship (1:20; 10:28–30; 13:12). The saying in Mark 10:29–30 indicates that, just as Jesus identified those who do God's will as his true relatives, so disciples of Jesus who have renounced their natural familial relationships find new relatives in the community of Jesus's true brothers and sisters.

The Gospel of Matthew

Matthew's is one of the two Gospels (along with Luke's) that provide an account of the birth and early infancy of Jesus. It is an account that focuses on Joseph much more than on Mary. The fate of the family depends upon Joseph's actions, which at each stage are directed by the angel of the Lord, who appears to Joseph in dreams and instructs him. Thus Joseph is instructed to go ahead with his marriage to Mary and is told about the unique identity and destiny of the child. He is also told to give the child the name *Jesus* (whereas usually, at least in the Hebrew Bible, it was the mother's role to name her child). It is Joseph who is instructed to take his wife and the child to Egypt to escape Herod's murderous intent, and it is Joseph who is later told that it is safe to return to the land of Israel and, then again, to avoid Judea and to settle in Nazareth. At each stage Matthew's hearers and readers are given Joseph's perspective on events.

Joseph's role of providing a family context for the birth and infancy of Jesus and of protecting Jesus against the serious threats to his life in these early days is clearly essential in the divine purpose. There are two reasons why Joseph is qualified for this supremely important role. First, he is descended from David. The genealogy that begins Matthew's Gospel (1:1–17) is designed to demonstrate that Jesus is "the Messiah, the son of David, the son of Abraham" (1:1). Joseph's descent through the royal line of the kings of Judah from David makes it possible for Jesus to inherit the throne of David and be the messianic "son of David" who is greater even than David (22:41–45). At the same time, Jesus's descent from Abraham enables him to be the messianic "seed of Abraham" through whom, according to God's promises to the patriarchs, all the nations of the world are to be blessed. For the sake of this latter role, any Israelite could have stood in Joseph's place, but for the sake of the former role, he had to be a Davidide. Matthew is clear that Joseph was not the biological father of Jesus, whose mother Mary conceived him miraculously (1:18, 20), and therefore the genealogy takes a novel turn at the end: "Joseph the husband of Mary, of whom Jesus was born" (1:16). But in Israel, tribal and family membership were inherited through the male line. If Mary had been a descendant of David (as later Christian tradition believed she was) it would not have made Jesus a descendant of David in a legally relevant way. According to the traditional view reflected in Matthew, Jesus could inherit the throne of David only because the Davidide Joseph was—legally though not biologically—his father. Thus Joseph's descent from David is not only the fact to which the Matthean genealogy leads but is emphasized early in the narrative, when the angel addresses him as "Joseph, son of David" (1:20). This address introduces the instruction that Joseph should take Mary as his wife, thereby becoming in effect the legal father of Jesus.

Joseph's second qualification for the extraordinary role that God gives him is that he is "a righteous man" (1:19). This description is related closely, in the narrative, to Joseph's initial decision to divorce Mary. The situation is that the couple was betrothed, which entailed the legal state of marriage (and therefore Joseph can already be called Mary's "husband" in verse 19), although sexual relations would not commence until the father relinquished responsibility for his daughter at the marriage ceremony, up to a year later, and the husband took her into his own household. When Joseph found that Mary was pregnant during this period, Jewish legal tradition required him to divorce her. Sexual relations with another man (even if she had been raped) would be considered to have broken the marriage bond. So Joseph is righteous, obedient to the law, in deciding to divorce her, but he goes beyond his strictly legal obligation in deciding not to subject her to a public trial to determine the cause of her pregnancy (cf. Deut. 22:22–29; Num. 5:11–31). Instead he intends to divorce her without publicity. Perhaps we should understand that Joseph's "righteousness" (a key term in this Gospel) goes beyond the minimum of literal obedience to the law (cf. 5:20), emulating rather the boundless compassion of God for the righteous and the unrighteous (5:45). While Joseph's righteousness is initially shown in his intentions toward Mary, before he knows the facts about her child, it certainly also characterizes the whole of his conduct throughout the events. At every stage he is unhesitatingly obedient to the commands of God.

Joseph's indispensable role in the purposes of God as they are worked out in the birth and early life of Jesus is especially emphasized in Matthew by the relationship between Joseph's obedient actions and the quotations from Scripture that Matthew inserts at every major stage of this narrative. The first such quotation (1:23, citing Isa. 7:14) is fulfilled by Joseph even to the extent that he abstains from sexual relations with Mary up to the birth of the child (1:25), so that, in literal accordance with the prophetic text, Mary is still a virgin when she gives birth. Joseph subsequently enables the fulfillment of prophecy when he takes his wife and the child to Egypt (2:13–15) and again when he takes them to settle in Nazareth (2:22–23).

There are certain parallels between Joseph in Matthew's narrative and the patriarch Joseph in the Genesis narratives. Both are associated with revelatory dreams, though the patriarch's skill in interpreting obscure, symbolic dreams is not paralleled in Matthew. Both go to Egypt, a move that in both cases has an important role in the unfolding of salvation history, though probably more so in the patriarch's case than in Matthew. It is difficult to know whether these parallels are significant. The Moses typology, in which what happens to the child Jesus resembles what happened to the child Moses (threatened by a tyrannical king, but escaping the fate that other children suffer at the time), and the exodus typology, in which Jesus escapes Egypt as the people of Israel did, are much more clearly part of the rich pattern of scriptural allusion that Matthew has woven into his narrative.

Though Joseph is the key player in Matthew's narrative of Jesus's birth and early life, Matthew does not tell us what happened to him thereafter, except for the almost incidental reference to the fact that he was an artisan (Matt. 13:55). It seems that, once the family is settled in Nazareth, Joseph has fulfilled his role in God's purpose and so also in Matthew's narrative. We see how Matthew's interest in Jesus's family is strictly limited.

In the rest of his Gospel, Matthew, by featuring Jesus's family only in the same two episodes as those in Mark (Matt. 12:46–50; 13:54–58), gives the same impression of a complete rift between Jesus and his mother and siblings, a rift not healed within the scope of his narrative. However, Matthew's Gospel lacks a parallel to Mark 3:19b–21, so that in this Gospel the relatives are not reported as considering Jesus deranged. Their request to see Jesus (Matt. 12:46) is not attributed to any specific motive, with the effect that Jesus's repudiation of them in favor of the new family of his disciples (12:48–50) appears even harsher than in Mark. But Matthew's interest, even more than Mark's, is focused on the new community that replaces natural family ties. The theme here links with other sayings of Jesus in Matthew that stress the need for disciples to renounce family loyalties for the sake of Jesus and the kingdom (Matt. 8:21–22; 10:34–38; 19:29).

Matthew's version of Jesus's rejection at Nazareth (13:54–58) is similar to Mark's, though briefer. (Like Mark, Matthew does not actually name Nazareth, but, although he regards Capernaum as Jesus's home in this period [4:13; 9:1], the Greek *patris* means native place or family home, while the presence of Jesus's relatives makes it clear that the scene is set in Nazareth.) Matthew's version of the proverb Jesus cites ("A prophet is not without honor except in his own country and in his own house" [RSV]) lacks Mark's phrase "and among his own kin," but since it does have "in his own house," the implication that Jesus's mother and siblings do not "honor" him is no less present.

The Gospel of Luke

Luke's narrative of the birth and infancy of Jesus differs from Matthew's in many ways, not only in the very different series of events that are recounted. The earlier part of Luke's story is dovetailed into a parallel story of the birth and infancy of John the Baptist, who is linked to Jesus not only by his future role as forerunner to Jesus but also because his mother Elizabeth is depicted as a relative of Mary (1:36) whom Mary goes to visit during the pregnancies of the two women (1:39–56).[7]

Another difference is that, whereas Matthew's focus is very much on Joseph, Luke's is very much on Mary. The minor role that Joseph does play is closely linked, as in Matthew, to his Davidic descent (1:27; 2:4; cf. 1:32; 2:11). But Mary is the main human subject whose actions are responsible, on the human level, for the events that occur in 1:26–56; 2:6–7. Moreover, in those passages

---

7. The relationship of the two women is left vague. For this reason, and because there is a chapter on John in this volume, I do not include a discussion of John and his parents in this chapter.

it is Mary's perspective on the events that the reader or hearer is invited to share. In the subsequent narrative (2:8–52), other characters take center stage in turn—the shepherds, Simeon, Anna, and the child Jesus himself. But all these events are, so to speak, gathered up into Mary's perspective by the statements that she "treasured all these words and pondered them in her heart" (2:19) and that she "treasured all these things in her heart" (2:51). These statements seem to present Mary as unable to take in the full significance of the remarkable events she witnessed and continuing to reflect on their significance as the years went by (cf. also her "ponder[ing]" in 1:29 and that of others in 1:66, in both cases provoked by perplexing events whose meaning was not immediately apparent). If that is the implication, then readers or hearers are being invited to ponder with her. But it is possible that these statements also identify Mary as the ultimate source of the stories Luke tells in these chapters and that the stories as Luke tells them incorporate the significance that Mary came to see in these events in her ongoing reflection and in the light of the whole life of her son Jesus.

In these early chapters of his Gospel, Luke has skillfully crafted a narrative that, by its language and its rich intertextual relationship with many parts of the Hebrew Bible, conveys the atmosphere of "biblical" Israel. Luke wants his readers and hearers to feel that his story of Jesus is deeply rooted in the biblical salvation history of God's dealings with his people Israel. He makes typological links with that history and draws out the prophetic hopes, explicit and implicit in the Scriptures, that point to the messianic redemption, the greatest salvation event of all, that is now happening in his narrative. Not only the angels but also such characters as Zechariah, the shepherds, Simeon, and Anna serve to identify the fulfillment of these prophetic hopes already underway with the births of John and Jesus. Elizabeth and Mary also serve this purpose, but, more importantly, they are the human agents through whom God is bringing his promised salvation into the world. Typological relationships that compare them as mothers with the mothers who are celebrated in the biblical histories help to define and enhance their roles as the mothers of the Messiah and his forerunner, and thus human agents of salvation. In this perspective, Mary emerges as the most greatly favored of all those biblical women who are called blessed because of their preeminent role in God's purposes for Israel and the world (cf. 1:42–45, 48).

In the annunciation scene (1:26–38), the emphasis is on the enormous privilege of the role to which God has called Mary (1:28: "favored one"; 1:30: "you have found favor with God"). The privilege, of course, carries with it enormous responsibility, and it is this that is presupposed in Mary's response, which is a paradigm of faith and obedience (1:38). Unlike Zechariah in the parallel scene preceding this one (1:18–20), and unlike even Sarah in a comparable situation (Gen 18:12–15), Mary believes the seemingly impossible (1:37; cf. 1:45). In calling herself the Lord's servant (1:38), she expresses humility in her willingness to do God's will (note Hannah's description of herself as the Lord's servant in her prayer in 1 Sam. 1:11), but the term also implies the privilege of her role, since the status of the servant or slave was determined in the ancient world by the status of her master. In the Old Testament, Moses in particular, the greatest of God's agents of salvation, is regularly called "the servant of the Lord" (e.g. Deut. 34:5). (Other great "servants" of God in the Old Testament are Abraham [Ps. 105:42], Joshua [Josh. 24:29], David [Ps. 89:3], and even the Davidic Messiah [Ezek. 34:23; 37:24].) So at the end of this passage we already glimpse the theme of Mary's song (1:46–55): Mary as the prime example of God's exaltation of the lowly.

As far as Old Testament precedents go, Mary belongs with Elizabeth among those who were enabled to bear children by the special favor and miraculous action of God: Sarah (Gen. 17–18; 21:1–7), Rebekah (Gen. 25:21), Leah and Rachel (Gen. 29:31–30:24), the mother of Samson (Judg. 13), and Hannah (1 Sam. 1:1–2:10). Mary both belongs to that succession and transcends it, in that in her case alone the miracle enables her to conceive a child while still a virgin. In Elizabeth and her son John the story of the Hebrew Bible culminates, while in Mary and her son Jesus the new creation begins. Consistently with this, whereas Luke's account of Mary certainly does put her in the succession of biblical mothers who conceive through God's power, it more especially and emphatically portrays her as in the succession of female human agents in God's deliverance of his people from their enemies. This succession includes some of the mothers just mentioned, especially Hannah, but also Deborah (Judg. 4–5), Jael (Judg. 4:17–22; 5:24–27), Esther, and (in the Apocrypha) Judith and the mother of the Maccabean martyrs (2 Macc. 7; 4 Macc. 14–18). This is conveyed especially by the references to Mary's blessedness. When Elizabeth, speaking prophetically in the Spirit, cries, "Blessed are you among women" (1:42), we are reminded of Jael, whom Deborah called "most blessed of women" (Judg. 5:24), and Judith, whom Uzziah called "Blessed by the Most High above all other women on earth" (Jdt. 13:18). When Mary says of herself that "from now on all generations will call me blessed" (Luke 1:48), we are reminded of Uzziah's words to Judith: "Your praise will never depart from the hearts of those who remember the power of God" (Jdt. 13:19). This perpetuity of reputation for Judith is connected with her own sense of the memorableness of the act of salvation God accomplishes through her: "I am about to do something that will go down through all generations of our descendants" (Jdt. 8:32). Similarly, that Mary will be called fortunate by all generations is due to the eternally enduring significance of her motherhood. Her child is to reign forever (Luke 1:33).

Mary's song (the Magnificat: 1:46–55) also stands in an Old Testament succession, in this case a succession of celebratory songs of praise sung by God's agents in salvation. The series begins with Moses's and Miriam's songs at the sea (Exod. 15:1–18, 21), and includes the song of Deborah and Barak

(Judg. 5), the song of Hannah (1 Sam. 2), the song of David (2 Sam. 22), and, in the Apocrypha, the songs of Judith (Jdt. 16), of Tobit (Tob. 13), and of the three young men (Add. Dan. 3). Of these the Magnificat most closely resembles the song of Hannah, which celebrates God's gift to her of a son who will lead the liberation of Israel from their enemies. The Magnificat is a collage of phrases drawn more or less verbatim from many parts of the Old Testament, but in both form and function it is strikingly parallel to Hannah's song. Both begin with personal declarations of praise and thanksgiving to God in view of his favor to the singer herself. Both continue with celebration of God's action for the humiliated in general (including, in both cases, the oppressed and the starving) and against the powerful in general (including, in both cases, the proud, the rulers, and the rich), effecting a reversal of status. By the end of the two songs both have in view God's saving action for his people Israel. In both cases it is understood, though not stated within the song, that the singer's motherhood of a significant son is the occasion for praise. In both cases it is understood that the singer's own lowly status makes her a representative example of God's characteristic activity of exalting the lowly. In both cases this reversal of status will be seen with reference not only to the lowly and exalted within Israel but also to Israel as God's humiliated servant and their powerful pagan oppressors. Mary represents God's faithful people in their oppressed condition, those whom her son the Messiah, according to Jewish hopes, will come to deliver.

Mary's lowly status (1:48) should be understood in terms both of socio-economic reality and of religious attitude. The biblical literature assumes a stereotypical relationship between the two: in the ordinary way of things, the rich and powerful are likely to trust arrogantly in themselves and disregard God, whereas those without worldly security tend to recognize their need of God and to approach him in humble trust. In the Magnificat, as usually else-where, the theme of reversal of status combines the attitudinal-religious and the socioeconomic. Luke tells us nothing directly about the social status of Joseph and Mary, but the sacrifice they offer for Mary's purification (2:22–24) is the two pigeons that the law prescribes for those who cannot afford a lamb (Lev. 12:8). While this need not put them among the truly destitute (who are "the poor" in the Gospels' usual terminology), it certainly puts them low on the socioeconomic scale, among those who could be called "lowly." It is possible that the lowly status to which Mary refers also reflects the fact that she is a woman.

Only one point about Mary in Luke's first two chapters still requires com-ment. When Simeon, speaking with prophetic inspiration, tells Mary that her son "is destined for the falling and rising of many in Israel"—alluding once more to the Magnificat's theme of reversal of status—and "to be a sign that will be opposed, so that the inner thoughts of many will be revealed," he adds a word about Mary's own future: "a sword will pierce your own soul too"

(2:34–35). The prophecy is mysterious because Luke himself never indicates how it was fulfilled. It seems to be indicating that when Jesus is "opposed," Mary too will suffer, and the image of the sword (cf. Ps. 22:20; Zech. 12:10; 13:7) implies that when that opposition to Jesus goes as far as his death, then Mary will suffer in her heart the death of her son.

After chapter 2, Jesus's mother appears only once in the narrative of Luke's Gospel, and this occasion accounts also for the sole mention of Jesus's brothers in Luke (though both mother and brothers reappear in Acts 1:14). Luke narrates the tradition we have noticed also in Mark and Matthew, according to which Jesus's mother and brothers come wanting to see him, whereupon Jesus says, "My mother and my brothers are those who hear the word of God and do it" (8:19–21). Like Matthew, Luke attributes no motive to Jesus's relatives here, and there is no need to infer any sort of rift between them and Jesus. But, on the other hand, Luke is not, as some have argued, presenting Jesus's relatives as model disciples. They simply provide the narrative occasion for Jesus to make the same point he makes in Mark's and Matthew's accounts: that in the renewed people of God it is not physical kinship but obedience to Jesus's teaching that counts. In the context, this reinforces the lesson of the parables that precede it (see especially 8:18).

The same point is made in a short anecdote unique to Luke's Gospel (11:27–28). A woman in the crowd expresses her admiration for Jesus by making a conventional point about the honor that thereby accrues to his mother: "Blessed is the womb that bore you and the breasts that nursed you!" On the face of it, this might seem to be no more nor less than what Elizabeth had said about Mary (1:42: "Blessed are you among women") and Mary had said about herself in the Magnificat (1:48: "all generations will call me blessed"). Jesus's reply— "Blessed rather are those who hear the word of God and obey it!"—therefore seems to contradict the words of Elizabeth, which were spoken under divine inspiration, and of Mary herself. However, we should remember that Luke 1 presents Mary as a paradigmatic example of those who hear the word of God and obey it. Not simply through being Jesus's mother, but through accepting her God-given task of motherhood in faith and obedience, Mary was blessed.

One other relative of Jesus appears in Luke's narrative: Cleopas (24:18), whom, in the first part of this chapter, we have seen reason to identify as Clopas, Joseph's brother and Jesus's uncle. That Luke gives his name and not that of his companion probably indicates that Cleopas was the source of the story, whether Luke heard it directly from him or transmitted by others. Luke does not mention Cleopas's relationship to Jesus, but it is likely that many of Luke's first readers and hearers could have known of this, because Cleopas's son Simon or Simeon was, when Luke was writing, the leader of the Jerusalem church, successor to his cousin James. In Luke's Gospel, where there is no hint of any tension between Jesus and his relatives, it is no great surprise to find Jesus's uncle among his disciples.

The Gospel of John

A distinctive feature of John's Gospel is the way in which it begins its narrative of Jesus's ministry (following the recruitment of his first five disciples) in a context where Jesus is evidently still behaving and treated as part of his family in Nazareth. The wedding at Cana, just a few miles from Nazareth, is one to which his mother and her whole family have been invited, most likely because the bridegroom's family is related to that of Jesus. Since Jesus's small group of disciples are guests of his family, they too have been invited (2:1–2). The miracle Jesus performs, the first of Jesus's "signs" (in John's terminology), is not really the beginning of Jesus's public ministry, since, like the steward, most of the guests evidently do not know that it has occurred (2:9–10). Only to Jesus's disciples does John say that it revealed Jesus's glory and gave rise to their belief in him (2:11). Following it, Jesus moves to Capernaum, along with his mother, his brothers, and his disciples. That Capernaum was the base for Jesus's Galilean ministry is probably one of those items of information that John assumes to be generally known to his readers and hearers, even though he himself does not explicitly say so. We should suppose that Jesus moves to Capernaum in order to begin his ministry of teaching and healing, and in that case John is portraying Jesus's mother and his brothers as, in effect, disciples. This is a perspective we do not get from any of the other Gospels.

Jesus's mother is never named in this Gospel (cf. 2:1, 5; 19:25–26), but this is perhaps not as surprising as is sometimes thought. She is similarly unnamed in Mark 3:31–32 (she is named by Mark only at 6:3, where he could not have written what he does without naming her); Matthew 2:20–21; 12:46–47; Luke 2:48, 51; 8:19–20; Acts 1:14. (Without the birth and infancy narratives in Matthew and Luke, we would know the name of Jesus's mother only from Matt. 13:55 and Mark 6:3.) In that society women were frequently identified, even in their own burial inscriptions, only as the wife or mother of a male relative. While this custom of course reflects the patriarchal culture, to follow it would not have been regarded as in any way disrespectful to the woman. Although John's narrative does create a close connection between Jesus's mother and the Beloved Disciple (19:26–27), who is similarly always anonymous, we probably do not need to look for some special reason for Mary's anonymity. John simply follows a common custom.

On both occasions on which Jesus addresses his mother in this Gospel, he does so as "Woman" (2:4; 19:26). This was a normal and polite way of addressing a woman, especially one the speaker does not know (Matt. 15:28; Luke 13:12; 22:57; John 4:21; 20:13, 15), but it is not at all clear whether it would be unremarkable to address one's mother in this way (evidence of Palestinian Jewish practice has not been adduced). It could imply that Jesus distances himself somewhat from his mother, in the same way that he demotes natural family relationships in the Synoptic Gospels (Mark 3:31–35 and elsewhere). Certainly the words that follow the address in 2:4 (literally, "what to me and you?") do rather forcefully create a distance. Jesus means that she cannot tell him what to do, since the work he has come to do and its timing are for his Father to determine. But, still, it would be going too far to say that he no longer regards her as his mother, for the scene in 19:26–27, where the dying Jesus gives his mother into the care of the Beloved Disciple, so that henceforth they are to be mother and son, would not make sense unless we were intended to understand that Jesus recognized his special responsibility for his mother up to his death.

What we can say about Mary herself from the story of the wedding at Cana is that she shows a remarkable belief that Jesus can do something about the shortage of wine (2:3) and an undeterred expectation that he will do so even after her implied request is rebuffed (2:5). On what basis she does so is not explained, but her behavior at this point makes it entirely natural that she should then accompany Jesus to Capernaum, along with his disciples. John gives us no reason to think that her attitude ever changed, and so it is also not surprising to find her at the cross (where she makes her only other appearance in the narrative of this Gospel).

Jesus's brothers are a different case. They are first mentioned in 2:12, where they accompany Jesus with his disciples as though they too are disciples, and when they reappear in 7:3 the reader or hearer will naturally suppose that they have remained supportive followers of Jesus up to that point. Now they urge him to go to Jerusalem for the feast of tabernacles and make a public display of miracles (7:3–4). John gives the parenthetical explanation that "not even his brothers believed in him" (7:5). It is possible that he means to indicate that from this point onward they are no longer followers of Jesus, like the many disciples who had given up following him some six months earlier (6:66). But this need not be the sense of the passage. In some sense the brothers do believe in Jesus: they have seen his miracles and have no doubt that he can perform such in Jerusalem. They are rather like those about whom Jesus laments that they will not believe unless they see signs and wonders (4:48), and they want Jesus to make such a display of his supernatural powers that people in general, including no doubt the Jerusalem authorities, will come to believe. In this way, from John's perspective, they seriously misunderstand Jesus and lack adequate faith in him. But this does not mean that from their own perspective they are not among Jesus's followers. Even about the belief of the Twelve, who distinguish themselves from the defectors by believing that Jesus is the Holy One (6:66–69), John is somewhat ambivalent (14:8–10; 16:30–31; but see also 17:8).

John's portrayal of the unbelief of the brothers of Jesus belongs to his quite complex account of belief and unbelief, inadequate and more adequate belief. But the main reason he introduces the brothers, with the attitude to Jesus he condemns as unbelief, at this point in his narrative (7:3–5) is that, as on many other occasions in this Gospel when people misunderstand Jesus, the misunderstanding affords a narrative opportunity for Jesus to clarify his own understanding and intentions (7:6–8). This narrative function is sufficient to explain John's inclusion of this passage about the unbelief of the brothers, and there is no need to resort, as some scholars have done, to the explanation that John was hostile to the Jerusalem church leadership of his time, in which the relatives of Jesus were prominent. In fact, this is wholly implausible in the light of the fact that John names Mary the wife of Clopas among the small group of faithful disciples present at the cross (19:25). She was almost certainly the wife of Jesus's uncle, Joseph's brother Clopas, and the mother of Simeon the son of Clopas, James's successor as head of the church of Jerusalem and the leader of Palestinian Jewish Christianity at the time John wrote.

Only in John's Gospel is the mother of Jesus among the women who stood close to Jesus at the cross (19:25). In fact the other Gospels refer to a group of women (Matt. 27:55–56; Mark 15:40–41) or of men and women (Luke 22:49) standing at some distance from the cross, and make it explicit that they are naming only a few of them. Only Mary Magdalene is common to the Synoptics and to John's group of four people—three women and the Beloved Disciple—who stand close to the cross. It is clear that they really are close to the cross because Jesus is able to converse with them. Roman soldiers would not have allowed people in general near the cross, but exception could have been made for a few women closely related to Jesus (as two of the three were) and for a mere youth (if it is right to think the Beloved Disciple was younger than the other disciples).

That John relates Jesus's entrusting of his mother to the Beloved Disciple, who "from that hour . . . took her into his own home" (19:27), has often been thought to suggest that, beyond its literal meaning, the passage must have some symbolic or allegorical meaning. The suggestion that is most plausible, because it avoids importing symbolic meanings that are nowhere indicated in John, is that the new relationship of Jesus's mother and the Beloved Disciple represents the new relationships that disciples of Jesus will have in the community that Jesus's death creates. (Mark 10:29–30 promises that those who have abandoned families for Jesus's sake will be compensated with "brothers and sisters, mothers and children" in the community of disciples. Early Christians did use these familial terms in their relations with each other.) But although the Beloved Disciple is often said to function in the Gospel as representing the ideal disciple, in my view his role is much better described as that of the ideal witness to Jesus. All his appearances in the Gospel contribute to his ability, at a later date and especially in writing the Gospel, to bear a distinctive kind of witness to Jesus. Consistently with this, Jesus's commendation of his mother to him may function to emphasize his closeness to Jesus, as the only male disciple present with Jesus at the cross and the one to whom Jesus saw fit to entrust his mother.

What do we learn of Jesus himself from these narrative portrayals of his family in the Gospels if we read them synthetically for the total impression they make? Evidently he came from a family that traced its descent from King David, though its relatively low social status implies it was a minor branch. He grew up in a pious Jewish family in which his messianic vocation was known and prized, but during his ministry he did not always enjoy the full support of his mother and siblings. Though they were often to be found among his disciples, there were also serious tensions that reflect how controversial a figure he was. But his own sense of vocation and the radical character of the kingdom of God that he preached led him to play down the importance of natural family ties and to see his own followers as a new kind of family that formed the nucleus of the renewed people of God.

Suggestions for Further Reading

Bauckham, Richard. *Gospel Women: Studies of the Named Women in the Gospels.* Grand Rapids: Eerdmans / Edinburgh: T&T Clark, 2002.

———. "James and the Gentiles (Acts 15:13–21)." In *History, Literature and Society in the Book of Acts*, edited by Ben Witherington III, 154–84. Cambridge: Cambridge University Press, 1996.

———. "James and the Jerusalem Church." In *The Book of Acts in Its Palestinian Setting*, edited by Richard Bauckham, 417–27. Carlisle, UK: Paternoster; Grand Rapids: Eerdmans, 1995.

———. *Jude and the Relatives of Jesus in the Early Church.* Edinburgh: T&T Clark, 1990.

———. "Traditions about the Tomb of James the Brother of Jesus." In *Poussières de christianisme et de judaïsme antiques: Études reunites en l'honneur de Jean-Daniel Kaestli et Éric Junod*, edited by Albert Frey and Rémi Gounelle, 61–77. Lausanne, Switzerland: Éditions du Zèbre, 2007.

Chilton, Bruce D., and Craig A. Evans, eds. *James the Just and Christian Origins.* NovTSup 98. Leiden: Brill, 1999.

———, eds. *The Missions of James, Peter and Paul.* NovTSup 115. Leiden: Brill, 2005.

Chilton, Bruce D., and Jacob Neusner, eds. *The Brother of Jesus: James the Just and His Mission.* Louisville: Westminster John Knox, 2001.

Gaventa, Beverly Roberts. *Mary: Glimpses of the Mother of Jesus.* Edinburgh: T&T Clark, 1999.

McHugh, John. *The Mother of Jesus in the New Testament.* London: Darton, Longman & Todd, 1975.

Painter, John. *Just James: The Brother of Jesus in History and Tradition.* Columbia: University of South Carolina Press, 1997.

5

Other Friends of Jesus

Mary Magdalene, the Bethany Family, and the Beloved Disciple

DIETER T. ROTH

This chapter presents five friends of Jesus: Mary Magdalene; the Bethany family of Mary, Martha, and Lazarus; and the Beloved Disciple. These friends have played important roles in church tradition and been the focus of considerable scholarly attention, and some of them have recently also captured the popular imagination. Each of them plays an important role in the Gospel narratives and contributes to our understanding of Jesus and his teachings as presented in the New Testament and as received in various early Christian communities.

Mary Magdalene

Though there has always been considerable interest in the figure of Mary Magdalene, the 1945 discovery of a number of fascinating texts at Nag Hammadi, in a few of which she figures prominently, led to a proliferation of

Nag Hammadi Library

In 1945, near Nag Hammadi, a city in Upper Egypt, thirteen codices were found that contained nearly fifty texts that likely were produced and read by groups of Christians often called "gnostics" (from the Greek word for knowledge, *gnōsis*), or at least by Christians interested in gnostic themes. Though the validity and appropriateness of the label "gnosticism" has been questioned,[1] in general it can be said that these groups understood salvation in terms of a revealed, esoteric knowledge that allowed the spiritual element in humanity to escape materiality. In the Christian forms of gnosticism, Jesus is viewed as the source of this esoteric knowledge, or *gnōsis*. Among the best-known texts included in the Nag Hammadi Library are the *Gospel of Thomas* and the *Gospel of Philip*.[2]

1. See, for example, Michael A. Williams, *Rethinking "Gnosticism": An Argument for Dismantling a Dubious Category* (Princeton: Princeton University Press, 1996). An accessible introduction to the challenges confronting contemporary scholarship on gnosticism can be found in Karen L. King, *What Is Gnosticism?* (Cambridge, MA: Harvard University Press, 2003), 5–19.
2. For an introduction to and English translation of the complete Nag Hammadi Library, see *The Nag Hammadi Library in English*, ed. James M. Robinson, 4th ed. (Leiden: Brill, 1996), or *The Nag Hammadi Scriptures*, ed. Marvin Meyer, rev. ed. (New York: HarperOne, 2009).

scholarly discussions in recent decades.[1] In addition, the popular fascination with this woman has steadily increased through her presence in, for example, the musical *Jesus Christ Superstar* (1971), the movie *The Last Temptation of Christ* (1988), and, most recently, the international best seller *The Da Vinci Code* (2003) and its cinematic presentation (2006). Despite what is found in some church traditions and popular presentations, the New Testament actually says very little about Mary Magdalene, and though the presentations of her in noncanonical texts are undoubtedly intriguing, they have often been misinterpreted.

Historical Considerations: Mary Magdalene outside the New Testament Gospels

When considering the presentation of Mary Magdalene outside the New Testament Gospels, it is worth beginning with traditions found in the church fathers, particularly since some of these traditions strongly influenced the portrayal of Mary Magdalene in the ensuing centuries.

1. François Bovon has rightly noted, "In recent years the literature concerning this woman has become immeasurable" (*Das Evangelium nach Lukas*, 4 vols., EKKNT 3 [Neukirchen-Vluyn, Germany: Neukirchener Verlag, 1989–2009], 4:529n80; unless otherwise noted, translations are my own).

The Name Mary

As seen in the citation from *Homily* 33 of Gregory the Great, the fact that Mary of Bethany and Mary Magdalene shared the name Mary appears to have contributed to his confusion. In fact, the Gospels mention numerous women named Mary, including, for example, Mary the mother of Jesus, Mary Magdalene, Mary of Bethany, Mary the [wife] of Clopas, and Mary the mother of James and Joseph. That several women with this name appear in the New Testament is not at all surprising since *Mary*, according to the available data, was the most common feminine name among Palestinian Jews, with more than one in five women bearing it.[1] It is precisely because the name was so common that additional information was appended to the name in order to identify the Mary in view. Most often the additional information related either to other family members or the city from which Mary hailed. Thus, for example, there is a Mary identified as the mother of James and Joseph (Matt. 27:56) and a Mary Magdalene, that is, the Mary from Magdala, a town on the west side of Lake Gennesaret.[2]

1. See Richard Bauckham, *The Testimony of the Beloved Disciple: Narrative, History, and Theology in the Gospel of John* (Grand Rapids: Baker Academic, 2007), 175. For charts of the data concerning masculine and feminine names, see Richard Bauckham, *Jesus and the Eyewitnesses: The Gospels as Eyewitness Testimony* (Grand Rapids: Eerdmans, 2006), 85–92.
2. For discussion of the town of Magdala, see Jane Schaberg, *The Resurrection of Mary Magdalene: Legends, Apocrypha, and the Christian Testament* (New York: Continuum, 2002), 47–64.

CHURCH FATHERS

In the Western church there arose a portrait of Mary Magdalene based on the establishment of the belief that Mary Magdalene, Mary of Bethany, and the sinful woman who anointed Jesus in Luke 7:37–38 were the same woman. Reference is often made to a homily by Pope Gregory the Great (540–604 CE) in which he stated, "The woman, whom Luke calls a sinner [Luke 7:37], John names Mary [John 12:3]. I believe that she is the same Mary of whom Mark says that seven demons had been cast out [Mark 16:9]. How should we interpret the seven demons except as the totality of vices?"[2] Gregory then described how Mary formerly used perfume, her eyes, her hair, and her mouth in a life of prostitution but has now offered them all to God in a praiseworthy manner. Even though the fusing of these women into one figure did not occur in the

2. Gregory the Great, *Homily* 33, in David Hurst, ed., *Forty Gospel Homilies*, Cistercian Studies Series 123 (Kalamazoo, MI: Cistercian Publications, 1990). For an extensive survey of patristic references to the question of the identity of Mary Magdalene, see Richard Atwood, *Mary Magdalene in the New Testament Gospels and Early Tradition*, European University Studies 23.457 (Bern: Peter Lang, 1993), 147–85, and Urban Holzmeister, "Die Magdalenenfrage in der kirchlichen Überlieferung," *ZKG* 46 (1922): 402–22, 556–84.

Eastern church,[3] this depiction of Mary Magdalene as a repentant prostitute profoundly shaped many later traditions about her.[4]

There are many references to Mary Magdalene in the church fathers and later church teaching that could be discussed; however, here I will highlight two traditions of particular interest. First, because of the early traditions about Mary Magdalene, in the Middle Ages she came to be called *apostolorum apostola* ("apostle to the apostles"), a title that underscores how important the tradition of this woman as a witness of the resurrected Jesus to the apostles was for the church.[5] Second, as if the confusion surrounding Mary Magdalene and other women in the New Testament Gospels were not great enough already, several church fathers posit that there may actually have been *two* Mary Magdalenes! One is the Mary Magdalene mentioned in John 20:1, 17–18, who came to the tomb while it was still dark and was not allowed to grasp the risen Jesus. The other Mary Magdalene is the one mentioned in Matthew 28:1 and Mark 16:1, who went to the tomb when it was light and, according to Matthew 28:9, was allowed to touch him. Thus, a perceived contradiction in the Gospel accounts was solved by multiple Mary Magdalenes.[6]

Noncanonical Gospels/Writings

Though Mary Magdalene does appear in writings of the church fathers, it is in noncanonical texts that Mary becomes a central and, at times, dominating figure. François Bovon has helpfully noted the variety of reasons for the interest in Mary Magdalene among groups at the margins of early Christianity:

1. her virtue and purity;
2. Jesus's affection for her;
3. her first, direct, and privileged contact with the resurrected Christ as a source of revelation;
4. the jealousy of the disciples in view of this privilege;

3. Carla Ricci notes that the distinction between these three women was maintained in the East as evidenced by their having three separate feast days (*Mary Magdalene and Many Others: Women who Followed Jesus*, trans. Paul Burns [Minneapolis: Fortress, 1994], 32n6). For a brief and helpful summary of why these women, as presented in the New Testament, cannot all be Mary Magdalene see Bart Ehrman, *Peter, Paul, and Mary Magdalene: The Followers of Jesus in History and Legend* (Oxford: Oxford University Press, 2006), 189.

4. For discussion of Mary Magdalene in the Middle Ages and the cult that grew up around her in southern France, see Robin Griffith-Jones, *Beloved Disciple: The Misunderstood Legacy of Mary Magdalene, the Woman Closest to Jesus* (New York: HarperOne, 2008), 177–207, and Ricci, *Mary Magdalene*, 151–54. Esther de Boer notes, "In 1969 the Roman Catholic Church officially decided to drop the image of Mary Magdalene as the reformed prostitute" (*The Mary Magdalene Cover-Up: The Sources Behind the Myth*, trans. John Bowden [London: T&T Clark, 2007], 13).

5. On the title, see Katherine Ludwig Jansen, *The Making of the Magdalen: Preaching and Popular Devotion in the Later Middle Ages* (Princeton: Princeton University Press, 2000), 62–65.

6. See, for example, Eusebius, *Quaestiones ad Marinum* 2.7; Ambrose, *Exp. Luc.* 10.144–67; and Jerome, *Epist.* 120, *ad Hedebiam* 4.

5. the responsibility with which she was charged to regroup the disciples and send them out on their mission; and
6. the virile character, in the spiritual sense, of this chosen and cherished woman.[7]

In the following I will consider Mary Magdalene in the *Gospel of Thomas*, the *Gospel of Philip, Pistis Sophia,* and the *Gospel of Mary.*[8]

In the *Gospel of Thomas*, Mary appears twice in the text, the first time only to ask Jesus, "Whom are your disciples like?" (*Gos. Thom.* 21).[9] In the final saying of this Gospel, however, Simon Peter says, "Let Mary go away from us, for women are not worthy of life," to which Jesus replies, "'Look, I will draw her in so as to make her male, so that she too may become a living male spirit, similar to you.' (But I say to you): 'Every woman who makes herself male will enter the kingdom of heaven'" (*Gos. Thom.* 114). It is worth noting Peter's animosity, a theme also present in other texts. In addition, regardless of precisely how Jesus's reply is interpreted,[10] it is clear that "maleness" is presented as a superior category *but* that Jesus is able to bring Mary into that category, qualifying her for the kingdom of heaven.

The *Gospel of Philip* contains passages, made famous by *The Da Vinci Code*, where Mary Magdalene appears as the "companion" of Jesus whom Jesus appears to have loved more than the disciples, and whom he used "to kiss [. . .] on her [. . .]" (*Gos. Phil.* 63–64). As indicated by the ellipses, there are some unfortunate lacunae in the manuscript, but it seems clear that Mary is presented in a particularly close relationship to Jesus and the recipient of his kisses. The conclusion, however, that the text is presenting some type of *sexual* intimacy between Jesus and Mary Magdalene is entirely erroneous. "Companion" here does not mean spouse,[11] and as Michael Penn notes, the *Gospel of Philip* "connects the ritual kiss with concepts of nourishment, mouth, speech, and impregnating 'the perfect' with grace," and the text emphasizes the kiss "as a vehicle for a transfer of spirit."[12] Thus, the text again highlights the special *spiritual* significance of Mary Magdalene.

---

7. See François Bovon, "Le privilège pascal de Marie-Madeleine," *NTS* 30 (1984): 56.

8. For extensive discussion of Mary Magdalene in these and other texts, see Antti Marjanen, *The Woman Jesus Loved: Mary Magdalene in the Nag Hammadi Library and Related Documents,* NHMS 40 (Leiden: Brill, 1996).

9. The translation is that found in Stephen J. Patterson, James M. Robinson, and Hans-Gebhard Bethge, *The Fifth Gospel: The Gospel of Thomas Comes of Age* (Harrisburg, PA: Trinity Press International, 1998).

10. For interpretive options, see Schaberg, *Resurrection of Mary Magdalene,* 156–60.

11. The Coptic uses a loan word from Greek (*koinōnos*), which is not the word for "spouse" and normally simply means "associate."

12. Michael Philip Penn, *Kissing Christians: Ritual Community in the Late Ancient Church,* Divinations: Rereading Late Ancient Religion (Philadelphia: University of Pennsylvania Press, 2005), 40. These points are explicitly made earlier in *Gos. Phil.* 59.

Was Mary Magdalene Jesus's Wife?

It is generally recognized, as will also be seen below, that the New Testament provides no grounds to see Mary Magdalene in a romantic relationship with Jesus, much less as his wife: Mary Magdalene is one of *many* women who followed Jesus (Luke 8:1–3). It is sometimes argued, however, that it is the noncanonical texts that have preserved the true relationship between Jesus and Mary Magdalene. Yet not one of these texts discusses a supposed marriage of Jesus to Mary Magdalene, and the attempt to read a sexual relationship into the "kissing" mentioned in the *Gospel of Philip*, for example, is simply misguided.[1]

1. See also Bart Ehrman, *Peter, Paul, and Mary Magdalene*, 214–16, 248–51, and Antti Marjanen, "Mary Magdalene, a Beloved Disciple," in *Mariam, the Magdalen, and the Mother*, ed. Deirdre Good (Bloomington: Indiana University Press, 2005), 54–56.

Turning to texts not included in the Nag Hammadi library,[13] in a lengthy text called *Pistis Sophia* ("Faith Wisdom") one again finds Mary's special status and the jealously of and rivalry with Peter. In one passage, Mary asks permission to speak openly, to which Jesus replies, "Blessed Mary, you whom I shall complete with all the mysteries on high, speak openly, for you are one whose heart is set on heaven's kingdom more than all your brothers" (*Pist. Soph.* 1.17).[14] After completing her discourse, Jesus says, "Well done, Mary. You are more blessed than all women on earth, because you will be the fullness of fullnesses and the completion of completions" (*Pist. Soph.* 1.19). Peter and the other disciples are apparently upset with Mary's conversing with Jesus, and Peter complains, "My master, we cannot endure this woman who gets in our way and does not let any of us speak, though she talks all the time" (*Pist. Soph.* 1.36). It seems that as a result of this attitude Mary herself later states that though she knows that she can come forward at any time to interpret the *Pistis Sophia*, she is afraid of Peter, who threatens her and hates the female gender (see *Pist. Soph.* 2.72).

In the *Gospel of Mary*,[15] Mary Magdalene appears on the scene after Jesus has departed and offers words of encouragement to the disciples (*Gos.*

13. Only two such texts are discussed here, but one could also mention others, such as the *Manichean Psalm-book*, for example, or the *Great Questions of Mary*, known only through the discussion of Epiphanius in *Pan.* 26.8.1–9.5.

14. Several excerpts from the *Pistis Sophia* dealing with Mary Magdalene are helpfully provided in Marvin Meyer and Esther de Boer, eds., *The Gospels of Mary: The Secret Tradition of Mary Magdalene, the Companion of Jesus* (San Francisco: HarperSanFrancisco, 2004), 66–69. English translations here are from this volume.

15. For discussion, commentary, and the translation of the Coptic text used here, see Christopher Tuckett, *The Gospel of Mary*, Oxford Early Christian Texts (Oxford: Oxford University Press, 2007).

Mary 9). In response, Peter says, "Sister, we know that the Saviour loved you more than the rest of women. Tell us the words of the Saviour which you remember, which you know but we do not, and which we have not heard" (*Gos. Mary* 10.1–6). Mary then recounts a vision she had of the Lord (unfortunately several pages of the vision are missing in the manuscript) and is met with a skeptical response. Andrew speaks up and says, "Say what you (wish to?) say about what she has said. I myself do not believe that the Saviour said this. For these teachings seem to be (giving) different ideas" (*Gos. Mary* 17.11–15). Peter then jumps in, adding, "He did not speak with a woman without our knowing, and not openly, did he? Shall we turn around and all listen to her? Did he prefer her to us?" (*Gos. Mary* 17.18–23). Mary begins to weep and asks Peter if he thinks that she has thought all this up in her heart or that she is lying about the Savior. At this point, Levi says, "Peter, you have always been hot-tempered. Now I see you are arguing against the woman like the adversaries. But if the Saviour made her worthy, who are you then to reject her? Certainly the Saviour knows her very well. That is why he loved her more than us" (*Gos. Mary* 18.7–15). Levi then exhorts them all to put on the perfect man and preach the gospel, and the text ends with the narrator indicating that they went out to proclaim and preach. It is noteworthy that Mary is identified by Peter as one whom Jesus loved more than other women, but Levi goes further and indicates she was loved more than the male disciples. Her vision and special place in the community is vindicated, and the "hot-tempered" Peter is rebuked.

Narrative Considerations: Mary Magdalene inside the New Testament Gospels

It is striking that although Mary Magdalene plays an important role as a witness to the crucifixion and resurrection of Jesus in all four New Testament Gospels, she makes only one appearance in a brief reference in Luke 8:1–3 prior to the passion and resurrection narratives. The New Testament Gospels, therefore, generally do not highlight her importance until they recount her role during the death and resurrection of Jesus.[16]

LUKE 8:1–3

In Luke 8:1–3, Luke's indication that this Mary is "called Magdalene" reveals that she is from Magdala, that is, she is a Galilean Jewish woman. In addition, Luke recounts that "seven demons had gone out" of this woman.

16. An extended discussion of Mary Magdalene in the New Testament Gospels can be found in Esther A. de Boer, *The Gospel of Mary: Beyond a Gnostic and a Biblical Mary Magdalene*, JSNTSup 260 (London: T&T Clark, 2004), 101–99. Focusing on Mary Magdalene in John is Susanne Ruschmann, *Maria von Magdala im Johannesevangelium: Jüngerin—Zeugin—Lebensbotin*, NTAbh 40 (Münster: Aschendorff, 2002).

Though the text does not specifically say that Jesus is the one who healed her, that he did so can probably be inferred. In the longer ending of Mark, where this bit of information appears again, it is stated that Jesus was the one who had cast out the demons (Mark 16:9). Mary Magdalene is also one of several women who had the means to support and provide financially for Jesus and the group traveling with him as they were proclaiming the good news of the kingdom of God (Luke 8:1; cf. Mark 15:40–41).[17] Luke literally says that the women "were serving [diēkonoun] them" out of their resources, a description that may be influenced by the later use of diakoneō words to describe Christian service.[18] At the same time, however, they are not simply identified as providers of physical needs but are said to have been, like the Twelve, "with" Jesus. As such, Mary Magdalene and the other women are identified by Luke as disciples.[19] Finally, Mary Magdalene is at the head of the list, just as she is in nearly every New Testament reference in which she is mentioned, likely because of the prominent and special place she has as a witness to Jesus's crucifixion, burial, and resurrection. It is in the passion and resurrection narratives where she, as Bovon puts it, "steps out of the shadows."[20]

MARY MAGDALENE AT THE CRUCIFIXION

The first mention of Mary Magdalene in Mark and Matthew occurs when these Gospels indicate that she was one of several women who were watching the crucifixion "from a distance" (Mark 15:40–41//Matt. 27:55–56). These verses, consonant with what Luke 8:1–3 reveals, mention that she was one of the women who had followed Jesus in Galilee and had ministered to him.[21]

---

17. For discussion of the relationship between Luke 8:1–3 and Mark 15:40, along with several other issues, see Martin Hengel, "Maria Magdalena und die Frauen als Zeugen," in *Abraham unser Vater: Juden und Christen im Gespräch über die Bibel: Festschrift für Otto Michel zum 60. Geburtstag*, ed. Otto Betz, Martin Hengel, and Peter Schmidt, AGJU 5 (Leiden: Brill, 1963), 243–56.

18. See I. Howard Marshall, *The Gospel of Luke*, NIGTC (Grand Rapids: Eerdmans, 1978), 317. The use of this word has engendered significant discussion, particularly in feminist readings focusing on how "service," usually referring to "waiting on tables" in Luke-Acts, serves as a metaphor for leadership. (The same issue arises in interpreting the Martha and Mary story in Luke 10:38–42; see n. 49 below.) Ben Witherington III, however, likely more accurately sets forth the perspective of the text in noting how traditional roles for women could become more than service for the physical family by serving the family of faith (see "On the Road with Mary Magdalene, Joanna, Susanna, and Other Disciples—Luke 8:1–3," *ZNW* 70 [1979]: 246–48).

19. The way in which Luke develops the idea that being "with Jesus" connotes discipleship can be seen in passages such as Luke 7:11–12; 8:38; 22:11, 14, 28.

20. Bovon, "Le privilege pascal," 50.

21. The description of the women as having "followed" Jesus again brings up images of discipleship (see the calling of the male disciples in Mark 1:16–20), and Craig Evans observes that these women "stand in stark contrast to the disciples who had fled, and so in some ways model discipleship better than do the Twelve themselves" (*Mark 8:27–16:20*, WBC 34B [Nashville: Nelson, 2001], 512).

The "Longer Ending" of Mark

The so-called longer ending of Mark is one of four endings to Mark found in manuscripts of this Gospel.[1] This ending, encompassing verses 9–20, has been judged by nearly all scholars to be a secondary addition.[2] When considering the manuscript evidence, we must observe that though a variety of witnesses, including some ancient witnesses, attest the longer ending, two of the oldest and most important manuscripts, Codex Sinaiticus (ℵ) and Codex Vaticanus (B), do not have verses 9–20. Even more significant is the internal evidence, as these verses contain numerous words found nowhere else in Mark and sometimes nowhere else in the New Testament. In addition, the transition from verse 8 to verse 9 is grammatically and stylistically awkward. The women are the subject of verse 8, and then suddenly Jesus is the implied subject of verse 9. Finally, Mary Magdalene appears to be introduced in verse 9 even though she had been mentioned previously in both chapters 15 and 16, and the other women present in verses 1–8 simply disappear from the narrative.

1. For a helpful overview of the four endings, see Bruce Metzger, *A Textual Commentary on the Greek New Testament*, 2nd ed. (Stuttgart: German Bible Society, 1994), 102–6. For the variety of ways in which the longer ending appears in the manuscripts, see Adela Yarbro Collins, *Mark*, Hermeneia (Minneapolis: Fortress, 2007), 804–6.
2. Modern English versions of the Bible indicate the questionable status of this ending by either adding a note or placing the text in brackets.

Luke 23:49 also indicates that there were women observing the crucifixion standing at a distance, and though his reference to these women being the ones who had followed Jesus from Galilee may be a reference to the women named in chapter 8 of his Gospel, Luke here does not mention the names of any of the women. John 19:25 mentions women "near the cross,"[22] one of whom is Mary Magdalene.[23] Thus, even though the four New Testament Gospels differ in some elements of their presentation of Jesus's crucifixion, they all, either explicitly or implicitly, indicate that Mary Magdalene was a witness to Jesus's death.

Mary Magdalene at the Burial

According to the Synoptic Gospels, having witnessed the crucifixion, Mary Magdalene, along with other women, next witnessed the burial of Jesus by

22. The proximity of the women to the cross is necessary for John, as it allows for the dialogue that Jesus has with Mary, his mother, and the Beloved Disciple in vv. 26–27.
23. There has been quite a bit of scholarly discussion concerning whether John's list refers to two, three, or four women. Regardless of one's view, that Mary Magdalene is one of them is clear. See further Richard Bauckham, "Mary of Clopas (John 19:25)," in *Women in the Biblical Tradition*, ed. George J. Brooke, Studies in Women and Religion 31 (Lewiston, NY: Edwin Mellen, 1992), 232–34; George R. Beasley-Murray, *John*, 2nd ed., WBC 36 (Nashville: Nelson, 1999), 348–49.

Joseph of Arimathea. (Mark 15:47//Matt. 27:61; Luke 23:55 again does not
name the women but identifies them as the ones who had come with Jesus
from Galilee.)[24] The importance for the Gospel writers of the women knowing where Jesus was entombed may be found in the fact that this knowledge
would preclude the possibility that the women had gone to the wrong tomb
when they returned and found it empty. Since Mary Magdalene saw the tomb
in which the body of Jesus was laid, she could later discover that the body
was no longer there.

Mary Magdalene at the Resurrection

Finally, Mary Magdalene is recounted as having come to the empty tomb,
with no one else mentioned, as in John 20:1,[25] or with other women, as in
Mark 16:1//Matthew 28:1 and Luke 24:1, 10. Then, John narrates that Mary
Magdalene is the first person to see the risen Christ (John 20:16), and Matthew has her in the group of women to have seen him first (Matt. 28:9).[26] In
Luke 24:9–10, Luke again highlights the importance of Mary Magdalene,
not only by naming her but also by naming her first among the women. At
the same time, however, Luke notes that the "eleven and all the rest" did not
believe what the women said (v. 11), which may have influenced some of the
later "rivalry" stories involving Mary Magdalene.

The Johannine account of Mary Magdalene's interactions with the risen
Jesus is particularly noteworthy. After somewhat abruptly noting that Mary
is back at the tomb in 20:11, John narrates her encounter with the resurrected
Jesus, whom she initially does not recognize (v. 14). After Jesus asks her the
same question the angels had asked ("Woman, why are you weeping?" [vv. 13,
15]) and follows it with "Whom are you seeking?" Mary Magdalene reveals
that she thinks Jesus is a gardener who may have moved Jesus's body and
asks him to tell her where it is so that she may take it away. The key exchange
occurs in verse 16, where Jesus's reply is simply "Mary," at which point Mary
Magdalene recognizes Jesus and exclaims "Rabbouni."[27] Mary is then given a
message to give to the disciples (v. 17), to whom she announces, "I have seen
the Lord," and then relates his words (v. 18). This encounter likely inspired
numerous elements of her depiction in the apocryphal Gospels and other

24. In John the women are not mentioned at the burial of Jesus, and it appears that it is
Nicodemus who functions as the witness to this event (John 19:38–42).
25. Though John mentions only Mary Magdalene in v. 1, in v. 2 she tells Peter and the Beloved
Disciple, "*We* do not know where they have laid him" [emphasis added], which may mean that
she was not alone at the tomb.
26. Mark does not recount an appearance of the risen Christ to the women, and Mark 16:8 states
that they did not say anything to anyone out of fear. Luke also does not record an appearance
to the women but recounts that they went and told what they had seen and heard at the empty
tomb "to the eleven and all the rest" (Luke 24:9).
27. There is a rather clear echo of John 10:3 here, where the Shepherd calls his own sheep by
name and the sheep hear/recognize his voice.

second-century "gnostic" texts discussed earlier. In any case, by the conclusion of the passion and resurrection accounts, the New Testament Gospels have established Mary Magdalene as present at Jesus's death, at his burial, and at his resurrection. In this way she serves as an eyewitness to key events confessed in the church: Jesus died, was buried, and rose again.

The Bethany Family (Martha, Mary, and Lazarus)

Though only John indicates that Martha, Mary, and Lazarus were from Bethany (John 11:1), it is generally recognized that these are the same Martha and Mary from an account in Luke (Luke 10:38–42). At the same time, however, Luke does not mention their brother Lazarus, and this fact has raised numerous historical questions about John's account and this family.[28] It is also John's account that tells us of the affinity that Jesus had for this family with the statement "Jesus loved Martha and her sister and Lazarus" (John 11:5). When considering these individuals, as was the case with Mary Magdalene, we find in early Christian traditions several texts that are interesting—if not nearly as extensive and not, till now, the object of even a fraction of the attention given to those dealing with Mary Magdalene.[29]

Historical Considerations: The Bethany Family outside the New Testament Gospels

The same two primary sources for traditions and teachings outside the New Testament Gospels concerning Mary Magdalene are also those for the Bethany family: the church fathers and noncanonical Gospels/writings.

Church Fathers

The best-known patristic interpretations of the account of Martha and Mary in Luke 10:38–42 see the two women as representing different kinds or levels of piety.[30] Origen (ca. 185–254 CE), for example, stated, "You might reasonably take Martha to stand for action and Mary for contemplation. For, the mystery of love is lost to the active life, unless one directs [one's] teaching and [one's] exhortation to action, toward contemplation."[31] For Origen, Martha's life is clearly problematic on its own and must be directed toward

---

28. See n. 44.

29. For a recent monograph on Martha see Allie M. Ernst, *Martha from the Margins: The Authority of Martha in Early Christian Tradition*, VCSup 98 (Leiden: Brill, 2009).

30. For the patristic exegesis of this passage in the first four centuries CE, see Daniel A. Csányi, "Optima Pars: Die Auslegungsgeschichte von Luke 10, 38–42 bei den Kirchenvätern der ersten vier Jahrhunderte," *StudMon* 2 (1960): 5–78.

31. Origen, *frg.* 171, in *Homilies on Luke; Fragments on Luke*, trans. J. T. Lienhard, Fathers of the Church 94 (Washington, DC: Catholic University of America Press, 1996).

Mary's. Seeing in them slightly different emphases, Augustine (early fifth century CE) stated that in these two women "two lives are figured, the life present, and the life to come, the life of labour, and the life of quiet, the life of sorrow, and the life of blessedness, the life temporal, and the life eternal. . . . In Martha was the image of things present, in Mary of things to come. What Martha was doing, that we are now; what Mary was doing, that we hope for."[32] In fact, he explicitly noted that both women were pleasing to the Lord and that both lives are praiseworthy. For Augustine, Martha and Mary are simply representatives of different phases in the Christian life.

Many church fathers also refer to the raising of Lazarus in John 11, though they at times paint quite different portraits of members of the Bethany family.[33] Origen, for example, in his *Commentary on John*, begins his comments on 11:41 by highlighting the "delay" in the moving of the stone.[34] Jesus commands the stone to be removed in verse 39, but Martha's protest that there will be a stench hinders its immediate removal. Origen understood Jesus to be rebuking Martha's unbelief in verse 40, and offers his opinion that someone intervening between a command of Jesus and its accomplishment should not be called an "imitator of Christ" (*Comm. Jo.* 28.18). On the other hand, Cyril of Jerusalem (ca. 313–387 CE), in his *Catecheses*, presents an argument for how one is saved by the faith of another. The example he uses to make his case is that Lazarus was dead, but that the faith that was lacking in the dead man was supplied by his sisters. When Jesus says, "Did I not tell you that *if you believed*, you would see the glory of God" (v. 40; emphasis added), the faith of *both* Mary and Martha is strong enough to recall their dead brother from the doors of hades (*Catecheses* 5.9).

Two particularly interesting traditions are found in the *Commentary on the Song of Songs*, attributed to Hippolytus (second–third century CE). First, though in the biblical account it is Mary who anoints Jesus (see John 12:3), Hippolytus referred to *Martha* having done the anointing. Second, in a comment on part of Song of Songs 3:1 ("at night I sought him whom my soul loves"), Hippolytus states, "See this is fulfilled in Martha and Mary."[35] As Hippolytus continues, it is clear that he sees this fulfillment in the Gospel narratives when the women go to seek Jesus at the tomb, and therefore he places Martha and Mary at the tomb. In addition, in *In Canticum canticorum* 25.2

---

32. Augustine, *Sermon* 54.4 (*NPNF*[1] 6:430).

33. For an interesting discussion of the raising of Lazarus in early Christian art, see Philip E. Esler and Ronald Piper, *Lazarus, Mary and Martha: Social Scientific Approaches to the Gospel of John* (Minneapolis: Fortress, 2006), 131–45.

34. Unfortunately, Origin's comments on John 8:53–11:38, which correspond to books 21–27 of the commentary, are lost. Thus, we are able to access Origen's comments only on the final events in the narrative of the raising of Lazarus.

35. Hippolytus, *In Cant.* 24.2, quoted in Yancy Warren Smith, "Hippolytus' Commentary on the Song of Songs in Social and Critical Context" (PhD diss., Texas Christian University, 2009).

Martha and Mary are said to have witnessed and recognized the risen Christ when he said, "'Martha, Mary' and they said 'Rabbouni,'"[36] and in 25.6 it appears that Martha and Mary are the women who are called "apostles to the apostles." Though an error or confusion on the part of Hippolytus cannot be excluded,[37] there is another tradition in a noncanonical text listing Martha as a resurrection witness.

A Noncanonical "Epistle"

In the *Epistle to the Apostles*, a mid- to late second-century polemical document combating "gnosticism" and purporting to have been written by the apostles to all the churches,[38] Martha again plays a significant role in the account of Jesus's resurrection. The Ethiopic text names the three women who went to the tomb to anoint Jesus as "Sarah, Martha, and Mary Magdalene" (*Ep. Apos.* 9).[39] When Jesus appeared to the women, according to the Coptic text he said, "But let one of you go to your brothers and say, 'Come, the Master has risen from the dead,'" and then the disciples who received her message said, "Martha came and told it to us" (*Ep. Apos.* 10).[40] The inclusion of Martha in both instances is at the very least noteworthy, even if the reason for this inclusion is debated.[41]

Narrative Considerations: The Bethany Family inside the New Testament Gospels

Having considered elements of the portrayal of members of the Bethany family outside of the New Testament Gospels, it is now important to give

36. This scene clearly parallels John 20:16, though, as was seen above, Jesus there is in conversation with Mary Magdalene and only says "Mary."

37. Ernst also rightly notes, "It is possible that Hippolytus has fused Mary Magdalene with Mary of Bethany, but such fusion should be argued rather than assumed" (*Martha from the Margins*, 99n6). Even if this "fusion" has occurred, however, the presence of Martha is still noteworthy.

38. Originally written in Greek, the text is extant only in an Ethiopic and fragmentary Coptic translation. For an introduction and English translation, see Ron Cameron, ed., *The Other Gospels: Non-Canonical Gospel Texts* (Philadelphia: Westminster, 1982), 131–62; or J. K. Elliott, ed., *The Apocryphal New Testament: A Collection of Apocryphal Christian Literature in an English Translation* (Oxford: Oxford University Press, 1993), 555–88. Citations here are taken from the translation found in the former volume.

39. The Coptic text refers to them as "Mary, she who belonged to Martha, and Mary [Magd] alene." That there may be a textual problem here is revealed by the text shortly thereafter, where it recounts "the Lord" speaking to "Mary and also to her sisters" (*Ep. Apos.* 11), which would imply at least three women.

40. The Ethiopic text says, "And Mary came to us and told us," a reading that may have arisen due to the influence of the canonical accounts.

41. Depictions of Mary and Martha as present at the resurrection are also found in liturgy, hymnody, and iconography. For discussion of these texts and images see Ernst, *Martha from the Margins*, 119–75.

attention to their portrayal within the New Testament Gospels. Members of
the Bethany family, as mentioned above, appear in Luke and John.

Luke 10:38–42

Questioning the traditional reading of this passage mentioning Martha and
Mary, feminist interpreters have subjected it to extensive scrutiny.[42] Nevertheless, John Collins's observation that the text most naturally sketches a scene of
a guest in a home where one woman is busy with preparing a meal and the other
is seated at the guest's feet listening to what he is saying is likely correct.[43] As
noted earlier, another issue with this text is that it does not mention Lazarus,
Martha and Mary's brother.[44] At the outset it may be stated, however, that
simply because Lazarus is not mentioned in this account is not an argument
against his historicity. As Richard Bauckham notes, "In Gospel pericopes as
brief and focussed as Luke 10:38–42, extraneous details unnecessary to the
story are not to be expected."[45]

Though Mary is clearly important in the narrative, Luke does not mention
her in verse 38, stating instead that "a woman named Martha welcomed him
[Jesus] into her home." Since Luke mentions Martha first and identifies the
house as hers, it is likely that she is the older sister.[46] Verse 39 begins with the
introduction of Mary as Martha's sister and immediately indicates that she
"sat at the Lord's feet and listened to what he was saying." It is significant
that Mary's posture here reveals her position as a female disciple of Jesus,
for, particularly in Luke, to listen to Jesus's words is central to discipleship
(e.g., Luke 6:47; 8:11, 21; 11:28).[47] Martha, however, distracted by her many

42. For a presentation of the feminist reading of this passage, see Elisabeth Schüssler Fiorenza,
But She Said: Feminist Practices of Biblical Interpretation (Boston: Beacon, 1992), 51–76.

43. John N. Collins, "Did Luke Intend a Disservice to Women in the Martha and Mary
Story?" *BTB* 28 (1998): 110.

44. Esler and Piper, for example, see an "obvious stumbling-block to his [Lazarus's] historical
existence" because in Luke 10:38–42 Martha and Mary "apparently had no living brother"
(*Lazarus, Mary and Martha*, 76).

45. Bauckham, *Testimony of the Beloved Disciple*, 178. Building on Gerd Theissen's idea of
"protective anonymity," Bauckham goes on to make the case that the silence of the Synoptics
concerning Lazarus may be explained by the need to protect him in the early Jerusalem church's
life (*Testimony*, 181–89).

46. Though Martha is here said to own a home, and Mary, in John 12:3, anoints Jesus with
a large amount of "costly perfume," the Bethany family need not have been wealthy or among
the privileged few (see Satoko Yamaguchi, *Mary and Martha: Women in the World of Jesus*
[New York: Orbis, 2002], 132–35).

47. On this discipleship theme, from slightly different perspectives, see Adele Reinhartz, "From
Narrative to History: The Resurrection of Mary and Martha," in *"Women like This": New
Perspectives on Jewish Women in the Greco-Roman World*, SBLEJL 1 (Atlanta: Scholars Press,
1991), 163–72, and Ben Witherington III, *Women in the Ministry of Jesus: A Study of Jesus's
Attitudes to Women and their Roles as Reflected in His Earthly Life*, SNTSMS 51 (Cambridge:
Cambridge University Press, 1984), 100–103.

tasks and distraught that she has been left alone to do all the work of serving, appeals to Jesus to tell her sister to help (v. 40).

In verses 41–42, Jesus begins his response to Martha's request with a sympathetic, though perhaps somewhat chiding, "Martha, Martha." Although the exact phrasing of Jesus's reply is textually uncertain,[48] it is clear he is not harshly rebuking Martha, merely indicating that her concern is misplaced. That which Mary has chosen is "the better part, which will not be taken away from her" (v. 42). The point is not the elevation of the "contemplative life" over the "active life," nor is the contrast between Martha's "service" (i.e., the active leadership of a woman) and Mary's "listening" (i.e., the passive role of a woman). It is rather an issue of hospitality and the type of welcome that Jesus seeks, a contrast between "worried" distraction and "listening to Jesus's word."[49] That is, Luke presents Jesus as seeking to help his friends Martha and Mary understand that when he is welcomed into a home he does not desire intense busyness in domestic activity in preparation for a meal, but rather an attendance to his words.[50] Thus, Luke understands the story in a spiritual sense, that is, as Jesus commending Mary for listening to his teaching and not allowing Martha, who is distracted by excessively elaborate preparations for a meal, to deprive Mary of the opportunity to hear his word.[51]

JOHN 11:1–44

Though commentators have differed on whether John 11 is the climax of the first half of John's Gospel, the opening of the second half, or both, it is quite clear that this fascinating chapter marks a turning point in the narrative, not least because John presents the raising of Lazarus as the reason for the Sanhedrin resolving to put Jesus to death (John 11:45–53; cf. John 12:9–11, 17). For present purposes, however, I will focus particularly on the presentation of the Bethany family, whom John introduces in 11:1–2 as Mary, her sister Martha, and Lazarus their brother.[52] Interestingly, verse 2 speaks of this Mary as the one who anointed Jesus *before* the account of this anointing is given in John 12:1–8.[53] It is likely that Mary was mentioned first because John

---

48. For discussion of the textual variants, see Marshall, *Luke*, 452–53.

49. The NRSV's "listened to what he was saying" in v. 39 is literally "was listening to his word."

50. So also Joel B. Green, *The Theology of the Gospel of Luke* (Cambridge: Cambridge University Press, 1995), 433–34.

51. See Marshall, *Luke*, 450–51.

52. Concerning the appearance of a Lazarus in the parable in Luke 16:19–31, Barnabas Lindars is likely correct in concluding, "The connection with the parable of the rich man and Lazarus seems very remote; John's telling of this story is in no way indebted to this parable" (*The Gospel of John*, NCB [London: Oliphant, Marshall, Morgan and Scott, 1972], 385).

53. For discussion and an argument that the curious explanatory gloss is intended for readers of John who are familiar with the anointing narrative in Mark 14:3–9, see Richard Bauckham, "John for Readers of Mark," in *The Gospels for all Christians: Rethinking the*

had a further identification for her; however, in verse 5 the order is reversed, with Martha coming first and Mary simply identified as "her sister," possibly suggesting that Martha will have the principal role in the following account.[54] Indeed, as Jesus approaches, it is Martha who goes out to meet him, leaving Mary in the house (v. 20). Martha engages Jesus with words of grief that, according to some commentators, contain overtones of reproach and three times confesses elements of her faith (vv. 22, 24, and 27). The brief exchange climaxes with the fifth "I am" statement of Jesus (vv. 25–26a), Jesus's question, "Do you believe this?" (v. 26b), and Martha's affirmative response (v. 27). Martha, however, does not simply say, "Yes, I believe," but rather goes on to make a confession of the identity of Jesus, stating, "Yes, Lord, I believe that you are the Messiah, the Son of God, the one coming into the world." Though elements of this confession have appeared as statements earlier in John (see 1:29, 41; 6:14), and Peter also made a "confession of faith" in John 6:69, it is noteworthy that Martha's words here are very similar to those used to describe the faith that this Gospel is intended to elicit (see 20:31). There is therefore good reason to see John giving Martha and her confession a role ascribed to Peter in the synoptic tradition.[55]

Martha then returns to the house and tells Mary "privately" that Jesus is calling for her. Mary thus goes out to meet Jesus and, falling at his feet, utters the same first words as Martha: "Lord, if you had been here, my brother would not have died" (v. 32). Here, however, there is no ensuing discussion— no statement of faith, no revelation from Jesus, no confession of faith. Yet it would be wrong to read a disparaging depiction of Mary into the brevity of the exchange.[56] It is Mary's tears that "greatly disturb" Jesus in spirit and deeply move him to shed his own tears (11:35).

Martha reappears in the narrative in verse 39, at Lazarus's tomb, when she protests the removal of the stone because of the stench. Whether Martha's words reflect a deficiency in her faith or not, her hesitation provides Jesus with the opportunity to remind her, "Did I not tell you that if you believed, you would see the glory of God?" (v. 40). After this brief delay, Jesus's prayer, and

Gospel Audiences, ed. Richard Bauckham (Edinburgh: T&T Clark; Grand Rapids: Eerdmans, 1998), 161–69.

54. So Gérard Rochais, *Les récits de resurrection des morts dans le Nouveau Testament*, SNTSMS 40 (Cambridge: Cambridge University Press, 1981), 118, who sees the Evangelist in this chapter expressing his theological considerations through Martha. John 11:19 also identifies the sisters as "Martha and Mary."

55. This ascription need not, however, be intended as polemical against Peter or his traditional position but rather may be supplemental. For helpful comments see Raymond E. Brown, "Roles of Women in the Fourth Gospel," *TS* 36 (1975): 693.

56. This is done by Rudolf Schnackenburg, for example, when he states, "Mary gives the impression of being nothing but a complaining woman" (*The Gospel according to St. John*, trans. Kevin Smyth, David Smith, and G. A. Kon, 3 vols., HTKNT [London: Burns and Oates, 1968–1982], 2:333).

The "I Am" Statements in John

Jesus makes seven statements in the Gospel of John that are referred to as the "I am" statements:

1. "I am the bread of life" (John 6:35, 48);
2. "I am the light of the world" (John 8:12; 9:5);
3. "I am the gate" (John 10:7, 9);
4. "I am the good shepherd" (John 10:11, 14);
5. "I am the resurrection and the life" (John 11:25);
6. "I am the way, and the truth, and the life" (John 14:6); and
7. "I am the true vine" (John 15:1).

Each of these statements reveals an important element of the Johannine Christology.

his command for Lazarus to come forth, Lazarus exits the tomb in verse 44. It may be observed that Jesus's words indicate that Lazarus must be unbound and freed from his graveclothes by others, a reality that will not apply to Jesus (cf. John 20:5–7).[57]

JOHN 12:1–8

In John 12:1, Jesus is said to have returned to Bethany, identified as the place where Jesus had raised Lazarus from the dead. A dinner was given for Jesus, at which Martha served, and Lazarus is specifically mentioned as one of those at the table. Mary is then said to have taken costly perfume and "anointed Jesus's feet, and wiped them with her hair" (v. 3).[58] For the reader familiar with Luke's account, the depiction of the actions of Martha and Mary would remind him or her of the similar picture of the roles taken in Luke 10:38–42. At the same time, here there is no dialogue between Jesus and Martha and no sense that any difficulties arise from Martha's serving. The narrative focuses instead on the anointing and its results. These verses do not give Mary's own perspective on the action. Jesus, however, in his rebuke of Judas, who expressed disapproval of Mary's action, sees in her act a devoted expression of preparation for his burial (v. 7).

57. Thus, R. Alan Culpepper concludes, "His [Lazarus's] is not a resurrection like Jesus's . . . for he is still bound by the grave clothes" (*Anatomy of the Fourth Gospel: A Study in Literary Design*, FF [Philadelphia: Fortress, 1983], 141).

58. There are several accounts of an anointing by a woman in the Gospels, but only here is the woman named (cf. John 12:1–8 with Mark 14:3–9//Matthew 26:6–13; and Luke 7:36–38). There are numerous challenges in attempting to ascertain the relationship(s) between these accounts. For discussion, see Raymond E. Brown, *The Gospel according to John*, 2 vols., AB 29 and 29A (Garden City, NY: Doubleday, 1966–1970), 1:449–52.

Anointing

There are numerous Old Testament examples of Israelite kings being designated through a ritual anointing on the head by a prophet, for example, Samuel anointing Saul (1 Sam. 10:1) and then David (1 Sam. 16:13) or Elisha anointing Jehu (2 Kings 9:1–3, 6). The Hebrew word *māšîaḥ* and the Greek word *christos* both mean "anointed one," and a "messiah" or "christ" is therefore someone who is considered to have been specially anointed by God. Christians believe Jesus to be *the* Christ in a unique way as the Son of God (see Matt. 16:16; John 11:27). Interestingly, in the New Testament Gospels there is an account of Jesus being anointed on the head (Mark 14:3–9//Matt. 26:6–13), as would be expected, and an account of his feet being anointed (John 12:3–8), where the anointing is understood by Jesus as an anointing for his burial.[1] A further passage in Luke 7:36–50 also recounts an anointing of Jesus's feet, though here the narrative focuses on the issue of forgiveness and the response to having received it.

1. Though the anointing of feet may not have been common, it is not unheard of in antiquity (see Witherington, *Women in the Ministry of Jesus*, 113).

The Beloved Disciple

The Gospel of John's "disciple whom Jesus loved" is as cryptic as he is significant. There have been many suggestions for the identity of this disciple, ranging from viewing him as a fictitious or symbolical figure to positing him as a real figure identified as John the son of Zebedee (the traditional view), or Matthias, or Apollos, or Paul, or Judas Iscariot, or Andrew, or Philip, or Thomas, or Lazarus, or John the Elder, or the rich young ruler, or Mary Magdalene, or any number of other figures.[59] Though the testimony of some of the church fathers concerning the identity of this disciple will be noted, rather than entering into the thorny debate of identifying the Beloved Disciple, I will focus on understanding the role of this disciple in the Gospel of John.

Historical Considerations: The Beloved Disciple outside the New Testament Gospels

James Charlesworth rightly notes that several individuals who were "highly influential in early Christianity, identified the Beloved Disciple with John the son

59. James Charlesworth's extensive, though by no means exhaustive, review of scholarly suggestions concerning this disciple's identity runs to nearly one hundred pages (*The Beloved Disciple: Whose Witness Validates the Gospel of John?* [Valley Forge: Trinity Press International, 1995], 127–224).

of Zebedee."[60] Two such individuals were Irenaeus of Lyon (ca. 125–200 CE) and Tertullian (ca. 155–225 CE). At the outset of book 3 of his work *Against Heresies*, Irenaeus argues that the gospel of Jesus is handed down in the Scriptures, and after referring to Matthew, Mark, and Luke, writes, "Afterwards, John, the disciple of the Lord, who also had leaned upon His breast, did himself publish a Gospel during his residence at Ephesus in Asia."[61] Irenaeus continues by listing a few teachings that in his estimation are the core of the Scriptures and argues that if anyone rejects these teachings, "he despises the companions of the Lord; nay more, he despises Christ Himself the Lord; yea, he despises the Father also."[62] Thus, for Irenaeus, rejecting the teaching of the Gospel of John is rejecting a companion of Jesus, and by extension, rejecting Jesus and the Father as well.

In Tertullian's own arguments against "heretics," he often appealed to the "rule of faith" that the apostles faithfully received and transmitted to the church. Though recognizing that it could be objected that the apostles did not know all things pertaining to the faith or to doctrine, Tertullian asked whether anything was "concealed from John, the Lord's most beloved disciple, who used to lean on His breast to whom alone the Lord pointed Judas out as the traitor, whom He commended to Mary as a son in His own stead?"[63] For Tertullian the apostolic identity and beloved status of John is part of what guarantees the completeness and veracity of the church's teachings.

Narrative Considerations: The Beloved Disciple inside the New Testament Gospels

Six passages in the Gospel of John refer to the "disciple whom Jesus loved": 13:21–26; 19:26–27; 20:1–10; 21:1–14; 21:20–23; and 21:24.[64] It is also generally recognized that the Beloved Disciple is in view in John 19:35, though the identification of this disciple as the anonymous disciple in 1:35–40 and/or 18:15–16 is more debated.[65] In any case, John first refers explicitly to the Beloved Disciple in the context of Jesus declaring that one of the Twelve will betray him (John 13:21). It is worth noting that what is said about this

---

60. Charlesworth, *Beloved Disciple*, 394. Charlesworth provides an overview of advocates for this view on pp. 394–99.

61. Irenaeus of Lyon, *Haer.* 3.1.1 (*ANF* 1:414).

62. Irenaeus of Lyon, *Haer.* 3.1.2 (*ANF* 1:415).

63. Tertullian, *Praescr.* 22.4 (*ANF* 3:253).

64. Interestingly, in 13:23; 19:26; 21:7; 21:20; and 21:20 the Greek is *hon ēgapa*; however, in 20:2 it is *hon ephilei*. Most scholars conclude that no distinction should be made on the basis of the use of different verbs for "love."

65. On these two passages, see Frans Neirynck, "The Anonymous Disciple in John 1," *ETL* 66 (1990): 5–37, and idem, "The 'Other Disciple' in John 18:15–16," *ETL* 51 (1975): 113–41.

disciple first is *not* that he is the one whom Jesus loved;[66] rather, the Evangelist first notes the position of this disciple. The mention of him reclining *en tō kolpō* ("on the bosom of Jesus") echoes the phrase describing Jesus as *eis ton kolpon* ("in the bosom of the Father") in John 1:18. This description of the disciple, therefore, points to the idea that just as Jesus's close fellowship with the Father allows Jesus to reveal the Father, the Beloved Disciple's close fellowship with Jesus allows that disciple to reveal Jesus.[67] Second, it is significant that this disciple is introduced in order to identify the one to whom Peter motions, the one who will ask Jesus which disciple he was speaking about. Nearly all of the subsequent appearances of the Beloved Disciple also involve Peter, a point to which I will return below.

In John 19:25–27, the Beloved Disciple is near the cross with Mary, Jesus's mother. Jesus says, "Woman, here is your son," and, "Here is your mother," again likely revealing a particularly close relationship with Jesus. In 20:1–10, John recounts the "race" of the Beloved Disciple and Peter to Jesus's tomb, where the former runs more quickly and arrives at the tomb first (v. 4). He looks into the tomb and sees the linen wrappings; however, he does not go inside (v. 5). Peter, on the other hand, arrives second at the tomb but enters it first (v. 6). No response by Peter to what he sees is mentioned, but when the Beloved Disciple enters the tomb he not only sees but also believes (v. 8). It is also the Beloved Disciple who, as he and six other disciples fish on the Sea of Tiberias, recognizes Jesus on the shore and says to Peter, "It is the Lord!" (21:7).[68] Finally, at the end of chapter 21 there are two further references to the disciple whom Jesus loved. In John 21:20–23, Peter inquires about the fate of the Beloved Disciple, and the explanatory comment in verse 23 is often interpreted as revealing that the Beloved Disciple had recently died. In verse 24, the Gospel of John draws to a close on the note that it is the Beloved Disciple who bore witness to these things and who wrote them, and that his witness is true. The very similar language of John 19:35 and 21:24 seems to confirm the view that it is also the Beloved Disciple in the former

66. The NRSV has brought this description, found at the end of the verse in Greek, forward in its translation.

67. Unfortunately, the renderings of these two verses in most English translations do not reveal the verbal parallels; nevertheless, the point is often mentioned in commentaries and is found as early as Origen. At the same time, however, one should not overemphasize this parallel, as John uses a different, but synonymous, expression in v. 25 by referring to this disciple as reclining *epi to stēthos* ("upon the breast of Jesus"). See also the caution by Ismo Dunderberg, *The Beloved Disciple in Conflict? Revisiting the Gospels of John and Thomas* (Oxford: Oxford University Press, 2006), 143–44, against pushing the analogy too far.

68. Chapter 21 of John's Gospel is often viewed as an appendix to a Gospel originally ending at 20:31; however, Paul S. Minear has argued that the chapter always was a crucial part of the design of the text ("The Original Functions of John 21," *JBL* 102 [1983]: 85–98). Bauckham also points out that though chapter 21 could be regarded as an epilogue, "an epilogue need not be an afterthought: it may be integral to the design of the work" (*Testimony*, 78).

verse who witnessed the spear thrust and the blood and water coming out of Jesus's side.

An interesting question to consider is why John's Gospel presents the Beloved Disciple in these passages and in this manner. Culpepper rightly notes, "The Beloved Disciple regularly appears in scenes where he is given some priority or advantage over Peter."[69] The Beloved Disciple is apparently able to ask Jesus a question that Peter cannot (John 13:24); he sees *and believes*, whereas Peter only sees (John 20:6–8); and he recognizes Jesus and informs Peter of Jesus's identity (John 21:7). Thus, a common view is that the Beloved Disciple represents a model for others as the "ideal disciple."[70] Bauckham, however, has argued that, though the Beloved Disciple does sometimes function in this way, as do others in the Fourth Gospel, "such a function cannot satisfactorily account for most of what is said about him."[71]

Andrew T. Lincoln draws attention to the Beloved Disciple's "function of being a key witness to significant moments in the last part of Jesus' ministry: the announcement of the identity of the betrayer (13:23–26), the meaning of the death [in 19:35–37], the significance of the empty tomb (20:8) and the recognition of the risen Lord (21:7)."[72] It is not so much that the Beloved Disciple is modeling something for others; indeed, in the passages explicitly mentioning him he seems to have "an exclusive privilege that is precisely not representative."[73] Rather, John's Gospel presents the disciple whom Jesus loved in such a way that by 21:24 the attribution of the written testimony to the Beloved Disciple is an attribution to one who is the "ideal witness" or the "ideal author."[74] Thus, the Beloved Disciple is given superiority to Peter, who through failure and restoration becomes a "shepherd" of the church (John 21:15–17), but only in ways that qualify the Beloved Disciple as the true and trustworthy witness to Jesus.

69. R. Alan Culpepper, *John, the Son of Zebedee: The Life of a Legend* (Columbia: University of South Carolina Press, 1994; repr. Minneapolis: Fortress, 2000), 62.

70. Brendan Byrne, for example, speaks of the faith of the Beloved Disciple as "both precursive and typical of that of later generations of believers" ("The Faith of the Beloved Disciple and the Community in John 20," *JSNT* 23 [1985]: 83). See also Kevin Quast, *Peter and the Beloved Disciple: Figures for a Community in Crisis*, JSNTSup 32 (Sheffield: JSOT Press, 1989), 162.

71. Bauckham, *Testimony of the Beloved Disciple*, 82. The difficulties of the "ideal disciple" view are discussed by Bauckham on pp. 82–84. See also Bauckham's earlier discussion, "The Beloved Disciple as Ideal Author," *JSNT* 49 (1993): 21–44, and Dunderberg, *Beloved Disciple*, 128–48.

72. Andrew T. Lincoln, "The Beloved Disciple as Eyewitness and the Fourth Gospel as Witness," *JSNT* 24 (2002): 13.

73. Bauckham, *Testimony of the Beloved Disciple*, 83.

74. The former term is used by Lincoln ("The Beloved Disciple," 11), and the latter by Bauckham (*Testimony*, 75). See also David R. Beck, who refers to the Beloved Disciple as "the witness par excellence to Jesus" (*The Discipleship Paradigm: Readers and Anonymous Characters in the Fourth Gospel*, Biblical Interpretation Series 27 [Leiden: Brill, 1997], 120).

Conclusion

Mary Magdalene, the Bethany family, and the Beloved Disciple all contribute to the picture of Jesus that emerges from the New Testament Gospels and from early Christian communities. Mary Magdalene functions in all four Gospels as a disciple of Jesus and a vital witness to the events of Jesus's passion and resurrection. Her place in the New Testament then becomes a springboard for numerous traditions about her in noncanonical texts. Jesus's interactions with Martha and Mary and, in John, with Lazarus provide Jesus with opportunities to teach about true discipleship, the resurrection, and spiritual life. It is also the raising of Lazarus that John identifies as setting the Jewish leadership on the path to seeking the death of Jesus, and it is the anointing by Mary that Jesus interpreted as preparatory for his burial. Finally, the Beloved Disciple is the figure for the Fourth Gospel who is present at key moments in Jesus's ministry and who, as a uniquely qualified witness, is presented as providing true and trustworthy witness of the life and ministry of Jesus. Undoubtedly, the narratives and traditions surrounding these friends of Jesus provide a richness to the depictions of Jesus found within and outside of the New Testament that would otherwise be lacking. As such, these friends rightly deserve attention and study when considering the person and influence of Jesus.

Suggestions for Further Reading

Bauckham, Richard. *The Testimony of the Beloved Disciple: Narrative, History, and Theology in the Gospel of John*. Grand Rapids: Baker Academic, 2007.

Charlesworth, James. *The Beloved Disciple: Whose Witness Validates the Gospel of John?* Valley Forge, PA: Trinity Press International, 1995.

Culpepper, R. Alan. *John, the Son of Zebedee: The Life of a Legend*. Columbia: University of South Carolina Press, 1994. Repr., Minneapolis: Fortress, 2000.

Ehrman, Bart. *Peter, Paul, and Mary Magdalene: The Followers of Jesus in History and Legend*. Oxford: Oxford University Press, 2006.

Ernst, Allie M. *Martha from the Margins: The Authority of Martha in Early Christian Tradition*. VCSup 98. Leiden: Brill, 2009.

Esler, Philip E., and Ronald Piper. *Lazarus, Mary, and Martha: Social Scientific Approaches to the Gospel of John*. Minneapolis: Fortress, 2006.

Marjanen, Antti. *The Woman Jesus Loved: Mary Magdalene in the Nag Hammadi Library and Related Documents*. NHMS 40. Leiden: Brill, 1996.

Witherington, Ben, III. *Women in the Ministry of Jesus: A Study of Jesus's Attitudes to Women and their Roles as Reflected in His Earthly Life*. SNTSMS 51. Cambridge: Cambridge University Press, 1984.

6

Secret Disciples

Nicodemus and Joseph of Arimathea

David M. Allen

The relationships of many Gospel figures with Jesus tend to be fairly self-evident. Whether they are portrayed as Jesus's friends and followers (loyal or otherwise) or as his enemies, those openly in opposition against him, it is normally straightforward to discern upon which side of the proverbial fence they sit. Some characters have a more ambiguous or undefined relationship, however; they lurk in somewhat more muddied territory, and it remains unclear exactly how they relate to Jesus and thus whether they should be counted as his "friend" or "enemy." It is not that they necessarily adopt a neutral position but rather that the Evangelists' depiction may be insufficient for one to be confident either way, and so the reader is left to ponder further as to the precise nature of the relationship.

The enigmatic young man of Mark 14:51–52 might be such a candidate. Even though he is said to be "following Jesus," his continued anonymity and absence from the other Synoptic accounts leaves the full extent of his relationship with Jesus unresolved. The matter is further colored by the young man's flight from the Gethsemane arrest scene. What happened to this "follower-cum-deserter," and what ultimately came of his relationship with Jesus? A more substantive example might be Simon of Cyrene, the apparently innocent passerby coerced into the role of mysterious cross bearer in the Synoptic accounts (Mark 15:21;

Matt. 27:32; Luke 23:26). Unlike the Markan young man, Simon is named by the Synoptic Gospel writers,[1] but his characterization remains somewhat mysterious. Although charged with a significant role in the Passion Narrative, Simon disappears from the Gospel accounts as soon as he arrives, perhaps mentioned because of the original readers' acquaintance with his sons.[2]

Similarly enigmatic characters are Nicodemus and Joseph of Arimathea, two other figures whose portrayal in the canonical narratives leaves the reader uncertain as to their status vis-à-vis Jesus. At one level, they are contrasting figures; canonically speaking, one is known only to John, while the other is that rarity, a figure beyond the Twelve who appears in all four Gospel accounts. Joseph's role in the Passion Narrative is almost as brief as that of Simon of Cyrene, while Nicodemus's head rises sporadically across the Johannine account. Despite their different "billing," both are interesting examples of the ambiguous persona, for they are also potentially significant people within the Jerusalem hierarchy. So as well as being apparently enigmatic or unusual figures, they may also serve to reflect Jesus's impact on certain significant, powerful Jews.

Nicodemus and Joseph become particularly entwined in John's account of Jesus's burial (19:38–42), and such intertwining continues within later Christian tradition. An interesting, if belated, portrayal of their evolving association is Michelangelo's Florence *Pietà*. The piece depicts four figures, three of whom are Mary Magdalene, the Virgin Mary, and Jesus himself. The fourth figure has traditionally been understood to be Nicodemus but could well be viewed as Joseph, and some have even ventured that this large figure—the Joseph/Nicodemus persona—represents Michelangelo himself.[3] Whatever the precise identification, the sculpture's evocative association of Joseph/Nicodemus with the body of Jesus, alongside other "supportive" figures like the two Marys, seemingly endorses the view that they were all his allies, friends tending to him in his postmortem state. The rest of this chapter will test out Michelangelo's assumption, examining whether the historical record, or the testimony of the canonical Gospels, supports such a conclusion.

Historical Considerations: Nicodemus outside the Canonical Gospels

Attempts to uncover or discern the "historical Nicodemus" have generally been greeted with some degree of skepticism. Because the figure appears only in

1. In John's account, Jesus notably carries his own cross (John 19:17).
2. On the historicity, or otherwise, of Simon of Cyrene, see William John Lyons, "The Hermeneutics of Fictional Black and Factual Red: The Markan Simon of Cyrene and the Quest for the Historical Jesus," *JSHJ* 4 (2006): 139–54.
3. See the discussion in Moshe Arkin, "'One of the Marys . . .': An Interdisciplinary Analysis of Michelangelo's Florentine Pieta," *The Art Bulletin* 79 (1997): 493–517.

the Gospel of John, and not in the Synoptic accounts, some scholars consider him to be merely a convenient literary creation, a typical "character" within the Johannine cast that suits John's literary purposes but lacks any particular historical referent. Just like the (unnamed) Samaritan woman at the well, or the revivified Lazarus, Nicodemus has been dismissed as a figurative means by which John might, for example, address insufficient or inadequate faith.[4] Such characterization would normally tend to negate any historical interest and permits Nicodemus to disappear into the proverbial literary sunset. But since he appears at several points in the Gospel account, in contrast to the other supposed symbolic figures whose respective roles are generally confined to one unit of John's discourse, attempts to reduce him to merely literary status are less compelling than they might otherwise seem.

The absence of Nicodemus from noncanonical Christian literature, however, until relatively late in the tradition, compounds the suspicion that he lacks any historical reference. Attempts to locate him in earlier texts remain unpersuasive. The content of Nicodemus's "confession" of Jesus's origins (John 3:2), for example, has some features common to Papyrus Egerton 2. In one fragment from the codex, a group acknowledges: "Teacher Jesus, we know that you have come from God, for the things you do bear witness beyond all the prophets."[5] Such an acknowledgment, however, bears only a passing resemblance to the Fourth Gospel, and Nicodemus himself is not mentioned with respect to the content, at least not in the surviving portions. The fragment continues with Jesus being questioned over payment of taxes to kings, the material akin to that found in Matthew 22:15–22 (Mark 12:13–17//Luke 20:20–26) rather than that of the Johannine pericope.

It takes some time for Nicodemus to take his place within extracanonical Christian texts, with perhaps the earliest significant reference found in the so-called *Gospel of Nicodemus*. Although identified in this writing as the "author" or recorder of the material, Nicodemus crops up in it only sporadically. Of particular note, however, is his involvement in the account of the trial of Jesus before Pilate. Initially a lone voice who distances himself from the other "Jews," Nicodemus speaks up for Jesus before Pilate, testifying to the many signs and wonders that he has performed (5:1). Other Jews address him, explicitly labeling him a disciple of Jesus, and Nicodemus's defense causes no end of antagonism on their part (5:2). Other figures subsequently bear witness to Jesus's achievements, but it is Nicodemus who emerges as the leader of the defense counsel and the one whom Pilate accordingly addresses during the trial (9:1). Consequently, after Jesus's death, the Jews are said to

4. For such a categorization, see, for example, Raymond F. Collins, *These Things Have Been Written: Studies on the Fourth Gospel* (Louvain, Belgium: Peeters, 1990), 57–58.

5. Translation taken from J. K. Elliott, ed. *The Apocryphal New Testament: A Collection of Apocryphal Christian Literature in an English Translation Based on M. R. James* (Oxford: Oxford University Press, 1993), 40.

The Gospel of Nicodemus

This amalgam of texts broadly relating to the events of the passion, also known as the *Acts of Pilate* because of its extended interest in him, purports to have been drawn up by Nicodemus in Hebrew, though such an ascription is certainly fictional and the original language is surely Greek. Although Justin Martyr (a second-century Christian writer) knew of a text by this name (*1 Apol.* 35, 48), it is unlikely to be the one known to us through surviving medieval manuscripts, and the scholarly consensus view is that the "Gospel" we possess dates from the fifth or sixth century.[1] The text is a diverse arrangement of material and includes vivid description of Christ's descent into hell, extended trial scene material, and letters between Pilate and various figures.

1. Elliott, *Apocryphal New Testament*, 164–65.

have sought out Nicodemus, designated a "ruler of the Jews" (12:1), for he is seen as a sympathizer of Jesus (12:1). He subsequently defends Jesus's cause before the council and before the priestly authorities, encouraging the Jews to embrace the risen Jesus (15:1, 5). He shares in this task with Joseph of Arimathea—indeed, Joseph seems to assume a superior status (15:5)—and the *Gospel of Nicodemus* thus expands, in some fashion, the "partnership" of Nicodemus and Joseph that John's account may imply (John 19:38–40).

Despite Nicodemus's high profile in the eponymous Gospel, such prominence is a rarity within extracanonical Christian accounts, and even here his portrayal remains highly mythical and probably derives from the Johannine juxtaposition with Joseph. Jewish sources, however, may be more fruitful on the question of Nicodemus's historicity. The key element here is the possible relevance of the figure known in rabbinic writings as Naqdimon ben Gurion. Naqdimon appears in several rabbinic texts (cf. *b. Giṭ.* 56a; *Lam. Rab.* 1.5.31; *Eccles. Rab.* 7.12.1), and he is portrayed as a wealthy and influential figure operative around 70 CE, the time of the Roman conquest of Jerusalem that ended the Jewish revolt.

The similarity of their names has created some speculation as to the relationship between "Nicodemus" and "Naqdimon," and this matter has recently been discussed in depth by Richard Bauckham.[6] Tracing various contemporary references to figures named Gurion and Naqdimon, and noting the Jewish custom of keeping the same male name across the generations to preserve family identity, Bauckham argues for the existence of a wealthy Pharisaical Gurion dynasty within first-century Jerusalem, with Naqdimon one of its most remembered figures. Because he shares a similar name, and is likewise

6. Richard Bauckham, *The Testimony of the Beloved Disciple: Narrative, History, and Theology in the Gospel of John* (Grand Rapids: Baker Academic, 2007), 137–72.

Arimathea

The precise location of Arimathea is not known, as, aside from its mention in the Gospel accounts, the place is not found in any other textual source. Luke describes it as a "Jewish town" (23:51), perhaps as clarification for a gentile audience, but this does not leave us much the wiser as to its location. It is commonly identified with Ramah or Ramathaim, home of Samuel and his family (1 Sam. 1:1, 19), though there is no certainty in this regard.

cast as a leading Pharisaical figure, Nicodemus, Bauckham suggests, may well have been part of this family.

The argument for a familial link between the two figures is possible, and Bauckham supplies a lot of documentary evidence in its support, but it must remain only a hypothesis. Certainly, to suppose that Nicodemus was the grandfather of Naqdimon, as John Robinson surmises,[7] is far too exact. However, even if Bauckham's assessment is just speculation, we might more confidently say that rabbinical and other first-century Jewish testimony gives sufficient basis for the *kind* of figure that we see portrayed in the Gospel, one counted among the council and with sufficient "funds" to bring forth the abundance of burial oil of John 19 (however rhetorical that description ultimately may be).

Historical Considerations: Joseph of Arimathea outside the Canonical Gospels

If the search for the historical Nicodemus has proved a difficult quest, one might equally observe the same of Joseph of Arimathea, with the caveat that doubts about him have come to the fore only relatively recently in critical inquiry. For many years, the "historicity" of Joseph was a given, even if little was confidently known about him. Perhaps because of the limited reference to him, or maybe even in spite of it, John Robinson observed, "No one seriously doubts that he was a historical character."[8]

This confidence in the historical Joseph has ebbed in recent years but mainly only in a secondary fashion. Suspicion has instead focused primarily on the events surrounding the burial *process* rather than on the figure of Joseph himself. But as soon as the burial itself is brought into question, Joseph's own authenticity is brought into doubt as well—he is tarnished by the association. Consequently, Joseph becomes, like Nicodemus in light of certain suggestions, merely a historical construction, a convenient figure to solidify a fictional burial/empty tomb narrative. Although not dismissing the burial

7. John A. T. Robinson, *The Priority of John* (London: SCM, 1985), 287.
8. Ibid., 284.

The Jesus Seminar

A predominantly American group of scholars, the Jesus Seminar attempted to discern what were real "historical Jesus" sayings/narratives and what were constructions of the early church. As part of this process, they codified the Gospel accounts (the canonical four plus the *Gospel of Thomas*) in terms of various colors: red (authentic Jesus material), pink (likely to be authentic), gray (not Jesus's words, but equivalent to his ideas), and black (a later construction of the church).[1]

1. See, for example, Robert W. Funk and Roy W. Hoover, *The Five Gospels: The Search for the Authentic Words of Jesus* (New York: Macmillan, 1993), 36–37.

tradition—and hence Joseph—entirely, Matti Myllykoski's summation perhaps encapsulates the skeptical approach: "It is difficult to imagine that Joseph the member of the Sanhedrin went to the abominable place of crucifixion and personally took care of the body of Jesus. His role as a historical figure was more likely much less concrete than the Markan burial story suggests."[9] It is unsurprising, therefore, that episodes involving Joseph have been categorized as black (i.e., fictional) within the Jesus Seminar's color scheme.

The Seminar's skepticism is not entirely unwarranted, and we might well have expected to know more of Joseph—or at least to have heard of his "conversion"—if he really was a key historical figure. Surely someone who had paid such close attention to Jesus at such a key time, someone whose actions are recorded across the canonical record, someone who stood with Jesus when others were deserting him, would have attracted some interest in other first-century writings. But at the same time, the comparison with Simon of Cyrene is worthy of note. Although burial may rank higher in hagiographic significance than cross bearing, it is noteworthy that there is comparatively less effort to sanctify or augment the role of Simon. Thus the lack of any mention of conversion is an argument from silence that does not yield any insight either way.

Whereas Nicodemus's path may be traced through Jewish sources, Joseph's hagiographical journey proceeds through more overtly Christian texts. Extracanonical narratives of Joseph's life postburial, however, offer little help in resolving the question of his historicity. In their retelling, he emerges as a character more at home in legendary tales than in the historical record. Joseph has a particular association with Glastonbury, where legend has him heading a team of missionaries dispatched by the apostle Philip from Gaul to establish Christianity in the British Isles thirty or so years after the resurrection. Landing

9. Matti Myllykoski, "What Happened to the Body of Jesus?," in *Fair Play: Diversity and Conflicts in Early Christianity: Essays in Honour of Heikki Räisänen*, ed. Ismo Dunderberg, C. M. Tuckett, and Kari Syreeni, NovTSup 103 (Leiden: Brill, 2002), 72.

in Somerset, he is portrayed as having made his way to Glastonbury Tor, at whose foot he buried the Holy Grail,[10] given him by Pontius Pilate and allegedly containing the crucified Jesus's blood. The factual basis for such discourse is minimal, and the account is probably the result of twelfth-century hagiographic speculation, but the capacity for Joseph to assume a key role in the Glastonbury narrative testifies to the general vacuum that exists in relation to him. He is a fleeting character within the Gospel narratives, but his proximity to Jesus at the moment of burial is enticing, and it is easy to understand how the character and role of such a figure might be fleshed out within subsequent narratives, however lacking in "historical" facticity.

At the same time, it is notable that Joseph does not figure within any other first-century texts. Instead, it is the *Gospel of Peter* that continues to ascribe a role to him, broadly following the pattern of the Synoptic testimony in portraying him as the primary actor within the burial narrative. But this apocryphal text goes beyond the canonical record in several ways. The location of the tomb is specifically termed "Joseph's Garden," probably derived from John's reference to a garden at the place of crucifixion (John 19:41). Joseph's character is also fleshed out; he asks Pilate for the body *before* the crucifixion (2:3–4), rather than after it, and becomes a "friend of Pilate and of the Lord" (2:3). Such characterization is, of course, highly spurious, and indeed, much of the account is infamously implausible. On the one hand, Pilate is portrayed as seeking *Herod's* assent for the body's release (2:4)—an unlikely scenario—while on the other hand, it is Herod, and not Joseph, who is concerned with legal observance, agreeing to hand Jesus over to expedite the death and burial before the advent of Sabbath (2:5). The narrative also assumes an anti-Semitic tendency, with "the Jews" rejoicing at Jesus's death (6:23). It is they (not Pilate) who give the body to Joseph for burial, in accordance with his prior request, and because he had witnessed Jesus's good deeds (6:23).[11] The Petrine Joseph is thus, at the very least, part of Jesus's retinue, and perhaps, by implication, one of his disciples.

Although noticeably absent from the *Epistle of the Apostles* (another apocryphal writing), which narrates Jesus's burial without naming the agent of it (9), Joseph does feature, alongside Nicodemus, as a key protagonist within the *Acts of Pilate/Gospel of Nicodemus*, but with a far more expanded role than he has in the canonical Gospels. As in the canonical record, Joseph asks for Jesus's body and places it in a previously unused, rock-hewn tomb (11:2). In this account, however, Joseph is imprisoned by the Jews over the Sabbath for doing this (12:1). Subsequently, when he is to be brought before the Jews, to receive an impending death penalty, he is found to be gone (12:2), his

10. See further R. F. Treharne, *The Glastonbury Legends* (London: Sphere Books, 1971), 4–6.
11. "Jewish" responsibility for the burial process is also alluded to in Acts 13:29: "They took him down from the tree and laid him in a tomb."

"disappearance" from a locked cell somewhat anticipating the empty tomb of Jesus. The Jews thereafter find Joseph back in Arimathea and acknowledge their sinful action, with Joseph thus becoming something of a Jesus prototype; he returns to Jerusalem to bring peace to the city and reestablishes a good relationship with his former captors (15:1–3). But in an interesting new development, he testifies before the chief priests to an appearance of the resurrected Jesus during his Sabbath imprisonment, during which, he says, Jesus transported him to the (now) empty tomb (15:6).

A similar "resurrection appearance" of sorts is found within a text generally known as the *Narrative of Joseph of Arimathea*. The earliest manuscript is from the twelfth century,[12] and the content is fairly rudimentary, but it likewise has Joseph imprisoned for burying Jesus. In more apocalyptic fashion than in the *Acts of Pilate*, however, Jesus appears to Joseph, accompanied by Demas, the "good" thief of the two crucified with Jesus, and the three journey to Galilee, ahead of the disciples.

Laying aside these apocryphal and hagiographical narratives, the question of Joseph's historicity still remains and is commonly focused on the reality of the burial practice accorded to him. As James Crossley puts it, "We simply have no genuine evidence as to the specifics of the burial, where it was, and what happened to Joseph in the years immediately following."[13] Some have rejected the very existence of a burial site because of the lack of any subsequent worship at such a place, a conceivable possibility were the tomb a reality.[14] Furthermore, it is sometimes claimed that the bodies of crucified criminals would have been merely discarded on a convenient rubbish heap: "The norm was to let crucifieds rot on the cross or be cast aside for carrion. The point was to deter lower-class violations of Roman law and order."[15] John Dominic Crossan, for example, has famously proposed that dogs ate the body of Jesus, and he thus opined that the Joseph-burial narrative is an entire work of fiction.[16] At one level, then, there may be good reason to concur that the intervention of Joseph would be "a remarkable departure from customary procedure since . . . the body of a crucified individual was not given an honorable burial."[17]

However, there is similarly good reason to conceive of the involvement of just such a figure. The narrative of Tobit recounts the activity of a faithful

12. Elliott, *Apocryphal New Testament*, 217.

13. James G. Crossley, "Against the Historical Plausibility of the Empty Tomb Story and the Bodily Resurrection of Jesus: A Response to N. T. Wright," *JSHJ* 3 (2005): 185.

14. Cf. A. J. M. Wedderburn, *Beyond Resurrection* (London: SCM, 1999), 63–65.

15. John Dominic Crossan and Jonathan L. Reed, *Excavating Jesus: Beneath the Stones, behind the Texts* (London: SPCK, 2001), 246.

16. John Dominic Crossan, *Jesus: A Revolutionary Biography* (San Francisco: HarperSanFrancisco, 1994), 123–58.

17. Marcus J. Borg and John Dominic Crossan, *The Last Week: What the Gospels Really Teach about Jesus's Final Days in Jerusalem* (London: SPCK, 2008), 153.

Burial Practice

The burial of a body, wrapped in a shroud and interred in either an earthen trench or a rock-hewn tomb, was a standard feature of first-century Jewish funereal practice. Particularly if the locus was a tomb, the custom was to return subsequently to the body and to enact a "second burial," whereby the deceased's bones would be collected and placed in a small container, commonly known as an ossuary.[1] In Jesus's case, Joseph would/should have collected the bones after decomposition of the body and relaid them in an ossuary.

1. Craig A. Evans, "The Silence of Burial," in *Jesus, the Final Days*, ed. Troy A. Miller (London: SPCK, 2008), 41–46.

figure who took it upon himself to bury dead bodies that had been cast outside the city (Tob. 1:17–19; 2:4–8), and Josephus acknowledges the requirement "not to leave a corpse unburied" (*Ag. Ap.* 2.211 [Thackeray, LCL]). Torah itself also teaches that bodies are not to hang on a tree/stake overnight but should be buried on that same day (Deut. 21:22–23), whether for purity or defilement reasons.[18] Normally Jesus, drawn from a poor family, would have been buried in a trench, but the drawing in of Sabbath precluded that possibility. An observant figure such as Joseph would presumably be keen to get the body and enclose it in a tomb as quickly as possible, and his "concern about Jesus was perfectly consistent with Jewish piety."[19]

Furthermore, the burial of the crucified is not without precedent, with the famous example of Yehohanan, whose ossuary contents testified to someone who had experienced crucifixion.[20] Josephus also records how "the Jews are so careful about funeral rites that even malefactors who have been sentenced to crucifixion are taken down and buried before sunset."[21] Philo likewise comments, "I have known cases when on the eve of a holiday of this kind [an emperor's birthday], people who have been crucified have been taken down and their bodies delivered to their kinsfolk, because it was thought well to give them burial and allow them the ordinary rites."[22] Thus, even if such a practice were the exception rather than the norm, there is no requirement to view Joseph as a literary construction merely on the grounds of burial practice, and it seems quite possible that Jewish concerns for piety and purity

18. Evans, "Silence of Burial," 46–53.
19. Raymond E. Brown, *The Death of the Messiah: From Gethsemane to the Grave; A Commentary on the Passion Narratives in the Four Gospels*, 2 vols. (New Haven: Yale University Press, 2008), 1216.
20. Evans, "Silence of Burial," 53–55.
21. Josephus, *J.W.* 4.317 (Thackeray, LCL).
22. Philo, *Flaccus* 83 (Colson, LCL).

trumped Roman practicalities.[23] Indeed, the inclusion of Jesus's burial within the kerygmatic tradition (1 Cor. 15:4)—albeit without naming Joseph—cautions against entirely removing it from the historical landscape.

Narrative Considerations: Nicodemus inside John's Gospel

The canonical portrait of Nicodemus forms a contrast to that of Joseph. Unlike the latter, Nicodemus features only in John's Gospel rather than in each of the Evangelists' testimonies. Attempts to associate him with other Synoptic figures—the rich man of Mark 10:17–22, for example—lack any real evidence to substantiate the link. Also, Nicodemus crops up at several points within John's retelling (3:1–10; 7:45–53; 19:38–42); he becomes an important figure in the Gospel narrative, somewhat different from Joseph, who departs the scene as quickly and as anonymously as he arrives. Yet Nicodemus's prominence is accompanied by an essential elusiveness. He is described in insufficient detail to convey precisely what his perspective on Jesus may have been, and "ambiguity is doubtless an important and deliberate part of the portrait of this obscure figure."[24] Jouette Bassler's summary statement captures the core enigmatic character well: "Rather like the Man in the Macintosh in James Joyce's *Ulysses*, Nicodemus makes a series of appearances that seem to be fraught with significance, but the nature of that significance remains elusive. He appears in the narrative often enough to evoke curiosity, but not, it seems, often enough to satisfy it."[25]

Nicodemus enters John's drama in three sequences, the first of which is notable for its nighttime setting (3:2). Labeled as a Pharisee and leader of the Jews (3:1), he comes to Jesus under cover of darkness with questions for his intended interlocutor, and John's reference to darkness is perhaps symptomatic of the ambiguity of the figure. The phrase "by night" may, of course, be no more than background detail, a mere temporal indicator. Bearing in mind John's interest in the light/dark dualism (for example, 1:4–5), however, it is hard to discount an intended symbolic significance. The darkness may suggest a furtive visit by Nicodemus, indicating someone who is potentially sympathetic to Jesus but unwilling to express that publicly, a secret, potential disciple. He does, after all, come *to* Jesus, not vice versa, and he may merely have sought an "an uninterrupted lengthy discussion."[26] It may well also have

---

23. John Dominic Crossan acknowledges that Joseph *could* have acted in this way, but conjectures that he actually *did not* (*The Birth of Christianity: Discovering What Happened in the Years Immediately after the Execution of Jesus* [Edinburgh: T&T Clark, 1999], 553–55). For him, Joseph's apparent involvement with Jesus's trial, and likewise Joseph's failure to deal with the other bodies, make the historical case implausible.

24. Wayne A. Meeks, "The Man from Heaven in Johannine Sectarianism," *JBL* 91 (1972): 54.

25. Jouette M. Bassler, "Nicodemus in the Fourth Gospel," *JBL* 108 (1989): 635.

26. Bauckham, *Testimony of the Beloved Disciple*, 165.

been an accompanied visit (cf. the "we" of 3:2), or he may have been the spokesperson of the group of 2:23–25, those who have believed in Jesus's signs but are still held at arm's length by Jesus. Were Nicodemus a representative figure of "interested" Pharisees, the exchange with Jesus could well be construed as a conversation between "church and synagogue,"[27] or "established religion meeting an emerging pneumatic movement."[28] The one who came in the darkness encounters the one who is the true Light.[29]

Alternatively, it may be that night was the time of Pharisaical study and that in his visit, Nicodemus bears the mantle of someone coming to confront Jesus rather than to laud or inquire of him. After all, John describes Nicodemus both as a Pharisee and as a leader of the Jews (3:1); bearing in mind the more negative construal the "Jews" receive elsewhere in the Gospel, Nicodemus's association with them has a potentially damaging aspect. Likewise, Jesus's labeling of him as "a teacher of Israel" (3:10) could be construed negatively; while Nicodemus does recognize the divine enabling of Jesus's signs and activity (3:2), he clearly does not grasp his discussion regarding being born "from above" (3:3–4, 9). Israel's "teacher" does not understand his own subject, one might say, and, with characteristic Johannine irony, the narrative soon makes it evident who is teaching whom. Nicodemus disappears from the narrative in 3:10, and it remains unclear whether 3:11–21 is actually directed at him. Even if he is seen as sympathetic to Jesus, any allegiance remains secretly expressed, and this first Nicodemus-Jesus encounter remains intriguingly unresolved.

The portrait of Nicodemus in John 3 is probably also to be interpreted in comparison with, or juxtaposed to, that of the Samaritan woman of the following chapter (4:1–42). John, so partial to setting characters and ideas in opposition to one another, seems to invite the comparison. On the one hand, Nicodemus represents the leadership of the Jews, a figure of high standing and authority. The (unnamed) woman, on the contrary, comes from the other end of the social spectrum, a woman, and a Samaritan one at that, with a history of several husbands (4:16–19). The contrast is so acute that one is invited to construe Nicodemus through the lenses of the Samaritan woman; because she embraces Jesus and affirms his messianic credentials, one might further view Nicodemus's response to Jesus as ultimately unbelieving and essentially inimical to Jesus and his purposes.[30]

After his nighttime encounter, Nicodemus reappears among the leadership grouping in the temple community who are debating the popular response

27. C. K. Barrett, *The Gospel according to St John: An Introduction with Commentary and Notes on the Greek Text*, 2nd ed. (London: SPCK, 1978), 202.

28. R. Alan Culpepper, *Anatomy of the Fourth Gospel: A Study in Literary Design*, FF (Philadelphia: Fortress, 1983), 135.

29. Barrett, *Gospel according to St John*, 205.

30. See further Winsome Munro, who describes the two figures as "parallel opposites" ("The Pharisee and the Samaritan in John: Polar or Parallel?," *CBQ* 57 [1995]: 710–28).

to Jesus's messianic claims (7:40–44). The Pharisees are cast in opposition to Jesus, accusing the temple police of being duped by Jesus's claims (7:47) and considering the crowd accursed by their (favorable) embrace of Jesus (7:49). Somewhat ominously, Nicodemus is described as "one of them" (7:50), namely, the Pharisees, and the generally negative portrayal of the Pharisees at this point potentially tarnishes him by his association with them. John does not distinguish Nicodemus from the Pharasaical opposition; indeed, within the Gospel's more dualistic worldview, one might understand this reference as a (not-so-subtle) articulation of where Nicodemus's loyalty lies.[31] The other identification of Nicodemus in the verse—the reminder that he had formerly visited Jesus—could perhaps be construed either way. On the one hand, it might be seen as placing Nicodemus in opposition to Jesus: although he had dealt with Jesus one-to-one (and thus had the primary evidence that the other Pharisees lacked), he remained still "one of them" and had not responded with faith to Jesus. On the other hand, it might be seen as a positive affirmation: Nicodemus—although "one of them"—has had courage to break ranks to hear and question Jesus for himself. This more positive sense also sits better with Nicodemus's subsequent response, namely, that Jesus should at least have some form of self-defense against the accusations levied against him. That this is somehow supportive of Jesus is evidenced by the other Pharisees' reaction and their suggestion that Nicodemus might equally be from Galilee (7:52). Yet, at the same time, even the author's possible defense of him remains somewhat tentative—Nicodemus's comments (7:51) are as much a response to competing interpretations of Torah's justification for Pharisaical due process as they are an outward affirmation of Jesus's status.[32] A parallel figure might be Gamaliel (Acts 5:34–40), someone who, while remaining part of the establishment, is sufficiently sympathetic to the apostles that they are given a fair hearing.[33]

Nicodemus's final appearance in the Johannine narrative is his participation in Jesus's burial (19:38–42), alongside Joseph, and it is in this third act that the seeds of the Joseph-Nicodemus association are set. Once again, John reminds the reader of Nicodemus's nocturnal visit (19:39), perhaps to reconfirm his identity, perhaps to affirm (once more) the ambiguous nature of his relationship with Jesus. Alternatively, the sense of "at first" (19:39) may indicate a change in Nicodemus's perspective; whereas he once came by night (3:1), the act of

31. Colleen M. Conway avers that Nicodemus's ambiguity is actually representative of John and questions the normal way of viewing John's characters as essentially binary in nature ("Minor Characters in the Fourth Gospel," *BibInt* 10 [2002]: 324–41). See also Susan E. Hylen, *Imperfect Believers: Ambiguous Characters in the Gospel of John* (Louisville: Westminster John Knox, 2009), 23–40.

32. Bassler, "Nicodemus," 639–40.

33. Thomas L. Brodie, *The Quest for the Origin of John's Gospel: A Source-Oriented Approach* (Oxford: Oxford University Press, 1993).

burial is a more public declaration of devotion to Jesus. Nicodemus seems to act as assistant to Joseph—it is the latter who requests Jesus's body—but he nevertheless arrives armed with a huge bundle of spices, the scale of which befits the burial of a king. The volume of spices brought has attracted a great deal of comment: Does Nicodemus's attentive conduct to Jesus's burial imply a refusal to believe in the resurrection? Is it the action of a mistaken follower rather than of one who has fully understood Jesus's significance?

Such criticism is hard to sustain, for there is little to suggest elsewhere in the Johannine account that the resurrection was eagerly anticipated by *any* of Jesus's followers. Instead, the final actions of Nicodemus perhaps support a more favorable characterization for him; here is someone who, even if in relative secret, participates in the honorable burial of Jesus, attending to him at his hour of need. Even if Nicodemus was one of the Pharisees (7:50), John would seem to be portraying him in a somewhat different fashion from the rest of his religious party.

The ambiguity, however, still persists for many commentators, and a survey of recent writers testifies to his ongoing inscrutability, the way in which he has been seen as manifesting the full gamut of responses to Jesus.[34] Raymond Collins, for example, conceives Nicodemus purely as representing "official Judaism" and thus as a prototype of an unbeliever.[35] He belongs to the Pharisees, is a leader of the Jews (3:1; 7:50), and is attentive to law observance (7:50–51) and ritual piety (19:39). Similarly negative is the conviction that Nicodemus represents "inadequate faith and inadequate courage"[36] (cf. the programmatic statement of John 20:31), a faith that recognizes Jesus's signs but is unwilling to embrace the full implications of Jesus and may be construed as insufficient or "non-saving."[37] More positively, but still with some reservation, Nicodemus could be seen as displaying a muted faith, a crypto-Christian who embraces Jesus but only in secret.[38] If association with Joseph is a factor, then that may be the case, as John specifically describes Joseph in those terms (19:38). Elsewhere in the Gospel also, John alludes to those whose profession is in secret (12:42–43), and Nicodemus may be one of their number, even if John himself desires a more open declaration of discipleship.

34. For Gabi Renz, Nicodemus's ambiguity contrasts heavily with John's otherwise general propensity to portray his characters in well-defined terms ("Nicodemus: An Ambiguous Disciple? A Narrative Sensitive Investigation," in *Challenging Perspectives on the Gospel of John*, ed. John Lierman, WUNT 2.219 [Tübingen: Mohr Siebeck, 2006], 255). For a contrasting view, cf. Conway, "Minor Characters in the Fourth Gospel," 324–41.

35. Collins, *These Things Have Been Written*, 14–16.

36. David Rensberger, *Johannine Faith and Liberating Community* (Philadelphia: Westminster, 1988), 40.

37. Meeks, "The Man from Heaven," 55.

38. J. Louis Martyn, *History and Theology in the Fourth Gospel* (Louisville: Westminster John Knox, 2003), 80. Cf. Culpepper, *Anatomy of the Fourth Gospel*, 136: Nicodemus is "'not far from the kingdom of God,' but he remains outside."

One might argue the alternative, however: that the declaration is actually in the open; the burial act is carried out in the daytime—before the Sabbath—and stands in contrast to the initial, nighttime visit of chapter 3. If this is the line taken, then Nicodemus becomes a genuine disciple of Jesus, the burial scene being the public declaration by which he finally nails his colors to the mast, the culmination of his journey from furtive hanger-on to devoted follower, from darkness to light.[39] After all, it is only Joseph whose discipleship is explicitly identified as "secret."

John's Nicodemus ultimately resists compartmentalization, however, and ambiguity remains. Some may read the ambiguity as resolved by John. Gabi Renz, for example, proposes that John's dualistic worldview and desire "to persuade the audience to become devoted disciples of Christ" preclude Nicodemus's remaining ambiguous.[40] Instead, he can be read profitably as either disciple or outsider, but only within the confines of John's narrative purposes: "All recipients recognize that within the narrative world of John, the right behavior for Nicodemus and for every character is to commit themselves to Jesus Christ the Son of God."[41] Others, however, will find an ongoing ambiguity congenial and will see Nicodemus as someone on a faith journey but without being absolutely certain as to where on that journey he ultimately resides.

Narrative Considerations: Joseph of Arimathea inside the Canonical Gospels

Joseph appears in all four canonical accounts, and at first sight, the respective portrayals are univocal in ascribing to him a role in Jesus's burial. Indeed, that is his only contribution; in all four accounts, he appears almost out of nowhere to fulfill the interment task, with no other role ascribed and no further account subsequently given of him. This thematic similarity, however, is only a surface one. Just as the Gospels give varying portrayals of Jesus, so Joseph receives a subtly different description in each of the four canonical Gospel texts. Although he fulfills more or less the same task before disappearing off the scene almost as quickly as he appears, the respective portraits of Joseph are as diverse as those of Jesus himself. Consequently, the debates generated by the character are in inverse proportion to the fairly minor role he occupies within the passion accounts, and it seems appropriate, therefore, to speak of a Markan, a Matthean, a Lukan, and a Johannine Joseph rather than to reduce him to one uniform depiction.

39. See, for example, Bauckham, *Testimony of the Beloved Disciple*, 163–66; Charles H. Talbert, *Reading John: A Literary and Theological Commentary on the Fourth Gospel and the Johannine Epistles*, rev. ed. (London: Smith and Helwys, 2005), 255.
40. Renz, "Nicodemus," 283.
41. Ibid.

The Markan Joseph of Arimathea

As with most attempts to understand Jesus, critical attention focuses on the Markan portrayal as representing probably the earliest textual account of Joseph's actions. Mark announces that Joseph goes to Pilate to request the body (15:43)—an action all four Gospels accord to him—and, given permission (15:44–45), Joseph himself removes it, wraps it in linen cloth, and places it in a sealed tomb (15:46). Why Joseph needs to go to Pilate—and not merely to the soldiers—to collect the body of a condemned criminal is not clear. But it may reflect the proper piety of Joseph, or the fact that he possessed sufficient political standing to obtain Pilate's assent.

Mark's depiction of Joseph is quintessentially ambiguous, and this has led to a variety of interpretations of his significance and role. Mark gives two pieces of information, both of which are somewhat enigmatic and both of which muddy the waters when we try to evaluate his relationship to Jesus. Joseph's description as a *bouleutēs* (15:43) likely implies a councilor role, but it remains unclear which council he would have belonged to. The term is different from that which Mark accords to those Sanhedrin councilors who have pronounced on Jesus's guilt (14:55; 15:1), and this may be an attempt to exonerate Joseph from that verdict. More likely, it merely reflects a different terminology or a plurality of sources, pieced together without the perceived need for smoothness (the existence of more than one council within Jerusalem seems unlikely). At the very least, the term suggests that Joseph is a figure of influence. That he had access to a tomb so close to Jerusalem and yet hailed from Arimathea is similarly suggestive; while Mark does not attribute the tomb's ownership to Joseph, to have access to the tomb at relatively short notice would make some form of possession highly likely. He is also described as a "respected" figure (15:43).

Second, and perhaps more intriguingly, Mark describes Joseph as "waiting expectantly for the kingdom of God" (15:43), and this could be construed as someone who supports Jesus. After all, Mark is clear that Jesus has announced God's kingdom (1:15), claiming that the time has been fulfilled. But it need not necessarily be so, and Mark's silence as to Jesus's relationship to Joseph is intriguing. While the Markan portrayal of Joseph is not *incompatible* with his being a disciple of Jesus, neither is it necessarily *compatible*. Joseph could instead be conceived as a good and faithful Jew, one expectantly awaiting the kingdom of God but not necessarily thinking that it is Jesus who fulfills it. It may be that Joseph is a pious Jew, who, just like Tobit, seeks to provide an appropriate burial place for those who have been executed. His inclusion in the tradition, then, would merely reflect the memory of a (pious) Jew who acted appropriately in matters of purity. As Morna Hooker observes: "Far from being a secret follower of Jesus acting out of devotion to him, . . . Joseph may have regarded Jesus's body as a curse to the land which needed to be disposed of as soon as possible."[42] To put the matter another way, it would seem implausible for Pilate to have given the body either to a disciple (as Matthew subsequently avers) or to someone who had not voted for Jesus's death (so the Lukan account), whereas a "non-disciple" who had been party to the Sanhedrin verdict makes for a more likely recipient.[43] For many interpreters, therefore, the Markan Joseph is merely a righteous Jew, one who acts independently of the onlooking women, and "all traditions of a Christian role in the burial are the creations of the later Evangelists."[44]

Others, however, ascribe a more overtly Christian emphasis to the Markan Joseph, particularly when his actions are contrasted with other figures within the Gospel. If he is indeed a Sanhedrin participant, the positive description of 15:42–46 makes him an exception to his fellow councilors[45] and to the Gospel's overall portrayal of them (just as the wise scribe is distinguished from the rest of his grouping in 12:28–34).[46] Although not described as such, Joseph *acts* as a disciple, just like those of John who bury their master (6:29). In this light, he is not merely open to the kingdom of God but also open to Jesus, and acts like a committed follower would, taking responsibility for the burial. He might therefore form a fitting parallel to the Roman centurion (15:39). Both are "faithful" within a broader constituency of unfaithfulness and "function as replacements for the disciples of Jesus who have long since fled from their master."[47] The failure, then, to describe Joseph as a disciple *is* significant; he is differentiated from the twelve "disciples" in order to show exactly what (true) discipleship entails.

The "observant Jew/nondisciple" argument may also be critiqued on other grounds. The reader, for example, does not hear about what is done, if anything, with the bodies of the other two figures crucified alongside Jesus (15:27). If Joseph ignores them, then the argument for his observance of ritual purity is weakened.[48] That Joseph is *named* may also be significant (why name such a relatively marginal and fleeting character?), particularly as Mark leaves some characters unnamed.[49] But even if the naming is acknowledged, it may

---

42. Morna D. Hooker, *The Gospel according to St Mark* (London: A and C Black / Peabody, MA: Hendrickson, 1991), 381.

43. Brown, *The Death of the Messiah*, 1217.

44. William John Lyons, "On the Life and Death of Joseph of Arimathea," *JSHJ* 2 (2004): 50.

45. R. T. France suggests that Mark's "all" (14:64) should not be taken absolutely, but such an interpretation ultimately depends upon one's prior convictions regarding Joseph's role (*The Gospel of Mark: A Commentary on the Greek Text*, NIGTC [Grand Rapids: Eerdmans 2002], 666). If Joseph is (merely) a pious Jew, one need not read the "all" in any more nuanced fashion.

46. Joel F. Williams, *Other Followers of Jesus: Minor Characters as Major Figures in Mark's Gospel*, JSNTSup 102 (Sheffield: JSOT Press, 1994), 190.

47. Ibid., 188.

48. This is, of course, an argument from silence. The omission may simply imply their secondary status in the narrative; it is really only Jesus's burial that concerns Mark.

49. Gerald O'Collins and Daniel Kendall, "Did Joseph of Arimathea Exist?," *Bib* 75 (1994): 240.

be attributed simply to Joseph's being a figure known to Mark's readership (without requiring that he had been known *as a disciple*), or else the naming may provide a fitting inclusio to the cross-bearing actions of Simon of Cyrene. Both are named, and both in terms of their hometown; one helps Jesus with the cross, and the other takes him down from it. The fact that it is two (relative) outsiders who offer service to Jesus—rather than those from within Jerusalem—may further indict the reputation of the holy city and its inhabitants.

Much then depends upon how one reads Mark's ultimate direction. It is difficult to resolve the argument either way, as much of the interpretive difficulty derives from Mark's silence. The reader simply is not told *why* Joseph acted as he did, and such minimalism leaves the reader (deliberately?) uninformed. This leads then to a diversity of thinking regarding Joseph's status, with some viewing Joseph's actions as those of someone who had already committed himself to following Jesus,[50] if not an "open" disciple. On the other hand, Crossan argues that Joseph was a Markan fiction, a convenient literary foil whereby Jesus's body is buried so that the resurrection hope can be verified.[51] In Crossan's view, Joseph fulfills an integral role in the narrative, but his relationship to Jesus is effectively incidental, even irrelevant. A slightly more positive assessment comes from Myllykoski, who argues for a *historical* Joseph, but a pre-Markan one, whose pious characterization is a later Markan overlay necessitated by Jesus's subsequent significance.[52]

William Lyons takes the process one stage further. He characterizes Joseph as a pious Jew, but no more than that, averring, "Mark's account . . . strongly suggests both that pious Jews buried the historical Jesus and that this proved no difficulty for at least one section of the early Church. The continuity between the historical Jesus and the risen Christ was viewed as sufficiently guaranteed by the witnesses to the burial *without the need for a disciple to have handled the body*."[53] Raymond Brown adopts a different tack. He depicts Joseph as a figure who was not a follower of Jesus at the time of the passion but who became one subsequently. Joseph is thus "remembered" in the Gospel accounts, but because of his pious activity, not because his actions demonstrated his discipleship at that time.

In summary, therefore, some agnosticism is required. The mystery with which Joseph appears on the scene and the ambiguity with which he is described are characteristically Markan, and these factors resist attempts to pronounce confidently on his relationship to Jesus.

50. France, *Mark*, 666–67.
51. See, for example, John Dominic Crossan, "Historical Jesus as Risen Lord," in John Dominic Crossan, Luke Timothy Johnson, and Werner H. Kelber, *The Jesus Controversy: Perspectives in Conflict*, The Rockwell Lecture Series (Harrisburg, PA: Trinity Press International, 1999), 16–26.
52. Myllykoski, "What Happened to the Body of Jesus?," 43–82.
53. Lyons, "Joseph of Arimathea," 50 (emphasis added).

The Matthean Joseph of Arimathea

Matthew's portrait, in contrast, is clear, seemingly ironing out the ambiguities present within Mark's retelling. Joseph is now a rich man (27:57) rather than a council member. The lack of reference to Joseph's councilor status may derive from Matthew's general antipathy toward the Jewish authorities[54] or perhaps be intended to disassociate Joseph from any involvement in Jesus's trial. Or it could merely be an omission on Matthew's part. Being wealthy and being a councilor are hardly mutually exclusive ascriptions, and they may indeed be entirely complementary.

Matthew's particular interest in Joseph's economic status would support the other detail the Evangelist supplies, namely, that he owned the tomb in which Jesus was laid (27:60). To possess a tomb in Jerusalem while hailing from Arimathea implies some significant wealth on Joseph's part. Matthew also confirms that the tomb was a new one (and, perhaps implicitly, that it was empty). Perhaps with the Easter narrative in mind, there was to be no possibility of confusion with any other body. To remove any semblance of doubt, therefore, Matthew adds that Joseph himself had actually hewn the rock (27:60), thereby adding an even more personal touch to the burial act. As W. D. Davies and Dale Allison note: "The only surprise is that Joseph purportedly interred Jesus in a family tomb, not a trench or common plot for criminals."[55] The reference to Joseph's wealth could actually be a literary device, harking back to Jesus's encounter with the rich young man, Matthew speculating that someone of wealth *can* enter the kingdom of God (19:24). It may also bring to mind the Isaianic prophecy regarding the one who "made his grave with the wicked and his tomb with the rich" (53:9); locating Jesus's body within the tomb of the wealthy Joseph sits well with Matthew's general interest in seeing prophecy "fulfilled."[56]

But perhaps more significant than Joseph's wealth and property is Matthew's clarification of his relationship with Jesus. Joseph is explicitly labeled as a disciple of Jesus—gone is the ambiguity of the Markan account. Whether this allegiance to Jesus comes before or after the passion, Matthew does not unambiguously declare, but the passive form (literally "was discipled") inclines more toward a present experience than a future one. Indeed, the sense in Matthew is that Joseph acts as a disciple, and this may, as some have suggested, effect a parallel between Jesus and John: Both are buried by disciples.[57] Furthermore, if Joseph

54. Cf. Helen K. Bond: "Clearly Matthew will not allow the man who buried Jesus to be an influential Jewish leader" (*Pontius Pilate in History and Interpretation*, SNTSMS 100 [Cambridge: Cambridge University Press, 1998], 126).

55. W. D. Davies and Dale C. Allison, *The Gospel according to Saint Matthew*, 3 vols., ICC (Edinburgh: T&T Clark, 1988), 3:648.

56. Cf. W. Boyd Barrick, "The Rich Man from Arimathea (Matt. 27:57–60) and 1Q1SA," *JBL* 96 (1977): 235–39.

57. Davies and Allison, *Matthew*, 3:649.

were a precrucifixion disciple of Jesus, then it would open up the possibility of Jesus exercising some form of ministry in Jerusalem prior to the passion visit.

The Lukan Joseph of Arimathea

Luke replicates Matthew's reworking of the Joseph tradition, but differently. He retains Mark's designation of Joseph as a council member (keeping the same term in 23:50–51, *bouleutēs*) but has also specified that Joseph did not consent to the verdict against Jesus (v. 51). This is perhaps akin to the innocent verdict that Luke elsewhere notes as being issued to both Jesus and Paul (Luke 23:4, 13–22; Acts 22:25–29; 26:30–31). Like Matthew, Luke notes that the tomb had yet to be used, presumably to remove any notion that another body got subsequently mixed up with that of Jesus. Yet at the same time, Luke does not completely resolve the mystery of Joseph, and retains something of the Markan enigma. Joseph remains someone "waiting . . . for the kingdom of God" (23:51), and there is no Matthean addition of discipleship status. As with Mark, there is no reason to impute any "Christian" identity to him; the Lukan Joseph is an innocent figure but is not explicitly, or necessarily, linked with Jesus. He may be a "disciple," but there is no pressing reason to conclude this from Luke's account. Joseph's function in Luke may therefore be to show that not all religious leaders are negative figures; like Zechariah (John the Baptist's father, Luke 1:5–7), he is construed as a righteous persona, and one who is faithfully hopeful.[58]

The Johannine Joseph of Arimathea

John's account is distinctive because of its pairing of Joseph with the figure of Nicodemus (19:38–42), already a familiar actor in the Johannine Gospel but, as observed above, not mentioned in the synoptic tradition. Partnered with Nicodemus, Joseph becomes a secret or furtive disciple (19:38), one who wishes to be associated with Jesus, but seemingly not in public. The extent to which their act of burial is private—and therefore how "secret" they were—is discussed above in regard to Nicodemus, but it remains the case in John that Joseph is explicitly a disciple, of whatever type. As with Matthew, the Markan ambiguity has been removed, but one suspects the motivation for so doing is different for John.[59] The juxtaposition with Nicodemus has an impact on the portrayal. Although Joseph initiates events, Nicodemus is the more prominent character in the Gospel, and John's retelling seems geared as much to the interests of Nicodemus as to those of Joseph.

58. Mark Allan Powell, "The Religious Leaders in Luke: A Literary-Critical Study," *JBL* 109 (1990): 107–8.

59. Lyons: "John's interest in presenting Nicodemus positively effectively compels him to convert the Markan Joseph, a conversion which is motivated by reasons wholly independent of those that concern Matthew" ("Joseph," 43–44).

Indeed, John offers correspondingly little biographical data regarding Joseph. The tomb, although described as new (19:41), is not identified as belonging to him, and there is no comment on Joseph's wealth or his involvement (or otherwise) in Jesus's trial. Instead, John specifically notes that the burial occurs within a garden located near the site of the crucifixion (19:41) and seems more concerned with the burial *process*. As noted earlier, the quantity of spices is voluminous, and the body is wrapped in more material than just the shroud.[60] In John's Gospel both Joseph and Nicodemus thus participate in a burial that befits a king.

Such canonical variation being acknowledged, what remains of the "historical" Joseph? One is tempted to conclude with Lyons that any changes are motivated by the agendas of the particular writers, and the historical Joseph—Markan or otherwise—is subsumed under the interpretative agenda of the other Gospel writers and their particular theological perspectives.[61] The canonical testimony thus manifests "a line of development that moved Joseph from being a pious Sanhedrist observing the law of burying the crucified toward a more sanctified status as a model disciple of Jesus."[62] Crossan's take is even more provocative: within the canonical testimony Jesus goes from being buried by an enemy to being buried by a friend, "from an inadequate and hurried entombment to one of regal magnificence."[63] On such a reading, Joseph—or at least the diverse portrayals of him by the canonical writers—becomes a particularly good exemplar of the title of our book, for he may be said to occupy the full gamut of roles that this book encapsulates.

Conclusion

Within the historical tradition, albeit somewhat belatedly, Nicodemus and Joseph develop as significant and influential disciples of Jesus. As they do, their roles are significantly fleshed out, and questions as to their relationship to Jesus are answered in no uncertain terms. While the historical basis for such expansion remains highly tenuous, it does reflect the desire of Christian writers formally to claim these "ambiguous" figures for themselves. The canonical record, while still retaining some of the ambiguity, also goes some way to clarifying the question. We see the gradual "discipling" of Joseph from Mark to John, and within the Fourth Gospel, we see the steady—if perhaps far from complete—evolution of Nicodemus's faith as the narrative progresses.

60. Craig Blomberg, *The Historical Reliability of John's Gospel* (Leicester, UK: Inter-Varsity, 2001), 258.
61. Lyons, "Joseph of Arimathea," 42.
62. Brown, *Death of the Messiah*, 1232.
63. Crossan, *Birth of Christianity*, 555.

But what do these characters add to the reader's knowledge of Jesus? In one sense, they reveal how he was received by some within the more affluent echelons of Jewish society. They confirm that Jesus interacted with influential figures, for good or for ill, and that his ministry gave prominent Pharisees such as Nicodemus food for intellectual thought. Jesus's engagement with them enables the Gospel writers to explore what his teaching might have entailed in the context of "official" Judaism. But perhaps more significantly, they also reveal how Jesus's claims were not always understood or embraced with immediate effect by those who encountered him, even those such as Nicodemus who were "teachers of Israel" and should therefore have grasped the significance more rapidly. Maybe part of their own inherent elusiveness as characters suggests that Joseph and Nicodemus (and others, by extension) actually found Jesus *himself* elusive. Joseph may have known Jesus before he died but—as Mark seems to suggest—could have been entirely ambivalent about him, still waiting for the kingdom of God and only becoming a disciple in the aftermath of the resurrection. John's Nicodemus is—at best—only slowly brought over to Jesus's side (if at all); he struggles to understand what an appropriate response to Jesus might be. Such elusiveness, then, such ambiguity of relationship, resists the temptation to place Jesus's ministry in simplistic terms.

Suggestions for Further Reading

Joseph of Arimathea

Brown, Raymond E. *The Death of the Messiah: From Gethsemane to the Grave; A Commentary on the Passion Narratives in the Four Gospels.* 2 vols. The Anchor Yale Bible Reference Library. New Haven: Yale University Press, 2008.

Evans, Craig A., and N. T. Wright. *Jesus, the Final Days.* Edited by Troy A. Miller. London: SPCK, 2008.

Lyons, William John. "On the Life and Death of Joseph of Arimathea." *JSHJ* 2 (2004): 29–53.

Nicodemus

Bauckham, Richard. *The Testimony of the Beloved Disciple: Narrative, History, and Theology in the Gospel of John.* Grand Rapids: Baker Academic, 2007.

Collins, Raymond F. *These Things Have Been Written: Studies on the Fourth Gospel.* Louvain, Belgium: Peeters, 1990.

Hylen, Susan E. *Imperfect Believers: Ambiguous Characters in the Gospel of John.* Louisville: Westminster John Knox, 2009.

PART 2

The Enemies of Jesus

7

Satan and Demons

Loren T. Stuckenbruck

Jesus's encounter with demonic forces in the New Testament Gospels presents readers today with a worldview that stands out in at least two respects: (1) it confronts many in the contemporary Western world with an existence of beings that seems hard to reconcile with rationalist sensibilities of cause and effect, and (2) when compared with the Hebrew Bible, it reflects a very different outlook in which the notion of "Satan" and demonic beings is far more developed. With regard to (1), we shall see during the course of this discussion that the value of reading Jesus's confrontation with malevolent forces does not depend on whether one shares an ancient understanding of the world; indeed, it is precisely by taking seriously a worldview in which angelic and demonic figures share social space with human beings that ancient discourse about the meaning of life from the perspective of faith can be better apprehended. With regard to (2), a look at the Hebrew Bible discloses traces of ideas that are taken up in the New Testament. However, when we come to the Gospels, it becomes apparent that the figure of "Satan" has become more than a personified force who in Israel's Scriptures incites sin (1 Chron. 21:1), puts humans to the test under God's auspices (Job 1–2), or stands as one who brings accusation against God's anointed (Zech. 3:1–2). Likewise, references to figures called "demons" (Heb. *šēdîm*, Gk. *daimonia*; cf. Deut. 32:17; Ps. 106:37) no longer simply denote deities of nations outside of Israel. Instead, the world of the Gospels yields a portrait of a being called Satan, for whom

Satan is now a proper name, who is identified outright as "the devil" (so Matt.
4:1–10; John 13:2, 27; cf. Mark 4:15//Luke 8:12//Matt. 13:39),[1] and who, as
such, is associated with a range of evil forces often called "demons" who come
under his authority (see Mark 3:22–26//Matt. 12:24–28//Luke 11:14–20; Luke
10:17–18). While some have attributed development of the notion of Satan-
with-subordinate-powers to the influence of Persian dualism (Zoroastrianism),
the more immediate background for the portrait of the demonic world in all
four Gospels can be traced to apocalyptic writings composed by Jews during
the Second Temple period. In order to understand better the kinds of inimical
beings Jesus encounters in the Gospels and what they signify for early Christian beliefs and practices, we should see how they functioned in ancient Jewish
thought. The following overview thus seeks to bring the Gospel portraits of
demonic opposition to Jesus into conversation with what may be regarded
as the most important formative Jewish traditions. Since, in Second Temple
literature, discourse about a single figure embodying evil is not always bound
up with talk about lower-level demonic beings, we shall consider these in turn
(first Satan, then demons), while recognizing that in a number of texts, both
from the Second Temple period and in the Gospels, the two overlap somewhat.

Historical Considerations

Several caveats and initial considerations should be kept in mind at the outset.
Whatever individual texts state, Jewish explanations of and approaches to
evil were wide ranging and diverse during the several centuries leading up to
the Common Era. In noting this, we do well to consider issues that apply as
much to our understanding of the Gospel tradition as to our look at Jewish
traditions. First, though some writers chose to emphasize humans (e.g., *1 En.*
98:4–6; Sir. 25:24; *4 Ezra* 7:118–25) or heavenly beings (e.g., *1 En.* 6–19, 85–88;
Jub. 5, 7; the Dead Sea Scroll *Book of Giants*) as responsible for the beginning
of evil, we are not to suppose that these same writers were thinking system-
atically.[2] It is misleading, then, for one to imagine it possible to extract from
any single text a view that represents what was generally thought among Jews
or even reflects what these writers themselves may have thought apart from

1. Unlike the New Testament, in which "Satan" and "the devil" are used side by side (see also
Rev. 12:9; 20:2), the Greek translators of the Jewish scriptures never transliterated "Satan," but
always translated or substituted it with *(ho) diabolos* (1 Chron. 21:1; Job 1:6–9, 12; 2:1–4, 6, 7;
Zech. 3:1–2). In the Old Testament "Satan" in the Hebrew is always, with one exception only
(1 Chron. 21:1), actually designated "*the* satan," so that a proper name is not in view.
2. Indeed, accounts about both human (based on Gen. 3–4—Adam and Eve, Cain and
Abel) and angelic (based on a rebellion related to Gen. 6:1–4) origins of evil could coexist or
be combined in some texts, such as, for example, several compositions belonging to *1 Enoch*
(Book of Watchers at chaps. 6–19 and 32:6; Similitudes at 69:6; Animal Apocalypse at 85:4 and
chap. 86), the *Book of Jubilees* (chaps. 4–5 and 7), and the *Life of Adam and Eve* (chaps. 12–17).

the compositions they produced. It is legitimate to ask, nonetheless, why a given emphasis about evil occurs in this or that text as well as to inquire into a writer's understanding of how evil can be coped with or negotiated in light of strongly held convictions about the God of Israel.

Second, although above we have noted differences between many parts of the Hebrew Bible and Second Temple literature, it is difficult to talk about a single, more generally held, chronological line of development. For example, while some circles cultivated a parlance that gave prominence to the activities of angelic and demonic powers (e.g., Jewish apocalyptic texts, many documents among the Dead Sea Scrolls), others were more content to say very little about or even minimize references to nonhuman, personified forces (e.g., 1 Macc., Sir., Josephus). It is not as though one of these, albeit in different times and places, developed into the other but rather that they were contemporary

The Qumran Community and the Dead Sea Scrolls

The "Dead Sea Scrolls" refers to a series of manuscript discoveries made in eleven caves off the northwest shore of the Dead Sea from 1947 until 1956. These mostly fragmentary documents—at least 20,000 fragments from at least 950 identifiable manuscripts—date from the late third century BCE until the mid-first century CE. While most of the materials were copied in Hebrew, many are written in Aramaic, and a few are in Greek. Individual manuscripts are commonly referred to by a number (1, 2, 3) or a title, sometimes abbreviated (*Thanksgiving Hymns* = H; *Community Rule* = S), preceded by identification of the cave designated according to the chronological sequence in which it was discovered (1Q, 2Q, 3Q . . .).

The Scrolls contain the earliest textual evidence for most of the Hebrew Bible (except for the book of Esther), including some Greek (for Deuteronomy) and Aramaic translations (for Leviticus and Job). In addition, many manuscripts belong to other previously known religious compositions (e.g., Tobit, *1 Enoch*, Sir., *Damascus Document*), while a majority of the manuscripts belong to documents unknown since antiquity before their discovery. Among the last-mentioned group of manuscripts, many were authored by members of a community that settled in the nearby ruins of Khirbet Qumran (e.g., *Community Rule*, *Thanksgiving Hymns*, commentaries on various biblical books called *pesharim*). Another large group of compositions, however, cannot be immediately traced to this particular community (e.g., *Two Spirits Treatise*, contained in the 1Q manuscripts of the *Community Rule*; *4QInstruction*; *Temple Scroll*; *Reworked Pentateuch*; and all the Aramaic documents). Therefore, given the differences in material culture among the eleven caves and the differences between archaeological phases of the ruins at Khirbet Qumran, the Dead Sea Scrolls provide important evidence, not only for a sectarian community and closely related communities, but also, more broadly, for religious groups using Hebrew and Aramaic during the Second Temple period.

perspectives, sometimes held apart and sometimes overlapping. Given this, it is better to ask what circumstances, social locations, and worldviews gave rise to particular ways of referring to evil.

Third, though the New Testament writings might lead one to think that the designations "Satan" or "the devil" were commonplace in contemporary Jewish thought, it does not appear that they were. What in Jewish tradition, then, informed particular ideas and practices as they surface in the Gospels?

Fourth, it is among apocalyptically oriented texts preserved among and related to documents recovered among the Dead Sea Scrolls that we find a good sampling of convictions that improve our grasp of the world of evil beings that readers encounter in the Gospel tradition. Since many writings preserved among the Scrolls were not composed by the group that settled at Khirbet Qumran, and since the documents were written, copied, and collected in eleven caves over a period of nearly two hundred years, we should not be surprised by the diversity of ideas about the demonic world that meet us there.

Fifth, and following from the last point, a discussion that anchors Jesus's conflict with evil powers within the world of Jewish apocalyptic thought has the opportunity to reflect on what "apocalyptic" thought is to begin with. We will take such an opportunity in the conclusion to this chapter.

Primary Demonic Figures in the Dead Sea Scrolls

If we focus on documents contained in or related to the Dead Sea Scrolls, at least five beings are presented as chief demonic figures. These are Melki-reša, "the Angel of Darkness," "S/satan," and Mastema and Belial.

Melki-reša

The designation Melki-reša, which means "king of wickedness," occurs twice, once in an Aramaic source and once in a Hebrew text. In the Aramaic *Visions of Amram* (4Q544 2 I, 3), Melki-reša is mentioned as one of two angelic beings who strive against one another to have authority over the patriarch Amram (called the father of Moses and Aaron [Exod. 6:18; 1 Chron. 6:3]). He is aligned with "darkness" and "deeds" associated with it. Melki-reša is contrasted with another chief angel whose name is not preserved but who is probably Melchizedek (meaning "king of righteousness"), who is aligned with "light" (4Q544 2 I, 3–6). Here the patriarch is asked to choose which of these two angels may have authority over him. Thus, although an angelic figure lies behind human wrongdoing, it is ultimately humans who bear responsibility for what they do. In a Hebrew text of *4QCurses* (= 4Q280) 1 I, 2–7, Melki-reša is expressly cursed in terms that anticipate how Belial is denounced in the Dead Sea group's *Community Rule* (1QS II, 5–9).

The Angel of Darkness

This figure is mentioned only in the *Two Spirits Treatise* of the *Community Rule* as a negative counterpart to "the Prince of Lights" (1QS III, 20–21). He is identified further as a "spirit . . . of deceit" who contends against "the spirit of truth" within human beings until the time of divine judgment. Similar to Melki-reša, the angel is bound up with darkness and its vices (IV, 9–14) in contrast with light and those virtues associated with it (IV, 2–8). However, what the angel does or does not do to human beings is not the result of human choice but rather has been determined from the beginning by "the God of knowledge" (III, 13–16) who knows beforehand how everything will turn out in each human being.

Satan

As a term, *śāṭān* means "accuser" or "one who brings charges against." In the Dead Sea Scrolls and related literature, it occurs five times. In three, perhaps four of these instances, the word is preceded by a term such as "all," "any" (after a negative), or "no" (1QHᵃ XXII [frag. 4], 6; XXIV [frag. 45], 3; 1Q28b I, 8; 4Q504 1–2 IV, 12) and therefore simply refers to someone—anyone, whether angelic or human—who engages in destructive activity. The word also occurs twice in the *Jubilees*, found among fragments from the Dead Sea Scrolls and composed during the middle of the second century BCE. *Jubilees* states that at the end of days "there will be neither satan nor any evil who [or better: "which"] will destroy" (23:29). Here *śāṭān* refers to someone—anyone—who destroys by cutting a human being's life short. In *Jubilees* 10:11, however, the word "satan" describes the activity of a figure called Mastema, whose power over a host of evil spirits is considered the cause of human suffering and idolatry after the time of the flood.

One passage in which *Satan* becomes a proper noun and is of significance for the Gospels is from a "Plea for Deliverance" (11Q5 XIX, 13–16). The text reads:

> Forgive my sin, O YHWH, and cleanse me from my iniquity.
> Bestow upon me a spirit of faithfulness and knowledge.
> Do not let me stumble in transgression.
> Do not let have authority over me *Satan* or a spirit of uncleanness;
> Let neither rain nor evil purpose take hold of my bones.

The use of *Satan* as a proper name here stands in contrast to a similar prayer in the older *Aramaic Levi Document* at 4Q213a 1 I, 17–18, which may be restored to read, "And do n]ot let have authority over me *any satan* [to lead me astray from your path]."

Mastema and Belial

These two designations sometimes occur together among the Dead Sea Scrolls, and only in Hebrew texts. As with *satan*, these words function not only as proper names but also as nouns: while *maṣṭemâ* means "enmity" or "animosity" and occurs eighteen times in the manuscripts, *belial* means "worthlessness" and occurs eighty-eight times. Because of the meanings of *Mastema* and *Belial*, their mere occurrence does not necessarily indicate that in each instance we are dealing with a proper name.

Mastema

While in *Jubilees* Mastema is the chief demonic power with jurisdiction over a contingent of evil spirits (see below), the function of the term in a number of the Qumran texts as well as its relation to *Belial* is unclear. We cannot, for example, assume that *Mastema* and *Belial* are but different names for the same figure, as the story line of *Jubilees* might lead one to infer. (*Belial* refers to the evil figurehead in 1:19–20.) For example, according to a document called *Blessings* in 4Q286, a curse is pronounced on Belial "in his inimical plan" (*ba*[*mmaḥa*]=*šebet maṣṭemātô*), so that *maṣṭema* is simply an abstraction presented as a feature of Belial's activity (see the parallel expression at 1QS III, 23, where a similar phrase—"and the times of their troubles are in his inimical dominion [*bammamšelet maṣṭematô*]"—applies to the "Angel of Darkness"). A more interesting example illustrates how the two can appear alongside each other as references to different beings. According to a fragmentary text from *Pseudo-Jubilees* at 4Q225 2 II, 14, "the Prince of An[im]osity/Mastema, and Belial listened to [," so that it is the "Prince," not "Mastema," that stands alongside Belial, who is likely another figure. A final example occurs in the *War Scroll* at 1QM XIII, 10–12. This text, formally part of a lengthy prayer, declares that God "made Belial for the pit, an angel of *maṣṭema*; and in dark[ness is] his [rule] and in his counsel is to bring wickedness and guilt about; and all the spirits of his lot are angels of destruction; they walk in the statutes of darkness." Here the equation is not between Belial and Mastema, but between Belial and an "*angel* of *maṣṭema*," where "*maṣṭema*" either characterizes the kind of angel that Belial is or is the proper name of the angel with whom Belial is being identified. A similar problem besets texts like *Pseudo-Jubilees* at 4Q225 2 II, 6 and 13–14 (angels of *hammaṣṭemâ*, i.e., inimical angels; see further *Apocryphon of Jeremiah* at 4Q387 2 III, 4; 4Q390 1.11 and 2 I, 7) and the *Damascus Document*, in which the expression "angel of *maṣṭema*" (*mal'ak hammaṣṭema*) may not so much mean "the angel Mastema," or even "the angel of/from Mastema" (i.e., the angel under Mastema's jurisdiction), but simply an inimical or adversarial angel (see CD XVI, 2–5 and pars. in 4Q270 6 II, 18 and 4Q271 4 II, 6).

Unfortunately, not a single text in *Jubilees* (in which *maṣṭema* occurs twelve times) is preserved from the Scrolls for us to know whether Mastema was affixed to a definite article. The most frequent expression is "Prince of Mastema/

Animosity" or, simply, "Prince Mastema" (*Jub.* 11:5, 11; 18:9, 12; 48:2, 9, 12, 15). This Prince is identified with the same Mastema who has been introduced in chapter 10 as the leader of the spirits who requests permission for a tenth of their number to carry out their work after the flood. In this way, "Prince" is a title for Mastema rather than the designation itself, much as Beelzebul is described as the "ruler of demons" by those who accuse Jesus of being allied to evil power (Mark 3:22//Matt. 12:24//Luke 11:15; cf. Matt. 9:34). In retelling selected traditions known from Genesis and Exodus, the author of *Jubilees* introduces Mastema into the story line: Mastema, not God, is the one who initiates the testing of Abraham to sacrifice Isaac (*Jub.* 17:16; 18:9, 12; cf. Gen. 22:1); he, not God, is the force behind an attempt to kill Moses (*Jub.* 48:2–4, contra Exod. 4:24–26); he is behind the work of Pharaoh's magicians to counteract Moses (*Jub.* 48:9, 12; cf. Exod. 7:11, 22; 8:7, 18); and he—not God, who hardened Pharaoh's heart—incites the Egyptians to pursue the Israelites in the wilderness (*Jub.* 48:15–18; cf. Exod. 14:4). Finally, "all the forces of Mastema" are sent to kill the firstborn in the land of Egypt (cf. Exod. 12:29, where the Lord does the striking). Significantly, in each of these passages where Prince Mastema is mentioned, the narrative makes clear that his activities happen only under the terms of allowance granted him and his reduced entourage in chapter 10. Interestingly, this Mastema seems to be identified with a figure that *Jubilees* also calls Beliar (1:20) and Satan (10:11).

BELIAL

As the statistics indicate, *Belial* is by far the most frequent designation used for any evil being in the Dead Sea Scrolls and, therefore, in Second Temple Jewish texts. In the New Testament, the only mention of the name, in its related form *Beliar*, occurs in 2 Corinthians 6:15, where Paul rhetorically asks, "What does Christ have to do with Beliar?" As with Mastema, there must have been a close connection between the figure and the meaning of the name. In phrases such as "dominion of Belial" (*mamšelet belîyaʿal*), "lot of Belial," "army of Belial," "spirits of Belial," "congregation of Belial," and "child/children of Belial" and "men of Belial," we may have to do with a proper name. Sometimes, however, the word is preceded by "any," in which case we have the same kind of language as that noted with "satan" above (see, for example, 1QHᵃ XI, 28). Most references to Belial occur in documents related to the community that settled at Qumran (*Community Rule, War Scroll, Thanksgiving Hymns, Blessings, Catena,* 11Q *Melchizedek*). On the other hand, in *Jubilees* "Beliar" only occurs twice: Moses petitions that future generations of Israel not be ruled by "the spirit of Beliar" (1:20), and the unfaithful of Israel are called "the people of Beliar" (15:33). Here the meanings of *Belial* as "worthlessness" and as a proper name are hard to distinguish.

Among the Qumran group's writings, *Belial* is most immediately applied in contexts referring to faithless or disobedient Jews (though it doubtless would have included gentiles as well). Here we can discern an extraordinary development that anticipates a pattern that emerges in the New Testament. Unlike in many earlier texts, which talk about demonic or malevolent beings in a variety of ways, often with proper names (as especially in the Enochic literature, Aramaic texts from the Dead Sea Scrolls 4Q180–81, 4Q510–11, and the *Two Spirits Treatise* preserved in the Qumran *Community Rule*), in these writings the name *Belial* becomes a gathering point around which discourse about personified evil is constructed. This primary focus on a single demonic figure appears in two ways. First, whereas in some earlier texts figures like the fallen angels (*1 En.* 12–13; 15–16; *Book of Giants* at 1Q24 VIII, 2 and 4Q203 XIII, 3), Melki-reša (4Q480 II, 2), and groups of demonic beings (4Q510 I, 5; 4Q511 III, 5; 11Q11 V) are denounced and cursed, in Qumran group's *Community Rule* Belial alone—and those errant Jews associated with him—is denounced (cf. 1QS II, 4–10 par. 4Q256 II, 12–III, 4; cf. 4Q286 7 II, 2). While the denunciations in some of the earlier texts are compatible with the practice of exorcism (see below), the Qumran group seems to have adopted more fixed curse formulae spoken by either a priestly figure or the community as a whole. Second, whereas the present world order was understood as one in which demonic powers have certain, though limited, sway, the focus on Belial now concentrated in a single figure the notion of a "dominion" (*mamšalâ*) that characterizes the present age of wickedness (1QS I, 23–24; II, 19; 1QM XIV, 9–10//4QMa = 4Q491 8–10 I, 6–7; cf. further 4Q177 = 4QCatena^a III, 8; 4Q390 2 I, 4).[3] To be sure, there are "spirits of Belial," but these have now become nameless, undifferentiated, and inconsequential in the larger scheme of things. The focus is more on dealing with Belial himself, who, presiding over evil forces, is to be cursed more than exorcised.

The observations thus far allow for the following summary: whether by exorcism or by formal curse, pious Jews in the Dead Sea texts and related literature held several convictions in tension:

1. the present world order is essentially a "dominion of wickedness" in which demonic power is by default in control;
2. in the midst of such a cosmos there are those who remain obedient to God's covenant; and
3. at the final judgment all forms of evil power will be eradicated and destroyed.

In the meantime, in view of knowing that such an outcome is assured, demonic power can be effectively negotiated, curbed, or addressed through temporary expedients such as exorcism and formal denunciations.

3. According to the *Songs of the Maskil* in 4Q510 I, 6–7 ("and you [viz., the demonic beings] have been placed in the age of the dominion of wickedness and in the periods of subjugation of the sons of ligh[t] . . ." [par. 4Q511 X, 3–4]). In the texts of the Qumran group, this era of wickedness is referred to as the time of "the dominion of Belial" (e.g., 1QS I, 18, 23–24; II, 19).

"Satan," "the Devil," and "the Evil One" in the Gospel Traditions

When we come to the New Testament, the Gospel writers show a remarkable unanimity in attributing manifestations of evil to a single figure. This focus on one organizing and personified principle mirrors what we have found to be the case with the growing prominence of Belial in the more sectarian Qumran literature. As occasionally found in the Qumran literature with Belial and Mastema, the proper names can occasionally be interchangeable. So, for example, the Gospel writers' reception of Jesus tradition equates what Jesus's opponents call "Beelzebul" with "Satan" (Mark 3:22–23//Matt. 12:24, 26–27// Luke 11:15, 18–19). On the whole, the tradition shows a clear preference for "Satan" (Matt. 12:26; 16:23; Mark 1:13; 3:23, 26; 4:15; 8:33; Luke 10:18; 11:18; 13:16; 22:3, 31; cf. Acts 5:3; 26:18), further describing the same being, except for in Mark, as "the devil" (Matt. 4:1, 5, 8, 11; 13:39; 25:41; Luke 4:2–3, 5–6, 9, 13; 8:12; John 8:44; 13:2; cf. Acts 10:38; 13:10) and in Matthew and John as "the evil one" (Matt. 5:37; 6:13; 13:19, 38; John 17:15).

The Gospels share another basic conviction with the Jewish texts just considered. The present world order is essentially an arena under one personified figure's control, an arena that, as such, they refer to as a "dominion" (*mamšalâ*) or "kingdom" (*basileia*). Thus, in Matthew and Luke's Gospels, before Jesus commences with his proclamation of God's kingdom, Satan offers, in the temptation narrative, to give Jesus "all the kingdoms of the world" if he will worship him (Matt. 4:8//Luke 4:5–7). Satan's ownership of the world has not resulted from a successful power struggle against God; Luke's version of the story has the devil clarify that such authority "has been given to me, and I give it to anyone I please," an allusion, in the passive voice, to the view that this authority has been granted by God. When did such a turnover of authority take place? It is not as likely that the text presupposes a story line such as the garden of Eden account as that it has in view an account such as in *Jubilees*, in which Mastema and some of his demonic minions are granted permission after the flood to afflict human beings and lead them astray. A similar understanding of satanic activity enabled by divine permission is expressed by Jesus's words to Simon (Peter) just before Jesus's death in Luke: "Satan has demanded to sift all of you like wheat" (Luke 22:31). Here, the permissive (and therefore derivative) nature of Satan's influence allows Jesus to state that he has gained the upper hand by praying (successfully) that Peter will not succumb to this power (22:32).

Satan's arena of control as a "kingdom" is also mentioned in Jesus's response to those who accuse him of acting on Beelzebul's behalf. While in Mark's version (cf. 3:24, 26) this is only implied, Matthew and Luke agree in having Jesus point out that Satan's kingdom would not be able to stand "if Satan [i.e., Jesus acting on his behalf] casts out Satan" (so Matt. 12:26; see par. Luke 11:17–18). Jesus's saying assumes as incontestable that Satan's kingdom in this world *does* stand and that, therefore, it must be fought against. The Johannine tradition expresses this understanding of Satan with the more fixed designation "the ruler of this world" (John 12:31; 14:30; 16:11). As such, Satan is said to be "coming" (14:30; i.e., probably through his involvement with Jesus's death), though as such he has no real power over Jesus (14:30) and, in fact, already stands condemned (16:11) and will be "driven out" (12:31), that is, be fully divested from the firm grasp he currently holds over the cosmos.

Alongside the principled acknowledgment of satanic rule in this world, the Gospels offer glimpses into the possibility that, in certain acute instances, Satan can be thought to inhabit or influence human beings directly. We have already noted the accusation that Jesus is in league with Beelzebul, which Mark's Gospel supplements with a further explanatory comment that Jesus was thought to have "an unclean spirit" (Mark 3:30). This was a serious charge that the Gospel writers could not ultimately leave unanswered. So, while Mark's Gospel is content to have Jesus be introduced as the one who will baptize in "the *Holy* Spirit" (1:8), to have the Spirit to descend upon him at his baptism (1:10), and to have this same Spirit bring Jesus into open conflict with Satan (1:12), the Gospels of Matthew and Luke may have drawn on a tradition that attempted to respond to the charge of satanic collaboration by emphasizing that Jesus, at his very conception, was generated by the *Holy* Spirit (Matt. 1:18, 20; Luke 1:35, 41). Within John's Gospel, the debate surrounding Jesus's alliance with Satan reaches a climax as Jesus and "the Jews" trade accusations, respectively, of having a demon and devilish parenthood in John 8:39–44 (esp. vv. 44, 48–49). Satan's particular embodiment within activities of people is illustrated in Jesus's response to Peter's wrong understanding of his own verbal confession of Jesus as Messiah ("Get behind me, Satan!"—Mark 8:33; Matt. 16:23), in the woman with "a spirit of illness" whom Satan had bound for eighteen years (Luke 13:11, 16), and in Judas's activity of betrayal that led to Jesus's death (Luke 22:3; John 13:27; see also Acts 5:3 and, further, the parable traditions in Mark 4:15//Luke 8:12//Matt. 13:39).

While the belief in the existence of a personified evil force is taken for granted as a constituent feature of the Gospels, its theological implications should not be overlooked. Although characters in the Gospel narratives, especially those who find themselves socially, religiously, and economically privileged, are frequently held accountable for their actions, the Gospels know very little about an "Adamic fall" as a condition inherited by all of humanity and hold up the possibility that people can be victims of the demonic. Instead, the world is regarded as an arena of conflict between Satan and his demonic forces, on the one hand, and God along with obedient followers who serve him, on the other, in anticipation of evil's complete annihilation. The tension between Jesus's continuing confrontation with evil during his ministry and evil's ultimate destruction is illuminated further when we consider more closely the exorcistic tradition and its background in Jewish thought.

Jesus's Exorcisms in Their Second Temple Jewish Context

In turning to the exorcisms of demonic beings, we will first note discernible patterns in the Gospel tradition, then consider what the Jewish apocalyptic traditions contribute to our reading of Jesus's activity. These characteristic features of Jesus's exorcisms will then guide our discussion of the apocalyptic Jewish traditions.

Within the Jesus tradition, three features stand out consistently and regularly: the dawning of God's rule, "demons" as evil or unclean spirits, and demonic possession as entry into the human body. Taken together, these add up to a worldview that regards divine activity, the nature of evil, and theological anthropology as different parts of a continuous whole.

The first feature is *the dawning of God's rule*. One of the most common ways of communicating the significance of Jesus's exorcisms in relation to our contemporary understanding has been to note their connection with Jesus's proclamation of the royal power of the God of Israel. Many are convinced that in addition to his healing miracles, Jesus regarded his expulsions of demons from people as concrete demonstrations that God's rule was breaking into this world. Exorcisms, insofar as they are presented as moments of conflict, would have provided poignant examples; they illustrated how through Jesus evil forces were being dispossessed by God from the foothold they were believed to have on people in the present age. However, none of the exorcism stories in the Gospels actually affirms the connection between what Jesus was doing, on the one hand, and God's kingship or rule, on the other. For this link the Gospels steer our attention to the sayings of Jesus.

In this respect, most scholarly attention has focused on the "Q" tradition in Luke 11:20 (par. Matt. 12:28). According to the Lukan version, Jesus claims, "But if it is by the finger [Matt.: "Spirit"] of God that I cast out the demons, then the kingdom of God has come upon you." The saying assumes that the vacuum that arises within a person dispossessed of demonic power is being filled by the protective power of God's rule. For those who have been exorcised, Jesus's ministry signals the beginning of a salvific process. Similarly, Jesus's declaration upon the return of the seventy disciples in Luke 10:18 that he "watched Satan fall from heaven like a flash of lightning" is offered as an explanation of why the disciples could be portrayed as successful exorcists. Exorcisms result from a power struggle in which Satan's power has been overcome by God. The association between casting out demons and the establishing of God's rule can be plausibly traced back to Jesus, or at least reflects Jesus's understanding of what was happening when he (and others whom he commissioned) emerged with success from exorcistic encounters. The final layers of redaction in both the Lukan and Matthean forms of the saying postpone the defeat of Satan or demons to a later stage, and so stand in tension with Jesus's claim. Jesus's statement, though form-critically independent from its context in the material shared by Luke and Matthew, cannot be understood apart from Jesus's own practice of exorcism, that is, from the *kind of activity* ascribed to him through the accounts conveyed to us through the Synoptic Gospels.

Though the link between exorcisms and God's rule may be traced back to Jesus, would it be correct to conclude that Jesus's activity in vanquishing the effects of Satan's rule is essentially different from and without precedent in the Jewish environment in which his ministry was conducted?

The second recurring feature in Jesus's episodic encounters with demonic forces is the presentation of *"demons" as evil and unclean spirits.* In the Synoptic Gospels the following designations occur, sometimes as a single term and sometimes in combination with one or more qualifying adjectives:

a. "demon"—*daimōn* or *daimonion* (Mark 1:34 2X, 39; 3:15, 22; 6:13; 7:26, 29–30; 9:38; Matt. 7:22; 9:33–34; 10:8; 11:18; 12:24 2X, 27–28; 17:18; Luke 4:33, 35, 41; 7:33; 8:2, 27, 30, 33, 35, 38; 9:1, 42, 49; 10:17; 11:14 2X, 15 2X, 18–20; 13:32)

b. "evil spirit"—*pneuma ponēron* (Luke 7:21; 8:2; cf. Acts 19:12–13, 15–16)[4]

c. "unclean spirit"—*akatharton pneuma* (Mark 1:23, 26–27; 3:11, 30; 5:2, 8, 13; 6:7; 7:25; 9:25; Matt. 10:1; 12:43 [Q]; Luke 4:36; 6:18; 8:29; 11:24 [Q])

d. "spirit of an unclean demon"—*pneuma daimoniou akathartou* (Luke 4:33 [cf. Mark 1:23])

e. "spirit of weakness"—*pneuma . . . astheneias* (Luke 13:11; "spirit that had crippled her")

f. "dumb" or "deaf-and-dumb spirit"—*pneuma alalon* (Mark 9:17), *alalon kai kōphon pneuma* (Mark 9:25)

g. "spirit"—*pneuma* (Matt. 8:16; 12:45; Luke 9:31 [cf. Mark 9:17], 38–39; 11:46)

With regard to the history of ideas, three aspects of these expressions are noteworthy. First, on the level of the Gospel narratives, the expressions "demon" and "unclean spirit" are used interchangeably (cf. Matt. 10:1, 8; Mark 3:22, 30; Luke 8:27, 29). Whereas these terms, respectively, flourished independently in sociocultural and religious Greco-Roman and Jewish spheres, they are here brought into a synonymity that, in a Jewish context, would associate impurity with demonic influence. While this might signify that exorcism functioned as a means of reintegrating into society someone whose presence in it had been proscribed, the early Enochic traditions (so *1 En.* 6–16) make clear that more than dealing with halakhic impurity is at stake.

4. The restricted distribution of the expression within Luke-Acts suggests that it is a Lukanism.

Second, it is well known that whereas among Greek writers during the preceding and subsequent centuries, *daimōn* is, on the whole, used neutrally to denote intermediary agents capable of carrying out good or ill in relation to humans,[5] in the Gospels—indeed, in the New Testament as a whole—the term has acquired an irrevocably negative meaning. The factors behind this development require a longer analysis than is possible here, though in anticipation of what follows, it suffices to say that the emphasis on *daimones* as evil powers was able to flourish within in a Jewish apocalyptic setting.

The third point to note is the remarkable distribution and frequency of the designation "unclean spirit." As far as I am able to ascertain, this expression is without parallel in non-Jewish literature from pre-Christian antiquity. Here, at least as far as the Synoptic Gospels are concerned, we find ourselves on unmistakably Jewish soil with which Jesus and those who spoke and wrote about him would have been familiar. This language extends back to Zechariah 13:2, where, in an association with idolatry, "unclean spirit" (Heb. *rûaḥ ḥaṭṭum'â*, Gk. *to pneuma to akatharton*) describes Judah and Jerusalem in an imperiled state of religious unfaithfulness; the removal of this spirit by God is envisioned on a national scale. The next references, preserved among the Dead Sea materials, bring us closer to the climate of the Gospels in that "spirit of uncleanness" pertains to a state of being from which *individuals* seek deliverance or relief (cf. 11Q11 XIX, 15; 4Q444 1 I, 8; 1QS IV, 22; perhaps also 4Q458 2 I, 5). The expression here suggests that the effect of the malevolent spirit is to render its victim ritually unclean and thus unable to participate in the religious life of Israel. While the origins of such spirits can be contemplated by considering the larger context of the Dead Sea Scrolls and their reception of Enochic tradition, the Gospels offer very little information about what made the exorcised spirits unclean; instead, the impurity of such spirits is taken for granted.

The third feature emerging from accounts about Jesus's exorcisms is an understanding of *demonic possession as entry into the human body*. Despite the diversity of traditions preserved in relation to the exorcisms of Jesus, his disciples, and others in the Gospels, the way demons are described in relation to their human victims is extraordinarily uniform. Almost all the texts portray exorcism as a *disembodiment* of spirits: they are "cast *out*" (*ekballein*) of the victims they have possessed.[6] The image of exit from within is reinforced by the notion of evil spirits either "entering" (*eiserchomai*)[7] into individual human

5. On this, see, e.g., Eric Sorensen, *Possession and Exorcism in the New Testament and Early Christianity*, WUNT 2.157 (Tübingen: Mohr Siebeck, 2002), 75–117; Lars Albinus, "The Greek δαίμων between Mythos and Logos," in *Die Dämonen / Demons*, ed. Armin Lange, Hermann Lichtenberger and K. F. Diethard Römheld (Tübingen: Mohr Siebeck, 2003), 425–46.

6. So in Mark 1:34, 39; 3:15, 22–23; 6:13; 9:18, 28; Matt. 7:22; 8:16, 31; 9:33–34; 10:1, 8; 12:24, 26–28; 17:19; Luke 9:40, 49; 11:14–15, 18, 19–20; 13:32.

7. Mark 3:27; 5:12–13; 9:25; Matt. 12:29; Luke 8:30, 32–33; 22:3.

beings or "departing" (*exerchomai*)[8] from them. Underlying this language is the assumption that people can be victimized by demons when the demons inhabit their bodies. There is no reason to think that Jesus's understanding of the relationship between demonic powers and human bodies was any different.

Among the Jesus sayings, this understanding of exit and entry is clearest in a passage from tradition shared by Matthew and Luke (Matt. 12:43–45// Luke 11:24–26) often referred to as "the return of the spirit." Luke's version, which is arguably earlier, reads as follows:

> When the unclean spirit has gone out of [*exelthē*] a person, it wanders through waterless regions looking for a resting place, but not finding any, it says, "I will return to my house from which I came." When it comes, it finds it swept and put in order. Then it goes and brings seven other spirits more evil than itself, and they enter and live there. And the last state of that person is worse than the first.

The saying simply concludes with a warning (v. 26b) without any accompanying exhortation. In its present form, this saying is remarkably open about the danger that, we may assume, follows an exorcism: the "last state" is not presented as a potential condition but rather as what can be expected to happen if, presumably, further measures are not undertaken. The scenario depicted here is that of exorcistic activity that is ultimately ineffectual, and no attempt is made in the saying to specify whether such activity is that of Jesus, the disciples, or others operating in Jesus's name. For this reason a number of interpreters regard this tradition as one that neither Jesus's disciples nor the early church would have been likely to create; the thrust of the saying, especially in the Lukan version, is counterintuitive to the portrait the Gospels provide of Jesus, whose exorcisms would more ideally have been portrayed as successful. If this saying can be traced back to Jesus, it is significant that, in line with the narrative accounts, the case as described presupposes that the human body can serve both as a demon's "house" (v. 24b; cf. the metaphorical use of "house" in Mark 3:25, 27//Matt. 12:25, 29) and as a natural abode for its return (v. 26a).

The uniformity of demonic corporeal indwelling in the Synoptic Gospels stands out given that it is relatively rare in Jewish sources that predate the New Testament writings. Far more widespread in Greco-Roman antiquity is language that depicts demonic activity more in terms of affliction or attack rather than as entry per se. Good examples of affliction rather than possession per se can be found in Tobit (cf. 3:8; 6:8, 14–15; 8:2—the demon Asmodeus's attacks on men at the wedding night), *Genesis Apocryphon* (1Q20 XX, 16–29— Abram's prayers to drive away an evil spirit), *Apocryphal Psalms* (11Q11 V, 4—words to say when a demon attacks during the night), the four songs

---

8. Mark 5:13; 7:29–30; Matt. 12:43 (Q); Luke 8:2, 33; 11:14, 24 (Q).

composed by David for "the afflicted" (11Q5 XXVII), and the songs to frighten away malevolent powers in *Songs of the Maskil* (4Q510 1.4–6//4Q511 10.1–3; 4Q511 8.4; 35.6–9; 48 + 49 + 51 II, 2–3). To be sure, it remains possible that these writers thought demons could inhabit bodies; however, it is conspicuous that the notion of corporeal habitation so prominent in the Gospels is absent here and, indeed, is far less widespread than is often assumed.

Less clear in distinguishing between affliction and possession is the text of *Jubilees* 10:7–14. According to this passage, the angels of the presence give instructions to Noah on how, for example, to use herbs to combat the malevolent effects of the remaining evil spirits (a tenth of their original number) who, following the great flood, were allowed to try to seduce human beings and cause illnesses. It is not clear whether the text assumes that the revealed herbal remedies have exorcistic effects (in dealing with physical ailments within the body), are prophylactic and simply ward the evil spirits off, or—as most likely is the case—both.

There are, in any case, only a few Jewish sources outside the New Testament and composed before the end of the first century CE that, analogous to the Synoptic Gospels, communicate demonic effects in terms of the inhabitation of demons within the human body. Perhaps the best-known instance of an exorcism is the story, recounted by Josephus, of "a certain Eleazar" who illustrates the continuing potency of exorcistic cures attributed to Solomon (*Ant.* 8.42–49).[9] Three further examples of this may be found among the Dead Sea Scrolls: (1) a text concerned with the location of a spirit that, residing under the surface of the skin, causes a skin disease (*Damascus Document* at 4Q266 = 4QD[a] 6 I, 5–7, with fragmentary parallels in 4Q269 = 4QD[d] 7; 4Q272 = 4QD[g] 1 I–II; and 4Q273 = 4QD[h] 4 II); (2) the *Two Spirits Treatise*, according to which "the spirit of deceit" and "the spirit of truth" battle each other "in the heart of man" (1QS IV, 23); and (3) a small text that refers to the entry of male and female forces of evil into the human flesh and heart (4Q560 1 I, 3–4; II, 5–6).

While the last three examples do not provide evidence for exorcistic practices that immediately underlie episodes recorded in the Gospels, they do preserve language that conceives of demonic influence in terms of corporeal invasion or habitation. On the basis of the Jewish evidence, we may at least conclude that they enhance the plausibility that the theological anthropology assumed in the Synoptic Gospels existed within a Jewish setting.

I have argued thus far that the motifs of God's reign, the belief that *daimones* are evil and unclean, and the view that they affect humans by gaining entry into their bodies are all linked in the early Jesus tradition. Taken

---

9. According to Josephus (*Ant.* 8.45), Solomon "composed incantations with which illnesses depart and by which illnesses are relieved, and left behind forms of exorcisms [*tropous exorkōseō*] with which those possessed by demons drive them out [*ekdiōkousi*], never to return" (Thackeray and Marcus, LCL).

together, they probably reflect *what* Jesus thought his exorcisms signified, *how* he thought demons affected the human body, and *what* he thought *happened* when demons were dealt with. This puts us in a better position to inquire into the nature of this convergence of ideas. For example, is the link between the kingdom of God and expulsion of demonic powers the creation of Jesus? While there is no doubt that the Gospel writers attribute to Jesus, even in his ministry, a distinctiveness that underscored his *own* extraordinary power and the power of exorcising in his name, we may still ask whether the notion of successful exorcisms as evidence of God's rule marked something *essentially* new.

The Demonic in Apocalyptic Perspective

Here it is possible to note the value of what the early Enoch and related traditions bequeathed to the New Testament world. In particular we may consider the Book of Watchers (in *1 En.* 1–36), the *Book of Giants*, and the Book of Dreams (in *1 En.* 83–90). These texts have gained increasing prominence during the last several decades for a number of reasons, including what their authors had to say about the introduction of evil into the world.[10] Those to be blamed for the presence of evil were thought to be rebellious angelic beings who, related to "the sons of God" in Genesis 6:2, gave instructions and engaged in activities (e.g., siring a race of giants) before the great flood that were fundamentally contrary to God's purpose for the created order.

The early Enochic traditions each draw heavily on an interpretation of the great flood as a decisive act of divine punishment carried out in response to the evils committed by the fallen angels and the giant offspring they sired through the women of the earth. Significantly, motifs and imagery associated with the deluge (cf. *1 En.* 10; 83–84; 91:5–10; 93:1–3, 12–15; 106:13–107:1; *Book of Giants* at 4Q530 2 II, + 6–7 + 8–12, lines 4–20) contribute to the way the Enochic authors attempted to describe God's final, eschatological triumph over evil. Perhaps the most influential form of this tradition is preserved in the Book of Watchers, which, as a whole, dates to the third century BCE while containing traditions that may be even earlier. The earliest extant copy of the Book of Watchers, 4Q201, already combines the once separate strands of tradition in *1 Enoch* 6–11 and 12–16. The resulting narrative, if one reads chapters 6–16 as a unit, focuses on the reprehensible instructions given to humanity during the antediluvian period by the fallen angels (*1 En.* 7:1; 8:3; 9:6–8a; 13:2b; cf. Ethiopic to 16:3), as well as on the violent activities of their progeny, the giants, who correspond to the "mighty men" and "Nephilim"

---

10. See, e.g., the discussion in Archie T. Wright, *The Origin of Evil Spirits*, WUNT 2.198 (Tübingen: Mohr Siebeck, 2005).

in Genesis 6:4. In contrast to Genesis 6, which makes no direct mention of the giants' involvement in the events leading up to the flood, the giants in the Book of Watchers are prominent among those being held accountable for the increase of oppression and suffering on the earth (*1 En.* 7:3–6; 9:1, 9–10). So, it is in response to the cries of the giants' human victims through four principal angels (8:4–9:3; cf. 7:6) that divine judgment is set in motion (chap. 10). The giants are then punished either through infighting among themselves (7:5; 10:9, 12)[11] or, though less clearly, through the great flood (10:15; *Jub.* 7:21–25).[12]

The emphasis placed by the Book of Watchers and, subsequently, the *Book of Giants* on divine judgment of the giant offspring of the rebellious angels was not simply based on the violence and oppressiveness of their deeds. More fundamentally, there was something inherently wrong with the very form of their existence. According to one strand of the narrative (that relating to the chief fallen angel, Shemihazah), the giants were the product of the illicit sexual union between the angels as heavenly beings and the human women as earthly beings (*1 En.* 6:1–4; 7:1–2; 9:7–8; 10:9, 11; 15:3–7, 12; cf. *Book of Giants* at 4Q531 1). In *1 Enoch* 15:3–7, the reason for the loathsomeness of this union is made explicit: the giants are a mixture based on acts of defilement in which beings assigned to essentially separate spheres in the cosmos (i.e., heaven and earth) had come together; by definition, then, the giants were an embodiment of the violation of the created order (15:4, 9–10; cf. *Jub.* 7:21). They were misfits and had no proper place. As the offspring of such an illegitimate union, they were neither fully angel nor fully human. Hence, they are called "bastards" in *1 Enoch* 10:9 (Cod. Panopolitanus, a codex from the sixth century, reads *tous mazereous*, a transliteration from Heb. or Aram. *mamzerayyâ/mamzerîm*)

Both the Book of Watchers and *Book of Giants* make it clear that through an act of divine intervention the giants had to be categorically and decisively held to account.[13] Nonetheless, although the giants are not spared, neither

11. See also *Jub.* 5:9; 7:22; *Book of Giants* at 6Q8 1 and 4Q531 7.

12. Within the early Enochic tradition, punishment of the giants through the deluge is clearest in the *Animal Apocalypse* at *1 En.* 89:5. In service of paradigmatic interests, the flood soon became the primary, if not only, means for the giants' destruction in Second Temple literature from the second century on. So esp. *4QExhortation Based on the Flood* (= 4Q370) I, 6; *Damascus Document* (CD A II, 19–20); Sir. 16:7(?); Wis. 14:6; 3 Macc. 2:4; *3 Bar.* 4:10.

13. It is possible that in taking this view, the apocalyptic Enochic writers were responding to the view, preserved among *Pseudo-Eupolemos* traditions cited by Eusebius (*Hist. eccl.* 9.17.1–9; 9.18.2), that retold the biblical story to allow for the giants' surviving the deluge and becoming a key link in the transmission and spread of revealed culture between pre- and postdiluvian times. See further Loren T. Stuckenbruck, "The Origins of Evil in Jewish Apocalyptic Tradition: The Interpretation of Genesis 6:1–4 in the Second and Third Centuries BCE," in *The Fall of the Angels*, ed. Christoph Auffarth and Loren T. Stuckenbruck, TBN 7 (Leiden: Brill, 2004), 87–118 (here 89–98).

Enochic Literature

During the Second Temple period a number of writings organized around and attributed to Enoch (see Gen. 5:21–24) were composed and, in stages, collected into a document that in the Ethiopian Orthodox tradition became known as "the Book of Enoch." Today this collection is variously titled *1 Enoch* (in order to distinguish it from subsequent writings under the patriarch's name) or *Ethiopic Enoch* (since it is only in classical Ethiopic, Ge'ez, that all 108 chapters are preserved as a collection in their entirety). Interest in this material has been stimulated in the West by a number of developments during the last two hundred years: (1) the study, editing, and translation of growing numbers of Ethiopic manuscripts, initiated when Richard Laurence brought a manuscript to Europe during the early nineteenth century; (2) discoveries of Greek materials in the nineteenth and twentieth centuries, confirming the existence of Enochic writings in this language and raising the question about the language(s) that may have been behind the Ethiopic version; (3) the identification and editing of smaller textual materials in Syriac, Coptic, and Latin that testify to the widespread use of the tradition; and (4) the recovery of Aramaic manuscripts among the Dead Sea Scrolls that confirm the early date of parts of *1 Enoch* and reveal that, even at an early stage, discrete Enochic compositions were beginning to be gathered and copied together in single-scroll manuscripts.

Since *1 Enoch* came to light through the Ethiopic tradition, it has been popular to talk about the collection in terms of "five books," plus two appendixes. This division would be as follows: (1) Book of Watchers (chaps. 1–36), (2) Book of Parables or Similitudes (chaps. 37–71), (3) Book of Heavenly Luminaries or Astronomical Book (chaps. 72–82), (4) Book

are they completely annihilated; though not escaping divine wrath, they end up surviving in a radically altered state: they are "evil spirits" (*1 En.* 15:8–9). The preserved textual witnesses to *1 Enoch* 15 do not state how this alteration of existence has occurred, but it is possible to reconstruct an etiology behind the existence of demons based on *1 Enoch* 15:3–16:3 and the *Book of Giants*, which may have been elaborating on parts of chapter 10. When the giants came under God's judgment, their physical nature was destroyed but their spirits or souls emerged from their dead bodies. In this disembodied state they continue to exist until the final triumph of God in the eschaton (16:1). After the great flood they engage in the sorts of activities that they previously did. In particular, as before, they wish to afflict human beings (15:12). Why? We may infer that they are jealous of humanity, who managed to escape the deluge with their bodies intact.

This story line explains how giants could become identified as demons not only among the Dead Sea Scrolls but also at a later stage. Among the Dead Sea materials several references to demonic beings reflect the direct influence of Dreams (chaps. 83–90), (5) Epistle of Enoch (chaps. 91–105). The appendixes would consist of Birth of Noah (chaps. 106–7) and Eschatological Admonition (chap. 108). In addition to these sections, there existed a number of closely related traditions or writings recovered from the Dead Sea Scrolls whose status as part of the Enochic collection is disputed; these include 1Q19 (Heb.) and the *Book of Giants* (10 mss.). If, for the moment, we restrict ourselves to the 108 chapters as they stand in the Ethiopic textual tradition, perhaps as many as nineteen discrete written traditions attributable to different authors survive in this collection: chaps. 1–5; chaps. 6–11 (with this section based, in turn, on several distinguishable sources); chaps. 12–16; chaps. 17–36; chaps. 37–71 (Similitudes; plus Noahic insertions and the possibility of chaps. 70–71 coming from a different author); chaps. 72–80 (Astonomical Book); 81:1–82:4; 82:4–20 (Astronomical Book); chaps. 83–84 (First Dream Vision); chaps. 85–90 (Animal Apocalypse); 91:1–10, 18–19 (Exhortation); 91:11–17; 93:1–10 (Apocalypse of Weeks); 92:1–5; 93:11–105:2 (Epistle of Enoch); chaps. 106–7 (Birth of Noah); and chap. 108 (Eschatological Admonition).

The earliest of these traditions come from the Astronomical Book (chaps. 72–79 and 82:4–20) and the Book of Watchers (esp. chaps. 6–11), which go back to the fourth and early third centuries BCE. The likelihood that a number of the writings can be dated to the second century (all the material from chaps. 85–107 and the *Book of Giants*) and evidence among the Dead Sea Scrolls that these were being collected and copied together in the same manuscript increases the likelihood that one can speak of an Enochic tradition with some socioreligious continuity (i.e., a community of different contemporary scribes who could assume the name of Enoch as the figure to whom to attach their activity).

of the Enochic tradition and have the giants' postdiluvian existence in view. According to *Songs of the Maskil* at 4Q510 1.5, the expression "spirits of the bastards" (*rûḥôt mamzerîm*) occurs within a longer catalogue of malevolent forces. This also avails in the same document at 4Q511 35.7; 48+49+51.2–3; and at 4Q444 2 I, 4, where the giants are beings who need to be brought under control by the hymns directed by the Maskil to God. Furthermore, in the above-mentioned *Apocryphal Psalms* text (section D.3), at 11Q11 V, 6, the demon visiting during the night is, if the text is correctly restored, addressed as "offspring of] Adam and seed of the ho[ly] ones."[14] This explanation of demons as disembodied spirits emanating from the giant offspring of the fallen angels continues in later Christian literature, picked up in *Testament of Solomon* (5:3; 17:1), the *Pseudo-Clementine Homilies* (8.12–18: giants designated as "bastards" and "demons"), Tertullian's *Apology* (22), Lactantius's *Divine Institutes* (2.15), and Commodianus's *Instructions* (3).

14. For the expression "holy ones" as referring to the fallen angels, see also *Genesis Apocryphon* (1Q20) II, 1; VI, 20; Book of Watchers at 4Q201 1 I, 3.

Jewish Apocalyptic Perspective and Exorcism in the Gospel Traditions

Before determining the significance of the Jewish traditions just reviewed for understanding Jesus's confrontations with demonic power in human beings, we can draw several negative conclusions. First, none of the Enochic traditions contains any of the more technical language such as "kingdom of God," which in the Gospels plays such a prominent role in Jesus's proclamation and, as we have seen, is related to Jesus's exorcistic ministry. Second, the Enochic traditions themselves do not provide any narrative accounts of exorcisms that may serve as background to narratives of Jesus's activity. Third, unlike the Dead Sea Scrolls, the Gospels contain not a single passage, be it narrative or saying, identifying a demon as a giant living in a postdiluvian state of its existence. What, then, might the early Enochic traditions and the trajectory of development they set within the Dead Sea documents contribute to our picture of Jesus the exorcist?

In relation to a better understanding of the ministry of Jesus in the Gospel tradition, the story of the giants could function in several ways. First, it could offer one way of explaining why demons were thought to be so intent on entering the bodies of human beings. Demonic entry is construed as an attempt to recover a form of existence the giants had lost and to make humans, who as a race came through the great flood unscathed, pay for their rescue.

Second, the story serves to locate the problem of demonic evil within an apocalyptic-eschatological framework. On the one hand, the giants' punishment was a decisive act of God. On the other hand, although the giants were allowed to survive into the postdiluvian period as disembodied spirits, their altered mode of survival was that of powers who are conscious of living in an already defeated state and whose obliteration is assured. Thus the flood is portrayed as a proleptic episode: imagery from the flood is adapted as the author of *1 Enoch* 10 looks forward to eschatological judgment, when evil will be destroyed once and for all (10:13–11:2). The meantime—that is, between the time when God's rule became manifest in the flood and the time when evil will be eradicated—is an age during which evil spirits that came from the giants can operate under restriction (cf. *Jub.* 10:7–9), knowing their time to wreak havoc on humanity is limited (*1 En.* 16:1; *Jub.* 10:7–9; see Matt. 8:29—"Have you come here to torment us before the time?" [pars. Mark 5:7; Luke 8:28]; cf. also Mark 1:24//Luke 4:34—"Have you come to destroy us?"—and James 2:19). Jewish contemporaries of Jesus who undertook means to curb the influence of demons could, against such a background, proceed with a certain measure of confidence. In relation to the discourse about the demonic world, then, the Jesus tradition does not so much introduce the notion of an eschatological tension between the "already" and "not yet" as intensify it as an activity that characterizes Jesus's ministry.

Third, God's act of delivering humanity in the deluge and punishment of evil is associated with royal power. The divine response happens following petitions in which the archangels address God as, among other things, "King of kings" (*1 En.* 9:4). Moreover, if it is correct to read one of the *Book of Giants* fragments (4Q203 9) as a petition (by Enoch?) that God intervene to punish the fallen angels and giants, then the reference in the prayer to "your great rule" (*malkût rebûtekâ*) suggests that God's kingship was being understood to have manifested itself in the past in the deluge. Indeed, Enoch's petition in the Book of Dreams (*1 En.* 84:2–6), which also appeals to God's kingship, anticipates—and is followed by—the punishment of antediluvian evil.[15]

Fourth, in view of the framework outlined here, one may then well ask: what do the Gospel stories of exorcisms performed by Jesus and others assume happens to demonic powers when they have been expelled? Those who understood themselves to live in a world inhabited by demons would not have thought exorcism is a matter of extermination or total destruction. Instead, spiritual forces are by these means *relocated*. This is the view affirmed in Luke 11:24–26 (par. Matt. 12:43–45; cf. discussion above) and presumed by all the accounts of Jesus's confrontation with malevolent spirits. Even the Gadarene demoniac episode provides another case in point, with its two-stage exorcism that builds on the presumption (articulated by "Legion" in Mark 5:12: "Send us into the swine; let us enter them") that this is what customarily happens. Therefore, despite the story's attempt to highlight the distinct authority with which Jesus has commanded the situation, the drowning of two thousand swine indwelled by the spirits (5:13) does not mark the end of those spirits. The final act of complete subjugation lies ahead.

Fifth, and following from the last point, the "return of the spirit" saying, as we have seen, acknowledged that exorcised powers can return and do so in such a way that the person's condition is worse than before. This reflects an outlook that evil power, once extricated from the human body, needs to be kept at bay or negotiated in order for the person to remain in an improved state of being.

Sixth and finally, the very idea that exorcism is needed at all is not based on an understanding of the plagued person as evil. The Enochic tradition and a number of texts that drew upon it regard demonic powers as inherently out of place in and alien to the world as God has set it up to be. The notion of possession, instead of undermining the dignity of this or that individual, could actually function to preserve it. Whatever their problems, human beings are and remain integral to the created order.

15. The presence of royal power in curbing or dealing with the effects of demonic power may be also implied in the *Songs of the Maskil*, mentioned above. The writer of the songs holds two convictions in tension: a belief that one now lives during a time of "a dominion of wickedness" during which "the sons of light" can be expected to suffer and be "plagued by iniquities," and a belief that, despite this, the threats posed by such evil powers, which are temporary in any case, can be neutralized until the present age is brought to an end (cf. 4Q510 1.6b–8//4Q511 10.3b–6).

Conclusion

In presenting Jesus as one in conflict with Satan and demonic beings subordinate to Satan, the Synoptic Gospels and John are heavily influenced by Jewish apocalyptic traditions. We have seen that discourse about a chief figure and discourse about demonic beings were not always integrated in the Jewish texts and that, therefore, the strategies for dealing with these beings—whether through liturgical denunciation or, in the case of lower-ranked demonic powers, through hymns, prayers, or exorcistic practices—could be distinguished. This distinction is largely, though not categorically, upheld in the Gospels, where the notion of exorcising "Satan" (cf. Mark 8:33//Matt. 16:18; John 12:31) seems to have been more the exception than the rule.

It is clear that the Synoptic Gospels underline the success of Jesus as one whose power is superior to that of demonic beings in the present age. Jesus's prominence as an exorcist par excellence is also reflected in the effectiveness attributed to the use of his "name" by others (Matt. 7:22; Mark 9:38; Luke 9:49; 10:17).[16] There is every reason to think, then, that the presentation of Jesus in the Gospels stressed the "miraculous," if not unique, character of his deeds.

At the same time, however, Jesus's counterdemonic maneuvers fit logically within the framework of an apocalyptic worldview that some, perhaps even many, of his pious Jewish contemporaries shared. The implications of this logical "fit" pose questions for New Testament interpreters, who fall heir to much of the scholarly discussion of "apocalyptic" as a worldview (as well as discussion of "apocalypse" as a literary genre) during the nineteenth and twentieth centuries. As is well known, discussion of apocalyptic that contextualized Jesus's ministry has been dominated by a model oriented around the future, a model that conceives of the future as a time of divine judgment to resolve evils that are irresolvable in the present world and that (sometimes) anticipates God's rule as an imminent reality.[17] This understanding has served New Testament scholarship as a convenient way not only to locate, for example, the historical Jesus and certain accents of Pauline theology within a Jewish frame of thought but also, for example, to draw attention to what marks them out as distinctive by comparison. For some, this understanding has provided a platform that regards Jesus within a "thoroughgoing eschatology," a view that attempts to take Jesus's place within apocalyptic Jewish ideology (as one who focused on the future) seriously.[18] For others, it is in Jesus's activity, both

16. The scope for successful exorcisms in Acts 19:13–16 is implicitly narrowed to Jesus's followers, though the sons of Sceva are presented as having wrongly assumed that their use of Jesus's name would be effective.

17. Such a framework assumed a certain prominence of ways to read works such as Daniel, John's Apocalypse, *4 Ezra*, and *2 Baruch*.

18. So the well-known work of Albert Schweitzer, *The Quest of the Historical Jesus: A Critical Study of Its Progress from Reimarus to Wrede*, trans. W. Montgomery, 3rd ed.

in how the Synoptic Gospels present him and perhaps even in the way Jesus understood himself, that God's rule is seen as breaking into this world in a definitive way, a moment after which "history" could no longer be the same.[19]

Scholars have, of course, observed the shortcomings of such a one-dimensional future orientation of Jewish apocalyptic, especially since the earliest recoverable apocalypses seem just as interested in a spatial understanding of the world made possible through revealed knowledge as in the conversion of the present into a future cosmos.[20] Other ways of understanding Jewish apocalyptic thought have therefore been suggested. For example, it is recognized that some apocalyptic writers demonstrated a concern with divine activity as a constant that shaped the unfolding story of Israel and that these writers thought the observation of this activity could help them understand and pose questions about the present. Furthermore, an influential way of understanding the temporal dimension of apocalyptic thought has been to notice the correspondence in apocalyptic literature between events of a primordial time (called *Urzeit*) and events leading up to the final judgment (called *Endzeit*), a framework construed as a means to reinforce eschatology:[21] the primordial past served as a repository of images that helped apocalyptic writers imagine the future.

We may observe, however, that out of the above discussion arises another emphasis that has been neglected, not only by New Testament scholars but

---

(London: Black, 1954). For a more recent take-up of this perspective, see Dale C. Allison, "A Plea for Thoroughgoing Eschatology," *JBL* 113 (1994): 651–68; idem, *Jesus of Nazareth: Millenarian Prophet* (Minneapolis: Fortress, 1998). Allison's argument is formulated against the "unapocalyptic" reconstruction of Jesus put forth by members contributing to the Jesus Seminar (esp. Marcus Borg, John Dominic Crossan, Burton Mack); on the latter, see Robert W. Funk and Roy W. Hoover, *The Five Gospels: The Search for the Authentic Words of Jesus* (New York: Macmillan, 1993), 34–38, 137.

19. See, e.g., C. H. Dodd, *The Founder of Christianity* (New York: Macmillan, 1970); Norman Perrin, *Jesus and the Language of the Kingdom: Symbol and Metaphor in New Testament Interpretation* (Philadelphia: Fortress, 1976), 204; James D. G. Dunn, *Jesus and the Spirit: A Study of the Religious and Charismatic Experience of Jesus and the First Christians as Reflected in the New Testament* (London: SCM, 1975), 41–67; idem, *Jesus Remembered*, CM 1 (Grand Rapids: Eerdmans, 2003), 478–84; Thomas P. Rausch, *Who Is Jesus? An Introduction to Christology* (Collegeville, MN: Liturgical Press, 2003), 77–93.

20. So the often-repeated definition by John J. Collins, "Introduction: Towards the Morphology of a Genre," in *Apocalypse: The Morphology of a Genre*, ed. John J. Collins, SemeiaSt 14 (Missoula, MT: Scholars Press, 1979), 1–20 (here p. 9), and *The Apocalyptic Imagination*, 2nd ed. (Grand Rapids: Eerdmans, 1998), 2–11, esp. 4–9.

21. The most important third- and second-century-BCE documents that draw on this correspondence between beginning and end include the Enochic Book of Watchers (*1 En.* 1–36), the Dream Visions (*1 En.* 83–84 and 85–90), Apocalypse of Weeks (*1 En.* 93:1–10 and 91:11–17), Exhortation (*1 En.* 91:1–10, 18–19), Birth of Noah (*1 En.* 106–7), Similitudes (*1 En.* 37–71), *Book of Giants*, and *Jubilees*. The impact of the perspectives upheld by these works in Second Temple literature (including writings among the Dead Sea Scrolls and Jewish literature composed in Greek) was significant.

also by specialists in ancient Jewish apocalyptic literature.[22] In addition to helping to describe deteriorating conditions in the world and how the God of Israel will inaugurate a new age, language about the *Urzeit* could also provide a basis for confidence in such an outcome: God's definitive response to demonic evil is not simply a matter to be imagined for the future; rather, God's clear-cut and unambiguous intervention to defeat evil *in the past* (e.g., at the time of the great flood) guarantees that Satan and his minions will be annihilated in the future (*1 En.* 10; 15–16; 91:5–10; 106:13–107:1; *Jub.* 5–10; *Book of Giants* at 4Q530 2 II, + 6–7 + 8–12, lines 4–20). Thus, in essence, evil, however rampant and overwhelming, is but a defeated power whose time is marked. The Jewish traditions Jesus inherited could conceive that, since God's rule has asserted itself in the cosmos on a global scale in the past, the "present era," though under satanic rule, is nevertheless a time when those who are pious can proceed confidently in dealing with demonic power, knowing that although it cannot be gotten rid of altogether before the ultimate end of things, it remains possible to address, curtail, or manage its effects.

Our brief consideration of the Second Temple context may provide one way of getting past the hermeneutical conundrum associated with Jesus's exorcisms. In parts of the Western world, readers of the Gospels have become accustomed to the dramatic, spectacular character with which the descriptions of these episodes are invested. While such a reading rightly picks up on the significance being attached by the Gospel writers to the person of Jesus, it may serve to make Jesus more remote or to focus on the misleading question of whether or not there is any place in religious communities today for such or similar activity. For those who seek direction from ancient texts received as sacred tradition, the discussion here refocuses the question as one of perspective. It is possible to comprehend a hermeneutically, cosmologically, and sociologically controversial part of Jesus's activity in combating demonic forces not only as miracle but also as a realistic approach. Informed by Jesus's apocalyptic Jewish context, readers of the Gospel narratives may more easily recognize that Jesus's encounters with Satan and subordinate evil demonic beings do not dispense with evil as an ongoing reality that cannot be wished away or altogether dispelled, but rather provide the assurance of divine victory by Israel's God, who will restore the entire created order—indeed, human beings who suffer—to the well-being with which it was originally endowed.

---

22. For an excellent overview of recent scholarship on Jewish apocalyptic thought and literature and its implications for New Testament scholarship, see Jörg Frey, "Die Apokalyptik als Herausforderung der neutestamentlichen Wissenschaft. Zum Problem: Jesus und die Apokalyptik," in *Apokalyptik als Herausforderung neutestamentlicher Theologie*, ed. Michael Becker and Markus Öhler, WUNT 2.214 (Tübingen: Mohr Siebeck, 2006), 23–94, though Frey does not press toward the emphasis of the present discussion.

Suggestions for Further Reading

Alexander, Philip J. "The Demonology of the Dead Sea Scrolls." In *The Dead Sea Scrolls after Fifty Years: A Comprehensive Assessment*, edited by Peter W. Flint and James C. VanderKam, 2:331–53. 2 vols. Leiden: Brill, 1998–1999.

Collins, John J. *Apocalypticism in the Dead Sea Scrolls*. New York: Routledge, 1997.

Klutz, Todd E. "The Grammar of Exorcisim in the Ancient Mediterranean World." In *The Jewish Roots of Christological Monotheism*, edited by Carey C. Newman, James R. Davila, and Gladys S. Lewis, 156–65. Journal for the Study of Judaism Supplement Series 63. Leiden: Brill, 1999.

Stuckenbruck, Loren T. "The 'Angels' and 'Giants' of Genesis 6:1–4 in Second and Third Century BCE Jewish Interpretation: Reflections on the Posture of Early Apocalyptic Traditions." *Dead Sea Discoveries* 7 (2000): 354–77.

VanderKam, James C. "1 Enoch, Enochic Motifs, and Enoch in Early Christian Literature." In *The Jewish Apocalyptic Heritage in Early Christianity*, 33–101. Compendium rerum iudaicarum ad Novum Testamentum 3.4. Assen, Netherlands: Van Gorcum, 1996.

8

The Jewish Leaders

ANTHONY LE DONNE

I had a red-letter edition Bible when I was a kid. In this version, direct quotations of Jesus were printed in red font. Looking back now, it seems a strange way to emphasize those passages. From my youthful perspective, the red words carried more authority than the others. I still wonder whether this helped or hurt my interpretation. Nevertheless, it was a visual indication of just how often Jesus is in dialogue in the Gospels. What is even more striking is how much of these red portions convey combative speech. I remember thinking that the red parts indicated heated arguments—and I was not that far off. If you were to remove all of the arguments from the canonical Gospels, most of those red letters would be gone. Without the Pharisees, Sadducees, scribes, and others, we would know considerably less about Jesus.

In the Gospels, these Jewish leaders are quite important. They are role players used to reveal who Jesus is and what he is all about. In the stories of Jesus, Christians learn how to pray, deal with persecution, interpret Scripture, care for one another, and so on. By contrast, the Jewish leaders most often show Christians how *not* to act. The storytellers behind the Gospels do this on purpose and thus purposely create a good guy/bad guy scenario. Often when the Gospels emphasize Jesus's righteousness, his counterparts are judged quite harshly in counterbalance.

History is full of characters with impure motives. The history of first-century Judaism is no different. But we must tread very lightly when we discuss good guys and bad guys in history. Where human agency is concerned, good versus bad is always complicated. Simplistic statements such as "the Jews plotted to kill Jesus" have led to bloody and shameful forms of oppression, pogroms, and holocausts. Such statements require both historical and literary contexts to be understood correctly. Taken out of context, those red letters will mislead us, especially when we use categories such as "friends" and "enemies." There can be no doubt, however, that some Jewish leaders considered Jesus an "enemy." Conversely, the Gospels portray most Jewish leaders as "enemies" of Jesus. Even though the canonical Gospels focus on opposition to him from Jewish critics and the Jewish temple leaders, *Jesus's true enemies were the enemies of Israel*. We will misunderstand Jesus historically, literarily, and theologically if we fail to understand this. Any proper reading of Jesus's words or the history behind his words must begin here.

As with most heated rivalries, Jesus argued most with the scribes and Pharisees (and, to a lesser extent, Sadducees) because he had the most in common with them. I am tempted to repeat this in red font. To state what should be obvious, Jesus was a Jew. Jesus's very identity was built upon his Jewishness. The historical Jesus is utterly unintelligible apart from his religion, ethnicity, citizenship, and culture. So when we see Jesus in heated debate and leveling harsh criticism at Israel's leaders, we are (most of the time) witnessing internal clashes with other Jews. As a deeply committed Jew, Jesus was in a position to rail against his fellows in ways that would be inappropriate for non-Jews. Many of Jesus's arguments were specific to his context and were not intended to be parroted by non-Jews.

With this foundation in place, and by proceeding cautiously, we can learn much about Jesus from the internal Jewish debates leading to and through the first century CE. Conversely, we can learn more about the Jewish leaders of Jesus's time by listening in on the arguments presented in the canonical Gospels. In doing so, we must remember that both windows into this history are narrow and tinted. Neither the New Testament nor the extracanonical historical documents available to us give a clear view. And neither is without partisan bias.

In this chapter, I will discuss the roles played by the Pharisees, Sadducees, and scribes in the time periods before and after Jesus. Then I will discuss the roles played by the Jewish leadership in the Gospels.

Historical Considerations: Pharisees, Sadducees, and Scribes outside the Canon

After the death of Alexander the Great in 323 BCE, four Greek generals divided his empire. Over the next 150 years, this empire decayed, slowly making inroads for a new empire, and the most powerful yet: Rome. For most of this history, Israel was an afterthought—an obscure land and people best kept quietly subdued. While the land itself was thought to be valuable, the people and culture(s) of Israel were less important from Greek and Roman political perspectives. Sandwiched between these two juggernauts of Western history was a mercurial era of independence for Israel (ca. 141–37 BCE).

Antiochus Epiphanes IV was a ruler of Persian descent but fluent in Greek culture and religion. Epiphanes banned circumcision, Hebrew Scripture, and Sabbath keeping. In effect, he attempted to fully assimilate Judaism to Greek culture and worship. While many Jews considered this an affront to Judaism, others saw Hellenization as advantageous.[1] Epiphanes was thus a polarizing figure, wedging an already rifted Israel into factions. When Epiphanes erected a statue of Zeus in the Jerusalem temple and ordered a pig to be sacrificed on the altar (1 Macc. 1:54; Dan. 11:31), hostilities were brought to a tipping point. Following a Jewish leader named Mattathias, many Jews revolted. The family of Mattathias and his son Judah (also called Judas Maccabeus) are called the Hasmoneans.

Under the leadership of the Hasmoneans, Israel governed itself for the first time in almost six hundred years. The Hasmoneans considered themselves a priestly family and took it upon themselves to govern Israel both politically and religiously. This marriage of royal and priestly offices was not uncommon in the ancient world, but it was controversial to Jewish sensibilities. The two offices were supposed to function hand in glove (for example, see Ps. 110), but the temple priesthood was supposed to be of the line of Aaron, whereas the kings were supposed to be of the line of David. The Hasmoneans claimed to have come from both genealogies.

According to the Jewish historian Josephus, the Sadducees and Pharisees rose to prominence under the Hasmoneans. The two groups were influential religious/political advisors. One might think of the Pharisees and Sadducees as rival cabinets divided by conservative and liberal agendas. Of course, "liberals" and "conservatives" in that context were divided by different interpretative postures concerning Jewish law. So we cannot take the modern analogy very far, but it is helpful to see these two groups as religious/political lobbies of a sort. The Sadducees were remembered for their "literalist" approach to Jewish law, while the Pharisees were remembered for being more "liberal" in their interpretation.

After the passing of Judah, his brother Jonathan (or Apphus) assumed Hasmonean leadership. Jonathan held political and priestly offices from 160 to 143 BCE. Josephus first mentions the Pharisees and Sadducees in his account of Jonathan's tenure, presumably because of their political/religious influence (*Ant.* 13.171–73). Later, we learn that when the Hasmoneans finally

1. 1 Macc. 1:11–15; cf. Elias Bickerman, *From Ezra to the Last of the Maccabees* (New York: Schocken, 1962), 106–8.

achieved kingship, the Pharisees held such sway with the common people that they could shape public opinion quite easily. It is clear that Josephus frowned on this degree of power in the hands of commoners.[2]

During the reign of John Hyrcanus (134–104 BCE), we are told, Hyrcanus was beloved by the Pharisees, with one notable exception. During a feast hosted by Hyrcanus, a Pharisee named Eleazar advised the king/high priest to give up his priestly office. When asked why, Eleazar accused Hyrcanus of being a half-gentile, bastard child of his raped mother. Apparently this comment was considered inappropriate for dinner conversation. Josephus is quick to emphasize that Eleazar was an ill-tempered man who delighted in stirring up trouble. It is clear that the historian does not think that Eleazar represents the general opinion of the Pharisees. Regardless, Hyrcanus reacts by shunning the Pharisees as a whole and by promoting the Sadducees to be his chief advisors (*Ant.* 13.288–98). This episode marks a major shift in the Hasmonean dynasty, and one that Josephus considers to have been devastating to their longevity.

The Sadducees were known for their rigid commitment to only the five books of Moses: Genesis, Exodus, Leviticus, Numbers, and Deuteronomy. They were advocates of human free will rather than the idea of predetermined fate. As a result, they held that every person's lot in life was the result of their own choices. Most importantly for Josephus, the Sadducees were quite severe when it came to punishing lawbreakers. Where penal codes were concerned, Josephus equates being a Sadducee with being "savage" (*Ant.* 20.199). In contrast, the penal code recommended by the Pharisees was much milder. This might explain the Pharisees' popularity with the common people.[3] It is worth noting, however, that everything we know of the Sadducees comes from their rivals. Both Josephus and the rabbis are quite hostile toward the Sadducees and color their portraits of them darkly. As a group, they left behind no writings of their own.

We hear very little from the Sadducees after Hyrcanus's feast episode, but assume that they remained influential throughout his tenure and the tenures of Aristobulus (104–103 BCE) and Alexander Jannaeus (103–76 BCE). It is probably no coincidence that Alexander Jannaeus left an altogether draconian legacy. Jannaeus was remembered as a bloodthirsty tyrant who mistreated and murdered his own people (*J.W.* 1.85–106).[4] It is unclear whether his legacy was colored by his association with the Sadducees, or whether the Sadducees'

---

2. Steve Mason, "Josephus' Pharisees: The Narratives," in *In Quest of the Historical Pharisees*, ed. Bruce D. Chilton and Jacob Neusner (Waco: Baylor University Press, 2007), 9–10. Josephus considers himself an aristocrat and draws a close relationship between noble birth and noble character. Whether or not Josephus thought the Pharisees themselves were of common birth is debatable. What is clear is that he considered contemptible their use of power by way of popular opinion.

3. Ibid., 19.

4. See also the corresponding legacy of Jannaeus in rabbinic literature (*Soṭah* 47a).

legacy was colored by their association with Jannaeus. Perhaps both are true. Whatever the case, Jannaeus was not lamented by the common people. He left his office to his wife Salome, who reigned as queen for almost a decade (ca. 76–ca. 67 BCE).

Whether Salome was shrewd, pious, or both, she brought back the Pharisees as her chief advisors. This act distanced her from her husband's legacy and discontinued the "savage" policies of the Sadducees. In contrast to her late husband, she endeared herself to the common people. According to Josephus, the Pharisees enjoyed enormous influence during this time.[5] Salome gave them authority to jail, banish, or execute as they pleased.[6] According to one portrait of Salome, she ceded so much power to the Pharisees that "while she governed others, the Pharisees governed her" (*J.W.* 1.107–12).

Salome made her son Hyrcanus II high priest and intended for him to take the throne also. However, her death in 67 BCE spurred a power struggle between Hyrcanus II, Aristobulus II (his younger brother), and Herod Antipater. Rome took advantage of this internal instability and seized Jerusalem in 63 BCE. Hyrcanus II eventually returned as Jerusalem's high priest under Roman rule. Meanwhile, the Pharisees fell from influence and never enjoyed so much power again. We learn from *Psalms of Solomon* 17 (most likely composed by Pharisees) that they were violently removed (17:4–6) and chased from the city (17:16–19).[7]

This brief sketch only hints at how complex and entangled the power structures were when Jesus was born. There were dividing lines between Jews and Samaritans. There were dividing lines between rural and city groups. Many Jews contested the Jerusalem-temple priesthood's claim to that office. The group that collected the Dead Sea Scrolls (probably the Essenes) believed that they were the "true" priesthood. This group established an alternative to the Jerusalem temple out in the desert. And we have not yet scratched the surface of the deceptive and power-grabbing world of Roman politics. Add to this the many cultural holdovers from the Greek Empire. In all of this, there were varying Jewish responses to the Roman Empire, Greek culture, and the hope for a renewed Israel. The structures of social and political governance of Jesus's day were labyrinthine.

In the world of Jewish hierarchy, the Pharisees and Sadducees were major players in this multifaceted social scene and power system. Both factions

---

5. See also the corresponding account in rabbinic literature (*b. Ta'an.* 23a)

6. Anthony Le Donne, *The Historiographical Jesus: Memory, Typology, and the Son of David* (Waco: Baylor University Press, 2009), 133.

7. It is both peculiar and noteworthy that the rabbis do not refer to the Pharisees' political rise and fall even once. Rather, rabbinic literature's general portrait of the Pharisees shows their concern for dietary laws, an agricultural purity. So Jacob Neusner, "The Rabbinic Traditions about the Pharisees before 70 CE," in Chilton and Neusner, *In Quest of the Historical Pharisees*, 299–300.

believed that their rightful place was among the governing elite. The above sketch also demonstrates that the Pharisees did not speak with a single voice. There were factions within factions. Some Pharisees were extremely wary of non-Jews and their cultural influences. These tended to side with a Pharisaic school linked with Shammai. Others were more liberal concerning foreign relations. These tended to side with the Pharisaic school linked with Hillel.

The disputes between the schools of Hillel and Shammai were diverse and profound. Indeed, the Talmud says that during the time of their conflict (ca. 30 BCE–70 CE), there were two legal and cultural foundations in Israel: "the Torah became as two Torahs" (*b. Sanh.* 88b). In one episode of this ongoing rivalry, Dosa ben Harkinas called a fellow Jew "the first born of Satan" for associating himself with the school of Shammai (*y. Yebam.* 5e). Harkinas's harsh words were spoken in the first century CE and directed at his own brother, Jonathan.[8] We may even have evidence that the followers of Shammai rose up to commit an act of mob violence against Hillel in the Jerusalem temple (*t. Ḥag.* 2.11). According to this Tosefta account, Hillel averted their violent intentions by distracting them with a discussion concerning sacrificial practice.[9] There can be no doubt that the rabbis have colored this story in favor of Hillel. Nonetheless, it shows the severity of the internal hostilities between Pharisaic schools.

As we move to the portraits of these groups within the canonical Gospels, it will be helpful to remember that Jesus's arguments with these Jewish leaders reflect an ongoing power struggle of partisan politics and religious division. It is also worth remembering that groups argue the most fiercely with those most like themselves. The houses of Hillel and Shammai had many more commonalities than differences and even more in common with each other than with the Greeks or the Romans. The Pharisees had much more in common with the Sadducees than they had with the Greeks or the Romans. In the same way, Jesus argued most with the Pharisees because he was most like them. He argued very little with Greek and Roman philosophers (indeed, we have no record of him ever doing so) because they had so very little in common.

A brief sketch of the "scribes" is also important. To be called a scribe was to refer to a person's function or occupation rather than to religious or political affiliation. In the same way that the title "secretary" has multiple meanings in English, the title "scribe" was wide ranging in the ancient world. To be a secretary in modern America, for example, could range from being a typist

8. Here *Yebam.* 5e is taken from the Jerusalem text. Harvey Falk recalls this episode (he points to *Yebam.* 16a of the Babylonian text) in connection to Jesus's similar words in John 8:44 and the phrase "synagogue of Satan" in Revelation 2:9; 3:9 (*Jesus the Pharisee* [Eugene, OR: Wipf and Stock, 1985], 118).

9. My thanks to Bruce Chilton, who pinpointed this episode for me via personal correspondence.

to being the secretary of state.[10] Because this chapter is interested in Jewish leadership, I will speak to the function of scribes with elite status.

"Scribes" is a category that overlaps with almost every aspect of the Jewish power matrix. Scribes could be priests, they could be political counselors, they could be Pharisees, and so on. The important thing to remember is that to function as an elite scribe was to be a power broker.[11] According to Ben Sira (the author of the book Sirach, ca. 180 BCE), scribes appeared before rulers, were sought for counsel, and functioned as judges (Sir. 38–39). According to Josephus, scribes served important functions under King Saul (*J.W.* 7.110), King David (*J.W.* 7.293), and several other rulers.[12] The prophet Jeremiah credits "Baruch" as his scribe (Jer. 36:26). Baruch seems to have been a very influential person with both royal and priestly offices.[13]

Elite scribes were much more than secretaries; they were dignitaries who mediated power. This was especially true for the Jews of Jesus's day because the culture and identity of Judaism were founded on a group of texts. Given that the vast majority of commoners were illiterate, to be a scribe was to be a guardian and authoritative interpreter of the sacred tradition. Elite scribes in ancient Jewish culture interpreted Jewish law and influenced how it was carried out. This means that they influenced how people farmed, ate, traveled, worshiped, and otherwise conducted their lives. Their influence was felt as they interpreted what actions broke these laws and how retribution or punishment was to be enforced. Of course, all these matters were mediated through established scriptural precedents and civic and priestly magistrates. The extent to which these magistrates heeded the voice of their scribes varied.

As with the Pharisees and Sadducees, in order to understand scribal function in Jewish leadership, you must understand the power matrices of which they were a part. As mentioned, this chapter can provide only a sketch of a much more complicated system. Pharisees, Sadducees, and scribes were influential on many different levels of society in different ways at different times. What they all had in common during Jesus's day was that they operated within a system of social power that could be manipulated in their favor. When they argued with each other, the sway of the people and (sometimes) the sway of the highest offices were at stake. It is difficult to say which of these held the most sway when Jesus entered the picture. What we can say is that if Jesus was to engage the power structures of his day, he would have had to contend with these groups. Indeed, this is the portrait provided by the Gospels.

10. John P. Meier, *A Marginal Jew: Rethinking the Historical Jesus*, vol. 3, *Companions and Competitors*, ABRL (New York: Doubleday, 2001), 550.

11. H. Gregory Snyder, *Teachers and Texts in the Ancient World: Philosophers, Jews and Christians* (London: Routledge, 2000), chap. 5.

12. For a fuller list see Synder, *Teachers and Texts*, 282n89.

13. Meier, *Marginal Jew*, 3:551.

Narrative Considerations: Pharisees, Sadducees, and Scribes
in the Earliest Gospel Narratives

The remainder of this chapter will describe the general characteristics of the
Jewish leaders in the Gospel narratives. After describing what is common to
these portraits in all four Gospels, I will briefly sketch the unique traits of
each Gospel.

As Chris Keith points out in his introductory essay, the four canonical
Gospels come to us in the form of stories. This is worth repeating because narration, even when rigidly attentive to the historical events, is always a revision
of what "really" happened. When telling stories, narrators produce accounts
that fall into typical patterns. These patterns obscure certain details, focus
on others, embellish/invent themes and motifs, and dramatically restructure
time lines. This is called "narrativization."

Narrativization is simply the process of creating a story. The process is similar (though not identical) to both memory stories and fictions. It is important
to realize that this process is at work even for courtroom testimonies and filmed
documentaries that try to capture authenticity as best they can. Even more so
for the canonical Gospels, which were not intended to be courtroom transcripts
but dramatic vehicles for veneration, evangelism, and religious instruction.

Because our knowledge of Jesus and his contemporaries comes to us in the
form of stories, we should expect several kinds of narrativization at the outset.
First, we can expect a projected story line. Events in time have no beginnings
and ends; they are continuous sequences of causes and effects that stretch
out indefinitely. When narrators translate these sequences into stories, they
choose beginnings and ends. They choose plotlines and characters. They choose
how the story will build to a climax and what details are important for this
purpose. Second, we should expect a general focus on details that move the
plot forward. Third, and most importantly for this chapter, we should expect
figures in the story to be characterized by the overarching plot. Jesus's story
is that of conflict, execution, and vindication. We should expect that Jesus's
"enemies" will enter and act within this story accordingly.

This happens on both the micro and macro levels of the narrative. In other
words, we can see narrative selectivity within smaller units (such as the argument about picking grains on the Sabbath) and within whole books (such as
the Gospel of Matthew). In both cases, the process of storytelling reduces
and dulls our picture of the Jewish leaders.

Most of the time, when Jesus is teaching or debating, the story is shortened.
In real life, certain dialogues stretch out over hours. In real life, the most important dialogues span lifetimes. In the American context, certain debates last for
generations: Should we choose social programs or smaller government? How
should a parent balance discipline and reward for their children's behavior?
Should baseball eliminate the designated hitter? In Jesus's context, the debate

about keeping the Sabbath was one of these ongoing social discussions. But in the Gospels the dialogues between Jesus and the Jewish leaders are just spliced and condensed summaries.

The Gospels reduce arguments that lasted generations into simple one-liners: "Look, your disciples do what is illegal on the Sabbath!" As we know from modern mass media, when long conversations are reduced to quick sound bites, the consumer is left to infer the context. Sound bites (or in this case, pithy quotations) cannot tell the whole story. The Gospels generally portray the Jewish leaders appearing suddenly, voicing their disapproval of Jesus, and then disappearing again, allowing Jesus to teach without interruption. Matthew 9:10–13 is an example of this recurring formula:

> And as he sat at dinner in the house, behold, many tax collectors and sinners came and were sitting with him and his disciples. When the Pharisees saw this, they said to his disciples, "Why does your teacher eat with tax collectors and sinners?" But when he heard this, he said, "Those who are well have no need of a physician, but those who are sick. Go and learn what this means, 'I desire mercy, not sacrifice.' For I have come to call not the righteous but sinners."

The narrative structure generally has three parts:

1. The setting is described.
2. A question or accusation is leveled by the Jewish leaders.
3. Jesus teaches.

Sometimes the storyteller will add a fourth part describing the subdued opponent of Jesus. Matthew 22:46 adds, "No one was able to give him an answer, nor from that day did anyone dare to ask him any more questions." On one of the rare times that Jesus's counterparts do respond (Matt. 21:27), the narrator describes them talking among themselves. After doing so, "they answered Jesus, 'We do not know.'" There is rarely any give-and-take in these arguments. With this in mind, calling them "arguments" hardly describes them. Many scholars prefer to call these episodes "controversies."

This 1, 2, 3 (and sometimes 4) structure shapes the characterization of Jesus and, by contrast, the Jewish leaders. Jesus is given a chance to talk about his understanding of God's kingdom, the instruction he has for his disciples, and his own identity because of the other role players in the drama. Jesus's "enemies" are painted darkly so that Jesus will be seen as the hero of these stories. In order for there to be no mistake that Jesus represents wisdom and innocence, Jesus's enemies are shown to have inept logic and evil motives.

In all four Gospels, Jesus's authority is on display. When dealing with the demonic world, Jesus is shown to be of heavenly status. When Jesus is dealing with Caiaphas at his trial, Jesus is shown to be allied with the heavenly Judge and ultimate authority. In the Gospels, each adversary occupies a different battleground. The battlegrounds occupied by the religious leaders are Scripture, worship, and purity. Each group claims to have the authority to interpret and guard what is holy in the life of Israel. The Pharisees use issues of ritual to gain leverage over Jesus (e.g., the proper keeping of Sabbath). The scribes quote Scripture to gain leverage over Jesus.[14] In both cases, Jesus is shown to be superior. As Jesus wins debate after debate, the storytellers demonstrate his authority to govern both the interpretation of Scripture and the practical keeping of this Scripture.

Another feature of narrativization in the Gospels involves the movement of the plot. Jesus's opponents are integral to the story being told. The narrators let us peek into the motives that eventually lead to Jesus's death. Mark 14:1 narrates: "It was two days before the Passover and the festival of Unleavened Bread. The chief priests and the scribes were looking for a way to arrest Jesus by stealth and kill him."

Without the Jewish leaders, according to the Gospels, Jesus would not have been executed by the Roman authorities. In short, without these "enemies," there would simply be no story. Imagine *Othello* without Iago, or *Star Wars* without Darth Vader. The stories about Jesus hinge on the words, motives, and actions of the Jewish leaders. It would be impossible to tell the story of Jesus without them.

Yet the portrait of the Jewish leaders in the Gospels is not monochrome. Some scribes are "not far from the kingdom of God" (Mark 12:34). Some Pharisees call Jesus a teacher "come from God" (John 3:2). Some rulers seek healing from Jesus (Luke 18:18). This is not to downplay the predominant antagonism portrayed in these stories. However, these exceptions hint that this good guy/bad guy contrast does not reflect the more complex history behind these stories. Indeed, these exceptions are the best evidence we have that the storytellers behind the Gospels did not simply invent all of these controversies. First-century Judaism was rife with conflict. Nothing in the Gospels is more historically plausible than hostility among like-minded fellows.

The Gospel of Mark: A Plot about and against Jesus

Mark introduces the Jewish leaders to readers with a story about Jesus at home, eating with tax collectors and sinners. We are told that "scribes of the Pharisees" question Jesus's disciples about his dinner company. The implication here is that, compared with other rabbis, Jesus might be less attentive to dietary purity (Mark 2:15–17).[15] Notice that these scribes are attached to the

---

14. Synder, *Teachers and Texts*, 184–85.
15. In addition, it is possible that a rabbi's table company reflected his level of erudition. See discussion in Adela Yarbro Collins, *Mark: A Commentary*, Hermeneia (Minneapolis: Fortress, 2007), 193–94.

Pharisees. This suggests that Mark is introducing scribes who are less than "elite." It is possible, but unlikely, that these are the same scribes with whom Jesus contends in Jerusalem (11:27). As discussed above, the scribes were not a cohesive group, and Mark's portrait reflects this.

It is also noteworthy, at this early stage in the narrative, that there is no apparent hostility between these leaders and Jesus. We are simply told that they have asked Jesus a question. Jesus answers by comparing himself to a physician who comes not for the healthy but for the sick. The storyteller gives us no indication that these Jewish leaders were unsatisfied with the answer. The narrative continues: "Now John's disciples and the Pharisees were fasting; and people came and said to [Jesus], 'Why do John's disciples and the disciples of the Pharisees fast, but your disciples do not fast?'" (Mark 2:18). The assumption here is that temporarily abstaining from food is an act of piety (i.e., a good thing). So this is a positive comparison between the Pharisees and John the Baptist's students. It is helpful to note that John is highly regarded in Mark's Gospel. No less than Herod feared John because John "was a righteous and holy man" (Mark 6:20). The questioner implies that both John and the Pharisees are more pious than Jesus. As mentioned above, we see evidence that these different Jewish sects had much more in common than not. Jesus answers again with an analogy. He compares his ministry with a wedding party and himself with the groom (i.e., the guest of honor, who requires celebrating). The storyteller includes two other analogies to justify the actions of Jesus's disciples (2:21–22). Again, Mark gives no indication of hostility.

The mood sours, however, in Mark 2:23–28. The Pharisees accuse Jesus's disciples of breaking sabbatical law by picking grain on the Jewish day of rest. This becomes an occasion for Jesus to compare himself to King David and claim that he is "lord even of the sabbath" (2:28). From a narrative perspective, Mark's Jesus is claiming that exceptions can be made for even the most sacred food laws. In addition, Mark is not-so-subtly revealing Jesus's divinely ordained authority and setting the stage for the crucial confrontation that follows.

From the Pharisees' perspective (one might imagine), Jesus's claim to be master of the Sabbath would have seemed outlandish. The Pharisees begin an argument concerning sabbatical law (this was a common argument if rabbinic literature is any indication), and they end up with a statement tantamount to megalomania! Who was this backwater revivalist to associate himself with King David?

In Mark 3:1–2 the storyteller reports that Jesus entered a synagogue (a local place of study and worship), and "a man was there who had a withered hand. They [presumably the Pharisees] watched him to see whether he would cure him on the Sabbath, so that they might accuse him." According to the storyteller, the key divide between the Jewish leaders and Jesus involves sabbatical interpretation. Jesus then instigates an even bigger argument:

And he said to the man who had the withered hand, "Come forward." Then he said to them, "Is it lawful to do good or to do harm on the sabbath, to save life or to kill?" But they were silent. He looked around at them with anger; he was grieved at their hardness of heart and said to the man, "Stretch out your hand." He stretched it out, and his hand was restored. The Pharisees went out, and immediately conspired with the Herodians against him, [about] how to destroy him. (Mark 3:3–6)

This is a crucial turn in Mark's plot and characterization. The Jewish leaders are shown to be quietly observing Jesus's behavior and wary of his sabbatical antics. In contrast, Jesus is shown to be intentionally provocative. He begins the argument and publicly heals (recall Jesus's medical analogy in 2:17) a man with a "withered" hand to provoke the Jewish leaders.

Notice that Mark's portrait is *not* of a passive, live-and-let-live Jesus who was simply minding his own business. By publicly healing on the Sabbath, and starting the argument in the synagogue, Jesus is picking a fight. Indeed, we are explicitly told that he is angry. No doubt, the storyteller's intention was to portray *righteous* anger. From this view, the Pharisees' elevation of Sabbath regulation over physical well-being demonstrates their "hardness of heart." These hard-hearted legalists then leave to conspire with the Herodians (the political supporters of King Herod).[16] Mark erases any previous ambiguity—the Pharisees mean to "destroy" Jesus. In this way, the characters and plot are clearly defined.

In general, Jesus's interactions with the Jewish leaders from this point on are predictable. Jesus is repeatedly at odds with them as the plot moves toward its Jerusalem climax. Jesus is confronted by various representatives from the different factions of the Jewish leaders in varying combinations.

The Sadducees are featured only once in Mark. The storyteller introduces them as "Sadducees, who say that there is no resurrection" (Mark 12:18). They present Jesus with a question to point out the absurdity of belief in life after death. The Sadducees tell a parable wherein a woman is married and widowed six times. They point out that Moses (the supposed author of the Law) commanded the remarriage of widows to continue the lineage of the deceased husband through his brother (Deut. 25:5–10). Jesus responds with a biting rhetorical question: "Is not this the reason you are wrong, that you know neither the scriptures nor the power of God?" (Mark 12:24). Jesus then appeals to Exodus 3:6, where the divine voice says, "I am the God of your father, the God of Abraham, the God of Isaac, and the God of Jacob." Then Jesus makes the uncontroversial claim that God "is not God of the dead, but

16. The group called "Herodians" is notoriously difficult to identify historically. For a concise appraisal, see John P. Meier, "The Historical Jesus and the Historical Herodians," *JBL* 119 (2000): 740–46.

of the living" (Mark 12:27).[17] Logically, if (a) the Lord claimed to be the God of these (dead) patriarchs, and (b) it is also true that God is (only) the God of the living, then (c) there must be some way to reconcile this apparent contradiction. For Jesus, the righteous dead were destined for resurrection and thus could be considered alive.

Notice that Jesus's appeal to Exodus (the second book of Moses) coheres with the Sadducees' canon of only five books. If Jesus had appealed to a prophetic text (such as Ezekiel), his appeal would have been rejected, since the Sadducees did not recognize the prophets or the writings as canonical. Again, Jesus is portrayed as a superior debater who can beat his adversaries on their own chosen battleground. In this case, the battleground involved the interpretation of God's words to Moses. In this way, Mark continues to portray Jesus as an authoritative interpreter of Scripture.

Mark connects the Pharisees to Herod and his supporters three times (3:6; 8:15; 12:13). In doing so, the storyteller reminds us of their collaborative plot against Jesus.[18] When Jesus gets to Jerusalem, he is confronted by "the chief priests, the scribes, and the elders" (11:27). "The elders," like "the scribes," is a somewhat ambiguous title. However, the connection of these particular scribes and elders to the temple priesthood suggests that they are among the more elite leaders in Israel.[19] After Jesus's confrontation in the Jerusalem temple, he is arrested, summarily tried, and executed. Ironically, Jesus's role as the superior debater is transformed as he stands before Pilate and Caiaphas in relative silence.

Mark 14 indicates that when Judas betrays Jesus, he conspires with the "the chief priests, the scribes, and the elders" (14:43). It is noteworthy that the Pharisees and Herodians are not represented in the group that arrests Jesus. Previously, the Pharisees and Herodians were sent to "trap [Jesus] in what he said" (Mark 12:13). We are not told who is doing the sending, but we presume that it is the Jerusalem temple establishment because of the list of three groups in Mark 11:27. Whoever is strategizing behind the scenes, the storyteller has

---

17. Similar claims can be found in rabbinic literature (*y. Ber.* 2.3; *b. Ber.* 18a), Philo (*Abraham* 50–55), and 4 Macc. 16:25. See Craig A. Evans, *Mark 8:27–16:20*, WBC 34B (Nashville: Nelson, 2001), 256–57.

18. Evans points out that it is highly unlikely that Herodians and Pharisees were historical allies. Mark associates the two groups, however, and probably does so to set up the debate over taxes in Mark 12:13–17. Evans notes that the two groups (probably) had opposite views on Jewish taxes to Caesar. The Herodians likely favored it; the Pharisees likely considered it idolatry. If so, their question about paying taxes to Caesar (Mark 12:14–15) had no right answer. If Jesus answers against Roman taxation, he fails the Herodians' test. If he answers in favor of Roman taxation, he fails the Pharisees' test. Jesus sidesteps both tests by saying, "Give to the emperor the things that are the emperor's, and to God the things that are God's" (12:17). In this way, Jesus confounds both groups. However, it must be restated that our ability to sketch the historical Herodians is very limited (Evans, *Mark 8:27–16:20*, 244–45).

19. For more on the Jerusalem temple establishment and Herod, see Helen Bond's chapter in this book.

demoted the Pharisees and Herodians to mere pawns on the chessboard. By the time Jesus is arrested, the Pharisees and Herodians are no longer significant characters. As we saw with the 1, 2, 3 structure of controversy narrative, Jesus's opponents were repeatedly silenced. As Mark's narrative climaxes, the storyteller silences the Pharisees by eliminating them from the narrative entirely.

Matthew, Mark, and Luke: Contrasting Portraits

Because Matthew and Luke take their cues from Mark, much of the above is repeated in both of these Gospels. Matthew, Mark, and Luke have many more commonalities than differences. However, a few prominent differences should be pointed out.

Matthew's portrait of the Pharisees is expanded, often mentioning Pharisees where Mark mentions scribes (e.g., Matt. 21:45). Matthew is all but entirely uninterested in the Herodians, substituting an increased script for the Sadducees (Matt. 3:7; 16:1, 6, 11–12; 22:23, 34). Matthew is not unaware of Herodians as a category, but they enter the picture only when taxes to Caesar are at issue (Matt. 22:16). Matthew's most prominent editorial move is that the Pharisees become lightning rods for criticism. In Matthew, Jesus has an extended monologue in the Jerusalem temple about the hypocrisy of the Pharisees.[20] In this passage, they are hypocrites, fools, blind guides, sons of hell, and so on. Matthew, like Mark, connects the Pharisees to the elite in Jerusalem. But Matthew's Pharisees are more connected with the Jerusalem temple establishment and receive much more venom.

When set in parallel, Luke's portrait of the Pharisees is almost mild in comparison. This is not due to Luke's sympathy for the Pharisees but because Matthew's references to them are simply so harsh. Luke offers a more complex picture of the Pharisees. For the most part, they are still cast as "enemies," but Luke nuances this caricature a bit. In Luke's parallel to Jesus's Sabbath healing (par. Mark 3:3–6), the Pharisees and scribes do not conspire to "destroy" Jesus. Rather, they discuss "what they might do to Jesus" (Luke 6:11). Amy-Jill Levine observes, "Compared to the reaction in the Nazareth synagogue [Mark 3:6] . . . and to Matthew's notice [Matt. 12:14] that the Pharisees sought to kill him, Luke's description is benign."[21] Indeed, whereas for Mark this episode concludes with the Pharisees attaching themselves with the Herodians, in Luke there is no such relationship. It cannot be denied, however, that Luke perpetuates Mark's antagonism. Luke takes Mark's portrait of the Pharisees and adds several more negative references (Luke 5:17, 21; 7:30, 45; 11:53; 14:1, 3; 16:14). But according to Luke, the Pharisees played no part in the plot to kill Jesus.

20. See Matt. 23; compare this with the much shorter Mark 12:38–40.
21. Amy-Jill Levine, "Luke's Pharisees," in Chilton and Neusner, In Quest of the Historical Pharisees, 119.

In fact, in Luke's account the Pharisees disappear altogether during Jesus's final conflict in Jerusalem, arrest, and execution. Both Matthew and Mark place the Pharisees in rural Galilee *and* urban Jerusalem. While Matthew and Mark differ on how connected they were to the Jerusalem elite, both storytellers connect the Pharisees to the plot against Jesus. Not so in Luke. Luke's Pharisees are set in rural Galilee almost exclusively. When Jesus approaches Jerusalem, Luke leaves the Pharisees at the city gate (19:39). If Luke were our only guide, we would have no reason to think that the Pharisees had any connection to the Jerusalem temple establishment.

Luke 13:31 departs from the general caricature altogether: "At that very hour some Pharisees came and said to him, 'Get away from here, for Herod wants to kill you.'" We are not given any indication that these Pharisees had ulterior motives for this warning. Perhaps this is a glimpse behind the friends-versus-enemies characterization.

Luke is the only Gospel to show Jesus dining with Pharisees (11:37). Luke also includes this exchange: "Once Jesus was asked by the Pharisees when the kingdom of God was coming, and he answered, 'The kingdom of God is not coming with things that can be observed; nor will they say, "Look, here it is!" or "There it is!" For, in fact, the kingdom of God is among you.'" (Luke 17:20–21). Not only is there no apparent hostility here; Jesus's response might also imply that the "kingdom of God" includes this particular Pharisee.

As does Mark, Luke shows very little interest in the Sadducees. They are featured only once (Luke 20:27). According to Luke, the plot to arrest Jesus was arranged by "chief priests, the officers of the temple police, and the elders" (Luke 22:52). In other words, it was the fault of the Jerusalem temple establishment, the Jewish leaders most influenced by Roman rule.

Still, when Luke's more "mild" version is considered in full, it is quite troubling to modern sensibilities. Luke, along with Mark and Matthew, implicates Jewish leaders in the plot to kill Jesus. By extension, in Luke's mind, this implicates the nation of Israel as a whole. The storyteller says as much in his sequel to Luke. "Let the entire house of Israel know with certainty that God has made him both Lord and Messiah, this Jesus whom you crucified" (Acts 2:36). Peter's words indict "the house of Israel" for Jesus's execution. For the storyteller, it is quite clear that Rome, and the temple establishment associated with Rome, executed Jesus. It is also quite clear that Jesus's life and death polarized Jewish Christians (represented by Peter) from Jews in general (represented by the Jewish leaders).[22] Jesus may have had exactly this in mind when he said, "Do not think that I have come to bring peace to the earth; I have not come to bring peace, but a sword. For I have come to set a

---

22. Joseph A. Fitzmyer thinks that the plural "you" in Peter's statement "refers above all to the Jews of Jerusalem who handed Jesus over to Pilate; it cannot refer to the diaspora Jews visiting Jerusalem for the feast" (*The Acts of the Apostles*, AB 31 [New York: Doubleday, 1998], 261). If so, one wonders if the phrase "house of Israel" might refer to the Jerusalem temple.

man against his father, and a daughter against her mother, and a daughter-in-law against her mother-in-law; and one's foes will be members of one's own household" (Matthew 10:34–36). They say that nothing divides like politics or religion. By clashing with the Jewish leaders of his time, Jesus was divisive on both levels. Matthew, Mark, and Luke have this in common.

The Gospel of John and "the Jews"

As we saw with Luke-Acts, characters can represent groups. Occasionally, Peter represents Jewish followers of Jesus and the Jewish leaders represent the nation of Israel as a whole. In John, this second category gets collapsed into a monolithic category: "the Jews." John's story refers to "the Jews" over 60 times. In comparison, John mentions "Pharisees" 20 times, "priest(s)" 21 times, and "scribes" only once.[23] The Sadducees are not mentioned in John. So while specific groups within the Jewish hierarchy are mentioned, John most commonly refers to Jesus's opponents quite vaguely.

John's vagueness is problematic on several levels. (1) It is possible that, in the first century, the term *Jew(s)* was a term used by outsiders. *Children of Israel* and *Israelites* were terms used by those within Judaism. Does this suggest that Jesus and his followers are not to be identified with "the Jews" in John?[24] If so, this might explain why Jesus calls the Torah "your law" in John 8:17 and 10:34, rather than "our law" or "the law." (2) Given that Jesus and his disciples were Jewish, are we dealing with heated arguments between Jewish factions, or do these arguments represent the concerns of later (non-Jewish) Christianity? (3) Do "the Jews" in John represent the Jewish leaders, or all Jews who are not followers of Jesus?

As previously discussed, the process of storytelling involves focusing on certain details and obscuring others. One by-product of such narrativization is reduction. In John, the narrator reduces many characters to an almost archetypal level. Jesus is not only wise; he is Wisdom itself. Judas is not simply demonized; he is possessed by the devil. Rather than painting with nuance and texture, John represents many of his characters as simply black or white. Indeed, John is fond of duality and simplicity: light versus dark, life versus death, above versus below, and so on. Once these abstract themes are boiled down to basics, the narrator works toward new complexity in using them. This is how John chooses to reveal Jesus's heavenly identity, or "Christology." Conversely, he casts those characters who oppose Jesus with a hellish identity.

23. The only time "scribes" are mentioned in John is in John 8:3. This section was added to the book long after the narrative had taken shape. For more on this passage, see Chris Keith, *The"Pericope Adulterae," the Gospel of John, and the Literacy of Jesus*, NTTSD 38 (Leiden: Brill, 2009).

24. The only time that Jesus is called a Jew is by the Samaritan woman (John 4:9). Thus, it applied to Jesus only by a perceived "outsider."

Adele Reinhartz writes that John "focuses extensively on Christology, that is, on the exploration of Jesus's identity as the Messiah and Son of God. Christology underlies all other elements of the Gospel, including its plot, its characterization, and its theology."[25] According to John's theology, "no knowledge or experience of God is possible except through him (14:6). The exclusiveness of this claim contributes considerably to the Gospel's attitude toward those Jews who refuse to believe in Jesus."[26] John 8:42–45 shows this world of stark contrasts dramatically:

> Jesus said to them, "If God were your Father, you would love me, for I came from God and now I am here. I did not come on my own, but he sent me. Why do you not understand what I say? It is because you cannot accept my word. You are from your father the devil, and choose to do your father's desires. He was a murderer from the beginning and does not stand in the truth, because there is no truth in him. When he lies, he speaks according to his own nature, for he is a liar and the father of lies. But because I tell the truth, you do not believe me."

This passage is among the most troubling for Jewish-Christian relations but also among the most important for John's portrait of Jesus. Here we see Jesus's identity as the Son of God set in contrast to the identity of his opponents, who are accused of being sons of the devil.[27] Jesus claims that these Jews do not believe in him because they simply have no relationship with the truth. In contrast, we are told that Jesus is the "Truth" (John 14:6). This struggle between heaven and hell is the real plotline in John. Jesus will be misunderstood and disbelieved because it is in the devil's nature to deceive. Jesus will be murdered because it is in the devil's nature to murder. As I argued above, the true enemies of Jesus were the enemies of Israel. In John, the real enemy is the devil—he who deceives Israel.

The storyteller behind John's Gospel writes so that his reader "may come to believe that Jesus is the Messiah, the Son of God" (John 20:31). There is no safe middle ground in John; you are either a child of God or a child of the devil. In the context of John 8, it is said that Jesus condemned "Jews who had believed in him" but no longer believed (8:31). In John's world, where believing means the difference between heaven and hell, those who once believed but do not any longer are considered traitors. John allies such people with the devil himself.

25. Adele Reinhartz, "The Gospel of John: How 'the Jews' Became Part of the Plot," in *Jesus, Judaism and Christian Anti-Judaism: Reading the New Testament after the Holocaust*, ed. Paula Fredriksen and Adele Reinhartz (Louisville: Westminster John Knox, 2002), 100.
26. Ibid.
27. In a passage that is most likely independent of John, Jesus accuses converts to Pharisaism of being children of hell (Matt. 23:15). We should also remember the similarly harsh words of Dosa ben Harkinah. As mentioned above, Harkinah calls his brother Jonathan "the first born of Satan" (*Yebam.* 5e).

The example of Nicodemus illustrates John's duality quite well. Nicodemus is described as a "Pharisee" and a "leader of the Jews" (John 3:1). This might imply that he was a member of the Sanhedrin (a judicial body related to the Jerusalem temple establishment). He comes to Jesus by night to discuss the great things Jesus is doing. Nicodemus calls what Jesus is doing "signs" (what we might call miracles). In John's narrative, "signs" are awesome actions that inspire belief. And yet, we know from the preceding narrative that people who believe only because of signs are not be trusted (John 2:23–25). Nicodemus says, "Rabbi, we know that you are a teacher who has come from God; for no one can do these signs that you do apart from the presence of God" (3:2).

Nicodemus is full of respect and admiration. In this, his portrait is rare in John. Not only does he lack hostility but he is also given a sympathetic tone and a level of intimacy with Jesus that John reserves for "friends" rather than "enemies." Jesus poses to him a riddle: "No one can see the kingdom of God without being born from above" (3:3).[28] Nicodemus questions the meaning of this riddle. Indeed, the thought of a grown man returning to his mother's womb is absurd without further explanation! What follows is quite unexpected: Jesus rebukes Nicodemus for not grasping the metaphor.

From John's perspective, Nicodemus has ambiguous loyalty and thus is not to be praised.[29] It is not enough to be open to belief in Jesus. What we might see as sincere open-mindedness, John considers indecisiveness. Nicodemus comes to Jesus as a fence-sitter, and John reveals this by highlighting his lack of wisdom.[30] This episode is important because it shows that John's Jesus is a polarizing figure.[31] If you come to Jesus undecided, he will force you to one side or the other. Even characters who are potentially sympathetic to Jesus are forced into black-and-white categories.

Conclusion

Over the course of this chapter, I have pointed out several contexts where hostility is just below the surface, if not openly manifested. The historical sketch of the generation immediately before that of Jesus showed that like-minded fellows often fought for influence and supremacy. The more neighboring groups

28. Jesus's riddle is most likely meant to frustrate Nicodemus. See discussion in Tom Thatcher, *The Riddles of Jesus in John: A Study in Tradition and Folklore*, SBLMS 53 (Atlanta: Society of Biblical Literature, 2000), 189–93.

29. For more on Nicodemus, see David Allen's chapter in this book.

30. Matthew Kraus, "New Jewish Directions in the Study of the Fourth Gospel," in *New Currents through John: A Global Perspective*, ed. Francisco Lozada Jr. and Tom Thatcher, RBS 54 (Atlanta: Society of Biblical Literature, 2006), 163.

31. After Jesus's death in John, Nicodemus returns to the narrative to help with Jesus's ceremonial burial (John 19:38–42). This might suggest that Nicodemus ultimately becomes an example of discipleship. However, such conclusions are best left understated.

had in common, the more ugly these fights became. This is exactly the picture given in the canonical Gospels.

In Mark, we are introduced to a Jesus who was argumentative and confrontational. Jesus starts a long chain of arguments and ultimately silences all who would question him. He argues most with those who are nearest him. Historically speaking, the Pharisees were among the least legalistic leaders in Israel. Yet, at every turn, Jesus's elevation of the well-being of his followers over that of Sabbath keeping is controversial.

Matthew is generally considered the most Jewish Gospel. Luke is generally considered the most concerned with non-Jews. Yet Matthew's venom for the Pharisees is unrivaled, while Luke includes glimpses of sympathy and common humanity. We must not lose sight of the overall narrative tendencies of Luke-Acts, but it seems that the more the storyteller identified with Judaism, the more unforgiving he was toward his coreligionists. John's Gospel carries this internal conflict to the breaking point. The storyteller forces us to question the very parameters of Judaism. In reading, John's readers are required to redefine the category "Jew" in uncomfortable ways.

In sum, both the historical and literary contexts wherein we find Jesus suggest that Jesus's closest religious/ideological relatives were the Pharisees. In all these cases, it is the kinsmen of Jesus who are most alienated and most likely to be called "enemies." According to these biblical portraits, there was a hostile rift between Jesus and the Jewish leaders. We are meant to see Jesus over and against the Pharisees, Sadducees, and scribes. But it is quite telling that Jesus debates time and again with these schools and never with Greek or Roman philosophers. While we are meant to see Jesus in contrast to the Jewish leaders of his time, there is no better evidence than this very contrast that Jesus was himself a Jewish rabbi in close proximity to the Pharisaic tradition. From this perspective, the narratives' portraits of the Jewish leadership lead the reader to see Jesus as a Jewish teacher and leader in his own right, as a formidable opponent to the recognized authorities who treads too closely onto their turf.

Suggestions for Further Reading

Chilton, Bruce D., and Jacob Neusner, eds. *In Quest of the Historical Pharisees*. Waco: Baylor University Press, 2007.

Meier, John P. *A Marginal Jew: Rethinking the Historical Jesus*. Vol. 3, *Companions and Competitors*. ABRL. New York: Doubleday, 2001.

Schürer, Emil. *The History of the Jewish People in the Age of Jesus Christ (175 BC–AD 135)*. Translated and edited by Geza Vermes, Fergus Millar, and Matthew Black. Vol. 1. Edinburgh: T&T Clark, 1973–1987.

9

Political Authorities

The Herods, Caiaphas, and Pontius Pilate

HELEN K. BOND

In ancient societies the divide between "religion" and "politics" was not nearly as clear as it appears to most people in the Western industrialized world. Religion permeated all aspects of people's lives, from private, individual decisions up to local and national government. Readers should not be surprised, then, to find a high priest listed alongside Herodian kings and Roman governors as part of the *political* landscape of first-century Israel. These different rulers, in varying combinations, directed political life at the time of Jesus. We shall look first at what we know about these men historically before turning in the second half of this chapter to their presentations in the Gospels.

Historical Considerations: Political Authorities in the First Century

In order to understand the political situation at the time of Jesus, we need to go back to the declining years of the Hasmonean dynasty in the mid-first century BCE. The Hasmoneans were the heirs of the Maccabees, the small but determined band of Jews who had shaken off rule by the Seleucids (the Syrian heirs of Alexander the Great) a century before and established Judea as an independent nation once again. Assuming the title of king and then of high priest, they expanded their territories, pushing into Galilee and Samaria in the north and Idumea in the south. By the 60s BCE, however, the dynasty was beset by dynastic struggle, and the country was forced into civil war. Both rivals appealed to Rome, their long-term ally and the emerging new superpower on the world stage. The Roman general Pompey supported first the warlike Aristobulus, then later the more docile Hyrcanus, installing him as high priest, reducing Judean territories and demanding the payment of heavy tribute. By 63 BCE Rome was no longer friend and ally, but master.

An Idumean Jew and loyal supporter of Hyrcanus named Antipater set about restoring order to the country, ably aided by his sons. One of these was to become Herod I, or Herod the Great as he is better known. The young man had favorably impressed a series of Roman generals with his energy and valor, and when the powerful eastern Parthian Empire installed one of Aristobulus's sons as king in 40 BCE, Mark Anthony and Octavian (later to become the emperor Augustus) decided to offer the young Herod the throne. Three years later and following a successful siege of Jerusalem, Herod claimed his crown. He took his place on Rome's eastern border as one of a series of other "client kings" (or "friendly kings"). These kingdoms acted as buffer states between areas of direct Roman rule and outside territories; their rulers enjoyed a certain amount of autonomy but typically were expected to pay taxes and offer military aid to Rome when required (see fig. 9.1).

Herod reigned from 37 to 4 BCE. In many respects his reign was a glorious one. Herod saw himself—and wanted to be seen—as a major player on the world stage, a confident and generous Hellenistic monarch quite at ease with his Roman patrons. His loyalty to successive Roman rulers ensured that the boundaries of his territory increased to rival the great kingdom of Solomon. He was a magnificent builder, incorporating the latest Italian designs into his architecture;[1] he gave benefactions to cities around the Mediterranean, strove to protect Jewish rights in the Diaspora, rebuilt Jerusalem, and refurbished its temple on a lavish scale, turning it into one of the wonders of the ancient world. His subjects enjoyed reduced taxation (there is no evidence that Herod or his successors paid tribute to Rome), and as a Jew himself (common claims to the contrary are unsupported), he tolerated and respected the customs of his Jewish subjects.

At the same time, however, Herod had come to the throne following a brutal civil war and had executed large sections of the Judean nobility. Since he was an absolute monarch, his reign was undoubtedly oppressive; he built a series of desert fortresses not to protect his borders but to maintain order among his people. His domestic life was troubled, largely because of his paranoid inability to name a successor (he killed his three eldest sons for suspected

---

1. See Ehud Netzer, *The Architecture of Herod the Great Builder* (Grand Rapids: Baker Academic, 2006).

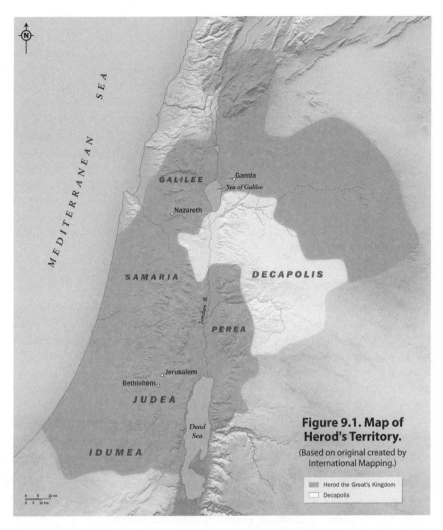

Figure 9.1. Map of Herod's Territory.
(Based on original created by International Mapping.)

Herod the Great's Kingdom
Decapolis

treason, besides his Hasmonean wife and her mother). It is perhaps ironic that Herod's most infamous act—the so-called massacre of the innocents—has no corroboration outside Matthew 2:1–18. Josephus gives a full and detailed account of Herod's last years, particularly in his *Jewish Antiquities*, but says nothing about this incident. Arguments from silence are not always strong ones, but Josephus was keen to paint as villainous a portrait of Herod as possible and would surely have incorporated the story had he known it. Yet Herod's reputation was clearly such that people would have believed such a story of him. When the king finally died, aged seventy, of a debilitating illness, the people vented their pent-up frustration through a series of uprisings the length and breadth of his realm.

Rome responded swiftly and aggressively to the uprisings. Sending two legions under the Syrian governor Varus, they swept down through the country, burning towns, crucifying protesters, and taking others into slavery. As a particular mark of honor, Herod had been granted the unusual privilege of selecting his own successor. The will, however, needed to be ratified by the emperor, and his sons quickly left their troubled homeland and presented themselves in Rome. Augustus decided to uphold Herod's wishes and divided the realm among three of his sons. He granted Archelaus almost half, incorporating Judea, Idumea, and Samaria with the title *ethnarch* (literally a "national ruler"), and promised that he would be made king if he proved himself worthy. Two other sons, Antipas and Philip, were to rule as "tetrarchs" (literally "ruler of a quarter"): Antipas received the noncontiguous territories of Galilee and Perea, while Philip was allotted largely gentile territories to the north and east of the Sea of Galilee. So it was that Galilee at the time of Jesus was ruled by a Jewish tetrarch, Herod Antipas.

Galilee and Herod Antipas

Antipas was born about 25 BCE, the second son of Herod I and his Samaritan wife, Malthace. His forty-three-year reign (from 4 BCE to 39 CE) presumably bears testimony to his abilities as a ruler. His father thought of making him sole heir at one time, though he later changed his mind (*J.W.* 1.616, 2.20). Antipas adopted the dynastic title of "Herod" (*J.W.* 2.167) and set about restoring Galilee after Varus's devastating campaigns. Proving himself a son of Herod, he refounded and fortified the city of Sepphoris and then later, in 19/20 CE, built a new capital by the Sea of Galilee, naming it Tiberias in honor of the emperor. Josephus notes that Tiberias's location on a former burial ground deterred many Jews from moving there (*Ant.* 18.38), though this does not seem to have prevented the city from becoming the site of a rabbinic academy at a later period. Despite his love of Hellenism, Antipas, like his father, refrained from putting images on his coins and seems to have regularly attended feasts in Jerusalem (see Luke 23:7 and the affair of the shields below).

Antipas's cities have been much debated by scholars. On one side it is argued that his "urbanization" policies were a huge drain on the local economy, that cities act as parasites on the surrounding towns and villages, demanding ever more in taxes and commodities, leading to dispossession of land, destitution, and banditry. On the other side it is argued, particularly by archaeologists, that Antipas's building projects were not nearly so grand as those of his father; that many of the most striking features, such as theaters, were probably built in the second century, when the cities were extended again by Roman rulers; and that Antipas's buildings simply brought his cities up to the level of those in neighboring regions. Archaeological evidence from surrounding villages and towns suggests a network of thriving local economies. No internal disturbances are recorded for this period, and Antipas's relations with his subjects seem to have been good. As Morten Jensen suggests, Antipas was probably a moderate and reasonably able ruler.[2] Though it would be naive to assume that he enjoyed universal support, many might well have preferred his rule to that of his father or direct Roman rule. The "Herodians" mentioned in the Gospels (Mark 3:6; Matt. 22:16) were probably Antipas's political supporters.

Of particular importance to the Jesus story is Antipas's execution of John the Baptist. The story is told in some detail by Josephus, who notes that Antipas feared that the large crowds surrounding the Baptist might lead to insurrection. Consequently, he had him imprisoned in the desert fortress of Machaerus (near Perea) and executed (*Ant.* 18.116–19). The Synoptic Gospels suggest that John was executed specifically because he criticized Antipas's *marriage*. Early in his reign, Antipas had entered into a politically expedient union with the daughter of King Aretas IV of Nabataea. On a visit to his half-brother Herod Philip (not the tetrarch), however, he had fallen in love with and later married Philip's wife, Herodias. Marriage to a brother's wife, if that brother was still living, was forbidden under the Mosaic law.[3] We shall see below that many of the details in the Synoptic accounts of the Baptist's death appear to be legendary embellishments (the banquet, the dancing girl, and so on), but it is quite likely that the Baptist's criticism of Antipas's marital affairs may well have contributed to his downfall. The Jewish tetrarch would not have wanted a holy man accusing him of unlawful actions, particularly if he was based in Perea and drawing attention to his recent divorce from the Nabataean princess. It is hardly surprising that Antipas acted quickly to curtail John's activities.[4]

So far as we know, Jesus seems to have completely avoided Antipas's cities, even though Sepphoris was only an hour's walk from his hometown of Nazareth, and Tiberias was close to the fishing towns on the banks of the Sea of Galilee. Was it simply that he preferred the small settlements and villages where people naturally understood his rural metaphors and images? Or was the fate of John the Baptist a warning to avoid too much confrontation with Antipas? The New Testament suggests that Antipas kept an eye on Jesus, and Luke maintains that at least two of his courtiers were attracted by

2. See Morten H. Jensen, *Herod Antipas in Galilee: The Literary and Archaeological Sources on the Reign of Herod Antipas and its Socioeconomic Impact on Galilee*, WUNT 2.215 (Tübingen: Mohr Siebeck, 2006).

3. Lev. 18:16; 20:21. See also Mark 6:17; Matt. 14:3; and Josephus, *Ant.* 18.109–11, 136.

4. Josephus indicates John's popularity in the sequel to this story. Some years later, King Aretas of Nabataea, still smarting at Antipas's treatment of his daughter, invaded Perea. The defeat of Antipas's army, Josephus notes, was popularly seen as retribution for his execution of the Baptist (*Ant.* 18.116, 119).

the new movement linked to Jesus (of particular interest is Joanna, the wife of Herod's steward Chuza, who accompanied Jesus [Luke 8:2–3]; see also Manaen in Acts 13:1). Antipas would have been alert to any kind of insurrectionary behavior—even if the crowds in the Gospels are exaggerated, Jesus's activities would clearly have been of some concern. Luke claims that Antipas wanted to kill Jesus (13:31–32) and gives Antipas a role in Jesus's trial (Luke 23:6–12). Although the historicity of this latter scene has been severely challenged—prisoners at the time were tried in the region where they committed the crime, not their home territory[5]—it is not impossible that Pilate might have asked the tetrarch's opinion on a difficult case. Antipas lost his realm in 39 CE. Shortly beforehand, the emperor Gaius Caligula appointed Herodias's brother Agrippa I as king over Philip's former territories. Herodias persuaded Antipas to go to Rome and ask that he might be granted the title king too. Agrippa, however, who had benefited from Antipas's generosity in the past, now turned against him and accused him of treason. Unable to deny that he had been stockpiling arms, Antipas was exiled to Gaul (accompanied by Herodias) and his land added to that of Agrippa. Within two years, Agrippa was king of the entirety of Herod I's former realm, though his reign was to be short-lived (41–44 CE). All this, however, takes us beyond the time of Jesus. To understand the political situation to the south, where Jesus met his death, we need to turn our attention to events following the appointment of Herod's son Archelaus over the region in 4 BCE.

Judea the Roman Province

Only a decade after his appointment, Archelaus was deposed for excessive brutality and exiled to Gaul. Augustus decided not to entrust the territory to another Herod but to impose direct Roman rule. A census was taken to determine tribute levels,[6] a Roman governor named Coponius was sent out from Rome to take charge of affairs, and the region was transformed into a Roman province in 6 CE. There were actually two phases of direct Roman rule of Judea separated by Agrippa's short reign: from 6 to 41 CE, and from 44 CE to the outbreak of revolt in 66 CE. It is the first of these that will occupy our attention.

In many respects, Judea was not an easy posting. Although it was small, its borders encompassed a variety of peoples and cultures—Jews, Samaritans, and gentiles—all of whom had their difficulties. An inscription found in Caesarea and relating specifically to Pilate gives the governor's title in this first phase as "prefect," a military title, emphasizing the governor's primary task

5. For discussion and bibliography, see Helen K. Bond, *Pontius Pilate in History and Interpretation*, SNTSMS 100 (Cambridge: Cambridge University Press, 1998), 148–49.
6. This is the census under Quirinius recorded by Luke 2:1–7, though the Evangelist erroneously puts it ten years earlier.

Caesarea Inscription

Figure 9.2. The Caesarea Inscription. (Photo courtesy of Helen K. Bond.)

The limestone block was reused in a later refurbishment of the theater at Caesarea and was found in the course of excavations in 1961. The missing left half of the inscription contained the first of Pilate's three names (now lost). The right half clearly gives his title as *praefectus Iudaeae*, "prefect of Judea."

as the maintenance of law and order in the newly established province.[7] The prefect commanded only auxiliary troops (presumably Herod's former army), amounting to five infantry cohorts and one cavalry regiment.[8] If things got out of hand, he could appeal to the legate of Syria, the highest-ranking Roman in the East, who would intervene with his legions. The Roman governor set up his headquarters in the airy gentile city of Caesarea Maritima ("Caesarea-on-Sea") rather than the traditional capital, Jerusalem. This respected the sensitivities of the local population and, more importantly, facilitated communication with both Rome and the Syrian legate in Antioch. He came to Jerusalem principally for the festivals, ready for trouble in the highly charged atmosphere, though, ironically, the presence of the governor and his troops often created friction among the people.

Rome had few officials in the provinces. The prefect, with a small team of bureaucrats in Caesarea, oversaw the collection of taxes, minted bronze coins when necessary, and held supreme judicial power. A network of spies and informers doubtless kept him abreast of potential disturbances. The day-to-day ruling of the province, however, was left in the hands of the native aristocracy in Jerusalem.

7. After Agrippa, the title changed to "procurator," now highlighting the financial side of his duties—a change that explains the confusion in some texts.

8. See Bond, *Pontius Pilate*, 5.

Caiaphas and the Jewish Priestly Aristocracy

The Jewish aristocracy had suffered greatly under Herod; nevertheless, it was to these men that Rome entrusted the daily governing of the country, with the high priest at their head. It is important to realize that the high priestly office encompassed both of what we might distinguish as "religious" and "political" dimensions.

Religiously, the high priest was the spokesman for Jews everywhere, the mediator between God and humans, and the head of the Jerusalem temple. This beautiful building was the holiest place in Israel, the focus of national hopes, and the symbol of God's election of the Jewish people. Offerings in the temple obtained mercy and forgiveness, and ensured the continuing order not just of Israel but of the whole world. The high priests were Sadducees, an aristocratic group who seem to have concerned themselves primarily with the temple, its purity, and particularly the maintenance of its cult. The Pharisee Josephus describes them twice, accusing them of being heartless in judgment, unpopular, boorish, and rude (*J.W.* 2.164–66; *Ant.* 18.16–17). Sadducean literature (had any survived) might have told a different story.

Politically, the high priest, along with his fellow aristocrats, was expected to mediate between the governor and the people, to settle local disputes, and to keep the peace. These men are often labeled as "collaborators," but it is difficult to see what options they had. Most of them had lived through the turbulent times following the death of Herod I and perhaps had witnessed firsthand the bloody battle in the temple itself, when parts were burned and the treasury was plundered (*J.W.* 2.39–50; *Ant.* 17.250–68). That time they had been lucky—the temple could be cleansed and the cult continued—but they must have been anxious not to let things get out of hand again. For many of these men, the only way to keep Roman troops out of the temple was to maintain peace, which meant acquiescing to Roman rule and paying tribute. It was a compromise, of course, and one that those of a more nationalist persuasion scorned.

It is difficult to know what common Jewish people thought about their high priests in this period. Certainly neither Josephus nor Philo portrays them as the natural spokesmen of the people, though most recorded uprisings took place at feasts when the high priest was busy with cultic matters and tensions may have been too high for diplomacy. One aspect of the high priests that may have tarnished their standing is the fact that they were *Roman appointments*. Originally, the high priesthood was for life, passed on from father to son. Things changed, however, with Herod I, who took it upon himself to appoint and depose high priests at will. Rome continued this policy; although they tended to respect established families, their meddling went further than Herod's, with some high priests holding office for only a year. (It is significant that during the revolt, when the rebels seized power, they appointed their own man in the traditional biblical manner, by drawing *lots*.⁹) An implication of Herodian/Roman policy toward the high priests was the emergence of a new group of "deposed high priests." Evidence suggests that these men continued to be called "high priest" long after they had left office, reflecting either deference to the post or the view that the high priesthood was a lifelong role. (Annas is referred to as "high priest" in the New Testament, even though the actual incumbent at the time was Caiaphas: Luke 3:2; John 18:19–24; Acts 4:6.) These men, together with their immediate families, formed the group known in the New Testament as the "chief priests."[10]

During the first phase of direct Roman rule, the high priesthood was almost exclusively in the hands of the family of Ananus (or Annas, as the New Testament calls him). He was the first Roman appointment, and after a nine-year period of service his five sons and, later in the century, a grandson succeeded him. Caiaphas was linked to this powerful priestly family through marriage (John 18:13). Nothing further is known of Caiaphas's early life, except that he must have been from a wealthy, aristocratic, and priestly family. He was appointed to the high priesthood in about 18 CE by Pilate's predecessor, Gratus, and was deposed by the Syrian legate in 37, shortly after Pilate himself had left office. The fact that Pilate saw no reason to change him suggests that the two men worked well together and that Pilate could trust him to pursue Roman interests. At the same time, he was the longest-serving high priest of the first century, and his lengthy tenure may have lent a certain air of much-needed stability to the post.

Caiaphas is important in the Jesus story, of course, as part of the priestly opposition, and perhaps even the prime mover, in his arrest and execution. But what caused him to take the step of handing over one of his compatriots to Rome? Others spoke out against the leading priests (the Essenes, for example, or the desert prophets later on), but there is no evidence that the priests tried to silence them. What made Jesus different was the fact that he brought his movement to a crowded Jerusalem at Passover, that he had a following (perhaps of a worryingly large size), and, perhaps most importantly of all, that he not only *spoke* but *acted* against the temple. The Synoptic Gospels locate Jesus's demonstration in the temple shortly before his death (Mark 11:15–19; Matt. 21:12–17; Luke 19:45–46), and Mark 11:18 (and perhaps Luke 19:47) specifically links this incident with the decision of the "chief priests and scribes" to kill him.[11] Precisely what occasioned Jesus's protest is debated. Was there too much commercial activity? Was his action intended as a prophecy of impending destruction? Perhaps, from the ruling

9. Josephus, *J.W.* 4.147–57.

10. There is actually no distinction between the words for "high priest" and "chief priests" in Greek; the former is used for the singular and the latter for the plural.

11. John puts the incident at the beginning of Jesus's public ministry (John 2:13–22). The Johannine sequence is likely less historical, since, as the Synoptic accounts suggest, the Jewish authorities would not have allowed Jesus's ministry to continue after such a defiant act in the temple.

Figure 9.3. Model of the Temple in Jerusalem. (Photo courtesy of David J. Reimer.)

priests' perspective, it did not matter much. Jesus had caused a disturbance in the temple at one of the holiest and busiest times of the year. His actions were fairly small in scale and, apparently, had eluded the gaze of the Roman soldiers stationed above the porticoes of the temple's outer courtyard. Next time, however, things might be different. Jesus might come back with more supporters, start a riot, and who knew where it might end? The last thing the Jewish leaders wanted was Roman intervention so close to the feast.

The Gospels suggest that Jesus was arrested at night and taken to the high priest's house, but this is as far as the agreement goes. Mark (followed by Matthew) presents a formal trial that night, John describes an informal interrogation in front of the former high priest Annas, and Luke maintains that the Jewish council met the following morning. It is difficult not to suspect that apologetic concerns are more important to the Evangelists at this point than historical accuracy (see below). But can we say anything about Caiaphas's role in the proceedings? Two points need to be made. First, the existence of a fixed Jewish council (the Sanhedrin) with responsibility for religious and legal matters has been seriously questioned in recent years. Instead, decisions were made by the high priest with a group of ad hoc advisors summoned specifically because of their expertise on particular matters.[12] Second, Jews may have retained some limited capital jurisdiction on religious matters, but

12. See, for example, Martin Goodman, *The Ruling Class of Judaea* (Cambridge: Cambridge University Press, 1987), 113–18; J. McLaren, *Power and Politics in Palestine* (Sheffield: Sheffield Academic Press, 1991); E. P. Sanders, *Judaism: Practice and Belief, 63 BCE–66 CE* (London: SCM,

Caiaphas Ossuary

Figure 9.4. Our only tangible link with Caiaphas is an ossuary (or bone box) found in Jerusalem in November 1990. (Photo courtesy of the Israeli Antiquities Authority.)

By the first century, Jews had adopted the Greco-Roman practice of secondary burial; the body was laid out in the family tomb for a year or so, then the bones were collected in a limestone ossuary. Some of these are quite plain, but the one in question is highly ornamented with a leaf pattern, two large circles and small rosettes, and traces of orange paint on both the front and the lid. The box has two roughly scrawled Aramaic inscriptions: a shorter one, *Yehosef bar Qapha*, and a longer one, *Yehosef bar Qayyapha*. Inside were the remains of six people: a sixty-year-old man, a young woman, and four children (multiple burials are common). Quite possibly the older man's name in Greek was Joseph (son of/belonging to the family of) Caiaphas.

the execution of a popular leader at Passover would certainly have required Pilate's authority. All that was needed in Jewish custody, then, was a brief interrogation and a clarification of the charge to be put before the prefect. John's Gospel is most plausible at this point, though whether he had better sources or simply had a better grasp of legal procedures is difficult to say. John may even be right to ascribe a prominent role here to Caiaphas's father-in-law, Annas; given Caiaphas's Passover duties and Annas's prominence, it would not be surprising to find him overseeing the affair. At all events, Caiaphas and Annas had no need to try Jesus formally; the only requirement was the decision to hand him over to Pilate for crucifixion.

Pontius Pilate

Pontius Pilate was the fifth Roman prefect of Judea, from 26 to early 37 CE.[13] Like most other governors of Judea, he belonged to the equestrian order; he

1992), 472–90; David Goodblatt, *The Monarchic Principle: Studies in Jewish Self-Government in Antiquity*, TSAJ 38 (Tübingen: Mohr Siebeck, 1994).

13. Daniel R. Schwartz, however, dates his arrival in the province to 19 CE ("Pontius Pilate," in *Anchor Bible Dictionary*, ed. David Noel Freedman [New York: Doubleday, 1992], 5:395–401).

was therefore a Roman knight, belonging to the lowest rung of the Italian nobility. His background is obscure, though, given the military nature of the post, he probably came to the emperor Tiberius's attention during military campaigns. The prefecture of Judea was not the most impressive post in the empire, but it was a provincial posting all the same and might prove a useful stepping stone to greater things if the incumbent showed himself worthy.

A number of incidents from Pilate's term of office are known to us from a variety of sources: Josephus, Philo of Alexandria, and the New Testament. None, however, are straightforward witnesses. The two Jewish writers (Josephus and Philo), though generally pro-Roman in their outlook, both present Pilate in a poor light. For Josephus, Pilate was one of the insensitive Roman governors whose misrule led the people to rebellion in 66 CE. For Philo, Pilate was a low-status Roman official whose lack of sensitivities toward the Jewish faith contrasts strongly with the sensitivity toward the law displayed by the emperor Tiberius. The New Testament witnesses (as we shall see below) have their own agendas too. Still, as long as we are aware of the rhetorical concerns of each writer, it is possible to piece together some events from Pilate's governorship.

Josephus tells us that around 26 CE, soon after his arrival in Judea, Pilate offended Jewish sensitivities by bringing into Jerusalem Roman troops carrying standards that featured images of the emperor. Jewish law did not allow graven images, particularly not in Jerusalem, and the people quickly took their grievances to Pilate at Caesarea, surrounding his residence for five days and imploring him to remove the offending standards. Pilate refused: to ask for the removal of the standards was to ask for the removal of the troops. He may have known that the images were offensive but refused to allow the people to dictate which troops he, as their new prefect, deployed. By the sixth day Pilate was thoroughly exasperated and threatened to cut the people down. At this, they bared their necks and declared that they would rather die than see their native laws transgressed. Amazed at their reaction, Pilate immediately ordered the troops to be removed to the Roman headquarters in Caesarea. Although there is clearly some idealization of Jewish devotion here, Pilate does seem to have been willing to compromise and anxious to avoid excessive bloodshed.[14]

A second incident, however, did not end so positively. Josephus tells how Pilate used temple money to build an aqueduct in Jerusalem. A rabbinic passage allows surplus temple money to be used "for all the city's needs."[15] The project was probably conceived as a joint venture, Roman and Jewish authorities cooperating with one another. At some point, however, things started to go wrong. Precisely what is unclear. Did Pilate drain the surplus and still

14. Josephus, *J.W.* 2.169–74; *Ant.* 18.55–59.
15. *m. Šeqal.* 4.2. For fuller discussion of this, and all the other incidents recorded by Philo and Josephus, see Bond, *Pontius Pilate*, 24–93.

Philo on Pilate

Philo offers a character sketch of Pilate, describing him as "a man of inflexible, stubborn and cruel disposition" and later as "a spiteful and angry person" (*Embassy* 301, 303). His administration was characterized by "his venality, his violence, his thefts, his assaults, his abusive behaviour, his frequent executions of untried prisoners, and his endless savage ferocity" (*Embassy* 303).

Written by a contemporary of Pilate, Philo's account needs to be taken seriously. Clearly he could not have characterized the prefect in this way if it was generally known that he was a model governor. Yet his account is highly tendentious at this point. It comes in the course of a letter encouraging its recipient (the emperor Gaius Caligula) to see how a good emperor like Tiberius defended the rights of Jews. The harsher the picture of Pilate, the better Tiberius looks in comparison. Every single adjective used to describe Pilate here has been used elsewhere by Philo to describe others who disregard the Jewish law. Of course, that does not mean that the list of Pilate's atrocities cannot be historical, but it does raise serious questions about its reliability.

demand more, treating temple resources as his own personal *fiscus* (as the account in the *Jewish War* seems to imply)? Or was it the *route* of the aqueduct that caused problems, possibly passing through a graveyard (as the parallel account in the *Jewish Antiquities* may suggest)? At all events, when Pilate next visited Jerusalem, large numbers of people protested, "besieging him with angry clamour." Having foreseen trouble, however, he had dispersed plain-clothesmen into the crowd, and, at a prearranged signal, they beat rioters with their clubs, and many lost their lives.[16]

Philo of Alexandria adds another story.[17] He tells how Pilate caused offense by setting up gilded shields in honor of Tiberius in his Jerusalem headquarters (Herod's former palace). The offense seems to have been caused by a reference to the emperor's full title, presumably including the phrase "son of the deified Augustus," in the holy city. Philo's account does not suggest sudden, mass outrage (as with the standards) but rather a slower realization on the part of the people that the standards were offensive—and perhaps too that they might be able to do something about it. Accordingly, they enlisted four Herodian princes to appeal to Pilate (Antipas and Philip were undoubtedly among them). A letter was sent to Tiberius, who ordered the shields to be removed to the temple of Augustus in Caesarea. Philo's account is highly negative toward Pilate; he accuses him of not really wishing to honor the emperor and being terrified that the Herodian princes might send an embassy

16. Josephus, *J.W.* 2.175–77; *Ant.* 18.60–62.
17. Philo, *Embassy* 299–305.

to Tiberius, which would expose his misgovernment (see box on previous page). More probably, the story dates to 31 CE, to the troubled time around the fall of Sejanus, Tiberius's closest advisor and prefect of the Praetorian Guard (the emperor's personal bodyguard). Many of Sejanus's associates were charged with treason; even if Pilate had no connection with him (and there is no evidence that he did), it was not a time to risk appearing to dishonor the emperor. If Pilate had erected the shields to show his loyalty to Tiberius, he would want a decree from the highest level before he risked removing them.

Most important for our purposes is Pilate's decision to send Jesus to the cross. The fact that Jesus was crucified, a specifically Roman penalty, is one of the surest facts about the historical Jesus (see the introductory chapter of this book). Yet the details surrounding his death are difficult to reconstruct. As we shall see below, the Roman trial scenes in the Gospels are just as divergent and theologically motivated as those depicting Jesus at the hands of the Jewish authorities. Many features, such as Pilate's question concerning truth, his hand washing, or the echoes of Second Isaiah that permeate the narratives, clearly were inspired by early Christian preaching. Other elements, such as the Passover amnesty, Barabbas, and the presence of a crowd cannot be substantiated by extracanonical evidence. In all probability, the earliest followers of Jesus had little idea of what happened before Pilate; their focus was on showing how Jesus came to be crucified as "King of the Jews" and on articulating the theological reasons for his death.

Quite probably, the Jewish high priests had a prior agreement with Pilate that troublemakers were to be dealt with swiftly and brutally. Both Caiaphas and Pilate were concerned to keep the peace, particularly in the crowded city during a festival. The fact that it was *Passover*, a feast celebrating national liberation from bondage in Egypt, only made matters more tense. Any popular leader who worried the priests would also have worried the prefect. Pilate was probably already watching Jesus: his spies and informers would have advised him what was happening in the Galilean villages, and Herod Antipas might have told him about his handling of John the Baptist, that he had moved swiftly to nip the movement in the bud, and that by executing the leader he had dissipated the danger. Pilate would not have deliberated long over Jesus. Rome showed a callous brutality when dealing with provincials. He might have questioned Jesus a little, but it is highly unlikely that he made any attempt to free the prisoner or that he would have allowed a crowd to assemble. Jesus would have been charged quickly as a troublemaker; the sign above the cross, "King of the Jews," albeit ironic, is found in all four Gospels and is likely authentic (Mark 15:26; Matt. 27:37; Luke 23:38; John 19:19–22). The prisoner would then be taken outside Jerusalem and crucified, a grim reminder that popular leaders were not to be tolerated.

Pilate lost his post some years later for alleged brutality. Josephus records a Samaritan uprising in which a messianic leader persuaded people to go with him to the top of Mount Gerizim, their holy mountain, where he promised to show them sacred vessels put there by Moses. Crowds of armed followers assembled in the village of Tirathana at the foot of the mountain, preparing to begin their ascent. Pilate, without waiting to see what happened, sent a detachment of cavalry who blocked their ascent, killed some in battle, and executed many of the ringleaders. The Samaritan leaders, however, complained to the Syrian legate, Vitellius, about Pilate's heavy-handed actions: "for, they said, it was not as rebels against the Romans but as refugees from the persecution of Pilate that they had met" (*Ant.* 18.89). Pilate was ordered to Rome to answer the charges but, despite hurrying back (doubtless to give his side of the story), reached the capital after Tiberius's death on the fourteenth of March, 37 CE. What became of Pilate is unknown. The fact that he did not return to Judea does not necessarily mean that the emperor found him guilty of the charges against him. After more than ten years in the province it was perhaps time for a new commission. Pilate may not have been the best Roman governor, but he was by no means the worst; he kept the province reasonably quiet and seems to have learned from some of his early mistakes. The emperor undoubtedly could use such a man elsewhere.

We have now looked at a number of Jesus's enemies—Herod, Caiaphas, and Pilate—all of whom are known to us from historical sources outside the Gospels. These sources allow us to build up a picture of these men, to understand their concerns and motivations, and to put their conflict with Jesus in clearer historical perspective. But what about their presentation in the Gospels? Does early Christian literature provide us with further historical material? Or do they tell us more about the pastoral and theological concerns of the earliest communities that produced them? To this we shall now turn.

Narrative Considerations—Political Authorities in the Gospels

In what follows I assume, with the scholarly majority, that Mark wrote first and was used as a major source by both Matthew and Luke. I shall look first, then, at Mark's depiction of political authorities before turning to Matthew, Luke, and finally John.

Political Authorities in Mark

Mark refers to three political authorities: Antipas and Pilate are mentioned by name, while Caiaphas is known only by the title of his office, high priest. We shall look at each in the order in which he is found in the text.

ANTIPAS

The tetrarch of Galilee (referred to simply as "King Herod") makes an appearance at Mark 6:14–16. He hears that people are linking Jesus with Elijah or one of the prophets of old; Antipas himself, however, imagines that Jesus is John the Baptist raised from the dead. The narrator then embarks on a relatively long digression, explaining events leading to John's death (6:17–29). The villain of the piece is Antipas's wife, Herodias, who has a grudge against John and wants to kill him because he criticized her marriage. Antipas, however, "feared John, knowing that he was a righteous and holy man, and kept him safe"; he liked to listen to him, though perplexed at his words (6:20). Herodias finally manages to eliminate John at Antipas's birthday party. Her daughter dances before the gathering, and when the enchanted tetrarch offers the girl anything she wants, her mother tells her to ask for the Baptist's head. Anxious not to lose face before his courtiers and the leading men of Galilee, Antipas reluctantly orders John's execution.

Within the context of Mark's narrative, the Antipas story fills a gap between Jesus sending out his disciples in 6:7–13 and their return in 6:30. The story itself is exotic and colorful and clearly contains legendary elements: the villainous wife, the dancing girl, the rash promise, and echoes of both the story of Esther and Jezebel's vendetta against Elijah. Yet Mark has not chosen to recount it simply because it is a good story. Jesus's ministry began after the arrest of John in 1:14; now, with the death of the forerunner, Jesus's own rejection and death will begin to come into sharper focus. And just as John was a good man who went to his death because of the machinations of others (here, Herodias), so Jesus will go to his death because of Jewish priestly opposition.

Caiaphas

The Markan Jesus has two trials: a Jewish one set at night (14:53–65) and a Roman one the following morning (15:1–15). Precisely why Jesus needs two trials is not made clear; presumably Mark assumed that the Jewish verdict needed ratification by the Roman governor. The effect of the narrative, however, is that it highlights the actions of both sets of political authorities, Jewish and Roman.

After his arrest Jesus is taken to the high priest (14:53). A curious aspect of Mark's trial narrative is that Caiaphas is never named but simply referred to throughout by his office: "the high priest" (14:53, 60–61, 63). For this Evangelist, all Jewish officials unite in condemning Jesus: the high priest, the chief priests, the elders, scribes, and, for good measure, "all the council." And what he presents can only be described as a kangaroo court. We know already that members of the court wish to see Jesus eliminated (14:1); now the judges convene with the sole intention of putting Jesus to death (14:55). Later on, after the verdict has been passed, it is members of the council themselves who spit on Jesus and ridicule him (14:65). Earlier generations of scholars debated the legality of the Jewish trial, but it is quite clear that Mark *intends* the trial to be a travesty of justice—it takes place at night on the eve of a feast, it is hurried, the witnesses are false, and the prisoner is convicted by nothing but his own confession. Only in this way can Mark explain Jesus's condemnation at the hands of the leaders of his own people.[18]

The trial turns on two charges. First is the accusation that Jesus will destroy the temple (14:58). Jesus has foretold its destruction in Mark 13:2 but not that he would destroy it himself. The false witnesses, however, cannot agree, and the charge is abandoned in favor of the much more significant question of Jesus's identity. Dramatically, the high priest stands in the midst of the courtroom and asks Jesus, "Are you the Messiah, the Son of the Blessed One?" to which Jesus replies, "I am; and 'you will see the Son of Man seated at the right hand of the Power,' and 'coming with the clouds of heaven'" (14:61–62). There is deep irony here in that, in a Gospel where even Jesus's closest followers do not fully understand who he is until after the resurrection, the hostile high priest has grasped Jesus's identity in terms of Mark's two central titles, Christ and Son of "the Blessed" (God). Jesus affirms his identity and continues by drawing upon phrasing from Daniel 7:13 and Psalm 110:1 to claim that, despite his present humiliation, he will be vindicated. Unlike Peter outside, who blusteringly denies his master, Jesus quietly and confidently proclaims his identity and perhaps serves as a model for Mark's readers, who may have found themselves on trial for their Christian identity. The high priest, however, accuses Jesus of blasphemy, a sentence endorsed by the rest of the council.

PILATE

The Markan narrator introduces Pilate abruptly in 15:1 without any indication of his title; presumably he and his role in Jesus's execution were well known to Mark's audience. The governor is often thought to be presented as a weakling in Mark's Gospel, but a careful reading of the text shows rather an astute governor who handles a difficult case with a certain amount of shrewdness. The whole of the Roman trial in Mark revolves around the theme of kingship (the title "king" is used six times in 15:1–32). Mark's question is, in what way was Jesus a king?

Pilate's initial question, "Are you the King of the Jews?" (15:2), picks up the findings of the Jewish court, translating the religious title "Christ" into the more political "King of the Jews." In response, Jesus answers evasively. He will not deny his kingship but also will not accept the Roman distortion of it. At this, the Jewish leaders accuse Jesus of many things, to which Jesus remains silent (possibly a reflection of the Suffering Servant of Isa. 53:7), and Pilate is said to be amazed (15:5).

The scene changes, and in 15:8 a crowd comes to Pilate, demanding that he honor his usual custom of releasing a prisoner to them at Passover. Pilate's offer is calculating; he knows that the chief priests have handed Jesus over

---

18. For fuller discussion, see Helen K. Bond, *Caiaphas: Friend of Rome and Judge of Jesus?* (Louisville: Westminster John Knox, 2004), 98–108.

out of envy (15:10), which implies that Jesus has a popular following. His question is a test of support: "Do you want me to release for you the King of the Jews?" (15:9). Who will back this messianic leader? Mark's readers of course would know that anyone supporting such a man would risk being crucified with him. Stirred up by the chief priests, the crowd asks for the release of another prisoner, Barabbas (15:11). In Mark, Barabbas is rather ambiguous: he is not specifically said to be a murderer and insurrectionary but rather to be in prison *alongside* such criminals. The precise question of his guilt is left open. Pilate continues: "Then what do you wish me to do with the man whom you call the King of the Jews?" (v. 12). Again, this is a test of public support; the severity of the punishment demanded will show how far the crowd is from supporting him, and the people shout for crucifixion (v. 13). Pilate even asks them to name the charge—"Why, what evil has he done?"—but the crowd simply shouts all the more for crucifixion (v. 14). Pilate is now in a strong position. As a messianic claimant, Jesus has to be eliminated, but the major obstacle—public opinion—has been removed. With deep irony, Mark notes in the final verse that Pilate, "wishing to satisfy the crowd, released Barabbas for them; and after flogging Jesus, he handed him over to be crucified" (15:15).

For Mark, Jesus's kingship stands in opposition to that claimed by nationalist leaders and insurrectionaries, though such men are clearly the choice of the Jewish leaders. He is a crucified messiah, sent to his death by the Jewish religious leadership and a harsh Roman governor. Mark may want to place primary responsibility on Jesus's Jewish antagonists, but Rome is not whitewashed, as Pilate plays his part in the events leading to the cross.

Political Authorities in Matthew

Following his Markan source, Matthew also includes Antipas, Caiaphas, and Pilate in his narrative. His birth narrative introduces two new characters: Herod I and his son Archelaus.

HEROD I AND ARCHELAUS

Herod I appears briefly but dramatically in Matthew's birth narrative (Matt. 2:1–18). The king is troubled when magi from the east appear, asking where they can find the newborn king of the Jews. After consulting his scribes, Herod asks the magi to report the child's whereabouts to him, but, warned in a dream, they return to their own land by a different route. Realizing he has been outwitted, Herod angrily orders the murder of all the male children two years old or under in Bethlehem. Meanwhile, Joseph also has a dream, warning him of Herod's intention and commanding him to take Jesus and Mary into Egypt. Only after Herod's death is the family told they can return (2:19–20); the reluctance of Mary and Joseph to live under Archelaus fits

Josephus's characterization of his rule as brutal and provides a reason why they settle in Nazareth (Matt. 2:22–23).

The historical difficulties with the story of Herod's massacre have been noted above. What is more important, however, is the theological use to which it is put in the context of the Gospel. Matthew presents Jesus as a new Moses; the parallels between Moses on Mount Sinai and Jesus at the Sermon on the Mount (Matt. 5–7) are quite striking, as too are the parallels here. Just as the evil pharaoh ordered the death of all newborn Israelite boys (Exod. 1:15–16), so the evil Herod orders the death of all the boys under two years of age in Matthew (2:16). And just as Moses came out of Egypt in Exodus, so does Jesus, symbolically reliving the history of his people.[19] These echoes would have been immediately apparent to Matthew's Jewish-Christian audience (and to all other readers familiar with the Exodus narratives). On a wider, literary level, the story also points forward to the Passion Narrative, foreshadowing conflict at the end of the Gospel, where once again "all Jerusalem" (2:3) will seek Jesus's life.

ANTIPAS

Matthew's presentation of Antipas (Matt. 14:1–2) broadly follows that of his Markan source, though he correctly labels him "Herod the tetrach" (14:1). The only major alteration is that Antipas is no longer sympathetic toward John the Baptist but wants to kill him. It is only fear of the people, who hold John to be a prophet, that stops him (14:5). Once again, opposition to John here points forward to the death of Jesus, where Jewish priestly rulers will similarly balance a desire to do away with Jesus with his popular support (26:3–5).

CAIAPHAS

Matthew's Jewish trial narrative follows Mark's very closely, diverting from its source only to add further blame to Jesus's Jewish opponents. So, whereas false witnesses presented themselves in Mark (14:56–57), in Matthew the Jewish leaders specifically seek them out (26:59). And this Evangelist always refers to the "elders *of the people*," perhaps a foreshadowing of the people's role in Jesus's death later on (see below, 27:25). The high priest is specifically named as Caiaphas by Matthew: the Jewish leaders meet in his palace to plot Jesus's death (26:3–5), and he is introduced at the beginning of the trial narrative (26:57), lending a certain prominence to his role.

PILATE

Pilate, in comparison, becomes a less central character in Matthew's retelling (27:2, 11–26). Although the first scene, with its accusation of kingship,

19. Matthew cites Hos. 11:1, "Out of Egypt I called my son," applying the text not to Israel as a whole (as in Hosea) but specifically to Jesus.

follows Mark closely (27:11–14), the scene with Barabbas departs from its source several times. Once again, the crowd gathers for the annual release of a prisoner, but the Matthean Pilate restricts the choice to two men: "Whom do you want me to release for you, [Jesus] Barabbas or Jesus who is called the Messiah?" (27:17). Jesus is no longer "King of the Jews" but "Christ"; clearly it is his *religious* significance that is at stake. Barabbas too has been drastically depoliticized; no longer is he associated with insurrection and murder but is simply a "notorious prisoner" (27:16). The fact that a number of ancient manuscripts give Barabbas's name as Jesus Barabbas only adds to the parallelism between the two men. Which Jesus should be released: a prisoner or the Christ?

As in Mark, the chief priests support Barabbas, but Jesus finds support in an unexpected quarter. Matthew (uniquely) reports that Pilate's wife sent him a message, imploring him to have "nothing to do with that innocent man," as she had unsettling dreams about him (27:19). Dreams, as we have seen, are an accepted manner of divine communication in Matthew (2:12–13, 19–20), so the reader knows that the gentile woman speaks the truth. Pilate, however, ignores her pleas and reiterates his earlier question, in answer to which the people, persuaded by the chief priests, ask for Barabbas (27:21). When the prefect asks what he should do with "Jesus who is called the Messiah" (note once again the religious title), the people ask for crucifixion. His final "What evil has he done?" leads only to a repetition of the people's verdict: "Let him be crucified!" (27:23).

At this point a riot threatens to break out, and Matthew adds a new element. His Pilate takes water and washes his hands in front of the crowd, with the words "I am innocent of this man's blood; see to it yourselves" (27:24). On one level this is an astonishing portrait of a Roman governor. Matthew's Jewish-Christian readers would recognize the ritual from Deuteronomy 21:1–9 (see also 2 Sam. 3:28; Ps. 26:6), which outlines the procedure for absolving oneself of the guilt of an unsolved murder. The gentile governor is behaving like a pious Jew! Significantly, he is not declaring *Jesus* innocent (though God has already done that through Pilate's wife's dream) but *himself*. One by one, characters in Matthew's Passion Narrative have sought to distance themselves from Jesus's death, first Judas (27:3–10) and now Pilate. Finally, in 27:25, it is the Jewish people who accept responsibility with the cry: "His blood be on us and on our children!"[20] At this, Pilate releases Barabbas and sends Jesus to the cross.

The emphasis in Matthew is not so much on the one chosen (Barabbas) as the one rejected (the Christ). The decision whether to accept Jesus as Christ

---

20. Written in roughly 80–90 CE, Matthew arguably has the fall of Jerusalem in mind here. For this Evangelist, the fall of the city and the destruction of its temple was God's retribution for the death of Jesus; he would certainly not have foreseen the terrible consequences these words were to have for generations of Jews.

would still have been an important one to Matthew's readers and lies at the heart of a number of seemingly anti-Jewish passages in this Gospel, an anti-Jewishness born out of controversy and conflict between Matthew's audience and their local Jewish synagogue. Clearly, for Matthew primary responsibility for Jesus's death lies with the Jewish people; but Pilate is not exonerated. He represents the kind of Roman governor many of the Evangelist's readers may have been familiar with: uninterested in religious questions, anxious to avoid a riot, and ready to work with Jewish leaders. Together, Pilate and Caiaphas mirror Herod and "all Jerusalem" in the infancy narratives; all political leaders are threatened by Jesus, and all want him eliminated.

Political Authorities in Luke

Luke was clearly interested in setting his account of Christian origins against the backdrop of imperial history. Jesus's birth takes place at the time of a Roman census (Luke 2:1–7), and the beginning of his ministry is dated with reference to Emperor Tiberius, Pontius Pilate, local client kings, and the high priest(s) (3:1–2). Throughout Acts too, events on the world stage have repercussions for the Christian community, for example, a famine in the time of Claudius (Acts 11:28) and the expulsion of Jews from Rome (18:2). Understanding their faith against the political realities of their day was obviously important for this Evangelist and his audience.

CAIAPHAS

Rather surprisingly, perhaps, Luke has very little interest in Caiaphas. He is introduced as part of the political landscape in 3:2, but even here his role seems to be marginal. Luke writes of "the high priesthood [singular] of Annas and Caiaphas." Did the Evangelist think that the two men shared the post? Or did he regard the deposed Annas as the lawful high priest? Or was he simply confused? A similar construction appears in Acts 4:6, where the priestly leaders act against Jesus's followers. Neither Caiaphas nor Annas, however, plays any specific part in the trial of Jesus, even though events take place at "the high priest's house" (22:54). And the unnamed high priest who appears briefly at the trial of Stephen in Acts 7:1 may be either man. Clearly, Luke was much more interested in Herodian and Roman rulers than Jewish high priests.

ANTIPAS

Although Luke sets the birth of Jesus "in the days of King Herod" (1:5), Herod I plays no further role in this Gospel (the massacre of the innocents is unique to Matthew). Other Herods play a role in Acts: Agrippa I, referred to as "King Herod" in Acts 12:1–6, 20–23, and Agrippa II and his sister Bernice in Acts 25:13–26:32. In the Gospel, however, the most prominent Herod is Antipas, who is introduced briefly in 3:1 as "Herod . . . tetrarch of Galilee."

Luke omits Mark's lengthy story of John the Baptist's death, though he gives a fuller account of his arrest (3:19–20). No longer is Herodias to blame for what happens to the Baptist; instead, the tetrarch acts alone, the reference to John's criticism of "the evil things he had done" casting him in a much less sympathetic light than his Markan counterpart. Later on, Herod Antipas hears about Jesus and expresses a desire to see him (9:7–9). The fact that Antipas links Jesus with "John (whom) I beheaded" sounds ominous, a worry reinforced by the warning of the Pharisees in 13:31 that Herod wants to kill Jesus. In response, Jesus refers to Antipas as "that fox" (13:32; denoting his cunning cleverness? or his inferiority as a ruler?) but acknowledges that he must leave Galilee, "because it is impossible for a prophet to be killed outside of Jerusalem" (13:33). By this stage in the narrative, then, we have encountered a cold and unscrupulous tetrarch, quite willing to put down critics and intent on killing Jesus. All this does not bode well for Antipas's final scene—his confrontation with Jesus at his trial.

Luke is the only Evangelist to include a hearing of Jesus held by Antipas (23:6–12). Within the context of the narrative, Pilate discovers that Jesus is a Galilean and sends him to be tried before the tetrarch. No reasons are given for this transferral, and, as we have seen above, there was no legal necessity for it. Many of the details here are reminiscent of Mark's Jewish trial scene, which Luke has reduced considerably (the mockery, the robing of Jesus, vague charges from the chief priests, and Jesus's silence). On a narrative level, the focus is on Antipas's reaction to Jesus. Herod, we are told, was "very glad" to see Jesus, for he had "been wanting to see him for a long time, because he had heard about him and was hoping to see him perform some sign" (23:8). Met with Jesus's lack of response, however, Antipas's reaction quickly turns to contempt and mockery. He finds Jesus ridiculous, the gorgeous robe shows his scorn for the prisoner's kingly claims, and his returning Jesus to Pilate shows that even as harsh a ruler as Antipas saw no crime in Jesus. The significance of this will become clear as we look at the Roman trial as a whole.

PILATE

As was the case with Antipas, Pilate has already been encountered within the narrative before Jesus's trial. In 3:1, we learn that he is "governor" of Judea, and in 13:1 we hear of some "Galileans whose blood Pilate had mingled with their sacrifices." No details are given here, but the gruesome expression prepares us for a ruthless man who is quite prepared to shed Galilean blood. Finally, in 20:20 the scribes and chief priests ask Jesus a question over payment of tribute with the intention of handing him over to the governor.

Luke's presentation of Jesus's trial is unique. Whereas Mark described two parallel trials, one Jewish, one Roman, Luke presents one composite trial in four scenes. There is no nighttime trial in this Gospel. Instead "the assembly of the elders of the people, both chief priests and scribes," gathers in the high

priest's house at daybreak, asks Jesus about his identity, then passes him on
to Pilate (22:66–23:1). The whole scene is much simpler than in Mark (and
many of the Markan details—false witnesses, temple accusations, blasphemy,
and the anger of the council—are transferred by Luke to the trial of *Stephen*
in Acts 7).

The Lukan Jesus is handed over to Pilate with specific charges: "perverting
our nation, . . . forbidding us to pay taxes to the emperor, and saying that he
himself is the Messiah, a king" (23:2). The reader knows that none of these is
true. Pilate picks up on the charge of kingship (23:3) but curiously responds to
Jesus's ambiguous "You say so" with the first of three declarations of Jesus's
innocence: "I find no basis for an accusation against this man" (23:4). The
Jewish assembly steps up its charges, accusing Jesus of stirring up the people
from Galilee to Jerusalem (23:5). Pilate seizes on the reference to Galilee,
perhaps hoping to rid himself of an irritating case, and sends the prisoner to
Antipas. The tetrarch, however, acts as a second witness, along with Pilate,
to Jesus's innocence (as required by Jewish law [Deut. 19:15]). In 23:12, Luke
notes that the two rulers became friends that day. What caused their former
enmity is not recounted (the Galilean deaths in 13:1?); what is important is
that both men are united in their assumption that Jesus has done nothing
deserving of death.[21]

Pilate now summons together the chief priests, rulers, and people and gives
his judgment. Both he and Herod have found Jesus innocent of the charges,
so Pilate will give Jesus a disciplinary beating and release him (23:13–17).
The Jewish crowd, however, will not accept Pilate's verdict. "Away with this
fellow," they cry, "and release Barabbas for us" (23:18). A curious feature
of Luke's account is that there has been no reference to a Passover amnesty
(23:17 is almost certainly a later harmonizing addition shaped by the accounts
in Matt. 27:15//Mark 15:6). The fate of Jesus is completely unconnected to
that of anyone else. The spontaneous cry of the crowd for Barabbas, then,
a man Luke quickly tells us is in prison for insurrection and murder, is inex-
plicable. Pilate addresses the crowd once again, attempting to release Jesus,
but in reply the people shout for crucifixion (23:20–21). Pilate repeats his
earlier verdict, but the cries of the crowd reach a dramatic crescendo, and
with great irony Luke notes that "their voices prevailed" (23:23). Luke is
the only Evangelist to admit that Pilate passed sentence, but it is clear that
it reflects the crowd's verdict rather than the prefect's. It is not so much a
condemnation of Jesus as a decision that what the priests, leaders, and people
want should be done. Once again, the lack of a Passover amnesty in Luke's
Gospel means that Pilate was under no compulsion to release Barabbas.
The final verse is almost pitiable: "He released the man they asked for, the

---

21. The link prepares for Acts 4:25–27 and the use of Ps. 2:1–2 there in connection with
Jesus's trial.

one who had been put in prison for insurrection and murder, and he handed Jesus over as they wished" (23:25). Pilate's weakness in the face of Jewish pressure has undermined both his own judgment and that of Herod. In the governor's court, injustice has triumphed.

It is clear that Luke had a particular interest in showing that, despite his shameful death on a Roman cross, Jesus had committed no crime. He dies as an innocent prophet and martyr, rejected by the people he came to save. Presumably Luke's community included Roman citizens and people who needed to be reassured that their leader was not an enemy of Rome. The Evangelist carefully lists the charges against Jesus and shows without a shadow of a doubt that the Roman political authorities of the day would have released him. Jesus goes to the cross in Luke because of Jewish animosity and Pilate's weakness in response to the people he is supposed to govern. He takes his place alongside Roman governors in Acts, who are often weak and self-seeking but who consistently find Jesus and his followers innocent of any political crime (Acts 18:12–17; 24; 25).

Political Authorities in John

John has no interest in any of the Herods, but both Caiaphas and Pilate play prominent roles in this Gospel.

CAIAPHAS

Caiaphas first appears at a council meeting that convenes after the raising of Lazarus to try Jesus in his absence (11:47–53). The councilors are concerned at the popular enthusiasm for Jesus's signs, an enthusiasm they worry will lead to Roman intervention and the destruction of both the temple and the nation (11:47–48). The discussion is dominated by Caiaphas, who, we learn, "was high priest that year" (11:49; see also 18:13; presumably meaning "high priest *that fateful year*"). "You know nothing at all!" he declares. "You do not understand that it is better for you to have one man die for the people than to have the whole nation destroyed" (11:49b–50). This is the voice of political expediency, the sober weighing of the situation (though the little phrase "better for you" may hint at self-preservation and self-interest). But Caiaphas's words are also deeply ironic: despite his hostility, the high priest has unconsciously given expression to both the sacrificial nature and the significance of Jesus's death. John attributes his words to prophecy, showing that he subscribed to the popular Jewish belief that prophetic powers were linked to the office of high priest.[22]

John mentions Caiaphas and his prophecy again after Jesus's arrest, though Caiaphas plays no further role in the narrative. Jesus is taken first

---

22. For discussion, see C. H. Dodd, "The Prophecy of Caiaphas (Jn xi 47–53)," in *Neotestamentica et Patristica*, NovTSup 6 (Leiden: Brill, 1962), 134–43.

to Annas, Caiaphas's father-in-law (18:12–13), who briefly questions Jesus in 18:19–23 "about his disciples and about his teaching" (he is referred to as "the high priest" in 18:19 and 22, presumably out of respect). The interrogation in front of Annas could hardly have been more different from Mark's formal trial. There are no assembled chief priests and scribes, no false witnesses, no charges, no accusations, and no verdict. Instead, John presents a quiet scene in which Jesus stands before the high priest and a number of guards. At first sight, it might appear odd that John, whose hostility toward "the Jews" is well known, should miss the opportunity to present a grand courtroom drama at the end. The reason is probably that, as many scholars have pointed out, the *whole of John's Gospel* is presented as Jesus's trial in front of the Jewish authorities, with frequent interrogations and constant appeal to witnesses.[23] In fact, many elements connected with Jesus's Jewish trial in Mark have already surfaced in John (1:51; 2:19–22; 10:24–39), and the council has already convicted him (11:47–53). To recount another Jewish trial at this point would have been superfluous. All that is necessary is to remind the reader of the earlier verdict (which the writer does in 18:14) and to have Jesus handed over to Pilate. John may imply knowledge of a further trial in front of Caiaphas: Jesus is sent to him in 18:24, but the Evangelist does not tell us what happened at this meeting (he recounts instead Peter's final two denials [18:25–27]).[24] The focus in John, then, will be on Jesus's *Roman* trial.

Pilate

John's trial before Pilate differs from those of the Synoptics both in structure and content. Structurally, it is composed of seven carefully formulated scenes dominated by two charges: first, that Jesus is king of the Jews; second, that he claims to be the Son of God. The opening verses set up the drama: "the Jews" bring Jesus to Pilate (who is introduced abruptly[25]) but refuse to enter the *praetorium* because it is Passover and they do not want to be defiled. This means that the Jewish leaders remain outside while Jesus is taken inside, and Pilate must go between the two.

The governor enters the *praetorium* and asks Jesus if he is the king of the Jews, admitting that the charge comes from Jesus's own people. Pilate's

23. See, for example, A. E. Harvey, *Jesus on Trial: A Study in the Fourth Gospel* (London: SPCK, 1976); Andrew T. Lincoln, *Truth on Trial: The Lawsuit Motif in the Fourth Gospel* (Peabody, MA: Hendrickson, 2000).

24. There is also the odd reference in this Gospel to "another disciple," "known to the high priest," who helps Peter enter the high priest's courtyard (18:15–18). Who is this other disciple? Is he the Beloved Disciple (referred to as "the other disciple" in 20:3–10)? Or an unknown Judean disciple? For discussion, see James H. Charlesworth, *The Beloved Disciple: Whose Witness Validates the Gospel of John?* (Valley Forge, PA: Trinity Press International, 1995).

25. The presence of Roman troops at Jesus's arrest in this Gospel (18:3) presumably implies some prior contact between the Jewish leaders and the governor, but John gives no details.

offhanded "I am not a Jew, am I?" (18:35) shows his contempt for the Judeans but contains a deeper irony. By his refusal to listen to Jesus, he will indeed align himself with "the Jews," who, for John, most often represent unbelief and those who reject Jesus. In response, Jesus explains that his kingship "is not from this world" (18:36). "So you are a king?" Pilate asks, perhaps grasping at straws. Jesus again answers in a manner that is beyond the governor's grasp: "You say that I am a king. For this I was born, and for this I came into the world, to testify to the truth. Everyone who belongs to the truth listens to my voice" (18:37). In response, Pilate utters his most infamous line—"What is truth?" (18:38)—and walks out to the waiting Jews. In Johannine thought, Jesus not only bears witness to the truth but is also himself that truth (14:6). The Roman governor has no idea that the Truth is standing before him and, by his failure to believe, shows that he really is "a Jew" (in the Johannine use of the term).

Outside once again, Pilate declares that he finds no crime in Jesus and offers to release him as part of a Jewish Passover amnesty. "Will you have me release for you the King of the Jews?" he asks. It is important to remember that there is no neutral crowd in John as there was in Mark; Pilate is speaking to the same people who have brought Jesus to him for execution. His words, therefore, are not a test of public support but mock Jewish national hopes and assert his power over "the Jews." With heavy condescension the Roman governor asks if he should release the Jewish king at Passover, a feast celebrating national liberation from slavery and foreign oppression. Not surprisingly, the Jewish leaders ask instead for a bandit named Barabbas (18:40).

In 19:1–3, Pilate has Jesus scourged, a severe beating rather than the disciplinary one suggested by the Lukan Pilate. Subsequently, Roman soldiers mock him by making fun of his kingly pretensions. A similar scene takes place more naturally *after* the trial in Mark 15:16–20 and Matthew 27:27–31. The presence of this derision in what forms the central scene of the Johannine trial, however, underscores the element of mockery throughout the entire narrative.

Pilate brings Jesus outside again, still dressed in kingly regalia, and declares that he is bringing him out "to let you know that I find no case against him" (19:4). "Here is the man" (19:5), he declares dramatically, and reveals the broken prisoner. Once again his words are contemptuous: Jesus is clearly no threat to Roman security because he is so completely humiliated and despised, a parody of Jewish messianic hopes. To the Jewish leaders (who have already shown their preference for Barabbas), Jesus is an embarrassment, and they shout for crucifixion. Pilate tells them to crucify him themselves, though this can hardly be a serious suggestion after the Jewish leaders made it clear in 18:31 that they were not able to crucify anyone. A third time the Roman governor declares Jesus innocent (19:6).

At this, Jesus's opponents change tactics and bring a religious charge, declaring that he has "claimed to be the son of God" (19:7). Pilate suddenly becomes afraid (19:8) and takes Jesus inside once again and asks him where he is from (19:9). Met with silence, the Roman asks, "Do you not know that I have power to release you, and power to crucify you?" (19:10). Jesus tells Pilate that his own power comes not from the emperor, as he supposes, but from God. "Therefore the one who handed me over to you is guilty of a greater sin" (19:11). This is presumably a reference to Caiaphas, or more generally the Jewish leaders as a whole. Clearly, primary responsibility for Jesus's death for John rests with "the Jews," but Pilate is part of the hostile world that rejects Jesus and will not be exonerated.

Now, for the first time, Pilate tries to release Jesus (19:12). Perhaps John wants to show that, like the soldiers in Gethsemane (18:4–6), the pagan governor could not remain unaffected by Jesus. The waiting Jewish leaders, however, seeing that their new ploy has backfired, revert to political threats: "If you release this man, you are no friend of the emperor; everyone who claims to be a king sets himself against the emperor" (19:12). This has the desired effect, and Pilate takes his place on the judgment seat. He is about to pass sentence but will not let the prisoner go before he has exacted a high price from the Jewish leaders. Continuing his earlier mockery, he says, "Here is your king" (v. 14). As expected, the Jewish leaders shout for crucifixion. "Shall I crucify your king?" Pilate asks, to which the chief priests alone respond, "We have no king but the emperor" (v. 15). Their words form a stark contrast to the Passover liturgy and the psalms that were being sung at that very moment in the temple, which praised the kingly rule of God (19:14). At their blasphemy, Pilate sends Jesus to the cross without further ado.

One last confrontation in John underlines Pilate's harshness once more. The Jewish leaders take offense at the title over Jesus's cross, which reads, "Jesus of Nazareth, the King of the Jews," in Aramaic, Latin, and Greek. Pilate, however, refuses to have it removed (19:19–22).

Pilate in John, like his representation in Luke, plays an important role in three times declaring Jesus innocent. The Roman governor refuses to take Jesus's kingship seriously and mocks both the pitiful prisoner and Jewish messianic hopes more generally. (Perhaps the futility of these had been exposed for John's readers by the recent Jewish revolt against Rome.) Yet Jesus, for John, really is a king, the savior of the world, even the Son of God. Within the trial narratives it is clear that the *true* judge is neither the high priest nor Pilate, but Jesus himself. Though despised by "the world," the Johannine Jesus goes to his death in full control and lays down his life for his friends (10:17–18; 15:13). Paradoxically, his humiliation on the cross is his hour of glorification. His majestic demeanor contrasts with the manipulative, aggressive, and mocking behavior of the political leaders. In the scenes with Pilate in particular, all earthly authority is judged and found wanting by its response to Jesus.

Conclusion

Jesus cannot simply be assigned to the category of "religious preacher"; his message was necessarily political too. To speak of the kingdom of God in a land ruled by Jewish client kings or Roman governors had clear political repercussions. So too did the selection of twelve men as representatives of the restored twelve tribes of Israel. And to perform symbolic acts, such as the entry into Jerusalem and the demonstration in the temple at the great feast of Passover, was something that clearly could not be ignored. It should come as no surprise, then, that Jesus annoyed the political leaders of the day. We saw in the first part of this chapter that these enemies were real, flesh-and-blood men who left their mark in the historical record—through inscriptions, archaeological finds, coins, and descriptions by contemporary authors. These sources need to be used with care, but they do allow us to piece together a reasonable picture of these rulers, to see why they saw Jesus as a threat, and why they dealt with him as they did.

Jesus's death on a Roman cross, however, very quickly needed explanation and reflection. The trial narratives in the Gospels all represent early Christian attempts to understand what happened to Jesus, how God's anointed one could be rejected by the leaders of his own people and executed as a political rebel by Rome. The Evangelists employ various strategies: demonizing the Jewish leaders, introducing a fickle crowd, using Pilate as an official witness to Jesus's innocence, and even adding the stories of Pilate's washing his hands and the hearing in front of Antipas. In varying ways, these narrative devices allow the Evangelists to present Jesus as the true "king of the Jews," unjustly condemned to death on a Roman cross by hostile Jewish leaders and a harsh Roman prefect (so Mark); as a second Moses and the Jewish Christ rejected by his own people (so Matthew); as an innocent martyr (so Luke); and as the true judge and majestic son of God (so John).

Suggestions for Further Reading

History

Most of our information for this period comes from Josephus's two accounts, the *Jewish War*, books 1–2, and the *Jewish Antiquities*, books 14–18. Although he has his own agenda, the Jewish aristocrat is generally a careful and entertaining writer, and his accounts are well worth reading. See also the following:

Goodman, Martin. *The Ruling Class of Judaea: The Origins of the Jewish Revolt against Rome, AD 66–70.* Cambridge: Cambridge University Press, 1987.
Grabbe, Lester L. *Judaism from Cyrus to Hadrian.* 2 vols. Minneapolis: Augsburg, 1992.

Jensen, Morten Hørning. *Herod Antipas in Galilee: The Literary and Archaeological Sources on the Reign of Herod Antipas and its Socio-Economic Impact on Galilee.* WUNT 2.215. Tübingen: Mohr Siebeck, 2006.

Kokkinos, Nikos. *The Herodian Dynasty: Origins, Role in Society and Eclipse.* Journal for the Study of the Pseudepigrapha: Supplement Series 30. Sheffield: Sheffield Academic Press, 1998.

McLaren, James S. *Power and Politics in Palestine: The Jews and the Governing of Their Land, 100 BC–AD 70.* JSNTSup 63. Sheffield: JSOT Press, 1991.

Richardson, Peter. *Herod: King of the Jews and Friend of the Romans.* Columbia: University of South Carolina Press, 1996.

Schürer, Emil. *The History of the Jewish People in the Age of Jesus Christ (175 BC–AD 135).* Translated and edited by Geza Vermes, Fergus Millar, and Matthew Black. 3 vols. Einburgh: T&T Clark, 1973–1986.

Gospels

Bond, Helen K. *Caiaphas: Friend of Rome and Judge of Jesus?* Louisville: Westminster John Knox, 2004.

———. *Pontius Pilate in History and Intepretation.* SNTSMS 100. Cambridge: Cambridge University Press, 1998.

Brown, Raymond E. *The Birth of the Messiah: A Commentary on the Infancy Narratives in the Gospels of Matthew and Luke.* Rev. ed. London: Chapman, 1993.

Darr, John A. *Herod the Fox: Audience Criticism and Lukan Characterization.* JSNTSup 163. Sheffield: Sheffield Academic Press, 1998.

Gillman, Florence M. *Herodias: At Home in That Fox's Den.* Collegeville, MN: Liturgical Press, 2003.

Mason, Steve. *Josephus and the New Testament.* 2nd rev. ed. Peabody, MA: Hendrickson, 2003.

Rensberger, David. *Johannine Faith and Liberating Community.* Philadelphia: Westminster, 1988.

10

Judas Iscariot

The Betrayer of Jesus

HOLLY J. CAREY

Even those who know practically nothing about the biblical story—much less the narrative of Jesus within that story—probably have heard of Judas Iscariot. One of Jesus's closest friends (a member of the inner twelve disciples), Judas hands over his teacher to those who are seeking to arrest and kill him, even as other disciples protest and weakly attempt to defend Jesus. Worse than an enemy is a friend who betrays, and this is exactly what Judas does.

He is an infamous character, so much so that his name has come to be synonymous with evil and betrayal. If someone were to accuse another of being "a Judas," the receiver of that barb would know that he or she is being accused of intimate deception and costly betrayal. And as far as popular baby names go, "Judas" would probably not even register on the list!

As we explore Judas in this chapter, we will do so from a variety of angles. In the first half of the chapter we will examine what can be gleaned historically about Judas and his relationship to Jesus. We will also consider how Judas has been depicted throughout the centuries by Christians. In the second half, we will explore Judas's depiction in the canonical Gospels, that is, how he functions in the narrative that centers on the significance of Jesus through his earthly ministry, suffering, death, and resurrection.

Historical Considerations of Judas and the Legends Associated with Him

Who was the historical Judas? It is always difficult to separate the man whom we read about in the canonical Gospels from the man who lived in history, since the Gospel writers were not writing history as we tend to think of it (a journalistic relaying of facts and events that happened in the past), and yet, in their theologically driven narratives, they *did aim to* include historically reliable information about people who really lived.[1] In other words, although the Gospel writers' primary goal was not to satisfy all the questions we might have about what happened, they do include information here and there that allows scholars to place their narratives in a historical setting.

It might help first to set the stage for a discussion of the historical Judas by briefly summarizing his role in the Gospels (a more detailed discussion of his function in the Gospels' narratives will come at the end of this chapter). As previously mentioned, Judas was one of the twelve disciples who were considered Jesus's closest companions, confidants, and students. We do not know any details about his calling to be a disciple (as we do about the calls of Andrew, Peter, James, and John, for instance: Mark 1:16–20); he simply appears on the scene in the first lists of the Twelve (Mark 3:16–19; Matt. 10:1–4). As Jesus heads toward Jerusalem, nearer to his suffering, death, and resurrection, the Gospel narratives increasingly foreshadow these final events in his ministry (Mark 8:31; 9:31; 10:33–34). The reader has already been told in the narrative that Judas will betray Jesus (the first time we meet him, Mark 3:19), and this indeed plays out in one of the most poignant scenes in all of the Gospels: the Judas kiss. Here Jesus has been agonizing over his fate while praying in the garden of Gethsemane, when Judas leads a crowd of soldiers and religious leaders to his place of refuge (John 18:1–3). Rather than say, "Here he is, boys! Have at him!" Judas's method of betrayal stings even more. He walks up to Jesus, calls him "Rabbi," and greets him with a kiss, the intimate greeting of a trusted friend (Mark 14:43–46; Matt. 26:47–50). Judas does not, however, get away with what he has done. Whether in true repentance and remorse, or by accident, Judas meets an awful—and lonely—end (Matt. 27:3–5; Acts 1:16–19).

What can we glean from the Gospels' accounts about the Judas Iscariot who lived during the first century and who betrayed Jesus? First, we know that Jesus did indeed have close companions with whom he lived during his short ministry, men with whom the Gospel writers tell us he shared special teachings (Mark 4:10–20) as well as the power to heal and exorcise demons (Matt. 10:1). These were the men who would become the first leaders of the early church (Acts 1). During his lifetime, Judas was one of these, and he

1. See the introductory chapter to this volume, which also deals with these issues with regard to the historical Jesus.

was quickly replaced by another after his death and Jesus's ascension (Acts 1:21–26). He appears in every list of the apostles in the canonical Gospels and was the subject of speculation and curiosity in the first few centuries of the early church, as we will see later.

There has been some debate as to the meaning of Judas's second name, "Iscariot." Of the options proposed, two carry the strongest weight. It is possible that "Iscariot" is a derivative of the noun *sikarios*, the Greek form of the Latin word meaning "assassin" or "one who holds a dagger." This term was used in the first century to refer to a group of Jewish nationalists called "Sicarii," who believed that the remedy to Roman oppression was through armed, and often violent, means.[2] We know that Jesus's ministry was often misunderstood to be a political one (Mark 11:7–11).[3] It is possible, then, that he attracted those who thought that being the Messiah meant war and military victory over the Romans. Judas could have been one of these.

The other—and perhaps more compelling—option is to understand "Iscariot" to refer to the place from which Judas came, that is, his hometown. In support of this is the fact that Judas's father is named "Simon Iscariot" several times in John's Gospel (6:71; 13:2, 26) and that some manuscripts have the addition of *apo karyōtou* ("from Kerioth").[4] The combination of the Hebrew term for man (*'îš*) and *karyōtou* could result in "Iscariot." Unfortunately, however, scholars are unsure of the exact location of Kerioth.[5]

One reason to be confident that Judas Iscariot was a real, historical person who followed and participated in Jesus's ministry is the difficulty of the story concerning his betrayal. The earliest Christians would not have wanted to make up a figure like this! How embarrassing to have to testify that the very person whom Jesus relied on and trusted was the one who ultimately led him into the hands of his enemies! Moreover, this was not just a random follower of Jesus. In the Gospel narratives, this was one of the elite, handpicked pupils whom Jesus molded to become the leaders of his followers. Imagine how the earliest Christians must have felt as they were spreading the gospel message and came to this part of the story. It is possible that potential converts would have heard the story and viewed Jesus as an incompetent, undiscerning teacher who did not have the sense to realize

2. Josephus, *Ant.* 20.8.10.

3. Even one of Jesus's disciples was a zealot (Luke 6:15), although it is unclear whether Simon was a member of the party that later became known as "Zealots." There is no clear evidence to suggest that this was a recognizable and distinctive group at the time of Jesus's ministry. See Martin Hengel, *The Zealots: Investigations into the Jewish Freedom Movement in the Period from Herod 1 Until 70 A.D.*, trans. D. Smith (Edinburgh: T&T Clark, 1997). An alternative is that this is a description of Simon's character, that he was zealous for God's law, perhaps in the tradition of Phineas (Num. 25:10–13).

4. On the other hand, this could merely indicate that there was early speculation about what Judas's second name might have meant.

5. See Williams, "Judas Iscariot," 406.

that one of his closest friends was his betrayer, rather than as the Messiah, God's son in human form. In short, this is *not* a story or character that early Christians would want to fabricate. This fact alone lends great credibility to the historical existence of Judas Iscariot.

As Christianity spread throughout the Mediterranean world, the story of Jesus's death and resurrection became increasingly well known. Judas's role in these events, of course, was integral to the story, and so his notoriety grew as well. Questions prompted by the Gospel narratives—but not explicitly answered—fueled speculation and a degree of fascination with Judas. Such questions concern the motivation for his action of betrayal (why did he do it?) and the degree to which he was responsible for his actions (was he merely God's pawn in the drama of salvation, or did he knowingly, willingly, and voluntarily betray Jesus?). Attempts to answer these questions can be seen in one important early Christian work, the *Gospel of Judas*. However, the contemplation of questions did not stop in the fourth century. Christians and non-Christians alike have been fascinated with Judas, and art, writings, and even modern film have provided their own interpretations of the life and fate of this man and have contributed to the legend of Judas Iscariot. It is to some of these interesting interpretations that we now turn.

The Legend of Judas in the Church Fathers

Several of the early church fathers had some strong things to say about Judas Iscariot. Providing a hint of his view of Judas, Origen (ca. 185–251 CE) more often refers to him as "the betrayer" rather than calling him by his proper name. He views Judas as the ultimate representative of those who hide behind the work of the church in providing for the poor in order to steal from its funds.[6] Judas, then, is a despicable thief who targets those who have no power to defend themselves. Later in the same work, Origen fumes at the audacity of Judas for taking advantage of the hospitality of a friend while simultaneously plotting his demise. Here he refers to Jesus's provision of the Passover meal, of which Judas takes full advantage before heading out to inform the religious leaders of Jesus's whereabouts. In both of these instances, Judas is regarded as a selfish and manipulative character. His betrayal is so despicable that Origen uses it as the template for understanding the heretical posture toward Christ: that of feigning allegiance and love to him.[7]

Origen is not alone in questioning the character of Judas. John Chrysostom (fourth century CE) notes that even Judas's coconspirators "branded [him] as

6. Origen, *Commentary on Matthew* 2.9. He is referring, of course, to Judas's pretense of caring for the poor while all the while pilfering from the funds that were designated for this purpose (John 12:4–6).
7. Ibid., 100.

a bad character."[8] Interestingly, he admires the Gospel writers for being entirely transparent concerning Judas's status as one of the twelve apostles—the initial leaders of the church—even though this could have been embarrassing for the early Christians.

According to Cyril of Alexandria (fourth century CE), Judas was capable of betraying Jesus because Satan found a door through which to enter him, his greed: "Those who seek to be rich, fall into numerous and unprofitable lusts, which sink people in pitfalls and destruction. The disciple who became a traitor is a clear proof of this, because he perished for the sake of a few miserable coins."[9] Moreover, Judas's guilt is even more profound because he had all of the privileges of the apostles and yet chose the path of murder.[10]

All of these later Christian writers portray Judas negatively. He is the stereotypical traitor, the backstabbing friend who cares nothing for those who trust him. He rejected his privileged place as one of Jesus's closest friends for a few meaningless coins. In their eyes, there is nothing redemptive about the character of Judas Iscariot.

The Legend of Judas in the Gospel of Judas

In 2006, a fourth-century manuscript containing the *Gospel of Judas* was published, creating a sudden firestorm concerning the true story of Judas Iscariot. As we will see below, the content of this text is contentious and much debated. Even the title of the work is challenging, combining the name of Judas with the genre of the Gospel (the good news about Christ), a combination usually reserved for reputable and respectable figures in the gospel story.

Discovered sometime in the 1970s in Egypt, the codex containing the *Gospel of Judas* has had a rough journey to the spotlight. In a story filled with mystery, intrigue, and a lot of luck, this ancient Coptic Christian manuscript has survived—albeit in extremely fragile condition—multiple exchanges of hands, theft, years spent in a safety deposit box, and even placement in a freezer![11] Finally landing in the care of Frieda Tchacos Nussberger, it was turned over to the Maecenas Foundation for Ancient Art, where it began to undergo the long process of restoration.

The *Gospel of Judas* does not stand on its own. It is bound together with several other works in a codex, an ancient book-form with leaves like those of modern books. Named Codex Tchacos after the woman who procured it and made its restoration possible, it contains at least four distinct works in

8. Chrysostom, *The Gospel of St. Matthew* 85.2.

9. Cyril of Alexandria, *Comm. Luke*, Homily 140. See also John 13:27.

10. Cyril of Alexandria, *Comm. Luke*, Homily 148.

11. See Herbert Krosney, *The Lost Gospel: The Quest for the Gospel of Judas Iscariot* (Washington, DC: National Geographic, 2006), for a detailed account of the journey of the *Gospel of Judas* from discovery to publication.

Gnostics

The term *gnostic* is derived from the Greek word *gnōsis*, meaning "knowledge." Although in recent years there has been some question of the usefulness of the term, most scholars continue to use it to refer to a diverse group of early Christians who held distinct views about God and the world. Simply put, these Christians believed that the path to God was given only to a select few who were privileged to receive special knowledge and revelation from God about this life and the life to come. One distinctive view of the gnostics was that this world and everything material was evil, while the spirit and the spiritual realm were good. In this schema, a lesser god created the world and was separate from the all-knowing, all-powerful God who sent his Son Jesus to save those select Christians by providing a way for them to escape their bodily prison and ascend in their spirit to the heavens. Many of the early church fathers condemned this sect as heretical, including Irenaeus, who spoke out against the *Gospel of Judas* and those who wrote it.

the following order: a copy of the *Letter of Peter to Philip*, a version of the *First Apocalypse of James*, the *Gospel of Judas*, and what is being referred to as the *Book of Allogenes*.

The *Gospel of Judas* is one of many early Christian gnostic writings discovered in the last century. The greatest collection of these texts, found in Upper Egypt in 1945 and called the Nag Hammadi library, consists of thirteen codices, some containing the only surviving copies of texts scholars had long thought were lost in the first few centuries of the church. As Christians struggled to define orthodoxy (i.e., the right teachings)—usually one group of Christians over against another—some groups debated certain theological perspectives by writing letters and works that espoused their beliefs while criticizing others. Long before the discovery of the Nag Hammadi library, scholars knew that these texts had once existed because they were mentioned in the works of the church fathers that have survived through the centuries. In fact, before the discovery of Codex Tchacos, scholars were aware that the *Gospel of Judas* existed because a bishop in the second century, Irenaeus of Lyon, spoke out against it.[12]

THE PLOT OF THE GOSPEL OF JUDAS

The *Gospel of Judas* opens with its self-description as the secret revelatory discussion that Jesus had with Judas three days before his arrest. The story begins with Jesus approaching his disciples while they are praying over the Eucharist. He laughs at them (in the *Gospel of Judas*, this is a form of mockery rather than amusement) because they do not realize that they are

12. Irenaeus of Lyon, *Haer.* 1.31.1.

not worshiping his God, the God he comes from, but another; he insists on this. This provokes them to anger because it implies that they do not truly know him. In response to a challenge from Jesus for anyone strong enough to stand before him, only Judas is able to do so. After correctly confessing Jesus's origins, Judas is told "the mysteries of the Kingdom." A similar scenario takes place the next day, when the disciples again do not understand Jesus's words, and after telling him of their dreams on the following day, he once again tells them that they worship the wrong god and receive teachings that they do not understand. Judas, on the other hand, tells Jesus his personal vision, and Jesus proceeds to interpret it for him and to explain to him the makeup of the cosmos, the fate of humanity, and Judas's own fate. The narrative ends with the simple statement that Judas handed Jesus over to the religious authorities.

INTERPRETING THE GOSPEL OF JUDAS

Although the general outline of the story is simple enough, some details of the narrative and the content of Jesus's teachings within the narrative have caused debate among scholars. There are two major interpretations of the *Gospel of Judas*, at opposite ends of the spectrum. Many scholars interpret it as a positive portrayal of Judas Iscariot, one that presents him as the only disciple who truly knows Jesus, understands his teachings, and is capable of carrying out the deed that ultimately releases him from the bonds of his human body.[13] This deed is the handing of Jesus over to the religious authorities. In other words, Judas is actually doing the will of Jesus by handing him over to his enemies so that he can be freed from his human body. According to this view, rather than being the black sheep of the disciples, Judas is the privileged, chosen one!

What elements within the *Gospel of Judas* support this interpretation? First, it is Judas Iscariot, not Peter, who of the Twelve receives special knowledge from Jesus. This could easily be seen as a claim that Judas was actually the greater of the two apostles, one who truly saw and understood Jesus's person and mission. This would be in contrast to the canonical Gospels' message, for in them it was Peter who recognized Jesus as the Messiah, even though he did not fully understand what that entailed (Mark 8:27–30; Matt. 16:13–20). Second, Jesus announces to Judas that he has a star that will rule over the thirteenth realm and lead the way for other stars (55:10–11; 57:19–20). Those who see Judas's portrayal in this Gospel as a positive one interpret this to be another sign of his leadership role and the honor placed upon him by Jesus. Third, at the end of the Gospel, Judas appears to be commissioned by Jesus to hand him over to the religious authorities (56:19–20; 58:25–26). Since this

---

13. This is the official position of the team that first translated and published the *Gospel of Judas*. Representative of this view is Bart Ehrman, *The Lost Gospel of Judas Iscariot: A New Look at Betrayer and Betrayed* (Oxford: Oxford University Press, 2006).

is a mission given him by Jesus (and God), it might indicate that he has not acted sinfully and against Jesus but rather has acted at his request and on his behalf (to liberate him from his earthly body).

Some scholars, however, read this Gospel in a wholly different light. Based on several statements within the text itself, these scholars regard the *Gospel of Judas* as a narrative full of biting irony that attacks the apostolic church.[14] In this view, Judas is a representative of the twelve apostles, those leaders who think that they are worshiping the God of Jesus but in fact are worshiping a lesser and evil god. This interpretation requires a sophisticated reading of the Gospel and takes seriously the context in which it was written and by whom it was written. In this case, a minority group of gnostic Christians are subtly attacking the majority (the church led by the apostles and their successors) by claiming that they do not know who they are really worshiping and that their true representative is not Peter the faithful disciple but Judas Iscariot the traitor of the Lord!

On almost every point made above, there is some agreement from the opposing side of the debate. Yet it is *how* one interprets the information that separates the two groups considerably. Those who argue that Judas is as bad a figure as ever in the *Gospel of Judas* also recognize that the text places Judas in the same position in which we find Peter in the canonical Gospels' accounts of Peter's confession. The distinction is that, rather than proving that Judas was considered the most important disciple, it demonstrates a gnostic parody of the apostolic succession. The church's forefather is not Peter but rather the ultimate betrayer of Christ, Judas Iscariot. The two interpretations also differ on the meaning of the content of the special knowledge that Judas receives. Whereas the majority of scholars interpret Jesus's statements about Judas's star as positive (he will be a leader and will rule), those who hold to the opposing view believe that *where* his star will rule is of utmost importance. According to this Gospel, Judas's star is located in the thirteenth realm, which, in some gnostic cosmologies, is the dwelling place of Ialdabaoth, an evil god who demands human sacrifice. This, coupled with the fact that Judas is called the "thirteenth *daimon*," may suggest not a place of honor but a position of evil, as a minion of Ialdabaoth. Thus, the significance of Judas's special revelation does not lie with the simple fact that he receives it. For the revelation contains a bleak picture of his role in Jesus's fate and of Judas's eternal status, so much so that he gets angry upon hearing it (46:5–47:1).

So, in the *Gospel of Judas*, do Jesus's statements concerning Judas's role in his death indicate a divine commission (he hands Jesus over because he is fulfilling a role that has been positively sanctioned by God and for which he will receive honor) or divine condemnation (he betrays Jesus because he serves an evil god and ultimately will receive his just reward)? The answer depends upon

14. See April D. DeConick, *The Thirteenth Apostle: What the Gospel of Judas Really Says*, rev. ed. (London: Continuum, 2007), for the most thorough exposition of this view.

whether one reads this as a defense of Judas or a parody of Judas as the true representative of the apostolic church; as an attack on orthodox Christianity using Judas as a counter to it, or as an attack on orthodox Christianity using Judas as an example of it. Both of these interpretations are possibilities, and neither is without problems. For example, can the minority theory explain why Irenaeus appears to miss the parody (if he was referring to the text we have)? He clearly believes the Gospel to be advocating a positive view of Judas rather than a negative one. On the other hand, the majority position does not adequately account for the negative aspects of Judas's fate in the Gospel.

THE SIGNIFICANCE OF THE GOSPEL OF JUDAS

The *Gospel of Judas* portrays a clear gnostic influence and likely contains the views of a gnostic sect, probably the Sethians or Cainites. Important elements that indicate this gnostic orientation are the cosmology and cosmological influences, the names of the gods of the realms of heaven and earth, the obsession with secret revelation, and the view of Jesus's death as accomplishing his escape from a bodily prison (56:19–20). There is little narrative to provide a context or backdrop by which to understand the sayings contained in the Gospel. In addition, the existing copy was written in the fourth century, with the earliest suggested date for the original sometime in the second century. All these factors indicate that the *Gospel of Judas*, though interesting in its portrayal of Judas Iscariot and helpful in understanding a certain minority gnostic sect in the second century, is not an equivalent alternative to the canonical Gospels or their portrayal of Judas the betrayer.[15]

Concerning the *Gospel of Judas*, this is what we know for certain. It contained a view of Judas Iscariot that was not mainstream in Christian history. As a text, if it is the same text that Irenaeus criticized, it drew his ire and was regarded by him as one of the many heresies that threatened the church. If it does contain a positive portrayal of Judas, then this is in contradiction to the canonical witnesses and one of the few perspectives in two thousand years that have tried to redeem Judas and his actions against Jesus. If it is a Gospel parody of Judas, then it is in agreement with the canonical Gospels that Judas was a villain, not a hero.

The Legend of Judas in Later Interpretations

The gnostic Christians responsible for the *Gospel of Judas* were not alone in their attempts to portray Judas in a particular light. A medieval sculptor known only as "Giselbertus" was tasked with the exterior decoration of the Cathedral of Saint-Lazare in Autun, France, built in 1120. In addition to

15. See Craig A. Evans, "The Gospel of Judas and the Other Gospels," in *The Gospel of Judas*, ed. R. Kasser, M. Meyer, and G. Wurst, 2nd ed.(Washington, DC: National Geographic, 2008), 103–24, for a more extensive treatment of this issue.

creating a masterpiece of story and sculpture in the *Last Judgment* of the west tympanum, he also carved a series of capitals (decorated tops of columns) for the Romanesque cathedral. One of these is the *Suicide of Judas*, created from 1130 to 1135. This carving reflects the horror of Judas's end, underscoring the fact that his final reward is not money but eternal damnation. He is depicted as a tortured man, hanging from a rope, with demons grabbing at his legs and feet and pulling him downward toward damnation. As is often the purpose of Romanesque sculptures, the intent of this piece appears to be (a) to tell a biblical story pictorially to a predominantly illiterate congregation and (b) to scare these peasants into piety (similar to the function of gargoyles on Gothic cathedrals). Judas's fate would have been the ultimate warning for what happens when people betray Christ and the church.

Between 1307 and 1321, Dante Alighieri, an Italian poet, wrote his most famous work, *The Divine Comedy*. This is an allegory about a fictional tour through hell, purgatory, and heaven with his guide, the ancient Italian writer Virgil. Dante envisions hell being made up of nine levels, called circles, with inner rings containing sinners. The severity of the person's sin is indicated by where they are placed in the descending levels: the further down one is located, the worse the sin that placed them there. In these rings Dante places various contemporary and historical figures, based on where he thinks their lives have landed them. In the very last circle, within the very last ring, is Satan himself. He is a beast tormented by his encasement in ice. In each of his three mouths he chews on the three worst sinners in all of history (according to Dante): Brutus and Cassius—the traitors of Julius Caesar—and Judas Iscariot.[16] As if being chewed on by Satan for all eternity is not punishment enough, Judas—called the "archtraitor"—also receives an additional torment: Satan continually scratches the skin off of his back with his claws, while Judas is positioned head first in his mouth.

According to Dante, Judas is the worst of those traitors in history, betraying his King just as Brutus and Cassius betrayed theirs. All three have committed treason against the very one who provided for them and with whom they had a relationship of trust. The common theme of this level, then, is that betrayal is worse when it comes from a friend.

Interestingly, Franco Zeffirelli's 1977 TV miniseries "Jesus of Nazareth" portrays Judas's involvement in Jesus's arrest and trial as a well-intentioned blunder on the part of the disciple. Zeffirelli envisions Judas's action as merely a misstep, a *misunderstanding* of what Jesus's messiahship was supposed to look like. Rather than knowingly setting Jesus up for a death sentence, this Judas's motivations are pure, if misplaced. He tries to force Jesus into a situation where he will have to use his power to gain political control, reflecting a common first-century view of what the Messiah ultimately would

16. Dante Alighieri, *The Divine Comedy*, canto 34.53–61.

accomplish.[17] However, once Judas realizes that this is not Jesus's intention, he is devastated by what he has done and commits suicide. According to Zeffirelli, the twelfth disciple is really a Judas who misunderstands and has himself been misunderstood.

As we have seen in this brief and selective survey, the majority of opinion throughout the centuries is consistent with the canonical Gospel message: Judas Iscariot was a betrayer who received his just reward in this life and will receive the torment he deserves in the life to come. There are some, however—perhaps early Christians as well as contemporary scholars—who have advocated a revisionist history concerning Judas. It is the richness of the canonical Gospel narratives, the diversity of Christian interpretation, and the polarizing actions of Judas himself that have led to this variety of perspectives on his story. In Christian history, however, the most weight has appropriately been given to the earliest and most reliable accounts of Judas—the canonical Gospels. It is to these that we now turn.

Narrative Considerations of Judas

Ultimately, the starting point for all of these interpretations (and many others) of Judas's acts throughout the centuries is the Gospel narrative accounts themselves. Although not a primary character until the end of these stories, Judas Iscariot is present throughout. As noted earlier, the canonical Gospels are written in narrative form and meant to be read as such in order to gain the most from the story in interpretation. Therefore, we will begin with a look at all of the passages relevant for our study of Judas—both those that mention him explicitly and those that imply his involvement through association—and then look at certain narrative elements that help the reader to understand Judas's role in the death of Jesus.

Judas in the Story of the Gospels

The very first thing that the Gospels say about Judas is that he is one of the twelve apostles, Jesus's most intimate friends and followers. Although Jesus has many followers, it is these twelve men that he handpicks (Mark 1:16–20; 3:13–19), sends on missions (Mark 6:7–13), and teaches the most difficult parables and predictions (Mark 4:10–20). Each Gospel writer focuses on particular aspects of the Twelve, depending on the overall aim of his Gospel. For example, in Mark the twelve disciples are continually misunderstanding Jesus, despite all of the special teachings and clues he gives about his death

17. For a helpful discussion on messianic expectations in the Old and New Testaments, see Stanley E. Porter, ed., *The Messiah in the Old and New Testaments* (Grand Rapids: Eerdmans, 2007).

(8:14–21; 9:30–32). There are rare glimpses of greatness in the Twelve (Mark 8:29), but these are always overshadowed by their great shortcomings and general ineptitude (Mark 8:31–33). Judas does not stand out in any positive way from the other eleven companions of Jesus. When they fail, he is lumped in with them. When one succeeds—albeit briefly—he is not mentioned explicitly (Matt. 16:13–20).

Judas is included in all of the Gospels' lists of the Twelve, and he is always last (Mark 3:16–19; Matt. 10:2–4; Luke 6:14–16). Despite this position, however, he was not regarded as the least important. In fact, during Jesus's ministry he held the office of treasurer for the group (John 12:6). This indicates that he was a trusted member of the group and makes his betrayal of Jesus even more piercing. The Gospel writers leave no room for confusion about his most important role in the Gospel narrative, however. In these lists he is not merely named, but his trademark is included as well: he is the one who betrayed Jesus. This is the literary device of foreshadowing. The reader—not the characters within the story—already knows that Judas is the one who will hand Jesus in to the religious authorities and Romans. Thus, the Judas of the canonical Gospels never gets the chance to surprise the reader. He is cast as a traitor from the very beginning.

Especially in the Gospel of Mark, the Twelve do not understand what Jesus means when he warns them about his suffering, death, and resurrection. By his membership in the Twelve, then, Judas is also depicted as one who does not understand what is going to be involved in Jesus's mission. Furthermore, he is one of those disciples who did not recognize Jesus as the Messiah or did not have the courage to declare him as such (Mark 8:27–30; Matt. 16:13–20; Luke 9:18–21). Only Peter confesses who Jesus truly is, while the others' feeble attempts fall sadly short.

As the movement of the canonical Gospels heads toward Jesus's death and resurrection, Judas's role in the narrative increases significantly. In the last few days before Jesus's death, while he is eating as a guest in a home in Bethany, a woman anoints him with an expensive perfume called nard (Mark 14:3–9; Matt. 26:6–13; John 12:1–8).[18] Each of the canonical Gospel accounts differs somewhat on the details, but all four agree that the woman was right to do what she did in Jesus's honor, even though some observers protested. If one examines Mark's, Matthew's, and John's accounts chronologically, one observes that the later the Gospel is written, the more details are given about the protestor(s). Mark gives the least information on these dissenters, stating only that "some" disapproved of her gift as a waste on Jesus of money that could have been given to the poor (Mark 14:4–6). Matthew tells his readers that it was the disciples who protested (Matt. 26:8–9). John gives us the most detailed information, however. According to him, it was Judas Iscariot who complained,

18. Luke places his account early in Jesus's ministry (Luke 7:36–50).

but not because he truly cared about the poor: "He said this not because he cared about the poor, but because he was a thief; he kept the common purse and used to steal what was put into it" (John 12:6). In John's account, Judas was motivated not by a disapproval of waste but by disappointment that he had lost some profit to be made upon the sale of the costly perfume. He was angry not at waste or injustice, but because of greed.

The story of Jesus's anointing at Bethany is juxtaposed with the narrative of Judas's plot to betray Jesus to the religious authorities in Matthew and Mark (Mark 14:10–11; Matt. 26:14–16). In these Gospels, the narrative flow contrasts the sacrificial love of the woman who anointed Jesus with Judas's selfish betrayal, which ultimately leads to Jesus's death. The placement of the anointing story in John's Gospel also has some interesting implications for the characterization of Judas. The woman's anointing (and Judas's reaction to it) is not contrasted with his plot to betray Jesus but is juxtaposed with the story of Lazarus's resurrection (John 11). The implication is that Judas does not understand that Lazarus's death and resurrection actually serve as a foreshadowing of Jesus's own death and resurrection, as Mary uses costly nard to anoint Jesus for his own burial.[19] Rather than being the fulcrum of God's plan for the salvation of humanity, the death of Jesus, in Judas's eyes, is just a way for him to acquire more money (John 12:6).

In the accounts of Luke and John, Judas's actions of betrayal are further explained by his possession by Satan himself (Luke 22:3; John 13:2, 27). Driven by demonic power, he conspires with the religious authorities to arrest Jesus (Luke 22:4–6) and is paid thirty pieces of silver for his services (Matt. 26:14–16). The opportunity presents itself during the Passover celebrations. After he accepts Jesus's offer to wash his feet—a humble example of servanthood that Jesus displayed toward all of the Twelve—and takes advantage of Jesus's provision and hospitality as host of the Passover meal, Judas's future dark deed is brought to light (John 13:21–30). It is at this meal that Jesus makes explicit what has been implicit throughout the Gospel narrative: one of his inner twelve disciples will betray him and set him on his course of suffering and death.

This betrayal is described in a number of ways in the canonical Gospels. The context of the Passover meal accounts in Mark 14:18 and John 13:18 (especially the eating of the bread, into which Jesus infuses new and profound meaning) provides an apt setting for Jesus to allude to Psalm 41:9: "Even my bosom friend in whom I trusted, who ate of my bread, has lifted the heel against me." In these instances of intertextuality, Jesus is drawing a parallel between the speaker of the psalm, who has suffered at the hand of his best

19. It is possible that Jesus's statement, "She bought it so that she might keep it for the day of my burial" (John 12:7), suggests that Mary was aware that Jesus was going to die soon and that her brother's resurrection was somehow related to Jesus's own death.

Intertextuality

The term *intertextuality*, first derived from literary studies to describe the way that new texts are continually shaped by those that have preceded them, has been adopted in biblical studies to refer specifically to the use of the Old Testament in the New Testament. It is an important concept because it acknowledges that the Scriptures of the New Testament writers (the Old Testament) profoundly shaped how they viewed Jesus and interpreted his life, death, and resurrection. Intertextuality can be manifested in three ways. *Citations* are clear references to the Old Testament that contain identical vocabulary and intentionally and deliberately use a particular Scripture. *Allusions* are more subtle references to a former text, often using similar vocabulary or circumstances that remind the reader of an Old Testament text or person. *Echoes* are faint allusions to the text, which may or may not be noticed by the reader. The importance of intertextuality is that it enables the New Testament writer to infuse a word, deed, or narrative with added meaning by comparing or contrasting it with former biblical examples. The goal of intertexuality, then, is never merely to recognize its presence but to understand the mutual relationship and significance of the Old Testament passage in its new context.

friend, and his own future situation: his betrayal, which leads to suffering, death, and resurrection. This is not the first time—nor will it be the last—that Jesus explains his passion by appealing to psalms that speak of a righteous person who suffers unjustly but who trusts that he will be delivered and vindicated by God. In this case, both the psalmist and Jesus are the victims of greedy, advantage-seeking "friends" who turn out to be interested only in their own gain, even at the expense of their host (Mark 14:18; John 13:18). Jesus does not come out and accuse Judas directly, however. He provides a somewhat cryptic sign that Judas is the one who will betray him: it is the one who dips his bread in the bowl with Jesus (Mark 14:20–21; Matt. 26:23–25) or the one to whom Jesus hands the dipped bread (John 13:26–27).[20] After this, Judas leaves the meal to make arrangements with the religious authorities (John 13:27–30). He is mentioned only once more before the account of Jesus's arrest in the garden, and only implicitly. In Jesus's prayer for the future protection and blessing of his followers, he refers to the "one destined to be lost" (John 17:12), a clear reference to Judas and one that brings up the intriguing issue of whether Judas's actions were a result of free will or fate—an issue that will be addressed below.

After the Passover meal, Jesus takes his disciples to the nearby garden of Gethsemane, where he intends to pray and urges his closest disciples to pray

20. The details vary here among the Synoptic Gospels and John, but the emphasis is the same: one who shares with Jesus in the intimate communal meal will be the one who betrays him.

as well (Mark 14:32–42). It is in this setting, after some agonizing on the part of Jesus, that Judas leads a crowd of soldiers, religious leaders, and others to Jesus. In a poignant act of betrayal, Judas uses a kiss to mark Jesus as the target and sets the wheels in motion toward his death. In Matthew, however, after seeing that Jesus has been condemned, Judas regrets what he has done and tries to return his payment to the religious authorities, who want nothing of it (Matt. 27:3–5). Out of regret and possibly repentance, Judas either commits suicide by hanging himself (Matt. 27:5) or by accident falls to his death (Acts 1:18). Either way, a sorry traitor meets a sorry end.

Judas in the Plot of the Gospels

In any narrative, it is not only what a person does that is significant but also how they are portrayed, which is often referred to as characterization. It is no different in the canonical Gospels, particularly in their portrayal of Judas Iscariot. We have already observed that it is only in the latter half of these narratives that Judas comes to the forefront as an antagonist of Jesus. Yet the way he is depicted gives Judas's story an added dimension of texture and richness and resists a positive view of his actions. Many aspects of his portrayal contribute to his role as a treacherous villain in the narrative. Most of these provoke and attempt to answer—although sometimes implicitly—three overarching questions: (1) Did Judas have a choice? (2) Why did he do it? and (3) What did he actually do to betray Jesus?

Did Judas Have a Choice?

Many readers of the Gospel narratives throughout the centuries have pondered this question. Could Judas help it? Could he have chosen to be faithful to Jesus, or was he destined to betray him and seal his own fate in the process? We have already seen how some later interpretations of the gospel story have viewed Judas as merely a pawn in God's endgame and thus take the blame off him. This was a minority view in some later communities but is not at all the perspective of the Gospel writers. There is indeed a tension between God's use of Judas's betrayal to bring about salvation and his involvement in Jesus's arrest and condemnation, but the conclusions are unambiguous: Judas was both responsible and held accountable for his betrayal of Jesus.

The allusion to Psalm 41 in Mark 14:18 and John 13:18 has already been mentioned in the previous section. In both of these Gospels, Jesus describes what is about to take place after the Passover meal—a betrayal by someone who is eating with him at the table. In the psalm, the act of the treacherous friend against the speaker is clearly intentional and is condemned as despicable. By Mark and John's use of it in this new context, they are indicating subtly that the "friend" who will betray Jesus is just as treacherous and deserving of judgment.

Judas's actions are also consistent with those of Jesus's arch enemies throughout the Gospel narratives: the religious authorities (Pharisees, Sadducees, scribes, and chief priests). From very early on in the narratives of his ministry, the reader has been told that there were those who were plotting Jesus's death (Mark 3:6). These religious authorities are jealous and offended by Jesus's authority to teach and the many wonders he is able to perform. Not only are Judas's actions like those of the religious authorities but he even conspires with them in his own act of betrayal! Judas and the religious authorities are contrasted with the other apostles, who—although they do not always understand Jesus or his purpose—have good intentions and strive to follow him and remain committed to him. Whereas their blunders are usually unintentional shortcomings and display ignorance and weakness, Judas's act of betrayal is intentional, premeditated, and driven by greed.

In the three passion-resurrection predictions of Mark's Gospel, Jesus formulaically anticipates his suffering, death, and resurrection (Mark 8:31; 9:31; 10:33–34). The latter two predictions also mention Jesus's betrayal as the starting point for this series of events. The Greek term for this act, *paradidōmi*, actually has two possible meanings: "betray" and, more neutrally, "hand over." At the heart of the issue is the agent of the verb: who is doing the handing over/betraying? Those who interpret this as a more neutral term believe that Jesus is referring to God, indicating that this series of events is orchestrated by God himself and thus inevitable.[21] Those who interpret this as a reference to betrayal see Judas as the agent.[22] If it is the former, this may be an indication that Judas has no control or freedom to choose his own path but must fill the role of betrayer because it has been orchestrated by God for him to do so. This provides the option to see Judas as merely a pawn in the gospel story and therefore not culpable for his actions.

There are, however, several reasons for understanding *paradidōmi* as a reference to Judas's act of betrayal rather than God's predestining of Jesus's arrest. First, Mark uses *paradidōmi* to describe what Judas will do in giving Jesus over to the religious authorities (Mark 10:33b; 14:10–11, 18, 21, 41–42, 44). Second, whoever is doing the betraying/handing over in these passages (and in the rest of the Gospel) is not depicted as a favorable character. The tone of this part of the prediction is not positive, and the agent is associated with the religious authorities, whom we have already seen to be antagonists of Jesus.

This does not mean that God plays no role in Judas's actions or the results of those actions in the suffering, death, and resurrection of Jesus. God is depicted as the one in control throughout all the canonical Gospels, and it is his will that Jesus must go through his passion in order to usher in his kingdom

21. See Morna D. Hooker, *The Gospel according to Saint Mark*, BNTC 2 (Peabody, MA: Hendrickson, 1991), 226, for an example of this argument.
22. Cf. Robert H. Gundry, *Mark: A Commentary on His Apology for the Cross* (Grand Rapids: Eerdmans, 1993), 503–7.

on earth (Mark 14:36). Jesus's words at the Passover meal also indicate that Judas's role cannot be avoided (Mark 14:21), and yet he is responsible for his actions and guilty for his betrayal of Jesus. Thus we see the tension between Judas's choice in betraying Jesus and his culpability for doing so, on the one hand, and, on the other, God's ultimate control over the situation and his involvement in Jesus's mission, which includes his suffering and death.[23]

This is not the first time that one encounters this tension in Scripture. There are several instances throughout the Old Testament where a villain has acted on his own against God's people and yet is understood to have been under the control of God, his plan consonant with God's plan of judgment and salvation. The most notable examples are of the Egyptian pharaoh in Exodus 5–14 and the Babylonian army in Habakkuk and Psalm 137. In both of these examples, God uses the villains for his purposes to secure the escape of his people (he "hardens Pharaoh's heart," which provides the opportunity for him to display his awesome power to his people through the plagues and in the crossing of the sea) or to enact judgment upon them for their idolatries (the prophets and the historical books repeatedly attribute the exile to God as his punishment of his wayward people). Yet he holds both Pharaoh and the Babylonians responsible for their actions against his people because these actions are consistent with their inclinations. There is no indication in these passages that they are puppets, made to do things that oppose their nature or common practice. There is, however, an emphasis on God's sovereignty in these passages, that is, on his utter control of the circumstances of his people no matter the situation, a notion that is not absent in the Gospel narratives and in the story of Judas particularly.

WHY DID HE DO IT?

As each of the canonical Gospels was written in its likely historical order of appearance, the answer to this question became more explicit. Mark is concerned to understand why Judas betrayed Jesus, but not from the standpoint of his personal motivation. Instead, Judas's betrayal is done in order to initiate the series of events that constitutes Jesus's passion and resurrection and its fulfillment of Scripture (Mark 9:31; 10:33; 14:21). In Matthew, Judas betrays Jesus in exchange for payment (Matt. 26:14–16), although it is unclear if he fully realized what he was doing (upon Jesus's condemnation, he appears to regret what he has done: Matt. 27:3). In Luke's Gospel, Judas betrays Jesus because he has been possessed by Satan and receives compensation for doing so (Luke 22:3–6). Last, in John Judas's greed is even further accentuated, as his character is made known to the reader even before he carries out his plot

---

23. Origen demonstrates his recognition of this tension throughout the Gospels when he writes that many people "delivered Jesus up," some positively (God), but most negatively (Judas and the religious leaders) (*Comm. Matt.* 75).

of betrayal with the religious authorities (John 12:4–6). The devil puts it into Judas's mind to betray Jesus (John 13:2), and he is possessed by Satan during Jesus's last meal with his disciples (John 13:27).

What Did He Do to Betray Jesus?

What exactly did Judas *do* to betray Jesus? As we have seen, the Gospel writers are very explicit that Judas betrayed his master, but the mode must be inferred from the texts. According to the narratives, there were three major elements of betrayal. First, Judas plotted with the Jewish religious authorities, who had it in for Jesus from the beginning of his ministry and whose zeal for his death intensified upon his entrance and activities in Jerusalem (Mark 3:6; 11:18; Luke 19:47–48; 22:1–2). Although they desired to put Jesus to death from the start, putting the event into motion proved to be more challenging. The difficulty was that they had to figure out a way to arrest Jesus without causing a riot (Luke 22:6), because they feared the people's reaction (the crowds were amazed by Jesus's teachings and miracle working).[24]

The second aspect of Judas's betrayal, then, was to take them to Jesus when he was away from the crowds. This is the reason that the religious authorities needed someone "on the inside." The garden in which Jesus was arrested was a favorite hideaway and place of prayer for him, so Judas somehow knew where to lead the soldiers and religious authorities (John 18:2). The betrayer needed to be someone whom Jesus trusted, who was close enough to know his pattern and to be allowed access to him by his other disciples. Judas fit the need perfectly.

The third aspect of betrayal was the acceptance of money for his role in leading Jesus's enemies to him. Not only does he betray Jesus by arranging for his arrest, but he profits by it as well! This added bit of information in Matthew and Luke makes his actions seem even more despicable, since he is not motivated by a deep sense that he is doing the right thing, but by material gain.

Conclusion

According to the canonical Gospels, Judas is no model disciple. He is the ultimate traitor. While appearing to remain committed to Jesus's ministry, Judas joins the ranks of those who oppose Jesus's mission. In the Gospel narratives he serves as a foil to all who are faithful to Jesus—even when they do not understand fully. More than any other single character, perhaps, Judas is the antagonist of these stories, while Jesus is the clear protagonist. And yet Judas serves an important purpose. In his attempt to thwart Jesus, he ultimately

---

24. Added to this was the fact that he had already avoided death from his enemies once before (Luke 4:29–30), a fact that might not have been known to the religious authorities but one that the Gospel's audience would have been aware of.

provides the opportunity for God's purpose to be worked out through his death and resurrection.

As a traitor, Judas meets an end that is fit for a villain. Whether out of regret and repentance or by accident, he dies an inglorious death by hanging and/or disembowelment. Whereas Jesus's own death is portrayed as gruesome yet selfless, sacrificial, redemptive, and victorious, Judas's is merely a sad and cautionary tale of the fate of the one who betrayed the ultimate friend, the Son of God.

Suggestions for Further Reading

Judas

Brown, Raymond E. *The Death of the Messiah: From Gethsemane to the Grave; A Commentary on the Passion Narratives in the Four Gospels.* 2 vols. ABRL. New Haven: Yale University Press, 2008.

Halas, R. B. *Judas Iscariot: A Scriptural and Theological Study of His Person, His Deeds, and His Eternal Lot.* Washington, DC: Catholic University of America, 1946.

Meyer, Marvin. *Judas: The Definitive Collection of Gospels and Legends about the Infamous Apostle of Jesus.* San Francisco: HarperOne, 2007.

Williams, D. J. "Judas Iscariot." In *The Dictionary of Jesus and the Gospels*, edited by Joel B. Green, Scot McKnight, and I. Howard Marshall, 406–8. Downers Grove, IL: InterVarsity, 1992.

The *Gospel of Judas*

DeConick, April D. *The Thirteenth Apostle: What the Gospel of Judas Really Says.* Rev. ed. London: Continuum, 2007.

Kasser, R., Marvin Meyer, and G. Wurst, eds. *The Gospel of Judas.* 2nd ed. Washington, DC: National Geographic, 2008.

Wright, N. T. *Judas and the Gospel of Jesus: Have We Missed the Truth about Christianity?* Grand Rapids: Baker Books, 2007.

Conclusion

Seeking the Historical Jesus among Friends and Enemies

Chris Keith with Larry W. Hurtado

As the studies of Jesus's friends and enemies collected in this book demonstrate, the Gospels' complete answers to the question of Jesus's identity are not fully intelligible apart from their portrayals of Jesus's social world, his friends and enemies, and their shared historical contexts. To take two examples from the previous chapters: readers gain insight into Jesus's true identity as the Messiah by watching John the Baptist's doubts over Jesus's messianic identity emerge in the context of John's Herodian imprisonment (Matt. 11:2–3); and readers better understand Jesus's identity as someone who "was betrayed" (1 Cor. 11:23) via the narrative portrayal of the follower who betrayed him, Judas. The canonical Gospels are thus multifaceted in their usage of Jesus's friends and enemies, among other methods, in order to answer the question "Who was (or is) Jesus?"

To what degree, however, does the answer the canonical Gospels give to the question of Jesus's identity—and, by extension, their employment of Jesus's friends and enemies in order to answer it—relate to how critical scholarship answers the question of Jesus's identity, specifically by questing for the "historical Jesus"? Thus far we have addressed the topic of the historical Jesus in a limited fashion. Since, however, as we noted in the introduction, critical questions about Jesus and the Gospel narratives almost inevitably arise for students who thoroughly study those texts and the sociohistorical contexts of Jesus and the early church, we turn in this final chapter to introduce readers to historical Jesus studies. Additionally, we will argue that the Gospels' portrayals of Jesus should be (and are) important to these studies.

The Historical Jesus

Who is the "historical Jesus"?[1] One can begin to answer this question by considering how historical Jesus studies began. Albert Schweitzer, the great chronicler of the First Quest for the historical Jesus (see sidebar on the quests for the historical Jesus), attributed the start of critical Jesus research to essays written by Hermann Samuel Reimarus (d. 1768), a professor of oriental languages in Hamburg, Germany.[2] Reimarus never published these essays during his life for fear of the reaction, so his disciple, Gotthold Lessing, published them following Reimarus's death. In one particularly important essay, titled "The Aims of Jesus and His Disciples," Schweitzer notes that Reimarus began by drawing a line of distinction between what Jesus *actually* said and did on the one hand and what his later followers *claimed* he said and did on the other.[3] James Charlesworth claims that such critical approaches to Jesus began slightly earlier and in Britain with English Deists such as John Locke, Matthew Tindal, and Thomas Chubb.[4] Regardless of its origins, the important concept to grasp at present is the distinction between the reality of Jesus's life and the claims of Christian Gospels. This distinction typically contains within it an implicit or explicit skepticism that the two are identical, thus giving birth to critical questioning of the canonical versions of Jesus's life and identity. Under such approaches to Jesus, the "historical Jesus" refers to the actual Jesus of the past rather than the portrayals of him by later Christians in the church's Gospels.

Students of Jesus and the Gospels are not necessarily dependent upon eighteenth- and nineteenth-century German and British theologians and philosophers to gain an initial grasp on the "historical Jesus," however. For, when claiming that Jesus's contemporaries often misunderstood him, the Gospels themselves reveal differences between what they thought about him during his earthly ministry and what they thought of him after his crucifixion and resurrection. These misunderstandings extend even—and especially—to those closest to him. For example, according to Mark 8:27–33//Matthew 16:13–23, Peter misunderstood Jesus's identity as "Christ"; according to John 2:22, the disciples did not understand Jesus's statements regarding the temple until after his resurrection; and according to John 7:5, Jesus's own brothers did not believe in him during his ministry. Mark 3:21 even indicates that at one point in his ministry, Jesus's family thought he was crazy! Admissions by the Gospel

---

1. The phrase "historical Jesus" itself is hotly debated. For some scholars, it means the Jesus who walked the earth, as it is used here. For others, since there has been no scholarly consensus on what this earthly Jesus looked like, "historical Jesus" refers to scholarly reconstructions of Jesus, which may or may not be what Jesus was "really" like; see further below in the main text.

2. Albert Schweitzer, *The Quest of the Historical Jesus: A Critical Study of Its Progress from Reimarus to Wrede*, trans. F. C. Burkitt (Baltimore: Johns Hopkins University Press, 1998), 13–26.

3. Ibid., 16.

4. James H. Charlesworth, *The Historical Jesus: An Essential Guide* (Nashville: Abingdon, 2008), 2.

Quests for the Historical Jesus

Scholars often divide historical Jesus research into three distinct quests—the First Quest (nineteenth century), Second (or New) Quest (1950s–1970s), and Third Quest (1980s–2000s)—with a period of "No Quest" between the First and Second Quests (1900–1950s).[1] Such division of historical Jesus research can be heuristically useful given many common traits between various Jesus researchers in each period. This division, however, has also received trenchant criticism for its oversimplification and particularly for the inaccurate suggestion that no positive work on Jesus was produced in the first half of the twentieth century (during the so-called No Quest).[2]

1. This triadic division appears, for example, in a recent introduction to Jesus and the Gospels, Mark L. Strauss, *Four Portraits, One Jesus: An Introduction to Jesus and the Gospels* (Grand Rapids: Zondervan, 2007), 347–82. Alternatively, Charlesworth identifies the precritical period of 26–1738 CE as the "No Quest" and the period of the 1900s to the 1950s as "The Moratorium on the Old Quest" (*Historical Jesus*, 1).

2. See especially Dale C. Allison, *Resurrecting Jesus: The Earliest Christian Tradition and Its Interpreters* (New York: T&T Clark, 2005), 1–26; Stanley E. Porter, *The Criteria for Authenticity in Historical-Jesus Research: Previous Discussion and New Proposals*, JSNTSup 191 (Sheffield: Sheffield Academic Press, 2000), 28–59, 238; and, most fully, Walter P. Weaver, *The Historical Jesus in the Twentieth Century: 1900–1950* (Harrisburg, PA: Trinity Press International, 1999). Note also the rejection of the whole three-quests schema by Fernando Bermejo Rubio, "The Fiction of the 'Three Quests': An Argument for Dismantling a Dubious Historiographical Paradigm," *JSHJ* 7 (2009): 211–53.

authors that what Jesus's closest associates thought about his identity *prior* to his death and resurrection was not strictly the same as what they thought *after* it also bring to light the enigmatic historical Jesus who walked the earth.

As has already been noted, for most scholars the historical Jesus stands in contrast to the Gospels' images of Jesus, often called the "Christ of faith" because the Gospels' portrayal of Jesus already reflects their faith in him as Christ.[5] The degree of contrast between the historical Jesus and the Christ of faith differs from one scholar to the next. For, although most scholars agree that the canonical Gospels reflect an already interpreted Jesus rather than a purely "historical" Jesus, they disagree considerably as to whether the Gospels' interpretation is an accurate image of the historical Jesus. In the words of perhaps the most influential New Testament scholar of the twentieth century, Rudolf Bultmann, "No sane person can doubt that Jesus stands as founder behind the historical movement whose first distinct stage is represented by the oldest Palestinian community. But how far that community preserved an objectively true picture of him and his message is another question."[6] Some

5. The classic presentation of the "historical Jesus" as something other than the "Christ of faith" is Martin Kähler, *The So-Called Historical Jesus and the Historic Biblical Christ*, trans. Carl E. Braaten, SemEd (Philadelphia: Fortress, 1964). The original German was published in 1896 as *Der sogenannte historische Jesus und der geschichtliche, biblische Christus*.

6. Rudolf Bultmann, *Jesus and the Word*, trans. Louise Pettibone Smith and Ermimie Huntress Lantero (New York: Charles Scribner's Sons, 1934), 13. For a sharp criticism of Bultmann

scholars view the historical Jesus as substantially the same as the Gospels' Jesus, and the Gospels thus as reliable witnesses to the past. Others view the historical Jesus as radically different from the Gospels' Jesus, and the Gospels as thus a corruption of past reality in the service of later Christian propaganda. (Still others reject these two alternatives, as we will see below.)

Since the historical Jesus stands in varying degrees of contrast with the Jesus of the Gospels, Jesus historians are left with a problem: what should one do with those Gospels and their Jesus? Most scholars would agree that one cannot simply set the Gospels aside when searching for the historical Jesus,[7] if for no other reason than that the canonical Gospels are the earliest sources for Jesus and thus invaluable for historical research. Since, therefore, the earliest sources for Jesus are (1) necessary and/or unavoidable but (2) already interpreted and serving an agenda, a primary concern in historical Jesus scholarship—if not *the* primary concern—has been establishing methodological means by which scholars can find the historical Jesus amid the interpreted Jesus of our earliest sources. They often do this by separating "authentic" Jesus tradition, thought to reflect the historical Jesus, from "inauthentic" tradition, thought to reflect the Christ of faith.

Sifting through the Jesus Tradition: Criteria of Authenticity

In recent historical Jesus studies the dominant approach to separating authentic Jesus tradition and inauthentic Jesus tradition is criteria of authenticity.[8] These criteria, which serve as filters for the Gospel tradition, have been shared by different quests for the historical Jesus but are a particular fixture of much Jesus research in the Third Quest (1980s–2000s). At the risk of oversimplification, we can say that these criteria attempt to establish whether particular events or sayings in the Gospels came from "history" (that is, actually happened) or were invented by Jesus's followers based on their theological convictions (that is, faith). The criteria thus assume a juxtaposition between history and the faith of early Christians. A brief look at two of the most popular criteria, the criterion of multiple attestation and the criterion of dissimilarity, will demonstrate how they are used.

---

in this regard, see Anthony Le Donne, *The Historiographical Jesus: Memory, Typology, and the Son of David* (Waco: Baylor University Press, 2009), 36–37.

7. Recently arguing this point is Dale C. Allison, *The Historical Christ and the Theological Jesus* (Grand Rapids: Eerdmans, 2009), 66; Craig S. Keener, *The Historical Jesus of the Gospels* (Grand Rapids: Eerdmans, 2009), xxxi.

8. Useful introductions to the standard criteria are Porter, *Criteria*, 63–123; and Robert H. Stein, "The 'Criteria' for Authenticity," in *Gospel Perspectives: Studies of History and Tradition in the Four Gospels*, ed. R. T. France and David Wenham (Sheffield: JSOT Press, 1980), 1:225–63.

The Criterion of Multiple Attestation

The criterion of multiple attestation asserts that the likelihood of a particular saying or action of Jesus being authentic increases if it appears in multiple, ideally independent, sources. These sources can be canonical Gospels, other New Testament texts, noncanonical Gospels, the first-century Jewish historian Josephus, or hypothetical sources such as Q, M, and L.[9] The criterion can be applied to particular events or particular sayings. An event that often passes the criterion of multiple attestation is Jesus's final meal, or Last Supper, with his disciples before his betrayal. This meal occurs in all four canonical Gospels (Matt. 26:20–29; Mark 14:17–25; Luke 22:14–23; John 13:1–30) and in Paul's first letter to the Corinthians (1 Cor. 11:23–26). A particular saying of Jesus that may pass this criterion is his rejoinder, "Let anyone with ears to hear listen," which occurs in Matthew 11:15 and 13:9, Mark 4:9 and 4:23, Luke 8:8 and 14:35, and *Gospel of Thomas* 21. Another example is Jesus's parable of the mustard seed, which occurs in Matthew 13:31–32, Mark 4:30–32, Luke 13:18–19, and *Gospel of Thomas* 20. The more sources a particular Jesus tradition appears in, the more confidence scholars have that it is authentic tradition and thus represents the historical Jesus.

The Criterion of Dissimilarity

Like the criterion of multiple attestation, the criterion of dissimilarity is a methodological means of sifting through the Gospels for authentic Jesus tradition. This criterion asserts that the likelihood of a particular saying or action of Jesus increases if it differs from Jesus's first-century Jewish context on the one hand and from the early church on the other hand.[10] That is, if scholars can demonstrate that a particular saying or event from the Gospels does not reflect Second Temple Judaism (what Jesus came from) or the early church (what came from Jesus), they feel more confident claiming it came from Jesus himself. Such a methodology is, of course, an effort at establishing a bedrock set of data, since ultimately very little Jesus tradition is dissimilar to Jesus's Judaism and Jesus's early followers. According to Ernst Käsemann, whose essay "The Problem of the Historical Jesus" launched the Second Quest for the historical Jesus, this criterion alone provides firm materials for recon-

---

9. On Q, see introduction, n. 47. "M" refers to "Special Matthew," a hypothetical source from which Matthew supposedly derived the material that appears in his Gospel alone. "L" similarly refers to a "Special Luke," which Luke alone used and accounts for the material in only his Gospel. See further Bart D. Ehrman, *Jesus: Apocalyptic Prophet of the New Millennium* (New York: Oxford University Press, 1999), 90–91. The Jesus Seminar famously included the *Gospel of Thomas* as one of its primary sources for the historical Jesus, along with the canonical Gospels; thus the title of their published results—*The Five Gospels*.

10. The criterion of dissimilarity is thus actually two criteria of dissimilarity—(1) dissimilarity with Second Temple Judaism and (2) dissimilarity with the early church.

structing the historical Jesus: "There is an almost complete lack of satisfactory and water-tight criteria for this material. In only one case do we have more or less safe ground under our feet; when there are no grounds either for deriving a tradition from Judaism or for ascribing it to primitive Christianity."[11] Examples of Jesus tradition that often pass the criterion of dissimilarity are Jesus's usage of *abba* for God (Mark 14:36) and his usage of "Son of Man" as a self-referential term, neither of which was featured prominently in Second Temple Judaism or early Christianity.[12]

The criteria of multiple attestation and dissimilarity are two of many criteria of authenticity. Among other suggested criteria of authenticity are the criteria of embarrassment, coherence, divergent traditions, Semitic influence, and multiple forms.[13] Each works differently in details and often goes by several names, but all share a common goal and general means of accomplishing that goal. Their common goal is the identification of authentic Jesus tradition and the means of accomplishing it is through separation of authentic Jesus tradition from inauthentic Jesus tradition. In addition, then, the practitioners of historical Jesus research who employ these criteria implicitly accept the assumptions that modern scholars are capable of distinguishing between authentic and inauthentic Jesus tradition and extracting one from the other. That is, under this methodology, which the majority of Jesus scholars still employ (some even in this book), the path to the historical Jesus is through dissection of the Gospels and separation into authentic and inauthentic bodies of Jesus tradition. Scholars then proceed to construct a historical Jesus with the authentic pile of tradition, which should then presumably be agreeable to critical historians, since in principle one is using only those pieces of tradition that have passed through the criteria of authenticity.

Dissatisfaction with the Criteria of Authenticity

It hardly needs to be said, however, that the end product that emerges from the criteria of authenticity—each scholar's historical Jesus—is never entirely agreeable with the field at large.[14] This disagreement results from innumerable prior disagreements as to which pieces of Jesus tradition belong in which cat-

11. Ernst Käsemann, "The Problem of the Historical Jesus," in *Essays on New Testament Themes*, trans. W. J. Montague, SBT 41 (London: SCM, 1964), 37. Similarly, Käsemann's mentor, Rudolf Bultmann, *The History of the Synoptic Tradition*, trans. John Marsh, rev. ed. (Peabody, MA: Hendrickson, 1994), 205. This example provides a similarity between the "No Quest" of Bultmann and the "Second Quest" initiated by Käsemann.

12. See discussion in Stein, "Criteria," 241.

13. Porter also suggests three new critieria: Greek language and its context, Greek textual variance, and discourse features (*Criteria*, 126–237).

14. Dale C. Allison: "It is certain that they [the criteria of authenticity] . . . have not led us into the promised land of scholarly consensus" (*Jesus of Nazareth: Millenarian Prophet* [Minneapolis: Fortress, 1998], 6). Similarly, Paula Fredriksen: "Dispute on the status of individual

egory, and for what reasons. A host of scholars, therefore, have become disillusioned with the prospect of the criteria of authenticity producing a neutral, historical, Jesus.[15] They are essentially skeptical of the criteria of authenticity's ability to perform the task for which they were designed, the separation of authentic and inauthentic Jesus tradition that enables the construction of a historical Jesus. This development in historical Jesus research is important and relates to the contribution that the current volume makes to Jesus studies.

Dissatisfaction with the criteria of authenticity has come in various shapes and sizes. Sometimes scholars attack a particular criterion, and here we note criticisms of the two criteria previously discussed, multiple attestation and dissimilarity.

DISSATISFACTIONS WITH THE CRITERION OF MULTIPLE ATTESTATION[16]

One major criticism of the criterion of multiple attestation is that it needs a solution to the Synoptic Problem (to know which sources are truly independent) in order to have any explanatory power.[17] This is a problem because, although there is in Synoptic Problem research currently a wide endorsement of Markan priority, the details of each theory of Markan priority (Two-Source, Four-Source, Farrar) are nowhere near a consensus and the problem itself has historically been one of the most debated issues in New Testament studies. Thus, problems emerge in trying to identify authentic tradition based upon multiple and/or independent occurrences. If a tradition occurs in all four canonical Gospels, can it claim four independent attestations? (The answer is almost always no.) Or, if Matthew and Luke used Mark (the current majority opinion), can a tradition in all four Gospels claim only two independent attestations (Mark and John)? To go down the rabbit hole one step further, if a tradition occurs in all four Gospels, can one claim for certain that Matthew and Luke followed Mark, or could they have possibly followed the hypothetical source Q despite the fact that Mark also had the tradition? (That is, do we know for certain that Mark and Q have no shared traditions?) In the latter hypothetical case, then, would there be three

---

passages seems virtually endless" (*From Jesus to Christ: The Origins of the New Testament Images of Jesus* [New Haven: Yale University Press, 1988], 96).

15. In addition to the studies cited below, see Scot McKnight, *Jesus and His Death: Historiography, the Historical Jesus, and Atonement Theory* (Waco: Baylor University Press, 2005), 45–46, and, most recently, Rafael Rodríguez, who suggests that, far from offering neutrality, the criteria are actually "vehicles of our subjectivity rather than checks against them" ("Authenticating Criteria: The Use and Misuse of a Critical Method," *JSHJ* 7 (2009): 152–67; see esp.157, 167). Similarly, M. D. Hooker had earlier charged, "The application of the method is bound to be subjective" ("On Using the Wrong Tool," *Theology* 75 [1972]: 576).

16. What follows expands and modifies work that appears in Chris Keith, *Jesus' Literacy: Scribal Culture and the Teacher from Galilee.* LHJS/LNTS 413 (London: T&T Clark, 2011).

17. See also Porter, *Critieria*, 87–89; Stein, "Criteria," 230–31.

independent sources (Mark, Q, John)? Alternatively, if a tradition occurs in all four canonical Gospels but one is convinced, as are some scholars, that John knew Mark,[18] is it possible that there is really only one independent tradition (Mark) despite the fact that, on the surface, there appear to be as many as four? The answers to these questions differ from one scholar to the next and from one bit of Jesus tradition to the next. So it is difficult to base affirmations of authentic Jesus tradition entirely on the criterion of multiple attestation.

Tom Thatcher's analysis of Jesus's usage of riddles in the canonical Gospels demonstrates an altogether different problem with this criterion.[19] Although all four canonical Gospels (and the *Gospel of Thomas*) agree that Jesus used the form of riddles in his teaching, "rarely does any single riddle appear in more than one context."[20] Thus, for example, when John 10:1–6 presents Jesus speaking a riddle to his audience that does not appear in any other Gospel, what should scholars do? Should scholars identify it as authentic because Jesus's usage of riddles is multiply attested? Or should they identify it as inauthentic because his usage of this particular riddle is not? An initially attractive middle ground would be to claim that, although scholars can be confident that Jesus used riddles, they cannot be confident that he used *this* riddle.[21] As this response answers one question, however, it implicitly asks another: if the criterion of multiple attestation inspires confidence that Jesus did just the *type* of thing that John 10:1–6 claims he did (and thus raises the possibility that this is authentic tradition), to what degree does the fact that the particular tradition is not multiply attested detract from that confidence (and thus raise the possibility that this is inauthentic tradition)? Which aspect of the criterion of multiple attestation should carry more weight in such judgments of authenticity?

Dissatisfactions with the Criterion of Dissimilarity

The criterion of dissimilarity has received perhaps more criticism than any other criterion of authenticity. Already in 1972, Morna Hooker published vehement disagreements with the usage of the criterion, identifying it as "the

18. Richard Bauckham, "John for Readers of Mark," in *The Gospels for All Christians: Rethinking the Gospel Audiences*, ed. Richard Bauckham (Edinburgh: T&T Clark, 1998), 147–71.

19. Tom Thatcher, *Jesus the Riddler: The Power of Ambiguity in the Gospels* (Louisville: Westminster John Knox, 2006), xix–xx.

20. Ibid., xix.

21. Thatcher argues along these lines: "I am not concerned about particular riddles recorded in the Gospels but about whether he engaged in riddling *at all*. I claim that if Jesus engaged in riddling *at all*, this fact is significant to key aspects of our understanding of his social posture and message" (ibid., xxi; emphasis original). Cf. also the comments of Gerd Theissen and Dagmar Winter, *The Quest for the Plausible Jesus: The Question of Criteria*, trans. M. Eugene Boring (Louisville: Westminster John Knox, 2002), 16, on indices of distinctiveness.

wrong tool."[22] By 1980, Robert Stein noted, "Despite the great optimism with which this tool was embraced, there has recently been a heavy barrage of criticism leveled at this tool."[23] The most damaging criticism of the criterion of dissimilarity is that it produces a Jesus who is a historical absurdity or, better yet, patently ahistorical. As already discussed, the criterion passes as authentic those traditions that could not have come from Second Temple Judaism or the early church, as judged by their presumed "discontinuity" with both contexts. As matters of historical fact, however, Jesus *was* a Second Temple Jew and Christianity *did* emerge from the activities of his life and death, and thus one should expect continuity between the historical Jesus and both contexts. The criterion thus severs the historical Jesus from the sociohistorical context in which he was born and lived, as well as from the historical aftermath of his life. This approach is hardly responsible historical methodology.[24]

Another criticism of this criterion is that scholars do not possess enough knowledge about Second Temple Judaism or early Christianity to claim what *could not* have emerged in either and thus should be attributed to Jesus himself.[25] "It requires exhaustive knowledge of Judaism and early Christianity to ensure accuracy, knowledge that we may never possess despite continual advances."[26] Thus, like the criterion of multiple attestation, whose power is limited by lack of an agreeable solution to the Synoptic Problem, the criterion of dissimilarity's persuasiveness is continually ebbing with the changing scholarly knowledge about Jesus's and the early church's context(s).

A more potent criticism of this criterion aims at its very root and concerns the traditioning process in the early church. The criterion assumes that the early church would have included a Jesus tradition in the canonical Gospels for one of two reasons: (1) it fit their theology and identity; or (2) it came from the historical Jesus. Elements of Jesus tradition in the first category are usually deemed inauthentic (or, at least, not authentic) because the continuity between the tradition and Christian identity suggests that the early church may have invented the tradition in order to buttress

---

22. Hooker, "On Using," 574–81.

23. Stein, "Criteria," 242.

24. Similarly, C. Stephen Evans: "One could only conclude that the picture of Jesus that emerged [from the criterion of dissimilarity] was accurate of him as a whole if one knew in advance that there was no continuity between Jesus and the Judaism that nourished him or between Jesus and the Church that grew up from his life and work. Far from being known to be true, both of these claims seem enormously implausible" (*The Historical Christ and the Jesus of Faith: The Incarnational Narrative as History* [Oxford: Clarendon, 1996], 328–29). See also Theissen and Winter, *Quest for the Plausible Jesus*, 10, for a judgment that such a procedure actually distances Jesus research from "general historical methodology."

25. Hooker, "On Using," 575; Theissen and Winter, *Quest for the Plausible Jesus*, 21–22.

26. Stanley E. Porter, "A Dead End or a New Beginning? Examining the Criteria for Authenticity in Light of Albert Schweitzer," in *Jesus Research: An International Perspective*, ed. James H. Charlesworth and Petr Pokorný (Grand Rapids: Eerdmans, 2009), 27.

278 Jesus among Friends and Enemies

its own theological position(s). Elements of Jesus tradition in the second category are often deemed authentic under the criterion (if they are also dissimilar to Second Temple Judaism) because their discontinuity with early Christian theology suggests that the church did not invent them but rather inherited them from Jesus himself and retained them, perhaps out of some sense of reverence.

Technically, the criterion of dissimilarity does not deny the historical possibility of a tradition that fits in both categories—came from Jesus *and* fits early Christian identity—but does hold as suspicious anything that comports with early Christianity, and so eliminates it from discussion of the historical Jesus. What becomes clear, therefore, is that the "authentic" body of Jesus tradition that the criterion of dissimilarity produces is really a default category consisting of anything that cannot readily be explained as arising from the character of the "early church." The dividing line between "authentic" and "suspicious/inauthentic" is early Christian identity itself.

One is fully justified, however, in asking at this point why continuity with early Christian identity *in itself* should qualify a tradition as "inauthentic" or why discontinuity *in itself* should qualify a tradition as "authentic." Why should scholars use Christian identity as a litmus test for *historical authenticity* at all, whether to pronounce confidence in it or to deny it?

Moreover, the assumption that early Christians placed various "authentic" Jesus traditions in the Gospels *despite* their lack of explicit support of, or agreement with, early Christian identity takes an overly narrow view of how early Christians saw themselves and their identity in relation to the Jesus tradition. To take one example, scholars often identify the term "Son of Man" as an element of discontinuity/dissimilarity between Jesus and the early church because early Christian writers (such as Paul) and early Christian creeds do not reflect the usage of it.[27] Upon this identification of "discontinuity," the expression "Son of Man" typically passes the criterion of dissimilarity as authentic tradition.[28]

Do we know for certain, however, *on the basis of the early church's restricted usage of the phrase alone*, that early Christians, either in liturgical practice or theological reflection, viewed Jesus's identity as Son of Man in discontinuity with their own identity as followers of him? That early Christians did not use

---

27. Cf. also Hooker, who argued that "Son of Man" exposed methodological problems with the criterion of dissimilarity on other grounds ("On Using," 577–79).

28. See, for example, the summary statement of Strauss in his textbook: "It seems beyond dispute that Jesus used the title, since it appears exclusively on his lips in the Gospels and since the later church did not adopt it as a messianic title (and so did not create it)" (*Four Portraits*, 484). For a recent treatment of various issues concerning the expression "the Son of Man," see the multiauthor volume *"Who Is This Son of Man?" The Latest Scholarship on a Puzzling Expression of the Historical Jesus*, ed. Larry W. Hurtado and Paul Owen, LNTS 390 (London: T&T Clark, 2011).

Dissimilar or Similar Usage of 'Son of Man' in the Early Church?

Was early Christians' usage of the term "Son of Man" dissimilar or similar to Jesus's own usage of the term?

(≠ represents a state of discontinuity/dissimilarity; = represents a state of continuity/similarity)

The Dissimilar Usage of "Son of Man" by Early Christians

State of Affairs in Jesus's Life		State of Affairs in the Early Church
Jesus used "Son of Man" to refer to himself.	≠	Early Christians do not use "Son of Man" to refer to Jesus.

The Similar Usage of "Son of Man" by Early Christians

State of Affairs in Jesus's Life		State of Affairs in the Early Church
Jesus alone used "Son of Man" to refer to himself.	=	Early Christians depict Jesus alone as using "Son of Man" to refer to himself.

"Son of Man" liturgically (for example, in ritual confession of him) does not necessarily lead to the conclusion that the term for Jesus is "dissimilar" to their full identities as Jesus followers. Assuming that the historical Jesus routinely used "Son of Man" (likely as a self-designation) and given that early Christians apparently did not routinely use it to confess or proclaim him,[29] one can indeed define this as a discontinuous practice between Jesus and the early church. However, on the same basis, one can also define early Christians' portrayal of Jesus alone using "Son of Man" as a self-designation in their Gospels as reflecting a certain continuity between Jesus and the early church. That is, according to "historical" reconstructions, only Jesus used "Son of Man," and according to the early church's portrayal of Jesus's life in the Gospels, only Jesus used "Son of Man." So, even if it was used distinctively by Jesus, nevertheless the phrase was important enough for early Christians to preserve its usage in the Gospels that also served as promoting their own group identity. This example demonstrates that "continuity" and "discontinuity" are much more complex in identity construction than the criterion of dissimilarity assumes.

Modifications to the Criterion of Dissimilarity

Despite its limitations, the criterion of dissimilarity has remained an important topic in historical Jesus research because of more recent attempts to

29. "Son of Man" occurs in the New Testament only four times outside the Gospels: Acts 7:56; Heb. 2:6; Rev. 1:13; 14:14.

challenge, rehabilitate, or enhance it. For example, in place of the criterion
of dissimilarity, N. T. Wright proposes the criterion of double similarity/
dissimilarity: "When something can be seen to be credible (though perhaps
deeply subversive) within first-century Judaism, *and* credible as the implied
starting-point (though not the exact replica) of something in later Christianity,
there is a strong possibility of our being in touch with the genuine history
of Jesus."[30] In other words, Jesus should "fit" in each context enough to be
recognizable but should fit with enough variance to be recognizably different
from others in each context. Wright's criterion thus recognizes the possible
coexistence of continuity and discontinuity in the Jesus tradition rather than
using either one as a sieve of historicity, or at least not in the same manner
as the criterion of dissimilarity. For, whereas the criterion of dissimilarity
isolates individual pieces of tradition for assessment, Wright does not intend
his criterion for isolated traditions: "It does not help very much at all to take
each saying, each parable, and work through a multiply hypothetical history
of traditions as though aiming thereby to peel the historical onion back to its
core. . . . Such a [method] serves only as a reminder that there is such a thing as
serious history, and this is not the way to do it."[31] In general, Wright employs
his criterion to place the historical Jesus, including his distinctiveness, back
in his sociohistorical context and the context of the early church rather than
distancing him from them.

After the most in-depth criticism of the criterion of dissimilarity to date,
Gerd Theissen and Dagmar Winter propose instead the criterion of historical plausibility: "What we know of Jesus as a whole must allow him to be
recognized within his contemporary Jewish context and must be compatible
with the Christian (canonical and noncanonical) history of his effects."[32] Like
Wright, in effect Theissen and Winter turn the criterion of dissimilarity on
its head. Whereas the criterion of dissimilarity severs Jesus from what he
came from and what came from him, the criterion of historical plausibility
views those contexts as precisely the paths to the historical Jesus. In this
light, one of the more significant points Theissen and Winter make regards
the "history of Jesus's effects." They insist that, rather than dissecting the
Jesus tradition and dispensing with parts of it, one must conceptualize
the historical Jesus in a manner that explains the existence of those texts.
"Historical research is not faced with the simple alternative 'authentic' or
'inauthentic,' but with the question of how the extant tradition may receive
the most satisfactory historical explanation."[33] In this way, the Gospels are

30. N. T. Wright, *Jesus and the Victory of God*, COQG 2 (Minneapolis: Fortress, 1996),
132 (emphasis original).
31. Ibid., 133.
32. Theissen and Winter, *Quest for the Plausible Jesus*, 212.
33. Ibid., 204.

not Jesus tradition to be chopped and discarded or retained, but rather Jesus tradition to be explained.[34]

Advancing the Critical Discussion by Returning to the Text

Further Jesus research claims that Wright's criterion of double similarity/dis-similarity and Theissen and Winter's criterion of historical plausibility are not so much challenges to the criterion of dissimilarity as important modifications or shifts of emphasis.[35] The manners in which these scholars have advanced the discussion are significant, however. For they agree that (1) the historical Jesus must be understood in light of Second Temple Judaism and the early church rather than in contrast to them and that (2) this is the case because searching for the historical Jesus should begin not by dividing the material in the Gospels into authentic and inauthentic piles but rather by asking what historical scenarios best explain the evidence we have. And, of course, the earliest evidence we have, as noted at the beginning of this chapter, is the four canonical Gospels. In this sense, historical Jesus research is currently witness-ing a forward progress characterized by a "return to the text." Rather than dividing the text and building the historical Jesus with what passes the criteria of authenticity, scholars are accounting for the corporate shape of the Gospel narratives and paying attention to their claims and sociohistorical contexts when answering the question of Jesus's identity.

Modifications of the criterion of dissimilarity like those of Wright, Theissen, and Winter are one trend demonstrating a return to the text in Jesus studies after abandoning efforts to divide the text into authentic and inauthentic tra-dition. At least two other trends similarly signal the return to the text: frank statements that the criteria of authenticity simply do not work and emphasis upon the Gospel tradition as Jesus memory.

The Criteria Simply Do Not Work: Allison et al.

The first additional trend marking the return to the text is frank statements that the criteria of authenticity do not work and that scholars therefore must work with what evidence they have, the Gospel texts as we have them. In a world of scholarly discourse of method and rigor, this trend is notable for its more-or-less autobiographical nature, with established scholars reflecting on their lack of conviction that the criteria of authenticity are useful.

---

34. For a similar emphasis, see below, under "The Narratives as Jesus Memory."
35. In particular, see Porter's assessments in his *Criteria*, 116–22; "Dead End," 29, 33; and "Reading the Gospels and the Quest for the Historical Jesus," in *Reading the Gospels Today*, ed. Stanley E. Porter, MNTS (Grand Rapids: Eerdmans, 2004), 52–53.

Perhaps leading this trend is Dale Allison. In his widely read *Jesus of Nazareth: Millenarian Prophet* (1998), Allison opens with a discussion of the criteria of authenticity and offers this condemnatory statement on their ability to deliver a pure historical Jesus:

> However much we better our methods for authenticating the traditions about Jesus, we are never going to produce results that can be confirmed or disconfirmed. Jesus is long gone, and we can never set our pale reconstructions beside the flesh-and-blood original. We should not deceive ourselves into dreaming that methodological sophistication will ever eventuate either in some sort of unimaginative scientific procedure or in academic concord. . . . Until we become literal time travelers, all attempts to find the historical Jesus will be steered by instinct and intuition. Appeals to shared criteria may, we can pray, assist us in being self-critical, but when all is said and done we look for the historical Jesus with our imaginations—and there too is where we find him, if we find him at all.[36]

Eleven years later, Allison's *The Historical Christ and the Theological Jesus* (2009) expresses a similar discontent with the criteria of authenticity. Reflecting on his own earlier work where, despite the previous quotation, he had attempted to rehabilitate authenticity criteria to a degree, Allison claims, "I also wish to say a little about recent suggestions for revising our criteria [for authenticity]—a trick I was still trying to perform ten years ago—or about replacing them with new and improved criteria. My question is not Which criteria are good and which bad? or How should we employ the good ones? but rather Should we be using criteria at all? My answer is No."[37]

Allison knows he is going against the majority of Jesus researchers but states rather autobiographically, "After years of being in the quest business, I have reluctantly concluded that most of the Gospel materials are not subject to historical proof or disproof, or even to accurate estimates of their probability."[38] Not surprisingly, then, Allison also expresses an uncertainty over anyone's ability to distinguish "history" in the Gospels from theological interpretation in the Gospels; that is, to distinguish authentic Jesus tradition in the Gospels from inauthentic tradition: "I must confess, however, that, with every year of further contemplation, I become more uncertain about anyone's ability, including my own, cleanly to extricate Jesus from his interpreters."[39]

In the latter study, however, Allison suggests that scholars are not left solely with their imaginations, as he had earlier intimated. He points searchers for

36. Allison, *Jesus of Nazareth*, 7.
37. Allison, *Historical Christ*, 55.
38. Ibid.
39. Ibid., 23.

Jesus to the oldest sources for his life, exhibiting the return to the text. "If the chief witnesses are too bad, if they contain only intermittently authentic items, we cannot lay them aside and tell a better story. . . . In order for us to find Jesus, our sources must often remember at least the sorts of things he did and the sorts of things that he said, including what he said about himself. . . . Although there is a canonical bias in all this, it is unavoidable."[40] For Allison, whether one likes it or not, the sources—not the criteria—are the starting point in questing for Jesus.

Like Allison, other scholars have confessed a lack of confidence in the criteria of authenticity. For example, Klaus Haacker notes that already by the end of his student days he "had come to the conclusion that a balanced overall picture of Jesus . . . cannot be built on the narrow basis of only those traditions which 'pass the exam' of dissimilarity."[41] Furthermore, similar returns to the full narratives of the Gospels in the search for the historical Jesus are the Identity of Jesus Project, of which Allison was a member, and the Princeton-Prague Symposium on Jesus Research, of which Haacker is a member. The first group published its findings in 2008 and claims,

> Many scholarly presentations of Jesus operate on assumptions that resemble those of an archaeological expedition. The "real" Jesus is thought to lie buried beneath historical artifacts—texts and traditions. . . . The Identity of Jesus Project came to believe that Jesus is best understood not by separating him from canon and creed but by investigating the ways in which the church's canon and creed provide distinctive clarification of his identity.[42]

Similarly, in the programmatic essay for the first published results of the ongoing Princeton-Prague Symposium, designed to assess the Third Quest, Charlesworth speaks for the group: "The historians in this volume do not imagine that they can find the 'real' Jesus behind the perceptions and theologies of the Evangelists."[43] In these two statements, one sees an abandonment of the assumption that the "real" Jesus of history lies hidden in the interpreted Jesus of

40. Ibid., 66.
41. Klaus Haacker, "'What Must I Do to Inherit Eternal Life?' Implicit Christology in Jesus's Sayings about Life and Kingdom," in Charlesworth and Pokorný, *Jesus Research*, 140. See further his "Die moderne historische Jesus-Forschung als hermeneutisches Problem," *TBei* 31 (2000): 60–74.
42. Beverly Roberts Gaventa and Richard B. Hays, "Seeking the Identity of Jesus," in *Seeking the Identity of Jesus: A Pilgrimage*, ed. Beverly Roberts Gaventa and Richard B. Hays (Grand Rapids: Eerdmans, 2008), 5.
43. James H. Charlesworth, "Introduction: Why Evaluate Twenty-Five Years of Jesus Research?" in Charlesworth and Pokorný, *Jesus Research*, 14. Petr Pokorný notes that the Princeton-Prague Symposium "avoid[s] the non-precise term 'historical Jesus'" (preface to Charlesworth and Pokorný, *Jesus Research*, xxii). Despite Charlesworth's claim, appeals to the criteria of authenticity occur throughout the volume (6, 7, 124, 173, 183n5, 186, 202, 216; cf. 143, 152n21).

the Gospels. Since the criteria of authenticity are built upon this assumption, and devised as a means of separating one from the other, this abandonment problematizes the usage of criteria of authenticity.

Although theirs is not the majority position, Allison, Roberts Gaventa, Hays, and Charlesworth are by no means alone in their various assertions concerning scholars' inability to construct knowledge concerning Jesus apart from the Gospel narratives via criteria of authenticity.[44] They are, nonetheless, examples of a second trend in Jesus research that signals a return to the text.

The Narratives as Jesus Memory

A second additional trend in Gospels studies that signals a return to the text in searching for Jesus is currently being led by scholars emphasizing that the Gospel texts are neither pure images of the past nor wholesale inventions but rather early Christian memories of Jesus. In addition to seeing the criteria of authenticity as the wrong tools to use for digging for the historical Jesus, this methodological perspective argues that the Jesus tradition itself is not the type of ground that can be dug.

A prominent representative of this trend is James Dunn. He cites the inadequacy of the criteria for reconstructing the actual words of Jesus,[45] but his more important contribution comes in his description of the Gospel tradition. The Gospels, according to Dunn, are not in the first instance evidence of "what really happened" but how Jesus's contemporaries remembered what happened. Since memory is necessarily selective, and thus a hermeneutical activity, "the Synoptic tradition provides evidence not so much for what Jesus did or said in itself, but for what Jesus was *remembered* as doing or saying by his first disciples, or as we might say, for the *impact* of what he did and said on his first disciples."[46] Thus, our earliest sources do not contain authentic/nonfaith traditions mixed in with inauthentic/faith traditions, which scholars must then separate one from another. To the contrary, "all we have is the impression actually made," and thus, "the only Jesus available to us . . . [is]

44. See Richard A. Horsley, *Jesus and Empire: The Kingdom of God and the New World Disorder* (Minneapolis: Fortress, 2003), 8; Rodríguez, "Authenticating Criteria," 156n15. Cf. also Larry W. Hurtado, who proposes that, like those who employ text-critical approaches to textual variants, historical Jesus scholars should attempt to explain "variants" in the Jesus tradition rather than "playing off one 'variant' in the Jesus tradition against another . . . thus producing a proposed reconstruction" in light of all the evidence rather than only that which passes criteria ("A Taxonomy of Recent Historical-Jesus Work," in *Whose Historical Jesus?* ed. William E. Arnal and Michel Desjardins, ESCJ 7 [Waterloo, ON: Wilfrid Laurier University Press, 1997], 295). This approach is similar to that of Theissen and Winter (see above, under "Modifications to the Criterion of Dissimilarity") and Schröter (see under "The Narratives as Jesus Memory") and receives a fuller articulation in light of social/cultural memory theory in Keith, *Jesus's Literacy*.

45. James D. G. Dunn, *Jesus Remembered*, CM 1 (Grand Rapids: Eerdmans, 2003), 97.

46. Ibid., 130 (emphases original).

the Jesus of faith, Jesus seen through the eyes and heard through the ears of the faith that he evoked by what he said and did."[47] From this perspective, criteria of authenticity are useless, because one cannot strip the interpretation of the Gospels from pure history—the latter never existed in the first place.[48] Similarly to Dunn, Elisabeth Schüssler Fiorenza describes the historical task as one of discerning early Christian memories of Jesus, and Larry Hurtado focuses upon the impact that Jesus had upon his followers and opponents.[49] Indeed, Terrence Tilley argues that Schüssler Fiorenza, Dunn, and Hurtado collectively represent "a new historical research program . . . [that] shifts from constructing theories about the Historical-Jesus to understanding the practices in which Jesus was remembered."[50]

Other scholars have appealed to the methodology of social/cultural memory theory in order to argue along essentially similar lines. This methodology views any act of commemoration, such as the Gospels, as an inextricable combination of the present and the past—"a complex interworking of the past putting pressure on the present's interpretation of it while the present simultaneously provides the only lens(es) through which the past can be viewed."[51] Thus, from the perspective of social memory theory, attempts at separating the "authentic" past from the "inauthentic" present of the early Christians who interpreted that past—such attempts as are made by those applying the criteria of authenticity—are futile. In the words of Alan Kirk and Tom Thatcher, "'Tradition' and 'memory' are not elements of the Gospel that can be pried apart through application of particular criteria. Rather, tradition is the indissoluble, irreducibly complex artifact of the continual negotiation and semantic interpenetration of present social realities and memorialized pasts."[52]

Although Kirk and Thatcher formally introduced this methodology to English-speaking Jesus scholarship in 2005,[53] it appeared in Georgia Keight-

47. James D. G. Dunn, A New Perspective on Jesus: What the Quest for the Historical Jesus Missed (London: SPCK, 2005), 30–31.

48. Ibid.: "When we strip away faith, we strip away everything and leave nothing." Dunn here speaks of the "faith" of the early Christians responsible for remembering Jesus by forming the Gospel tradition.

49. Larry W. Hurtado, Lord Jesus Christ: Devotion to Jesus in Earliest Christianity (Grand Rapids: Eerdmans, 2003), 53–64; Elisabeth Schüssler Fiorenza, Jesus and the Politics of Interpretation (New York: Continuum, 2000), 75–76.

50. Terrence W. Tilley, "Remembering the Historic Jesus—A New Research Program?" TS 68 (2007): 3–35 (quotation from 5).

51. Chris Keith, "The Claim of John 7.15 and the Memory of Jesus' Literacy," NTS 56, no. 1 (2010): 56.

52. Alan Kirk and Tom Thatcher, "Jesus Tradition as Social Memory," in Memory, Tradition, and Text: Uses of the Past in Early Christianity, ed. Alan Kirk and Tom Thatcher, SemeiaSt 52 (Atlanta: Society of Biblical Literature, 2005), 33.

53. Kirk and Thatcher, Memory, Tradition, and Text. This is the most useful English-language introduction to social memory theory with reference to the Jesus tradition.

ley's article in 1987.[54] Additionally, Jens Schröter was already applying the
insights of cultural memory to the sayings tradition in a monograph in 1997,[55]
preceded by an English article on the main methodological points in 1996.[56]
He emphasizes the difficulties plaguing assumptions that "purely historical
data" are accessible to historians and insists that one cannot therefore simply discard certain elements of the Jesus tradition: "Every approach to the
historical Jesus behind the Gospels has to explain how these writings could
have come into being as the earliest descriptions of this person."[57] Schröter's
argument, in this sense, foreshadowed Theissen and Winter, who emphasize
the "later effects" of the historical Jesus and their need to be explained. More
recently, Anthony Le Donne observes, similarly on the basis of social memory
emphases, "The historian's task is not simply to sift through the data looking
for facts . . . but to account for these early interpretations by explaining the
perceptions and memories that birthed them."[58]

According to these scholars, therefore, since the Gospels are Jesus memories,
and remembrance is an inherently hermeneutical activity, one cannot reduce
the material in the Gospels to separate boxes of authentic and inauthentic
tradition. Rather, historians must seek to explain the texts/memories as we
have them rather than dissect them with criteria of authenticity.[59] Importantly,
this method is naive neither in its abandonment of the idea of a pure past
nor in its return to the interpreted tradition. The explanation of such texts
as memories may include the notion that they are historically inaccurate but
insists that the job of the Jesus historian is not to pronounce them to have
such a status and end his or her day but to explain what type of person the
historical Jesus must have been to generate such a (false) memory.

In these ways, these scholars represent a third trend in Jesus research that,
alongside the trends of modifying the criterion of dissimilarity (Wright, Theissen, Winter) and offering frank confessions that the criteria do not work
(Allison et al.), reveals a forwarding of the critical discussion by returning to

54. Georgia Masters Keightley, "The Church's Memory of Jesus: A Social Science Analysis
of 1 Thessalonians," *BTB* 17 (1987): 149–56.

55. Jens Schröter, *Erinnerung an Jesu Worte: Studien zur Rezeption der Logienüberlieferung in
Markus, Q und Thomas,* WMANT 76 (Neukirchen-Vluyn, Germany: Neukirchener Verlag, 1997).

56. Jens Schröter, "The Historical Jesus and the Sayings Tradition: Comments on Current
Research," *Neot* 30, no. 1 (1996): 151–68.

57. Schröter, "Historical Jesus," 153. See further Jens Schröter, "Von der Historizität der
Evangelien: Ein Beitrag zur gegenwärtigen Diskussion um den historischen Jesus," in *Von Jesus
zum Neuen Testament: Studien zur urchristlichen Theologiegeschichte und zur Entstehung des
neutestamentlichen Kanons,* WUNT 204 (Tübingen: Mohr Siebeck, 2007), 105–46.

58. Anthony Le Donne, "Theological Distortion in the Jesus Tradition: A Study in Social
Memory Theory," in *Memory in the Bible and Antiquity,* ed. Loren T. Stuckenbruck, Stephen
Barton, and Benjamin G. Wold, WUNT 212 (Tübingen: Mohr Siebeck, 2007), 165.

59. Not all scholars applying social memory theory to the historical Jesus have abandoned
the criteria of authenticity. For example, Le Donne appeals to them in his larger study,
Historiographical Jesus, 87–88, 176, 195, 252n107, 265, 267.

the text. All three trends are rooted in previous and emerging dissatisfactions with the criteria of authenticity as a means of answering the question of Jesus's identity. In light of the widespread usage of the criteria of authenticity in the Third Quest for the historical Jesus, these scholarly opinions may also be signaling that quest's last breaths.[60] As something of a "second naiveté" writ large upon Jesus studies, the return to the text may be pointing toward the next era of Jesus scholarship.[61]

Conclusion

Jesus among Friends and Enemies contributes to Jesus studies against this larger background of scholars returning to the texts of the Gospels in order to understand the identity of (the historical) Jesus. This background is not necessarily a methodological requirement for the volume, for the individual contributors were not required to affirm the current authors' apprehension over the criteria of authenticity or their insistence that the narratives themselves must be the launching pad for discussing the historical Jesus. Rather, this background is appropriate because of the emphasis of the entire volume on the role of Jesus's friends and enemies in the Gospels' ultimate answers to the question "Who was (or is) Jesus?" As scholars advance discussion on Jesus's identity by first accounting for the narratives' respective answers to that question, these chapters highlight a crucial aspect of the narratives' answers—the characters of the Gospels. For, ultimately, whoever (the historical) Jesus was, he was not merely a speaker of wisdom, teacher of the law, or apocalyptic prophet. He was a person surrounded by contemporaries his whole ministry.

60. Similarly, Tilley claims the new research program evident in the work of Schüssler Fiorenza, Dunn, and Hurtado will "possibly supplant the third quest" ("Remembering the Historic Jesus," 5).

61. Paul Ricoeur, *The Symbolism of Evil*, trans. Emerson Buchanan (Boston: Beacon, 1967), 347–57, esp. 351. Ricoeur's concept of the second naiveté is concerned with philosophical, theological, and hermeneutical approaches to meaning and language as myth. He uses it to propose where readers (can) go once the introduction of criticism has destroyed the "primitive naiveté" of precritical textual encounters. Its relevance in the current discussion is due not so much to its theological/philosophical import as to its description of the critical enterprise. Jesus studies, as we have described them, have paralleled the path Ricoeur describes. After the introduction of critical approaches such as the criteria of authenticity disrupted the narratives of the Gospels and their interpretations of Jesus in search of "history," scholarship has returned to the surface level of the text. This return, however, is not to the original precritical position vis-à-vis the text but to a new understanding in light of what the criteria of authenticity, and scholars' attempts to use them, have taught us. Cf. Fredriksen, *From Jesus to Christ*, 94–97, on the difference between the "first reading" and "second reading," the latter of which is different from insistences upon explaining plausibly how Gospel tradition historically emerged but similar in its abandonment of the authentic/inauthentic dichotomy.

If we are to answer for ourselves the question of his identity, we must surely seek (the historical) Jesus among his friends and enemies.

Suggestions for Further Reading

Keener, Craig S. *The Historical Jesus of the Gospels*. Grand Rapids: Eerdmans, 2009.

Powell, Mark Allan. *Jesus as a Figure in History: How Modern Historians View the Man from Galilee*. Louisville: Westminster John Knox, 1998.

Witherington, Ben, III. *The Jesus Quest: The Third Search for the Jew of Nazareth*. 2nd ed. Downers Grove, IL: InterVarsity, 1997.

Bibliography

Abelson, J. *Jewish Mysticism: An Introduction to Kabbalah*. London: Bell and Sons, 1913.

Albinus, Lars. "The Greek δαίμων between Mythos and Logos." In *Die Dämon / Demons*, edited by Armin Lange, Hermann Lichtenberger, and K. F. Diethard Römheld, 425–46. Tübingen: Mohr Siebeck, 2003.

Alexander, Philip J. "The Demonology of the Dead Sea Scrolls." In *The Dead Sea Scrolls after Fifty Years: A Comprehensive Assessment*, edited by Peter W. Flint and James C. VanderKam, 2:331–53. 2 vols. Leiden: Brill, 1998–1999.

Allison, Dale C. "The Continuity between John and Jesus." *JSHJ* 1 (2003): 6–27.

———. *The Historical Christ and the Theological Jesus*. Grand Rapids: Eerdmans, 2009.

———. *Jesus of Nazareth: Millenarian Prophet*. Minneapolis: Fortress, 1998.

———. "A Plea for Thoroughgoing Eschatology." *JBL* 113 (1994): 651–68.

———. *Resurrecting Jesus: The Earliest Christian Tradition and Its Interpreters*. New York: T&T Clark, 2005.

The Ante-Nicene Fathers. Edited by Alexander Roberts and James Donaldson. 1885–1887. 10 vols. Repr., Peabody, MA: Hendrickson, 1994.

Arkin, Moshe. "'One of the Marys . . .': An Interdisciplinary Analysis of Michelangelo's Florentine Pieta." *The Art Bulletin* 79 (1997): 493–517.

Atwood, Richard. *Mary Magdalene in the New Testament Gospels and Early Tradition*. European Studies 23, no. 457. Bern: Peter Lang, 1993.

Augustine. *The City of God*. Translated by Marcus Dods. In vol. 2 of *The Nicene and Post-Nicene Fathers*, Series 1.

———. *The Harmony of the Gospels*. Translated by S. D. F. Salmond. In vol. 6 of *The Nicene and Post-Nicene Fathers*, Series 1.

The Babylonian Talmud: A Translation and Commentary. Vol. 16, *Tractate Sanhedrin*. Translated by Jacob Neusner. Peabody, MA: Hendrickson, 2005.

Barrett, C. K. *The Gospel according to St John: An Introduction with Commentary and Notes on the Greek Text*. 2nd ed. London: SPCK, 1978.

Barrick, W. Boyd. "The Rich Man from Arimathea (Matt. 27:57–60) and 1Q1SA." *JBL* 96 (1977): 235–39.

Bassler, Jouette M. "Nicodemus in the Fourth Gospel." *JBL* 108 (1989): 635–46.

Bauckham, Richard. "The Beloved Disciple as Ideal Author." *JSNT* 49 (1993): 21–44.

———. *Gospel Women: Studies of the Named Women in the Gospels.* Grand Rapids: Eerdmans / Edinburgh: T&T Clark, 2002.

———. "James and the Gentiles (Acts 15:13–21)." In *History, Literature and Society in the Book of Acts,* edited by Ben Witherington III, 154–84. Cambridge: Cambridge University Press, 1996.

———. "James and the Jerusalem Church." In *The Book of Acts in Its Palestinian Setting,* edited by Richard Bauckham, 417–27. Carlisle, UK: Paternoster / Grand Rapids: Eerdmans, 1995.

———. *Jesus and the Eyewitnesses: The Gospels as Eyewitness Testimony.* Grand Rapids: Eerdmans, 2006.

———. "John for Readers of Mark." In *The Gospels for All Christians: Rethinking the Gospel Audiences,* edited by Richard Bauckham, 147–71. Edinburgh: T&T Clark, 1998.

———. *Jude and the Relatives of Jesus in the Early Church.* Edinburgh: T&T Clark, 1990.

———. "Mary of Clopas (John 19:25)." In *Women in the Biblical Tradition,* edited by George J. Brooke, 231–55. Studies in Women and Religion 31. Lewiston, NY: Edwin Mellen, 1992.

———. *The Testimony of the Beloved Disciple: Narrative, History, and Theology in the Gospel of John.* Grand Rapids: Baker Academic, 2007.

———. "Traditions about the Tomb of James the Brother of Jesus." In *Poussières de christianisme et de judaïsme antiques: Études reunites en l'honneur de Jean-Daniel Kaestli et Éric Junod,* edited by Albert Frey and Rémi Gounelle, 61–77. Lausanne, Switzerland: Éditions du Zèbre, 2007.

Beasley-Murray, George R. *John.* 2nd ed. WBC 36. Nashville: Nelson, 1999.

Beck, David R. *The Discipleship Paradigm: Readers and Anonymous Characters in the Fourth Gospel.* Biblical Interpretation Series 27. Leiden: Brill, 1997.

Berenson MacLean, Jennifer K. "The Divine Trickster." In *Feminist Companion to John,* edited by Amy-Jill Levine and Marianne Blickenstaff, 1:48–77. 2 vols. London: Sheffield Academic Press, 2003.

Berger, Klaus. *Die Auferstehung des Propheten und die Erhöhung des Menschensohnes: Traditionsgeschichtliche Untersuchungen zur Deutung des Geschickes Jesu in frühchristlichen Texten.* SUNT 13. Göttingen: Vandenhoeck and Ruprecht, 1976.

Best, Ernest. *Following Jesus: Discipleship in the Gospel of Mark.* JSNTSup 4. Sheffield: JSOT Press, 1981.

Bickerman, Elias. *From Ezra to the Last of the Maccabees.* New York: Schocken, 1962.

Bird, Michael F. *Are You the One Who Is to Come? The Historical Jesus and the Messianic Question.* Grand Rapids: Baker Academic, 2009.

———. "Jesus and the Revolutionaries: Did Jesus Call Israel to Repent of Nationalistic Ambitions?" *Colloquium* 38 (2006): 129–30.

Blomberg, Craig. *The Historical Reliability of John's Gospel*. Leicester, UK: Inter-Varsity, 2001.

Bock, Darrel L. *Jesus according to Scripture: Restoring the Portrait from the Gospels*. Grand Rapids: Baker Academic, 2002.

Boer, Esther A., de. *The Gospel of Mary: Beyond a Gnostic and a Biblical Mary Magdalene*. JSNTSup 260. London: T&T Clark, 2004.

———. *The Mary Magdalene Cover-Up: The Sources Behind the Myth*. Translated by John Bowden. London: T&T Clark, 2007.

Bond, Helen K. *Caiaphas: Friend of Rome and Judge of Jesus?* Louisville: Westminster John Knox, 2004.

———. *Pontius Pilate in History and Interpretation*. SNTSMS 100. Cambridge: Cambridge University Press, 1998.

Borg, Marcus J., and John Dominic Crossan. *The Last Week: What the Gospels Really Teach about Jesus's Final Days in Jerusalem*. London: SPCK, 2008.

Bovon, François. *Das Evangelium nach Lukas*. 4 vols. EKKNT 3. Neukirchen-Vluyn, Germany: Neukirchener Verlag, 1989–2009.

———. "Le privilege pascal de Marie-Madeleine." *NTS* 30 (1984): 50–62.

Brodie, Thomas L. *The Quest for the Origin of John's Gospel: A Source-Oriented Approach*. Oxford: Oxford University Press, 1993.

Brown, C. "What Was John the Baptist Doing?" *BBR* 7 (1997): 37–50.

Brown, Raymond E. *The Death of the Messiah: From Gethsemane to the Grave; A Commentary on the Passion Narratives in the Four Gospels*. 2 vols. ABRL. New Haven: Yale University Press, 2008.

———. *The Gospel according to John*. 2 vols. AB 29 and 29A. Garden City, NY: Doubleday, 1966–1970.

———. "Roles of Women in the Fourth Gospel." *TS* 36 (1975): 688–99.

Bruce, F. F. *Jesus and Christian Origins outside the New Testament*. Grand Rapids: Eerdmans, 1974.

Bucur, Bogdan G. "Matthew 18:10 in Early Christology and Pneumatology: A Contribution to the Study of Matthean *Wirkungsgeschichte*." *NovT* 49 (2007): 209–31.

Bultmann, Rudolf. *The History of the Synoptic Tradition*. Translated by John Marsh. New York: Harper & Row, 1963.

———. *The History of the Synoptic Tradition*. Translated by John Marsh. Rev. ed. Peabody, MA: Hendrickson, 1994.

———. *Jesus and the Word*. Translated by Louise Pettibone Smith and Ermimie Huntress Lantero. New York: Charles Scribner's Sons, 1934.

Burchard, Christopher. "*Joseph and Aseneth*: A New Translation and Introduction." In *The Old Testament Pseudepigrapha*, edited by James H. Charlesworth, 2:177–247. Garden City, NY: Doubleday, 1985.

Burridge, Richard A. *Four Gospels, One Jesus? A Symbolic Reading*. 2nd ed. Grand Rapids: Eerdmans, 2005.

Byrne, Brendan. "The Faith of the Beloved Disciple and the Community in John 20." *JSNT* 23 (1985): 83–97.

Caird, G. B. *The Language and Imagery of the Bible*. London: Duckworth, 1980.

Cameron, Ron, ed. *The Other Gospels: Noncanonical Gospel Texts*. Philadelphia: Westminster, 1982.

Carter, Warren. "Embodying God's Empire in Communal Practices: Matthew 6:1–18." In Fleer and Bland, *Preaching the Sermon on the Mount*, 22–35.

———. *John: Storyteller, Interpreter, Evangelist*. Peabody, MA: Hendrickson, 2006.

———. *Matthew: Storyteller, Interpreter, Evangelist*. Rev. ed. Peabody, MA: Hendrickson, 2004.

———. *Matthew and the Margins: A Sociopolitical and Religious Reading*. Maryknoll, NY: Orbis, 2000.

———. "Power and Identities: The Contexts of Matthew's Sermon on the Mount." In Fleer and Bland, *Preaching the Sermon on the Mount*, 8–21.

Charlesworth, James H. *The Beloved Disciple: Whose Witness Validates the Gospel of John?* Valley Forge, PA: Trinity Press International, 1995.

———. *The Historical Jesus: An Essential Guide*. Nashville: Abingdon, 2008.

———. "Introduction: Why Evaluate Twenty-Five Years of Jesus Research?" In Charlesworth and Pokorný, *Jesus Research*, 1–15.

———, ed. *The Old Testament Pseudepigrapha*. 2 vols. Garden City, NY: Doubleday, 1983–1985.

Charlesworth, James H., and Petr Pokorný, eds. *Jesus Research: An International Perspective*. Grand Rapids: Eerdmans, 2009.

Chilton, Bruce D., and Craig A. Evans, eds. *James the Just and Christian Origins*. NovTSup 98. Leiden: Brill, 1999.

———, eds. *The Missions of James, Peter and Paul*. NovTSup 115. Leiden: Brill, 2005.

Chilton, Bruce D., and Jacob Neusner, eds. *The Brother of Jesus: James the Just and His Mission*. Louisville: Westminster John Knox, 2001.

———, eds. *In Quest of the Historical Pharisees*. Waco: Baylor University Press, 2007.

Clivaz, Claire. "The Angel and the Sweat like 'Drops of Blood' (Luke 22:43–44): P69 and f13." *Harvard Theological Review* 98, no. 4 (2005): 419–40.

Collins, Adela Yarbro. *Mark*. Hermeneia. Minneapolis: Fortress, 2007.

Collins, John J. *The Apocalyptic Imagination*. 2nd ed. Grand Rapids: Eerdmans, 1998.

———. *Apocalypticism in the Dead Sea Scrolls*. New York: Routledge, 1997.

———. "Introduction: Towards the Morphology of a Genre." In *Apocalypse: The Morphology of a Genre*, edited by John J. Collins, 1–20. SemeiaSt 14. Missoula, MT: Scholars Press, 1979.

Collins, John N. "Did Luke Intend a Disservice to Women in the Martha and Mary Story?" *BTB* 28 (1998): 104–11.

Collins, Raymond F. *These Things Have Been Written: Studies on the Fourth Gospel*. Louvain, Belgium: Peeters, 1990.

Conway, Colleen M. "Minor Characters in the Fourth Gospel." *BibInt* 10 (2002): 324–41.

Cook, David. "Joseph and Aseneth." In *The Apocryphal Old Testament*, edited by H. F. D. Sparks, 473–503. Oxford: Oxford University Press, 1984.

Crossan, John Dominic. *The Birth of Christianity: Discovering What Happened in the Years Immediately after the Execution of Jesus*. Edinburgh: T&T Clark, 1999.

———. *The Cross That Spoke: The Origins of the Passion Narrative*. San Francisco: Harper & Row, 1988.

———. *Jesus: A Revolutionary Biography*. San Francisco: HarperSanFrancisco, 1994.

Crossan, John Dominic, Luke Timothy Johnson, and Werner H. Kelber. *The Jesus Controversy: Perspectives in Conflict*. The Rockwell Lecture Series. Harrisburg, PA: Trinity Press International, 1999.

Crossan, John Dominic, and Jonathan L. Reed. *Excavating Jesus: Beneath the Stones, behind the Texts*. London: SPCK, 2001.

Crossley, James G. "Against the Historical Plausibility of the Empty Tomb Story and the Bodily Resurrection of Jesus: A Response to N. T. Wright." *JSHJ* 3 (2005): 171–86.

Csányi, Daniel A. "Optima Pars: Die Auslegungsgeschichte von Luke 10, 38–42 bei den Kirchenvätern der ersten vier Jahrhunderte." *StudMon* 2 (1960): 5–78.

Culpepper, R. Alan. *Anatomy of the Fourth Gospel: A Study in Literary Design*. FF. Philadelphia: Fortress, 1983.

———. *John, the Son of Zebedee: The Life of a Legend*. Columbia: University of South Carolina Press, 1994. Repr., Minneapolis: Fortress, 2000.

Cureton, William, ed. and trans. *Spicilegium Syriacum: Containing Remains of Bardesan, Meliton, Ambrose and Mara Bar Serapion*. London: Rivingtons, 1855. Repr., Lexington: American Theological Library Association, 1965.

Dapaah, D. S. *The Relationship between John the Baptist and Jesus of Nazareth: A Critical Study*. Lanham, MD: University of America Press, 2005.

Darr, John A. *Herod the Fox: Audience Criticism and Lukan Characterization*. JSNTSup 163. Sheffield: Sheffield Academic Press, 1998.

Davidson, Maxwell G. *Angels at Qumran: A Comparative Study of 1 Enoch 1–36, 72–108 and the Sectarian Writings from Qumran*. Journal for the Study of the Pseudepigrapha: Supplement Series 11. Sheffield: JSOT Press, 1992.

Davies, W. D., and Dale C. Allison. *The Gospel according to Saint Matthew*. 3 vols. ICC. Edinburgh: T&T Clark, 1988.

DeConick, April D. *The Thirteenth Apostle: What the Gospel of Judas Really Says*. Rev. ed. London: Continuum, 2007.

Dodd, C. H. *The Founder of Christianity*. New York: Macmillan, 1970.

———. "The Prophecy of Caiaphas (Jn xi 47–53)." In *Neotestamentica et Patristica*, 134–43. NovTSup 6. Leiden: Brill, 1962.

Donaldson, Terence L. "Guiding Readers–Making Disciples: Discipleship in Matthew's Narrative Strategy." In *Patterns of Discipleship in the New Testament*, edited by Richard N. Longenecker, 30–49. Grand Rapids: Eerdmans, 1996.

Dunderberg, Ismo. *The Beloved Disciple in Conflict? Revisiting the Gospels of John and Thomas*. Oxford: Oxford University Press, 2006.

Dunn, James D. G. *Jesus and the Spirit: A Study of the Religious and Charismatic Experience of Jesus and the First Christians as Reflected in the New Testament.* London: SCM, 1975.

————. *Jesus Remembered.* CM 1. Grand Rapids: Eerdmans, 2003.

————. *A New Perspective on Jesus: What the Quest for the Historical Jesus Missed.* London: SPCK, 2005.

Edwards, Richard A. "Uncertain Faith: Matthew's Portrait of the Disciples," in *Discipleship in the New Testament,* edited by Fernando F. Segovia, 47–61. Philadelphia: Fortress, 1985.

Ehrman, Bart. *Jesus: Apocalyptic Prophet of the New Millennium.* New York: Oxford University Press, 1999.

————. *The Lost Gospel of Judas Iscariot: A New Look at Betrayer and Betrayed.* Oxford: Oxford University Press, 2006.

————. *Peter, Paul, and Mary Magdalene: The Followers of Jesus in History and Legend.* Oxford: Oxford University Press, 2006.

Elliott, J. K. ed. *The Apocryphal New Testament: A Collection of Apocryphal Christian Literature in an English Translation Based on M. R. James.* Oxford: Oxford University Press, 1993.

Ernst, Allie M. *Martha from the Margins: The Authority of Martha in Early Christian Tradition.* VCSup 98. Leiden: Brill, 2009.

Ernst, Josef. *Johannes der Täufer: Interpretation–Geschichte–Wirkungsgeschichte.* Beihefte zur Zeitschrift für die neutestamentliche Wissenschaft 53. Berlin: De Gruyter, 1989.

————. *Johannes der Täufer: Der Lehrer Jesu?* Freiburg, Germany: Herder, 1994.

Esler, Philip E., and Ronald Piper. *Lazarus, Mary, and Martha: Social Scientific Approaches to the Gospel of John.* Minneapolis: Fortress, 2006.

Evans, C. Stephen. *The Historical Christ and the Jesus of Faith: The Incarnational Narrative as History.* Oxford: Clarendon, 1996.

Evans, Craig A. "The Gospel of Judas and the Other Gospels." In *The Gospel of Judas,* edited by R. Kasser, M. Meyer, and G. Wurst, 103–24. 2nd ed. Washington, DC: National Geographic, 2008.

————. "Inaugurating the Kingdom of God and Defeating the Kingdom of Heaven." *BBR* 15, no. 1 (2005): 49–75.

————. "Jesus in Non-Christian Sources." In Green, McKnight, and Marshall, *Dictionary of Jesus and the Gospels,* 364–65.

————. *Mark 8:27–16:20.* WBC 34B. Nashville: Nelson, 2001.

Evans, Craig A., and N. T. Wright. *Jesus, the Final Days.* Edited by Troy A. Miller. London: SPCK, 2008.

Falk, Harvey. *Jesus the Pharisee.* Eugene, OR: Wipf and Stock, 1985.

Fitzmeyer, Joseph A. *The Acts of the Apostles.* AB 31. New York: Doubleday, 1998.

Fleer, David, and David Bland, eds. *Preaching the Sermon on the Mount: The World It Imagines.* St. Louis: Chalice, 2007.

Foster, Paul. "Are There Any Early Fragments of the So-Called *Gospel of Peter*?" *NTS* 52 (2006): 1–28.

France, R. T. *The Gospel of Mark: A Commentary on the Greek Text*. NIGTC. Grand Rapids: Eerdmans 2002.

Fredriksen, Paula. *From Jesus to Christ: The Origins of the New Testament Images of Jesus*. New Haven: Yale University Press, 1988.

Frey, Jörg. "Die Apokalyptik als Herausforderung der neutestamentlichen Wissenschaft. Zum Problem: Jesus und die Apokalyptik." In *Apokalyptik als Herausforderung neutestamentlicher Theologie*, edited by Michael Becker and Markus Öhler, 23–94. WUNT 2.214. Tübingen: Mohr Siebeck, 2006.

Funk, Robert W., and Roy W. Hoover. *The Five Gospels: The Search for the Authentic Words of Jesus*. New York: Macmillan, 1993.

Garrett, Susan R. "Jesus and the Angels." *Word and World* 29, no. 2 (Spring 2009): 162–69.

———. *No Ordinary Angel: Celestial Spirits and Christian Claims about Christ*. New Haven: Yale University Press, 2008.

Gaventa, Beverly Roberts. *Mary: Glimpses of the Mother of Jesus*. Edinburgh: T&T Clark, 1999.

Gaventa, Beverly Roberts, and Richard B. Hays. "Seeking the Identity of Jesus." In *Seeking the Identity of Jesus: A Pilgrimage*, edited by Beverly Roberts Gaventa and Richard B. Hays, 1–24. Grand Rapids: Eerdmans, 2008.

Gillman, Florence M. *Herodias: At Home in That Fox's Den*. Collegeville, MN: Liturgical Press, 2003.

Goodblatt, David. *The Monarchic Principle: Studies in Jewish Self-Government in Antiquity*. TSAJ 38. Tübingen: Mohr Siebeck, 1994.

Goodman, Martin. *The Ruling Class of Judaea: The Origins of the Jewish Revolt against Rome, AD 66–70*. Cambridge: Cambridge University Press, 1987.

Goodspeed, Edgar J. *The Twelve: The Story of Christ's Apostles*. New York: Collier, 1962.

Grabbe, Lester L. *Judaism from Cyrus to Hadrian*. 2 vols. Minneapolis: Augsburg, 1992.

Green, Joel B. *The Theology of the Gospel of Luke*. Cambridge: Cambridge University Press, 1995.

Green, Joel B., Scot McKnight, and I. Howard Marshall, eds. *Dictionary of Jesus and the Gospels*. Downers Grove, IL: InterVarsity, 1992.

Gregory the Great. *Forty Gospel Homilies*. Edited by David Hurst. Cistercian Studies Series 123. Kalamazoo, MI: Cistercian Publications, 1990.

Griffith-Jones, Robin. *Beloved Disciple: The Misunderstood Legacy of Mary Magdalene, the Woman Closest to Jesus*. New York: HarperOne, 2008.

Gundry, Robert H. *Mark: A Commentary on His Apology for the Cross*. Grand Rapids: Eerdmans, 1993.

———. "New Wine in Old Wineskins: Bursting Traditional Interpretations of John's Gospel (Part I)." *BBR* 17, no. 1 (2007): 115–30.

Haacker, Klaus. "Die moderne historische Jesus-Forschung als hermeneutisches Problem." *TBei* 31 (2000): 60–74.

———. "'What Must I Do to Inherit Eternal Life?' Implicit Christology in Jesus's Sayings about Life and Kingdom." In Charlesworth and Pokorný, *Jesus Research*, 140–53.

Hanson K. C., and Douglas E. Oakman. *Palestine in the Time of Jesus*. Minneapolis: Fortress, 1998.

Harvey, A. E. *Jesus on Trial: A Study in the Fourth Gospel*. London: SPCK, 1976.

Heard, W. J., and Craig A. Evans. "Revolutionary Movements, Jewish." In *Dictionary of New Testament Background*, edited by Craig A. Evans and Stanley E. Porter, 937–42. Downers Grove, IL: InterVarsity, 2000.

Hengel, Martin. "Maria Magdalena und die Frauen als Zeugen." In *Abraham unser Vater: Juden und Christen im Gespräch über die Bibel: Festschrift für Otto Michel zum 60. Geburtstag*, edited by Otto Betz, Martin Hengel, and Peter Schmidt, 243–56. AGJU 5. Leiden: Brill, 1963.

Hillmer, Melvyn R. "They Believed in Him: Discipleship in the Johannine Tradition." In Longenecker, *Patterns of Discipleship*, 77–97.

Holzmeister, Urban. "Die Magdalenenfrage in der kirchlichen Überlieferung." *ZKG* 46 (1922): 402–22, 556–84.

Hooker, Morna D. *The Gospel according to Saint Mark*. BNTC 2. London: A and C Black / Peabody, MA: Hendrickson, 1991.

———. "On Using the Wrong Tool." *Theology* 75 (1972): 570–81.

Horsley, Richard A. *Jesus and Empire: The Kingdom of God and the New World Disorder*. Minneapolis: Fortress, 2003.

Hurtado, Larry W. *The Earliest Christian Artifacts: Manuscripts and Christian Origins*. Grand Rapids: Eerdmans, 2006.

———. "Following Jesus in the Gospel of Mark—and Beyond." In Longenecker, *Patterns of Discipleship*, 9–29.

———. "God." In Green, McKnight, and Marshall, *Dictionary of Jesus and the Gospels*, 270–76.

———. *Lord Jesus Christ: Devotion to Jesus in Earliest Christianity*. Grand Rapids: Eerdmans, 2003.

———. "A Taxonomy of Recent Historical-Jesus Work." In *Whose Historical Jesus?* edited by William E. Arnal and Michel Desjardins, 272–95. ESCJ 7. Waterloo, ON: Wilfrid Laurier University Press, 1997.

———. "The Women, the Tomb, and the Climax of Mark." In *A Wandering Galilean: Essays in Honour of Seán Freyne*, edited by Zuleika Rodgers, Margaret Daly-Denton, and Anne Fitzpatrick McKinley, 427–51. Leiden: Brill, 2009.

Hylen, Susan E. *Imperfect Believers: Ambiguous Characters in the Gospel of John*. Louisville: Westminster John Knox, 2009.

Irenaeus. *Against Heresies*. In vol. 1 of *The Ante-Nicene Fathers*.

Jansen, Katherine Ludwig. *The Making of the Magdalen: Preaching and Popular Devotion in the Later Middle Ages*. Princeton: Princeton University Press, 2000.

Jensen, Morten Hørning. *Herod Antipas in Galilee: The Literary and Archaeological Sources on the Reign of Herod Antipas and Its Socioeconomic Impact on Galilee.* WUNT 2.215. Tübingen: Mohr Siebeck, 2006.

Jonge, Marinus, de. "Messiah." In *Anchor Bible Dictionary*, edited by David Noel Freedman, 4:777–88. New York: Doubleday, 1992.

Josephus. Translated by H. St. J. Thackeray et al. 12 vols. LCL. Cambridge, MA: Harvard University Press, 1926–1981.

Joynes, Christine E. "The Returned Elijah? John the Baptist's Angelic Identity in the Gospel of Mark." *SJT* 58, no. 4 (2005): 455–67.

Justin Martyr. *Writings of Saint Justin Martyr.* Translated by Thomas B. Falls. Fathers of the Church 6. Washington, DC: Catholic University of America Press, 1948.

Kähler, Martin. *The So-Called Historical Jesus and the Historic Biblical Christ.* Translated by Carl E. Braaten. SemEd. Philadelphia: Fortress, 1964.

Käsemann, Ernst. *Essays on New Testament Themes.* Translated by W. J. Montague. SBT 41. London: SCM, 1964.

Keener, Craig S. *The Historical Jesus of the Gospels.* Grand Rapids: Eerdmans, 2009.

Keightley, Georgia Masters. "The Church's Memory of Jesus: A Social Science Analysis of 1 Thessalonians." *BTB* 17 (1987): 149–56.

Keith, Chris. "The Claim of John 7.15 and the Memory of Jesus' Literacy." *NTS* 56, no. 1 (2010): 44–63.

———. *Jesus's Literacy: Scribal Culture and the Teacher from Galilee.* LHJS/LNTS 413. London: T&T Clark, 2011.

———. *The "Pericope Adulterae," the Gospel of John, and the Literacy of Jesus.* NTTSD 38. Leiden: Brill, 2009.

Kelhoffer, James A. *The Diet of John the Baptist: "Locusts and Wild Honey" in the Synoptic and Patristic Interpretation.* WUNT 176. Tübingen: Mohr Siebeck, 2005.

King, Karen L. *What Is Gnosticism?* Cambridge, MA: Harvard University Press, 2003.

Kingsbury, Jack Dean. *Conflict in Luke: Jesus, Authorities, Disciples.* Minneapolis: Fortress, 1991.

———. *Conflict in Mark: Jesus, Authorities, Disciples.* Minneapolis: Fortress, 1989.

———. *Matthew as Story.* Philadelphia: Fortress, 1986.

Kirk, Alan. "The Johannine Jesus in the Gospel of Peter: A Social Memory Approach." In *Jesus in Johannine Tradition*, edited by Robert T. Fortna and Tom Thatcher, 313–21. Louisville: Westminster John Knox, 2001.

Kirk, Alan, and Tom Thatcher. "Jesus Tradition as Social Memory." In Kirk and Thatcher, *Memory, Tradition, and Text*, 25–42.

———, eds. *Memory, Tradition, and Text: Uses of the Past in Early Christianity.* SemeiaSt 52. Atlanta: Society of Biblical Literature, 2005.

Klutz, Todd E. "The Grammar of Exorcisim in the Ancient Mediterranean World." In *The Jewish Roots of Christological Monotheism*, edited by Carey C. Newman, James R. Davila, and Gladys S. Lewis, 156–65. Journal for the Study of Judaism Supplement Series 63. Leiden: Brill, 1999.

Kokkinos, Nikos. *The Herodian Dynasty: Origins, Role in Society and Eclipse*. Journal for the Study of the Pseudepigrapha: Supplement Series 30. Sheffield: Sheffield Academic Press, 1998.

Kraeling, C. H. *John the Baptist*. New York: Scribner's, 1951.

Kraus, Matthew. "New Jewish Directions in the Study of the Fourth Gospel." In *New Currents through John: A Global Perspective*, edited by Francisco Lozada Jr. and Tom Thatcher, 141–66. RBS 54. Atlanta: Society of Biblical Literature, 2006.

Krosney, Herbert. *The Lost Gospel: The Quest for the Gospel of Judas Iscariot*. Washington, DC: National Geographic, 2006.

Kurek-Chomycz, Dominika, and Reimund Bieringer. "Guardians of the Old at the Dawn of the New: The Role of Angels according to the Pauline Letters." In *Angels: The Concept of Celestial Beings—Origins, Development and Reception*, edited by Friedrich V. Reiterer, Tobias Nicklas, and Karin Schopflin, 325–55. Deuterocanonical and Cognate Literature Yearbook 2007. Berlin: De Gruyter, 2007.

Le Donne, Anthony. *The Historiographical Jesus: Memory, Typology, and the Son of David*. Waco: Baylor University Press, 2009.

———. "Theological Distortion in the Jesus Tradition: A Study in Social Memory Theory." In *Memory in the Bible and Antiquity*, edited by Loren T. Stuckenbruck, Stephen Barton, and Benjamin G. Wold, 163–77. WUNT 212. Tübingen: Mohr Siebeck, 2007.

Levine, Amy-Jill. "Luke's Pharisees." In *In Quest of the Historical Pharisees*, edited by Bruce Chilton and Jacob Neusner, 113–30. Waco: Baylor University Press, 2007.

Lincoln, Andrew T. "The Beloved Disciple as Eyewitness and the Fourth Gospel as Witness." *JSNT* 24 (2002): 3–26.

———. *Truth on Trial: The Lawsuit Motif in the Fourth Gospel*. Peabody, MA: Hendrickson, 2000.

Lindars, Barnabas. *The Gospel of John*. NCB. London: Oliphant, Marshall, Morgan and Scott, 1972.

Longenecker, Richard N. "Taking Up the Cross Daily: Discipleship in Luke-Acts." In Longenecker, *Patterns of Discipleship*, 50–76.

———, ed. *Patterns of Discipleship in the New Testament*. Grand Rapids: Eerdmans, 1996.

Lucian. *The Works of Lucian*. Translated by A. M. Harmon. 8 vols. LCL. Cambridge, MA: Harvard University Press, 1913–1967.

Lyons, William John. "The Hermeneutics of Fictional Black and Factual Red: The Markan Simon of Cyrene and the Quest for the Historical Jesus." *JSHJ* 4 (2006): 139–54.

———. "On the Life and Death of Joseph of Arimathea." *JSHJ* 2 (2004): 29–53.

Marjanen, Antti. "Mary Magdalene, a Beloved Disciple." In *Mariam, the Magdalen, and the Mother*, edited by Deirdre Good, 49–61. Bloomington: Indiana University Press, 2005.

———. *The Woman Jesus Loved: Mary Magdalene in the Nag Hammadi Library and Related Documents*. NHMS 40. Leiden: Brill, 1996.

Marshall, I. Howard. *The Gospel of Luke*. NIGTC. Grand Rapids: Eerdmans, 1978.

Martyn, J. Louis. *History and Theology in the Fourth Gospel.* Louisville: Westminster John Knox, 2003.

Mason, Steve. *Josephus and the New Testament.* 2nd rev. ed. Peabody, MA: Hendrickson, 2003.

———. "Josephus' Pharisees: The Narratives." In Chilton and Neusner, *In Quest of the Historical Pharisees,* 3–40.

Matera, Frank. *What Are They Saying about Mark?* New York: Paulist Press, 1987.

McDonald, Lee Martin. *The Biblical Canon: Its Origin, Transmission, and Authority.* 3rd ed. Peabody, MA: Hendrickson, 2007.

McHugh, John. *The Mother of Jesus in the New Testament.* London: Darton, Longman & Todd, 1975.

McKnight, Scot. *Jesus and His Death: Historiography, the Historical Jesus, and Atonement Theory.* Waco: Baylor University Press, 2005.

McLaren, James S. *Power and Politics in Palestine: The Jews and the Governing of Their Land, 100 BC–AD 70.* JSNTSup 63. Sheffield: JSOT Press, 1991.

Meeks, Wayne A. "The Man from Heaven in Johannine Sectarianism." *JBL* 91 (1972): 44–72.

Meier, John P. "The Historical Jesus and the Historical Herodians." *JBL* 119 (2000): 740–46.

———. *A Marginal Jew: Rethinking the Historical Jesus.* Vol. 2, *Mentor, Message, and Miracles.* ABRL. New York: Doubleday, 1994.

———. *A Marginal Jew: Rethinking the Historical Jesus.* Vol. 3, *Companions and Competitors.* ABRL. New York: Doubleday, 2001.

Metzger, Bruce. *A Textual Commentary on the Greek New Testament.* 2nd ed. Stuttgart: German Bible Society, 1994.

Metzger, Bruce M., and Bart D. Ehrman. *The Text of the New Testament: Its Transmission, Corruption, and Restoration.* 4th ed. New York: Oxford University Press, 2005.

Meyer, Marvin, and Esther de Boer, eds. *The Gospels of Mary: The Secret Tradition of Mary Magdalene, the Companion of Jesus.* San Francisco: HarperSanFrancisco, 2004.

Miller, Robert J., ed. *The Complete Gospels: Annotated Scholars Version.* Rev. and exp. ed. Santa Rosa, CA: Polebridge, 1994.

Minear, Paul S. "The Original Functions of John 21." *JBL* 102 (1983): 85–98.

Munro, Winsome. "The Pharisee and the Samaritan in John: Polar or Parallel?" *CBQ* 57 (1995): 710–28.

Murphy, Catherine M. *John the Baptist: Prophet of Purity for a New Age.* Collegeville, MN: Liturgical Press, 2003.

Murphy-O'Connor, Jerome. "John the Baptist and Jesus: History and Hypothesis." *NTS* 36 (1990): 359–74.

Myllykoski, Matti. "What Happened to the Body of Jesus?" In *Fair Play: Diversity and Conflicts in Early Christianity: Essays in Honour of Heikki Räisänen,* edited by Ismo Dunderberg, C. M. Tuckett, and Kari Syreeni, 43–82. NovTSup 103. Leiden: Brill, 2002.

The Nag Hammadi Library in English. Edited by Marvin W. Meyer. Leiden: Brill, 1977.

The Nag Hammadi Library in English. Edited by James M. Robinson. 4th ed. Leiden: Brill, 1996.

The Nag Hammadi Scriptures. Edited by Marvin Meyer. Rev. ed. New York: HarperOne, 2009.

Neirynck, Frans. "The Anonymous Disciple in John 1." *ETL* 66 (1990): 5–37.

———. "The 'Other Disciple' in John 18:15–16." *ETL* 51 (1975): 113–41.

Netzer, Ehud. *The Architecture of Herod the Great Builder*. Grand Rapids: Baker Academic, 2006.

Neusner, Jacob. "The Rabbinic Traditions about the Pharisees before 70 CE." In Chilton and Neusner, *In Quest of the Historical Pharisees*, 297–313.

The Nicene and Post-Nicene Fathers. Series 1. Edited by Philip Schaff. 1886–1889. 14 vols. Repr. Peabody, MA: Hendrickson, 1994.

Oakeshott, Philip. "How unlike an Angel: The Youth in Mark 16." *Theology* 111, (September/October 2008): 321–69.

O'Collins, Gerald, and Daniel Kendall. "Did Joseph of Arimathea Exist?" *Bib*. 75 (1994): 235–41.

The Old Testament Pseudepigrapha. Edited by James H. Charlesworth. 2 vols. Garden City, NY: Doubleday, 1983–1985.

Olson, Ken. "A Eusebian Reading of the *Testimonium Flavianum*. Paper presented at the annual meeting of the Society of Biblical Literature. New Orleans, LA, November 23, 2009.

Origen. *Contra Celsum*. Translated by Henry Chadwick. Corrected ed. Cambridge: Cambridge University Press, 1965.

———. *Homilies on Luke; Fragments on Luke*. Translated by J. T. Lienhard. Fathers of the Church 94. Washington, DC: Catholic University of America Press, 1999.

Painter, John. *Just James: The Brother of Jesus in History and Tradition*. Columbia: University of South Carolina Press, 1997.

Patterson, Stephen J., James M. Robinson, and Hans-Gebhard Bethge. *The Fifth Gospel: The Gospel of Thomas Comes of Age*. Harrisburg, PA: Trinity Press International, 1998.

Penn, Michael Philip. *Kissing Christians: Ritual Community in the Late Ancient Church*. Divinations: Rereading Late Ancient Religion. Philadelphia: University of Pennsylvania Press, 2005.

Perrin, Norman. *Jesus and the Language of the Kingdom: Symbol and Metaphor in New Testament Interpretation*. Philadelphia: Fortress, 1976.

Philo. Translated by F. H. Colson and G. H. Whitaker. 10 vols. LCL. London: Heinemann, 1929–1962.

Pliny the Younger. *Letters and Panegyricus*. Translated by Betty Radice. 2 vols. LCL. Cambridge, MA: Harvard University Press, 1972–1975.

Plisch, Uwe-Karsten. *The Gospel of Thomas: Original Text with Commentary*. Translated by Gesine Schenke Robinson. Stuttgart: Deutsche Bibelgesellschaft, 2008.

Pokorný, Petr. Preface to Charlesworth and Pokorný, *Jesus Research*, xxi–xxii.

Porter, Stanley E. *The Criteria for Authenticity in Historical-Jesus Research: Previous Discussion and New Proposals.* JSNTSup 191. Sheffield: Sheffield Academic Press, 2000.

———. "A Dead End or a New Beginning? Examing the Criteria for Authenticity in Light of Albert Schweitzer." In Charlesworth and Pokorný, *Jesus Research*, 16–35.

———. "Reading the Gospels and the Quest for the Historical Jesus." In *Reading the Gospels Today*, edited by Stanley E. Porter, 27–55. MNTS. Grand Rapids: Eerdmans, 2004.

Porter, Stanley E., ed. *The Messiah in the Old and New Testaments.* Grand Rapids: Eerdmans, 2007.

Powell, Mark Allan. "The Religious Leaders in Luke: A Literary-Critical Study." *JBL* 109 (1990): 93–110.

Przybylski, Benno. *Righteousness in Matthew and His World of Thought.* SNTSMS 41. Cambridge: Cambridge University Press, 1980.

Quarles, Charles L. "The Gospel of Peter: Does It Contain a Precanonical Resurrection Narrative?" In *The Resurrection of Jesus: John Dominic Crossan and N. T. Wright in Dialogue*, edited by Robert B. Stewart, 106–20. Minneapolis: Fortress, 2006.

Quast, Kevin. *Peter and the Beloved Disciple: Figures for a Community in Crisis.* JSNTSup 32. Sheffield: JSOT Press, 1989.

Rausch, Thomas P. *Who Is Jesus? An Introduction to Christology.* Collegeville, MN: Liturgical Press, 2003.

Reinhartz, Adele. "From Narrative to History: The Resurrection of Mary and Martha." In *"Women Like This": New Perspectives on Jewish Women in the Greco-Roman World*, 161–84. SBLEJL 1. Atlanta: Scholars Press, 1991.

———. "The Gospel of John: How 'the Jews' Became Part of the Plot." In *Jesus, Judaism and Christian Anti-Judaism: Reading the New Testament after the Holocaust*, edited by Paula Fredriksen and Adele Reinhartz, 99–116. Louisville: Westminster John Knox, 2002.

Rensberger, David. *Johannine Faith and Liberating Community.* Philadelphia: Westminster, 1988.

Renz, Gabi. "Nicodemus: An Ambiguous Disciple? A Narrative Sensitive Investigation." In *Challenging Perspectives on the Gospel of John*, edited by John Lierman, 255–83. WUNT 2.219. Tübingen: Mohr Siebeck, 2006.

Rhoads, David, Joanna Dewey, and Donald Michie. *Mark as Story: An Introduction to the Narrative of a Gospel.* 2nd ed. Minneapolis: Fortress, 1999.

Ricci, Carla. *Mary Magdalene and Many Others: Women Who Followed Jesus.* Translated by Paul Burns. Minneapolis: Fortress, 1994.

Richardson, Peter. *Herod: King of the Jews and Friend of the Romans.* Columbia: University of South Carolina Press, 1996.

Ricoeur, Paul. *The Symbolism of Evil.* Translated by Emerson Buchanan. Boston: Beacon, 1967.

Robinson, John A. T. *The Priority of John.* London: SCM, 1985.

Rochais, Gérard. *Les récits de resurrection des morts dans le Nouveau Testament.* SNTSMS 40. Cambridge: Cambridge University Press, 1981.

Rodríguez, Rafael. "Authenticating Criteria: The Use and Misuse of a Critical Method." *JSHJ* 7 (2009): 152–67.

Rothschild, Clare K. *Baptist Traditions and Q.* WUNT 190. Tübingen: Mohr Siebeck, 2005.

Rowe, C. Kavin. *Early Narrative Christology: The Lord in the Gospel of Luke.* Grand Rapids: Baker Academic, 2006.

Rubio, Fernando Bermejo. "The Fiction of the 'Three Quests': An Argument for Dismantling a Dubious Historiographical Paradigm." *JSHJ* 7 (2009): 211–53.

Ruschmann, Susanne. *Maria von Magdala im Johannesevangelium: Jüngerin–Zeugin–Lebensbotin.* NTAbh 40. Münster: Aschendorff, 2002.

Sanders, E. P. *Jesus and Judaism.* Philadelphia: Fortress, 1985.

———. *Judaism: Practice and Belief, 63 BCE–66 CE.* London: SCM, 1992.

Schaberg, Jane. *The Resurrection of Mary Magdalene: Legends, Apocrypha, and the Christian Testament.* New York: Continuum, 2002.

Schäfer, Peter. *Jesus in the Talmud.* Princeton: Princeton University Press, 2007.

Schnackenburg, Rudolf. *The Gospel according to St. John.* Translated by Kevin Smyth, David Smith, and G. A. Kon. 3 vols. HTKNT. London: Burns and Oates, 1968–1982.

Scholem, Gershom. *Major Trends in Jewish Mysticism.* New York: Schocken, 1995.

Schröter, Jens. *Erinnerung an Jesu Worte: Studien zur Rezeption der Logienüberlieferung in Markus, Q und Thomas.* WMANT 76. Neukirchen-Vluyn, Germany: Neukirchener Verlag, 1997.

———. "The Historical Jesus and the Sayings Tradition: Comments on Current Research." *Neot* 30, no. 1 (1996): 151–68.

———. "Von der Historizität der Evangelien: Ein Beitrag zur gegenwärtigen Diskussion um den historischen Jesus." In *Von Jesus zum Neuen Testament: Studien zur urchristlichen Theologiegeschichte und zur Entstehung des neutestamentlichen Kanons*, 105–46. WUNT 204. Tübingen: Mohr Siebeck, 2007.

Schürer, Emil. *The History of the Jewish People in the Age of Jesus Christ (175 BC–AD 135).* Translated and edited by Geza Vermes, Fergus Millar, and Matthew Black. 3 vols. Edinburgh: T&T Clark, 1973–1986.

Schüssler Fiorenza, Elisabeth. *But She Said: Feminist Practices of Biblical Interpretation.* Boston: Beacon, 1992.

———. *Jesus and the Politics of Interpretation.* New York: Continuum, 2000.

Schwartz, Daniel R. "Pontius Pilate." In *Anchor Bible Dictionary*, edited by David Noel Freedman, 5:395–401. New York: Doubleday, 1992.

Schweitzer, Albert. *The Quest of the Historical Jesus: A Critical Study of Its Progress from Reimarus to Wrede.* Translated by W. Montgomery. 3rd ed. London: Black, 1954.

———. *The Quest of the Historical Jesus: A Critical Study of Its Progress from Reimarus to Wrede.* Translated by F. C. Burkitt. Baltimore: Johns Hopkins University Press, 1998.

Scobie, C. H. H. *John the Baptist.* Philadelphia: Fortress, 1964.

Segovia, Fernando F. "'Peace I Leave with You; My Peace I Give to You': Discipleship in the Fourth Gospel." In Segovia, *Discipleship in the New Testament*, 76–102.

———, ed. *Discipleship in the New Testament*. Philadelphia: Fortress, 1985.

Smith, Yancy Warren. "Hippolytus' Commentary on the Song of Songs in Social and Critical Context." PhD diss., Texas Christian University, 2009.

Snyder, Graydon F. *Ante Pacem: Archaeological Evidence of Church Life before Constantine*. Macon, GA: Mercer University Press, 1985.

Snyder, H. Gregory. *Teachers and Texts in the Ancient World: Philosophers, Jews and Christians*. Religion in the First Christian Centuries. New York: Routledge, 2000.

Sorensen, Eric. *Possession and Exorcism in the New Testament and Early Christianity*. WUNT 2.157. Tübingen: Mohr Siebeck, 2002.

Stein, Robert H. "The 'Criteria' for Authenticity." In *Gospel Perspectives: Studies of History and Tradition in the Four Gospels*, edited by R. T. France and David Wenham, 1:225–63. Sheffield: JSOT Press, 1980.

Strauss, Mark L. *Four Portraits, One Jesus: An Introduction to Jesus and the Gospels*. Grand Rapids: Zondervan, 2007.

Stroker, William D. *Extracanonical Sayings of Jesus*. RBS 18. Atlanta: Scholars Press, 1989.

Stuckenbruck, Loren T. "The 'Angels' and 'Giants' of Genesis 6:1–4 in Second and Third Century BCE Jewish Interpretation: Reflections on the Posture of Early Apocalyptic Traditions." *Dead Sea Discoveries* 7 (2000): 354–77.

———. "The Origins of Evil in Jewish Apocalyptic Tradition: The Interpretation of Genesis 6:1–4 in the Second and Third Centuries BCE." In *The Fall of Angels*, edited by Christoph Auffarth and Loren T. Stuckenbruck, 87–118. TBN 7. Leiden: Brill, 2004.

Suetonius. Translated by J. C. Rolfe. 2 vols. LCL 31, 38. Cambridge, MA: Harvard University Press, 1997–1998.

Tacitus. The Histories and the Annals. Translated by Clifford H. Moore and John Jackson. 4 vols. LCL. Cambridge, MA: Harvard University Press, 1956–1962.

Talbert, Charles. "Discipleship in Luke-Acts." In Segovia, *Discipleship in the New Testament*, 62–75.

———. *Reading John: A Literary and Theological Commentary on the Fourth Gospel and the Johannine Epistles*. Rev. ed. London: Smith and Helwys, 2005.

Tannehill, Robert. "The Disciples in Mark: The Function of a Narrative Role." *JR* 57 (1977): 386–405.

Taylor, Joan E. *The Immerser: John the Baptist within Second Temple Judaism*. Grand Rapids: Eerdmans, 1997.

Thatcher, Tom. *Jesus the Riddler: The Power of Ambiguity in the Gospels*. Louisville: Westminster John Knox, 2006.

———. *The Riddles of Jesus in John: A Study in Tradition and Folklore*. SBLMS 53. Atlanta: Society of Biblical Literature, 2000.

Theissen, Gerd, and Dagmar Winter. *The Quest for the Plausible Jesus: The Question of Criteria*. Translated by M. Eugene Boring. Louisville: Westminster John Knox, 2002.

Tilley, Terrence W. "Remembering the Historic Jesus—A New Research Program?" *TS* 68 (2007): 3–35.

Treharne, R. F. *The Glastonbury Legends*. London: Sphere Books, 1971.

Tuckett, Christopher. "Forty Other Gospels." In *The Written Gospel*, edited by Donald A. Hagner and Markus Bockmuehl, 238–53. Cambridge: Cambridge University Press, 2005.

———. *The Gospel of Mary*. Oxford Early Christian Texts. Oxford: Oxford University Press, 2007.

Twelftree, G. H. "Jesus the Baptist." *JSHJ* 7 (2009): 103–25.

VanderKam, James C. "1 Enoch, Enochic Motifs, and Enoch in Early Christian Literature." In *The Jewish Apocalyptic Heritage in Early Christianity*, 33–101. Compendium rerum iudaicarum ad Novum Testamentum 3.4. Assen, Netherlands: Van Gorcum, 1996.

Van Voorst, Robert E. *Jesus outside the New Testament: An Introduction to the Ancient Evidence*. SHJ. Grand Rapids: Eerdmans, 2000.

Verbrugge, Verlyn D. "The Heavenly Army on the Fields of Bethlehem (Luke 2:13–14)." *Calvin Theological Journal* 43 (2008): 301–11.

Watts, Rikki E. *Isaiah's New Exodus in Mark*. Grand Rapids: Baker Academic, 2000.

Weaver, Walter P. *The Historical Jesus in Twentieth Century: 1900–1950*. Harrisburg, PA: Trinity Press International, 1999.

Webb, Robert A. "John the Baptist and His Relationship to Jesus." In *Studying the Historical Jesus: Evaluations of the State of Current Research*, edited by Bruce Chilton and Craig A. Evans, 179–230. NTTSD 19. Leiden: Brill, 1994.

———. *John the Baptizer and Prophet: A Socio-Historical Study*. JSNTSup 62. Sheffield: Sheffield Academic Press, 1991.

Wedderburn, A. J. M. *Beyond Resurrection*. London: SCM, 1999.

White, Lawrence G., trans. *The Divine Comedy of Dante Alighieri*. New York: Pantheon, 1948.

Wilkins, Michael J. *Discipleship in the Ancient World and Matthew's Gospel*. Grand Rapids: Baker, 1995.

Williams, D. J. "Judas Iscariot." In Green, McKnight, and Marshall, *Dictionary of Jesus and the Gospels*, 406–8.

Williams, Joel F. *Other Followers of Jesus: Minor Characters as Major Figures in Mark's Gospel*. JSNTSup 102. Sheffield: JSOT Press, 1994.

Williams, Michael A. *Rethinking "Gnosticism": An Argument for Dismantling a Dubious Category*. Princeton: Princeton University Press, 1996.

Wink, Walter. *John the Baptist in the Gospel Tradition*. SNTSMS 7. Cambridge: Cambridge University Press, 1968.

Witherington, Ben, III. "John the Baptist." In Green, McKnight, and Marshall, *Dictionary of Jesus and the Gospels*, 383–91.

———. "On the Road with Mary Magdalene, Joanna, Susanna, and Other Disciples—Luke 8:1–3." *ZNW* 70 (1979): 242–48.

————. *Women in the Ministry of Jesus: A Study of Jesus's Attitudes to Women and Their Roles as Reflected in His Earthly Life.* SNTSMS 51. Cambridge: Cambridge University Press, 1984.

Wright, Archie T. *The Origin of Evil Spirits.* WUNT 2.198. Tübingen: Mohr Siebeck, 2005.

Wright, N. T. *Jesus and the Victory of God.* COQG 2. Minneapolis: Fortress, 1996.

Yamaguchi, Satoko. *Mary and Martha: Women in the World of Jesus.* New York: Orbis, 2002.

Ancient Sources Index

Author Index

Subject Index

323